Federal Rules of Evidence

(2024 Edition)

With Rules Explanatory Notes, Advisory Committee Notes and Landmark Cases Supplement.

Includes Recent Amendments and Practical Exercises

Winston Mullins

Table of Contents

Overview of the Federal Rules of Evidence

The Federal Rules of Evidence (FRE) represent a codified set of legal standards governing the admission and use of evidence in United States federal courts. Enacted in 1975, these rules have undergone various amendments to address evolving legal standards and technological advancements. The primary objective of the FRE is to ensure the fair and efficient administration of justice by providing clear and consistent guidelines for what evidence is admissible in court. This chapter provides an overview of the origins, purpose, and structure of the Federal Rules of Evidence, setting the stage for the detailed analysis of individual rules in subsequent chapters.

Historical Context

The Federal Rules of Evidence emerged from a broader movement in the mid-20th century to standardize and reform procedural law in federal courts. Prior to their enactment, evidence law was largely governed by common law principles, leading to significant variations in practice across different jurisdictions. The Advisory Committee on Rules of Evidence, established by the Judicial Conference of the United States, played a crucial role in drafting the rules. The committee's work was influenced by the Model Code of Evidence (1942) and the Uniform Rules of Evidence (1953), both of which sought to harmonize evidentiary practices across the United States.

After extensive deliberation and public commentary, Congress enacted the Federal Rules of Evidence in 1975. Since then, the rules have been amended several times, reflecting changes in legal doctrine, societal norms, and the needs of modern litigation. Notable amendments include those addressing issues such as the admissibility of electronic evidence, the treatment of hearsay exceptions, and the standards for expert testimony.

Purpose and Objectives

The Federal Rules of Evidence are designed to achieve several key objectives:

1. **Fairness in Adjudication:** The rules aim to ensure that evidence admitted in court is both relevant and reliable, thus promoting a fair adjudicative process. By setting standards for admissibility, the FRE help to prevent prejudicial or misleading evidence from influencing the outcome of trials.

2. **Efficiency in Litigation:** The rules provide clear guidelines for the presentation of evidence, thereby reducing the likelihood of disputes and delays during trial. This promotes judicial efficiency and conserves resources for both the courts and litigants.

3. **Uniformity Across Jurisdictions:** By establishing a standardized set of rules, the FRE promote uniformity in the treatment of evidence across federal courts. This consistency helps to ensure that similar cases are treated similarly, regardless of the jurisdiction in which they are heard.

4. **Adaptability to Change:** The FRE are designed to be flexible and responsive to new developments in law and technology. This adaptability is evident in the periodic amendments to the rules, which

address emerging issues such as digital evidence and scientific testimony.

Scope and Application

The Federal Rules of Evidence apply to all federal courts in the United States, including district courts, courts of appeals, bankruptcy courts, and magistrate courts. The rules govern the admissibility of evidence in both civil and criminal proceedings, although certain rules may have different implications depending on the context. For instance, the standards for admissibility of hearsay evidence may vary between civil and criminal trials, reflecting the different stakes and constitutional protections involved.

The FRE do not apply in certain specialized proceedings, such as grand jury proceedings and administrative hearings. In these contexts, different evidentiary standards may be in place, reflecting the unique nature of these proceedings.

Structure and Organization

The Federal Rules of Evidence are divided into 11 articles, each covering a distinct aspect of evidentiary law:

- **Article I: General Provisions** - This article lays the foundation for the rules, including definitions and the purpose of the FRE.

- **Article II: Judicial Notice** - Covers the circumstances under which a court may recognize certain facts as true without requiring formal evidence.

- **Article III: Presumptions in Civil Actions and Proceedings** - Addresses the role of presumptions in shifting the burden of proof.

- **Article IV: Relevancy and Its Limits** - Discusses what constitutes relevant evidence and the limitations on admissibility of certain types of evidence.

- **Article V: Privileges** - Codifies the rules related to evidentiary privileges, such as attorney-client privilege.

- **Article VI: Witnesses** - Governs the qualifications, examination, and credibility of witnesses.

- **Article VII: Opinions and Expert Testimony** - Sets forth the rules for the admissibility of opinion evidence and expert testimony.

- **Article VIII: Hearsay** - Defines hearsay and its exceptions, which is a complex and critical area of evidentiary law.

- **Article IX: Authentication and Identification** - Establishes the requirements for authenticating evidence before it can be admitted.

- **Article X: Contents of Writings, Recordings, and Photographs** - Addresses the requirements for proving the content of documents and other recorded media.

- **Article XI: Miscellaneous Rules** - Includes rules on the applicability of the FRE, amendments, and other miscellaneous matters.

Each article is further divided into individual rules, which are numbered sequentially. For example, Rule 401 defines relevant evidence, while Rule 702 governs the admissibility of expert testimony. This structure allows for systematic analysis and application of the rules in legal proceedings.

Key Definitions and Concepts

Understanding the Federal Rules of Evidence requires familiarity with several key definitions and concepts:

1. **Admissibility:** Refers to whether evidence can be presented to the jury or judge in a court proceeding. Admissible evidence must meet the criteria set forth in the FRE, including relevance and reliability.

2. **Relevance:** Under Rule 401, evidence is considered relevant if it has any tendency to make a fact more or less probable than it would be without the evidence, and the fact is of consequence in determining the action.

3. **Hearsay:** Defined in Rule 801 as an out-of-court statement offered to prove the truth of the matter asserted. Hearsay is generally inadmissible unless it falls under one of the recognized exceptions.

4. **Privilege:** Certain communications are protected from disclosure in court under the concept of privilege. For example, communications between an attorney and client are generally privileged and cannot be compelled as evidence.

5. **Authentication:** Before evidence can be admitted, it must be authenticated—that is, shown to be what the proponent claims it is. Rule 901 outlines the requirements for authentication.

6. **Expert Testimony:** Rule 702 permits a witness qualified as an expert by knowledge, skill, experience, training, or education to testify in the form of an opinion, provided that the testimony is based on sufficient facts or data and is the product of reliable principles and methods.

Conclusion

The Federal Rules of Evidence serve as a cornerstone of the American legal system, providing a comprehensive framework for the admission and use of evidence in federal courts. Their careful balance between fairness, efficiency, and adaptability has made them an essential tool for judges, attorneys, and scholars alike. As we proceed to examine each rule in detail, it is crucial to keep in mind the overarching principles and objectives that guide the application of these rules in practice.

This chapter has provided an overview of the historical context, purpose, and structure of the FRE. The following chapters will delve into the specifics of each rule, offering a detailed analysis that is essential for understanding and applying the Federal Rules of Evidence in legal proceedings.

AUTHORITY FOR PROMULGATION OF RULES
TITLE 28, UNITED STATES CODE

§ 2072. Rules of Procedure and Evidence; Power to Prescribe

(a) The Supreme Court shall have the power to prescribe general rules of practice and procedure and rules of evidence for cases in the United States district courts (including proceedings before magistrate judges thereof) and courts of appeals.

(b) Such rules shall not abridge, enlarge, or modify any substantive right. All laws in conflict with such rules shall be of no further force or effect after such rules have taken effect.

(c) Such rules may define when a ruling of a district court is final for the purposes of appeal under section 1291 of this title.

(Added Pub. L. 100–702, title IV, § 401(a), Nov. 19, 1988, 102 Stat. 4648, eff. Dec. 1, 1988; amended Pub. L. 101–650, title III, §§ 315, 321, Dec. 1, 1990, 104 Stat. 5115, 5117.)

§ 2073. Rules of Procedure and Evidence; Method of Prescribing

(a)(1) The Judicial Conference shall prescribe and publish the procedures for the consideration of proposed rules under this section.

(2) The Judicial Conference may authorize the appointment of committees to assist the Conference by recommending rules to be prescribed under sections 2072 and 2075 of this title. Each such committee shall consist of members of the bench and the professional bar, and trial and appellate judges.

(b) The Judicial Conference shall authorize the appointment of a standing committee on rules of practice, procedure, and evidence under subsection (a) of this section. Such standing committee shall review each recommendation of any other committees so appointed and recommend to the Judicial Conference rules of practice, procedure, and evidence and such changes in rules proposed by a committee appointed under subsection (a)(2) of this section as may be necessary to maintain consistency and otherwise promote the interest of justice.

(c)(1) Each meeting for the transaction of business under this chapter by any committee appointed under this section shall be open to the public, except when the committee so meeting,

in open session and with a majority present, determines that it is in the public interest that all or part of the remainder of the meeting on that day shall be closed to the public, and states the reason for so closing the meeting. Minutes of each meeting for the transaction of business under this chapter shall be maintained by the committee and made available to the public, except that any portion of such minutes, relating to a closed meeting and made available to the public, may contain such deletions as may be necessary to avoid frustrating the purposes of closing the meeting.

(2) Any meeting for the transaction of business under this chapter, by a committee appointed under this section, shall be preceded by sufficient notice to enable all interested persons to attend.

(d) In making a recommendation under this section or under section 2072 or 2075, the body making that recommendation shall provide a proposed rule, an explanatory note on the rule, and a written report explaining the body's action, including any minority or other separate views.

(e) Failure to comply with this section does not invalidate a rule prescribed under section 2072 or 2075 of this title.

§ 2074. Rules of Procedure and Evidence; Submission to Congress; Effective Date

(a) The Supreme Court shall transmit to the Congress not later than May 1 of the year in which a rule prescribed under section 2072 is to become effective a copy of the proposed rule. Such rule shall take effect no earlier than December 1 of the year in which such rule is so transmitted unless otherwise provided by law. The Supreme Court may fix the extent such rule shall apply to proceedings then pending, except that the Supreme Court shall not require the application of such rule to further proceedings then pending to the extent that, in the

opinion of the court in which such proceedings are pending, the application of such rule in such proceedings would not be feasible or would work injustice, in which event the former rule applies.

(b) Any such rule creating, abolishing, or modifying an evidentiary privilege shall have no force or effect unless approved by Act of Congress.

§ 2075. Bankruptcy Rules

The Supreme Court shall have the power to prescribe by general rules, the forms of process, writs, pleadings, and motions, and the practice and procedure in cases under title 11. Such rules shall not abridge, enlarge, or modify any substantive right. The Supreme Court shall transmit to Congress not later than May 1 of the year in which a rule prescribed under this section is to become effective a copy of the proposed rule. The rule shall take effect no earlier than December 1 of the year in which it is transmitted to Congress unless otherwise provided by law.

The bankruptcy rules promulgated under this section shall prescribe a form for the statement required under section 707(b)(2)(C) of title 11 and may provide general rules on the content of such statement.

HISTORICAL NOTE

The Supreme Court prescribes Federal Rules of Evidence pursuant to section 2072 of Title 28, United States Code, as enacted by Title IV "Rules Enabling Act" of Pub. L. 100–702 (approved November 19, 1988, 102 Stat. 4648), effective December 1, 1988, and section 2075 of Title 28. Pursuant to section 2074 of Title 28, the Supreme Court transmits to Congress (not later than May 1 of the year in which a rule prescribed under section 2072 is to become effective) a copy of the proposed rule. The rule takes effect no earlier than December 1 of the year in which the rule is transmitted unless otherwise provided by law.

Pursuant to sections 3402, 3771, and 3772 of Title 18, United States Code, and sections 2072 and 2075 of Title 28, United States Code, as then in effect, the Supreme Court through the Chief Justice submitted Federal Rules of Evidence to Congress on February 5, 1973 (409 U.S. 1132; Cong. Rec., vol. 119, pt. 3, p. 3247, Exec. Comm. 359; H. Doc. 93–46). To allow additional time for Congress to review the proposed rules, Public Law 93–12 (approved March 30, 1973, 87 Stat. 9) provided that the proposed rules "shall have no force or effect except to the extent, and with such amendments, as they may be expressly approved by Act of Congress."

Public Law 93–595 (approved January 2, 1975, 88 Stat. 1926) enacted the Federal Rules of Evidence proposed by the Supreme Court, with amendments made by Congress, to be effective July 1, 1975.

Section 1 of Public Law 94–113 (approved October 16, 1975, 89 Stat. 576) added clause (C) to Rule 801(d)(1), effective October 31, 1975.

Section 1 of Public Law 94–149 (approved December 12, 1975, 89 Stat. 805) enacted technical amendments which affected the Table of Contents and Rules 410, 606(b), 803(23), 804(b)(3), and 1101(e).

Section 2 of Public Law 95–540 (approved October 28, 1978, 92 Stat. 2046) added Rule 412 and inserted item 412 in the Table of Contents. The amendments apply to trials that begin more than thirty days after October 28, 1978.

Section 251 of Public Law 95–598 (approved November 6, 1978, 92 Stat. 2673) amended Rule 1101(a) and (b) by striking out "referees in bankruptcy," and by substituting "title 11, United States Code" for "the Bankruptcy Act," effective October 1, 1979, pursuant to section 402(c) of Public Law 95–598.

Section 252 of Public Law 95–598 would have amended Rule 1101(a) by inserting "the United States bankruptcy courts," immediately after "the United States district courts," effective April 1, 1984, pursuant to section 402(b) of Public Law 95–598. However, following a series of amendments (extending the April 1, 1984, effective date) by Public Laws 98–249, § 1(a), 98–271, § 1(a), 98–299, § 1(a), 98–325, § 1(a), and 98–353, § 121(a), section 402(b) of Public Law 95–598 was amended by section 113 of Public Law 98–353 to provide that the amendment "shall not be effective."

An amendment to Rule 410 was proposed by the Supreme Court by order dated April 30, 1979, transmitted to Congress by the Chief Justice on the same day (441 U.S. 970, 1005; Cong. Rec., vol. 125, pt. 8, p. 9366, Exec. Comm. 1456; H. Doc. 96–112), and was to be effective November 1, 1979. Public Law 96–42 (approved July 31, 1979, 93 Stat. 326) delayed the effective date of the amendment to Rule 410 until December 1, 1980, or until and to the extent approved by Act of Congress, whichever is earlier. In the absence of further action by Congress, the amendment to Rule 410 became effective December 1, 1980.

Sections 142 and 402 of Public Law 97–164 (approved April 2, 1982, 96 Stat. 45, 57) amended Rule 1101(a), effective October 1, 1982.

Section 406 of Public Law 98–473 (approved October 12, 1984, 98 Stat. 2067) amended Rule 704.

Additional amendments were adopted by the Court by order dated March 2, 1987, transmitted to Congress by the Chief Justice on the same day (480 U.S. 1023; Cong. Rec., vol. 133, pt. 4, p. 4448, Exec. Comm. 713; H. Doc. 100–41), and became effective October 1, 1987. The amendments affected Rules 101, 104(c), (d), 106, 404(a)(1), (b), 405(b), 411, 602 to 604, 606, 607, 608(b), 609(a), 610, 611(c), 612, 613, 615, 701, 703, 705, 706(a), 801(a), (d), 803(5), (18), (19), (21), (24), 804(a), (b)(2), (3), (5), 806, 902(2), (3), 1004(3), 1007, and 1101(a).

Additional amendments were adopted by the Court by order dated April 25, 1988, transmitted to Congress by the Chief Justice on the same day (485 U.S. 1049; Cong. Rec., vol. 134, pt. 7, p. 9154, Exec. Comm. 3517; H. Doc. 100–187), and became effective November 1, 1988. The amendments affected Rules 101, 602, 608(b), 613(b), 615, 902(3), and 1101(a), (e).

Sections 7046 and 7075 of Public Law 100–690 (approved November 18, 1988, 102 Stat. 4400, 4405) amended the Tables of Contents and Rules 412, 615, 804(a)(5), and 1101(a). Section 7075(a) of Public Law 100–690, which directed the amendment of Rule 615 by inserting "a" before "party which is not a natural person," could not be executed because "party which is not a natural person" did not appear. However, the word "a" was inserted by the intervening amendment adopted by the Court by order dated April 25, 1988, effective November 1, 1988. Section 7075(c)(1) of Public Law 100–690, which directed the amendment of Rule 1101(a) by striking "Rules" and inserting "rules," could not be executed because of the intervening amendment adopted by the Court by order dated April 25, 1988, effective November 1, 1988.

An additional amendment was adopted by the Court by order dated January 26, 1990, transmitted to Congress by the Chief Justice on the same day (493 U.S. 1173; Cong. Rec., vol. 136, pt. 1, p. 662, Exec. Comm. 2370; H. Doc. 101–142), and became effective December 1, 1990. The amendment affected Rule 609(a).

Additional amendments were adopted by the Court by order dated April 30, 1991, transmitted to Congress by the Chief Justice on the same day (500 U.S. 1001; Cong. Rec., vol. 137, pt. 7, p. 9721, Ex. Comm. 1189; H. Doc. 102–76), and became effective December 1, 1991. The amendments affected Rules 404(b) and 1102.

Additional amendments were adopted by the Court by order dated April 22, 1993, transmitted to Congress by the Chief Justice on the same day (507 U.S. 1187; Cong. Rec., vol. 139, pt. 6, p. 8127, Ex. Comm. 1104; H. Doc. 103–76), and became effective December 1, 1993. The amendments affected Rules 101, 705, and 1101(a), (e).

An additional amendment was adopted by the Court by order dated April 29, 1994, and transmitted to Congress by the Chief Justice on the same day (511 U.S. 1187; Cong. Rec., vol. 140, pt. 7, p. 8903, Ex. Comm. 3085; H. Doc. 103–250). The amendment affected Rule 412 and was to become effective December 1, 1994. Section 40141(a) of Public Law 103–322 (approved September 13, 1994, 108 Stat. 1918) provided that such amendment would take effect on December 1, 1994, but with the general amendment of Rule 412 made by section 40141(b) of Public Law 103–322.

Section 320935(a) of Public Law 103–322 (approved September 13, 1994, 108 Stat. 2135) amended the Federal Rules of Evidence by adding Rules 413 to 415, with provisions in section 320935(b)–(e) of Public Law 103–322 relating to the effective date and application of such rules. Pursuant to Pub. L. 103–322, § 320935(c), the Judicial Conference transmitted a report to Congress on February 9, 1995, containing recommendations different from the amendments made by Pub. L. 103–322, § 320935(a). Congress did not adopt the recommendations submitted or provide otherwise by law. Accordingly, Rules 413 to 415, as so added, became effective on July 9, 1995.

Additional amendments were adopted by the Court by order dated April 11, 1997, transmitted to Congress by the Chief Justice on the same day (520 U.S. 1323; Cong. Rec., vol. 143, pt. 4, p. 5551, Ex. Comm. 2798; H. Doc. 105–69), and became effective December 1, 1997. The amendments affected Rules 407, 801, 803, 804, and 806 and added Rule 807.

An additional amendment was adopted by the Court by order dated April 24, 1998, transmitted to Congress by the Chief Justice on the same day (523 U.S. 1235; Cong. Rec., vol. 144, pt. 6, p. 8151, Ex. Comm. 8996 to Ex. Comm. 8998; H.

Doc. 105–268), and became effective December 1, 1998. The amendment affected Rule 615.

Additional amendments were adopted by the Court by order dated April 17, 2000, transmitted to Congress by the Chief Justice on the same day (529 U.S. 1189; Cong. Rec., vol. 146, pt. 5, p. 6328, Ex. Comm. 7333; H. Doc. 106–225), and became effective December 1, 2000. The amendments affected Rules 103, 404, 701, 702, 703, 803, and 902.

An additional amendment was adopted by the Court by order dated March 27, 2003, transmitted to Congress by the Chief Justice on the same day (538 U.S. 1097; Cong. Rec., vol. 149, pt. 6, p. 7689, Ex. Comm. 1494; H. Doc. 108–57), and became effective December 1, 2003. The amendment affected Rule 608.

Additional amendments were adopted by the Court by order dated April 12, 2006, transmitted to Congress by the Chief Justice on the same day (547 U.S. 1281; Cong. Rec., vol. 152, pt. 6, p. 7213, Ex. Comm. 7320; H. Doc. 109–108), and became effective December 1, 2006. The amendments affected Rules 404, 408, 606, and 609.

Section 1 of Public Law 110–322 (approved September 19, 2008, 122 Stat. 3537) added Rule 502 and inserted item 502 in the Table of Contents. The amendments apply in all proceedings commenced after September 19, 2008, and, insofar as is just and practicable, in all proceedings pending on that date.

An additional amendment was adopted by the Court by order dated April 28, 2010, transmitted to Congress by the Chief Justice on the same day (559 U.S. 1157; Cong. Rec., vol. 156, pt. 6, p. 8139, Ex. Comm. 7475; H. Doc. 111–113), and became effective December 1, 2010. The amendment affected Rule 804.

Additional amendments were adopted by the Court by order dated April 26, 2011, transmitted to Congress by the Chief Justice on the same day (563 U.S. 1075; Cong. Rec., vol. 157, pt. 6, p. 7770, Ex. Comm. 1662; H. Doc. 112–28), and became effective December 1, 2011. The amendments affected Rules 101 to 1103.

An additional amendment was adopted by the Court by order dated April 13, 2013, transmitted to Congress by the Chief Justice on April 16, 2013 (569 U.S. 1167; Cong. Rec., vol. 159, pt. 5, p. 6968, Ex. Comm. 1492; H. Doc. 113–26), and became effective December 1, 2013. The amendment affected Rule 803.

Additional amendments were adopted by the Court by order dated April 25, 2014, transmitted to Congress by the Chief Justice on the same day (572 U.S. 1233; Cong. Rec., vol. 160, pt. 11, p. 15506, Ex. Comm. 7580; H. Doc. 113–164), and became effective December 1, 2014. The amendments affected Rules 801 and 803.

Additional amendments were adopted by the Court by order dated April 27, 2017, transmitted to Congress by the Chief Justice on the same day (581 U.S. 1055; Cong. Rec., vol. 163, pt. 6, p. 7574, Ex. Comm. 1256; H. Doc. 115–34), and became effective December 1, 2017. The amendments affected Rules 803 and 902.

An additional amendment was adopted by the Court by order dated April 25, 2019, transmitted to Congress by the Chief Justice on the same day (587 U.S.——; Cong. Rec., vol. 165,

p. H7864, Daily Issue, Ex. Comm. 2225; H. Doc. 116–67), and became effective December 1, 2019. The amendment affected Rule 807.

An additional amendment was adopted by the Court by order dated April 27, 2020, transmitted to Congress by the Chief Justice on the same day (590 U.S.——; Cong. Rec., vol. 166, p. H4223, Daily Issue, Ex. Comm. 4922; H. Doc. 116–144), and became effective December 1, 2020. The amendment affected Rule 404.

Additional amendments were adopted by the Court by order dated April 24, 2023, transmitted to Congress by the Chief Justice on the same day (599 U.S.——; Cong. Rec., vol. 169, p. H1944, Daily Issue, Ex. Comm. 794; H. Doc. 118–33), and became effective December 1, 2023. The amendments affected Rules 106, 615, and 702.

Committee Notes

Committee Notes prepared by the Committee on Rules of Practice and Procedure and the Advisory Committee on the Federal Rules of Evidence, Judicial Conference of the United States, explaining the purpose and intent of the amendments are set out in the Appendix to Title 28, United States Code, following the particular rule to which they relate. In addition, the notes are set out in the House documents listed above.

ARTICLE I. GENERAL PROVISIONS

Rule 101 - Scope and Definitions

Text of Rule 101

Rule 101. Scope; Definitions

(a) **Scope.** These rules apply to proceedings in United States courts. The specific courts and proceedings to which the rules apply, along with exceptions, are set out in Rule 1101.

(b) **Definitions.** In these rules: (1) "civil case" means a civil action or proceeding; (2) "criminal case" includes a criminal proceeding; (3) "public office" includes a public agency; (4) "record" includes a memorandum, report, or data compilation; (5) a "rule prescribed by the Supreme Court" means a rule adopted by the Supreme Court under statutory authority; and (6) a reference to any kind of written material or any other medium includes electronically stored information.

Introduction to Rule 101

Rule 101 of the Federal Rules of Evidence serves as the foundational provision that defines the scope of the rules and provides essential definitions that are applied throughout the Federal Rules of Evidence. This rule is critical because it establishes the boundaries within which the rules operate and clarifies the terms that are used consistently in subsequent provisions. Understanding Rule 101 is crucial for any practitioner or scholar, as it provides the interpretative framework for the entire body of evidentiary law within the federal system.

Scope of the Federal Rules of Evidence (Rule 101(a))

Application to Federal Courts

Rule 101(a) succinctly states that the Federal Rules of Evidence apply to proceedings in United States courts. This phrase encapsulates the breadth of the rules, indicating that they govern the admissibility and use of evidence across the entire federal judiciary, including district courts, courts of appeals, and specialized federal courts like bankruptcy courts and magistrate courts. The scope of the rules is not restricted by the nature of the case—whether civil, criminal, or administrative in nature—so long as the proceeding takes place within the jurisdiction of the federal courts.

Exceptions and Specific Applications

While Rule 101(a) sets the general applicability, the exceptions to the rule, as well as specific applications, are detailed in Rule 1101, which will be discussed in a subsequent chapter. These exceptions may include certain specialized proceedings where the rules may not apply in full or where modified evidentiary standards are used. Rule 1101 outlines these circumstances, ensuring clarity on when and how the rules should be applied in diverse legal contexts.

Definitions (Rule 101(b))

The definitions provided in Rule 101(b) are integral to the proper interpretation and application of the Federal Rules of Evidence. Each term defined in this subsection has significant implications for how the rules are understood and employed in legal proceedings.

"Civil Case"

The term "civil case" is defined broadly to encompass any civil action or proceeding. This definition ensures that the rules apply uniformly across the spectrum of civil litigation, including but not limited to tort cases, contract disputes, and other matters where private parties seek judicial resolution of non-criminal disputes. By clarifying that a "civil case" includes all forms of civil actions and proceedings, Rule 101(b)(1) ensures that there is no ambiguity in the rules' application to civil matters.

"Criminal Case"

Similarly, the term "criminal case" is defined to include any criminal proceeding. This broad definition ensures that the rules apply to all stages of criminal litigation, from pre-trial motions and evidentiary hearings to trials and appeals. The inclusion of the term "criminal proceeding" within the definition reflects the comprehensive nature of criminal litigation, which may involve various pre-trial and post-trial processes where evidentiary rules are critical.

"Public Office"

The term "public office" is defined to include public agencies. This definition extends the application of evidentiary rules to various governmental entities and ensures that any reference to a public office within the rules also encompasses the broader category of public agencies. This is particularly relevant in cases where evidence involves records or actions of government bodies, ensuring that the rules apply consistently to entities that function as extensions of public offices.

"Record"

The term "record" is broadly defined to include any memorandum, report, or data compilation. This expansive definition is crucial in modern litigation, where the nature of evidence has evolved to include a wide variety of documentary forms. By defining "record" in this manner, the rules accommodate the inclusion of diverse types of documentary evidence, from traditional paper records to modern digital data compilations.

"Rule Prescribed by the Supreme Court"

This definition clarifies that a "rule prescribed by the Supreme Court" refers to a rule adopted by the Supreme Court under statutory authority. This definition is particularly important for understanding the hierarchical nature of legal rules and the authority under which they are promulgated. It underscores the role of the Supreme Court in shaping the procedural and evidentiary framework within the federal judiciary.

"Written Material or Other Medium"

Finally, Rule 101(b)(6) provides a forward-looking definition by including electronically stored information (ESI) in the reference to any kind of written material or any other medium. This definition is critical in the digital age, where much of the evidence presented in court is stored electronically. By explicitly including ESI, the rules ensure that the evidentiary standards apply to modern forms of data storage and communication, reflecting the realities of contemporary litigation.

Practical Implications of Rule 101

The practical implications of Rule 101 are profound. By defining the scope and key terms of the Federal Rules of Evidence, Rule 101 establishes a clear framework within which all subsequent rules operate. This framework ensures that practitioners have a consistent and predictable set of standards for the admission and use of evidence across federal courts.

Moreover, the definitions provided in Rule 101(b) facilitate a uniform understanding of the terms used throughout the rules. This uniformity is essential for ensuring that the rules are applied consistently in different cases and jurisdictions, thereby upholding the principles of fairness and justice that underpin the Federal Rules of Evidence.

Rule 102 - Purpose

Rule 102. Purpose

These rules should be construed so as to administer every proceeding fairly, eliminate unjustifiable expense and delay, and promote the development of evidence law, to the end of ascertaining the truth and securing a just determination.

Introduction to Rule 102

Rule 102 of the Federal Rules of Evidence articulates the overarching purpose and guiding principles that underpin the entire body of evidentiary rules. It serves as a foundational rule, emphasizing the objectives that the Federal Rules of Evidence are designed to achieve within the federal judiciary. Rule 102 is brief in its wording but profound in its implications, as it encapsulates the essential goals of fairness, efficiency, and truth-seeking that the rules are intended to promote. This chapter provides an in-depth analysis of Rule 102, exploring its language, purpose, and the broader impact it has on the interpretation and application of the Federal Rules of Evidence.

Analysis of Rule 102

Rule 102 establishes the interpretative framework for the Federal Rules of Evidence, guiding judges and practitioners in how the rules should be applied in legal proceedings. The rule's language emphasizes three core principles: fairness in administration, efficiency in litigation, and the development of evidence law to ascertain truth and secure just outcomes. Each of these principles is essential to understanding the broader purpose of the Federal Rules of Evidence.

Fair Administration of Proceedings

The first principle articulated in Rule 102 is the fair administration of legal proceedings. This principle reflects the fundamental requirement that the rules of evidence must be applied in a manner that ensures fairness to all parties involved in litigation. Fairness in this context means that evidence must be handled and adjudicated without bias, prejudice, or favoritism, and that the rules are applied consistently across different cases and litigants.

Fair administration also implies that all parties have an equal opportunity to present their evidence and challenge the evidence presented by their opponents. This principle is central to the adversarial system of justice that underpins the American legal system, where the truth is sought through the contestation of evidence by opposing parties.

Elimination of Unjustifiable Expense and Delay

The second principle emphasized in Rule 102 is the elimination of unjustifiable expense and delay in legal proceedings. The Federal Rules of Evidence are designed not only to ensure fairness but also to promote efficiency in the judicial process. Unjustifiable expense and delay can impede the delivery of justice, burden litigants with excessive costs, and strain judicial resources.

By emphasizing the need to eliminate unnecessary expenses and delays, Rule 102 encourages courts to apply the rules of evidence in a manner that facilitates the timely and cost-effective resolution of disputes. This principle is particularly important in the context of modern litigation, where the complexity of cases and the volume of evidence can often lead to protracted and costly proceedings.

Courts are thus encouraged to interpret and apply the rules in a way that avoids procedural pitfalls and unnecessary technicalities that could lead to protracted litigation. For example, this principle supports the use of streamlined procedures for the admission of evidence and discourages frivolous objections that serve only to delay proceedings without advancing the interests of justice.

Promotion of the Development of Evidence Law

The third principle outlined in Rule 102 is the promotion of the development of evidence law. The Federal Rules of Evidence are not static; they are intended to evolve in response to changes in legal doctrine, societal values, and technological advancements. This principle underscores the role of the judiciary in interpreting and applying the rules in a way that contributes to the ongoing development of evidence law.

The promotion of the development of evidence law involves adapting the rules to address new challenges and complexities in the legal landscape. For example, the increasing prevalence of digital evidence and advances in forensic science require courts to interpret the rules in ways that accommodate these developments while maintaining the integrity of the evidentiary process.

This principle also supports the idea that courts should not only apply the rules mechanically but should also contribute to the broader understanding and refinement of evidentiary principles. Judicial interpretations and rulings help to clarify ambiguous aspects of the rules, create precedents that guide future cases, and ensure that the rules remain relevant and effective in achieving their purpose.

Ascertainment of the Truth and Securing a Just Determination

The ultimate goal of Rule 102, as reflected in its concluding phrase, is the ascertainment of the truth and the securing of a just determination in every legal proceeding. This goal is the cornerstone of the Federal Rules of Evidence, reflecting the fundamental objective of the American legal system: to uncover the truth and achieve justice.

The emphasis on truth-seeking ensures that the rules are applied in a way that prioritizes the discovery of factual accuracy. Evidence that is relevant, reliable, and probative should be admitted, while evidence that is misleading, prejudicial, or irrelevant should be excluded. This truth-seeking function is essential to the legitimacy of the judicial process and the public's confidence in the legal system.

Securing a just determination involves ensuring that the outcome of legal proceedings is fair and equitable, based on a thorough and impartial consideration of the evidence. The rules of evidence are thus designed to balance the rights of all parties, protect against miscarriages of justice, and uphold the integrity of the judicial process.

Practical Implications of Rule 102

The principles enshrined in Rule 102 have significant practical implications for the interpretation and application of the Federal Rules of Evidence. Judges and practitioners are guided by these principles in making decisions about the admissibility and use of evidence in federal courts.

Judicial Discretion

Rule 102 grants judges a degree of discretion in how they interpret and apply the rules of evidence. This discretion allows judges to tailor their rulings to the specific circumstances of each case, ensuring that the principles of fairness, efficiency, and truth-seeking are upheld. However, this discretion is not unlimited; it must be exercised in a manner consistent with the overarching goals of the rules as articulated in Rule 102.

For instance, a judge might exclude evidence that, while technically admissible, could lead to undue delay or confusion, thus undermining the efficiency and fairness of the proceedings. Similarly, a judge might allow the admission of evidence that is crucial to establishing the truth, even if it presents some procedural challenges.

Interpretation of Ambiguous Rules

In cases where the language of a specific evidentiary rule is ambiguous or where new legal questions arise that the rules do not explicitly address, Rule 102 provides a guiding framework for interpretation. Judges can refer to the principles of fairness, efficiency, and truth-seeking to resolve ambiguities in a manner that aligns with the purpose of the Federal Rules of Evidence.

For example, in the context of emerging forms of evidence, such as digital or scientific evidence, judges may look to Rule 102 to determine how best to interpret existing rules in a way that promotes the development of evidence law and facilitates the ascertainment of truth.

Balancing Competing Interests

Rule 102 also plays a crucial role in balancing competing interests that often arise in the context of evidence law. For example, the need to protect the rights of criminal defendants must be balanced against the need to admit evidence that is vital to the prosecution's case. Similarly, the interest in maintaining confidentiality or privilege must be weighed against the interest in disclosing evidence that could be crucial to a fair determination of the case.

By emphasizing the goals of fairness, efficiency, and truth-seeking, Rule 102 provides a framework for resolving these conflicts in a manner that serves the broader interests of justice.

Rule 103 - Rulings on Evidence

Text of Rule 103

Rule 103. Rulings on Evidence

(a) **Preserving a Claim of Error.** A party may claim error in a ruling to admit or exclude evidence only if the error affects a substantial right of the party and: (1) **If the ruling admits evidence,** a party, on the record: (A) timely objects or moves to strike; and (B) states the specific ground, unless it was apparent from the context; or (2) **If the ruling excludes evidence,** a party informs the court of its substance by an offer of proof, unless the substance was apparent from the context.

(b) **Not Needing to Renew an Objection or Offer of Proof.** Once the court rules definitively on the record—either before or at trial—a party need not renew an objection or offer of proof to preserve a claim of error for appeal.

(c) **Court's Statement About the Ruling; Directing an Offer of Proof.** The court may make any statement about the character or form of the evidence, the objection made, and the ruling. The court may direct that an offer of proof be made in question-and-answer form.

(d) **Preventing the Jury from Hearing Inadmissible Evidence.** To the extent practicable, the court must conduct a jury trial so that inadmissible evidence is not suggested to the jury by any means.

(e) **Taking Notice of Plain Error.** A court may take notice of a plain error affecting a substantial right, even if the claim of error was not properly preserved.

Introduction to Rule 103

Rule 103 of the Federal Rules of Evidence addresses the procedures and principles governing judicial rulings on evidentiary matters. This rule is critical in ensuring that objections to evidence, as well as the court's rulings on such objections, are handled in a manner that preserves the integrity of the judicial process and the rights of the parties involved. Rule 103 outlines the conditions under which a party may object to or seek to admit evidence, the requirements for preserving errors for appellate review, and the circumstances under which evidentiary errors may be deemed harmless. Understanding Rule 103 is essential for any legal practitioner, as it provides the framework for effectively managing evidentiary disputes during trial.

Analysis of Rule 103

Rule 103 is structured to ensure that objections to evidence and judicial rulings on those objections are properly documented and preserved for potential appellate review. The rule's provisions are designed to balance the need for a fair trial with the procedural requirements necessary to manage evidentiary disputes effectively. Each subsection of Rule 103 addresses a specific aspect of how evidentiary rulings should be handled in the context of a trial.

Preserving a Claim of Error (Rule 103(a))

The first subsection of Rule 103 focuses on the preservation of a claim of error regarding a court's evidentiary ruling. This provision is crucial for ensuring that any error in admitting or excluding evidence can be raised on appeal, provided that it affects a substantial right of the party involved.

Rulings Admitting Evidence (Rule 103(a)(1))

When a court rules to admit evidence, a party must timely object or move to strike the evidence on the record to preserve the issue for appeal. The objection or motion must be specific, stating the grounds for the objection unless the grounds are apparent from the context. This requirement ensures that the trial court is fully informed of the basis for the objection, allowing it to address the issue properly. It also creates a clear record for appellate courts to review, should the case be appealed.

A timely objection typically means that the objection is made as soon as the grounds for it become apparent, often immediately after the evidence is offered or the objectionable question is posed. Failure to object timely or to specify the grounds for the objection generally results in the waiver of the right to contest the admissibility of the evidence on appeal.

Rulings Excluding Evidence (Rule 103(a)(2))

When a court rules to exclude evidence, the party seeking to admit the evidence must inform the court of the evidence's substance through an offer of proof unless the substance is apparent from the context. An offer of proof is a procedural step that allows the party to explain what the evidence would have shown had it been admitted. This procedure is essential for creating a record that appellate courts can review to determine whether the exclusion of the evidence was proper and whether it affected the outcome of the trial.

An offer of proof typically involves a description of the evidence, the testimony that would have been elicited, or the document that would have been introduced, along with an explanation of its relevance and admissibility. The offer of proof must be detailed enough to allow the court to understand the significance of the excluded evidence and to make an informed ruling.

Not Needing to Renew an Objection or Offer of Proof (Rule 103(b))

Rule 103(b) provides that once a court has ruled definitively on an evidentiary issue, either before or during the trial, a party does not need to renew its objection or offer of proof to preserve the issue for appeal. This provision is designed to prevent unnecessary repetition and to streamline the trial process. By removing the requirement to repeatedly object or make offers of proof once a definitive ruling has been made, the rule allows the trial to proceed more efficiently while still protecting the parties' rights to appeal evidentiary decisions.

This rule applies to rulings made in motions in limine (pre-trial motions to admit or exclude evidence) as well as rulings made during the trial. The key is that the ruling must be definitive; if the court leaves the door open to reconsidering the issue later, the party may need to renew the objection or offer of proof when the issue arises again.

Court's Statement About the Ruling; Directing an Offer of Proof (Rule 103(c))

Rule 103(c) allows the court to make a statement on the record regarding the character of the evidence, the objections made, and the court's ruling. This provision is important for creating a clear and complete record of the evidentiary proceedings, which is essential for appellate review. The court's statement can provide insight into the rationale behind its ruling, which can be critical for understanding the context in which the ruling was made.

Additionally, Rule 103(c) permits the court to direct that an offer of proof be made in question-and-answer form. This method of making an offer of proof is particularly useful when the excluded evidence involves witness testimony. By presenting the offer of proof in this format, the court and the record are provided with a more precise understanding of the testimony that would have been presented, which aids in assessing the impact of the court's ruling.

Preventing the Jury from Hearing Inadmissible Evidence (Rule 103(d))

Rule 103(d) emphasizes the importance of preventing inadmissible evidence from being suggested to the jury by any means, to the extent practicable. This provision reflects the fundamental principle that the jury should base its verdict solely on admissible evidence that has been properly presented during the trial.

To enforce this principle, courts are required to manage the trial process in a way that minimizes the risk of the jury being exposed to evidence that has been deemed inadmissible. This may involve conducting bench conferences outside the presence of the jury, issuing clear instructions to counsel, and promptly addressing any attempts to introduce or reference inadmissible evidence.

In the event that inadmissible evidence is inadvertently presented to the jury, the court may provide curative instructions, strike the evidence from the record, or, in extreme cases, declare a mistrial. The goal is to protect the integrity of the trial and ensure that the jury's decision is based solely on evidence that meets the standards of admissibility.

Taking Notice of Plain Error (Rule 103(e))

Rule 103(e) allows a court to take notice of a plain error affecting a substantial right, even if the error was not properly preserved by an objection or offer of proof. Plain error review is a doctrine that provides an exception to the general rule requiring timely objections. It allows appellate courts to correct errors that are so obvious and prejudicial that they affect the fairness, integrity, or public reputation of judicial proceedings, even if the error was not brought to the trial court's attention.

For an appellate court to take notice of plain error, the error must be clear or obvious, it must affect the appellant's substantial rights, and it must have seriously affected the fairness, integrity, or public reputation of the judicial proceedings. This provision is a safeguard that ensures that justice is served, even in cases where procedural requirements were not strictly followed.

Practical Implications of Rule 103

Rule 103 has significant practical implications for trial practice and appellate review. It establishes the procedures that parties must follow to properly object to evidence and preserve claims of error, and it provides guidance on how courts should manage evidentiary issues during trial.

Importance of Timely and Specific Objections

For trial attorneys, Rule 103 underscores the importance of making timely and specific objections to preserve the right to appeal. An objection must be raised as soon as the grounds for it become apparent, and the objection must clearly state the specific reason for the challenge to the evidence. Failure to do so may result in the waiver of the objection, leaving the party without recourse on appeal.

Creating a Complete Record for Appeal

Rule 103 also highlights the need to create a thorough and complete record of the trial proceedings. Offers of proof, court statements, and rulings on objections must be clearly documented to ensure that appellate courts have all the information they need to review the case. This is particularly important in cases where the exclusion or admission of evidence could have a significant impact on the outcome of the trial.

Managing Evidentiary Issues During Trial

For trial judges, Rule 103 provides guidance on how to manage evidentiary issues in a way that protects the rights of the parties and ensures a fair trial. Judges must balance the need to make prompt and definitive rulings on evidence with the requirement to prevent the jury from being exposed to inadmissible evidence. This involves making clear and reasoned decisions, providing explanations on the record, and taking appropriate measures to mitigate any potential prejudice.

Plain Error Review as a Safety Net

Finally, Rule 103(e) provides a safety net through the plain error doctrine, allowing courts to correct egregious errors that affect the fundamental fairness of a trial, even if those errors were not preserved by an objection. This provision ensures that justice is not compromised by procedural oversights, maintaining the integrity of the judicial process.

Rule 104 - Preliminary Questions

Text of Rule 104

Rule 104. Preliminary Questions
(a) In General. The court must decide any preliminary question about whether a witness is qualified, a privilege exists, or evidence is admissible. In so deciding, the court is not bound by evidence rules, except those on privilege.
(b) Relevance That Depends on a Fact. When the relevance of evidence depends on whether a fact exists, proof must be introduced sufficient to support a finding that the fact does exist. The court may admit the proposed evidence on the condition that the proof be introduced later.
(c) Conducting a Hearing So That the Jury Cannot Hear It. The court must conduct any hearing on a preliminary question so that the jury cannot hear it if: (1) the hearing involves the admissibility of a confession; (2) a defendant in a criminal case is a witness and so requests; or (3) justice so requires.
(d) Cross-Examining a Defendant in a Criminal Case. By testifying on a preliminary question, a defendant in a criminal case does not become subject to cross-examination on other issues in the case.
(e) Evidence Relevant to Weight and Credibility. This rule does not limit a party's right to introduce before the jury evidence that is relevant to the weight or credibility of other evidence.

Introduction to Rule 104

Rule 104 of the Federal Rules of Evidence addresses the process by which a court determines preliminary questions related to the admissibility of evidence. These questions often concern foundational matters, such as the qualification of a witness, the existence of a privilege, or the admissibility of evidence under specific legal standards. Rule 104 is essential in guiding judges through the procedures for resolving these preliminary issues, ensuring that the evidence presented in court meets the necessary legal standards before it is considered by the jury. This chapter provides a detailed analysis of Rule 104, examining its text, interpretation, and the broader implications it has for the administration of justice.

Analysis of Rule 104

Rule 104 establishes the procedures and standards by which courts resolve preliminary questions related to evidence. This rule is critical in ensuring that only admissible and relevant evidence is presented to the jury, thereby upholding the integrity of the trial process. Each subsection of Rule 104 addresses specific aspects of how these preliminary questions should be handled by the court.

In General (Rule 104(a))

The first subsection of Rule 104 grants the court the authority to decide preliminary questions concerning the qualification of a witness, the existence of a privilege, or the admissibility of evidence. This authority is fundamental to the court's gatekeeping role in ensuring that the evidence considered by the jury meets the necessary legal standards.

The Court's Role as Gatekeeper

Rule 104(a) underscores the court's role as a gatekeeper in determining whether the evidence presented meets the foundational requirements necessary for admissibility. The court's decision on these preliminary questions is a critical step in the trial process, as it ensures that the evidence that ultimately reaches the jury is both relevant and reliable.

In making these determinations, the court is not bound by the rules of evidence, except those relating to privilege. This flexibility allows the court to consider a wide range of information in making its determination, including hearsay, affidavits, and other materials that might not be admissible before the jury. The only limitation is that the court must respect any privileges that protect certain communications or information from being disclosed.

Judicial Discretion

Rule 104(a) gives judges broad discretion in how they handle preliminary questions. This discretion allows judges to consider all relevant information in making a determination about admissibility. For example, a judge might consider evidence that is otherwise inadmissible under the hearsay rule to decide whether a witness is qualified to testify as an expert. The judge's role is to ensure that the trial proceeds on a sound evidentiary basis, which is crucial for maintaining the integrity of the judicial process.

Relevance That Depends on a Fact (Rule 104(b))

Subsection (b) of Rule 104 addresses situations where the relevance of evidence depends on the existence of a particular fact. In such cases, the proponent of the evidence must introduce sufficient proof to support a finding that the fact does exist. This concept is often referred to as "conditional relevance."

Conditional Relevance

Conditional relevance arises when the relevance of a piece of evidence is contingent upon the establishment of a specific fact. For example, in a criminal trial, evidence of a defendant's previous conduct may be relevant only if it can be shown that the conduct is sufficiently similar to the conduct at issue in the current case. The court may admit the evidence on the condition that the party introducing it will later provide proof of the necessary fact.

Under Rule 104(b), the court's role is to assess whether the proponent has provided sufficient evidence for a reasonable jury to find that the fact in question exists. The standard is not whether the judge personally believes the fact exists but whether the evidence is sufficient for the jury to make such a finding. If the evidence meets this threshold, it is admitted; if not, it is excluded.

The Court's Discretion

While Rule 104(b) allows the court to admit conditionally relevant evidence, it also provides the judge with the discretion to require that the necessary proof be introduced later in the trial. This approach is often used to allow the trial to proceed efficiently, with the understanding that if the condition is not later met, the evidence may be stricken from the record or the jury instructed to disregard it.

Conducting a Hearing So That the Jury Cannot Hear It (Rule 104(c))

Rule 104(c) requires that hearings on preliminary questions be conducted outside the presence of the jury in specific circumstances. This provision is designed to protect the fairness of the trial by preventing the jury from being exposed to potentially prejudicial information that may not ultimately be admissible.

Admissibility of Confessions

One of the critical situations where a hearing must be conducted outside the jury's presence involves the admissibility of a confession. Given the significant impact that a confession can have on a jury, it is essential that the court first determine whether the confession was made voluntarily and in compliance with legal standards before allowing it to be presented to the jury. This procedure ensures that the jury does not hear a confession that might later be excluded as a result of the court's ruling.

Defendant's Request in Criminal Cases

In criminal cases, if the defendant is a witness, they may request that a preliminary hearing on the admissibility of evidence be conducted outside the presence of the jury. This provision protects the defendant from being prejudiced by the jury hearing inadmissible evidence that might otherwise influence their perception of the defendant's testimony.

Justice Requirement

The rule also allows the court to conduct a hearing outside the jury's presence whenever justice so requires. This broad discretion enables the judge to prevent the jury from hearing evidence that could unfairly prejudice one of the parties or that might be excluded after the preliminary hearing.

Cross-Examining a Defendant in a Criminal Case (Rule 104(d))

Rule 104(d) specifically addresses the rights of a defendant in a criminal case who testifies during a preliminary hearing. According to this rule, by testifying on a preliminary question, the defendant does not open themselves up to cross-examination on other issues in the case.

Protecting the Defendant's Rights

This provision is designed to protect the defendant's Fifth Amendment right against self-incrimination. When a defendant testifies during a preliminary hearing on an issue such as the admissibility of evidence, they should not be subject to broader cross-examination that extends to the merits of the case. This rule ensures that the defendant can challenge the admissibility of evidence without compromising their broader defense strategy.

Limiting Cross-Examination

The court must carefully manage the scope of cross-examination during preliminary hearings to ensure that it is limited to the issues relevant to the preliminary question. Any attempt by the prosecution to expand the cross-examination beyond these limits would be inconsistent with Rule 104(d) and could unfairly prejudice the defendant.

Evidence Relevant to Weight and Credibility (Rule 104(e))

Finally, Rule 104(e) clarifies that the rule does not limit a party's right to introduce evidence that is relevant to the weight or credibility of other evidence. This provision ensures that parties retain the ability to challenge or bolster the evidence presented in court through the introduction of additional evidence.

Addressing Weight and Credibility

While Rule 104 primarily concerns the admissibility of evidence, Rule 104(e) acknowledges that even after evidence has been admitted, parties may still present additional evidence that affects the weight or credibility of that evidence. For example, if a witness's testimony is admitted, the opposing party may introduce evidence that challenges the credibility of that witness, such as prior inconsistent statements or evidence of bias.

Jury's Role in Evaluating Evidence

The jury is the ultimate arbiter of the weight and credibility of the evidence presented at trial. Rule 104(e) ensures that once evidence is admitted, the parties have the opportunity to present additional relevant evidence that could influence the jury's assessment of that evidence. This provision reinforces the principle that the jury's role is to evaluate the entirety of the evidence in determining the facts of the case.

Practical Implications of Rule 104

Rule 104 has significant practical implications for how trials are conducted, particularly in managing the admission of evidence and ensuring that only legally sound evidence is presented to the jury.

Judicial Discretion in Admissibility Decisions

Rule 104 provides judges with considerable discretion in making determinations about the admissibility of evidence. This discretion allows judges to consider all relevant factors and to make informed decisions that balance the interests of justice with the need for a fair trial. Practitioners must be prepared to present compelling arguments during preliminary hearings to persuade the court of the admissibility or inadmissibility of evidence.

Strategic Use of Preliminary Hearings

For trial attorneys, understanding when and how to request a preliminary hearing is critical. These hearings can be used strategically to exclude damaging evidence before it reaches the jury or to secure the admission of evidence that is vital to the case. Effective use of Rule 104 can significantly impact the outcome of a trial by shaping the evidence that the jury ultimately considers.

Protecting the Rights of Defendants in Criminal Cases

Rule 104(d) is particularly important in protecting the rights of defendants in criminal cases. Defense attorneys must be vigilant in ensuring that their clients' rights are protected during preliminary hearings and that the scope of cross-examination remains limited to the issues relevant to the preliminary question.

Managing Conditional Relevance

Conditional relevance under Rule 104(b) requires careful attention from both judges and attorneys. When evidence is admitted on the condition that further proof will be provided, attorneys must be diligent in ensuring that the necessary proof is introduced. Failure to do so could result in the evidence being excluded, potentially weakening the party's case.

Ensuring a Complete Record for Appeal

Rule 104 decisions often play a significant role in appellate review. Judges and attorneys must ensure that the record of preliminary hearings and rulings is complete and well-documented to facilitate any potential appeals. This includes making clear offers of proof and ensuring that the court's rationale for its rulings is recorded.

Rule 105 - Limiting Evidence

Rule 105. Limiting Evidence That Is Not Admissible Against Other Parties or for Other Purposes

If the court admits evidence that is admissible against a party or for a purpose—but not against another party or for another purpose—the court, on timely request, must restrict the evidence to its proper scope and instruct the jury accordingly

Introduction to Rule 105

Rule 105 of the Federal Rules of Evidence addresses the court's duty to limit evidence to its proper scope when it is admissible for one purpose but not for another. This rule is essential in ensuring that evidence is used appropriately within the specific context for which it is admitted, thereby protecting against unfair prejudice, confusion, or misuse by the jury. Rule 105 empowers the court to provide juries with limiting instructions, which direct them to consider evidence only for its intended purpose. This chapter provides an in-depth analysis of Rule 105, exploring its text, interpretation, and the broader implications it has for the administration of justice.

Analysis of Rule 105

Rule 105 serves a crucial function in the trial process by ensuring that evidence is used only for its legally permissible purpose. The rule recognizes that certain evidence, while admissible for one purpose or against one party, may not be admissible for other purposes or against other parties. This limitation is essential to maintaining fairness in the trial process and ensuring that the jury's verdict is based solely on relevant and legally permissible considerations.

Scope and Purpose of Rule 105

The primary purpose of Rule 105 is to prevent the misuse of evidence by restricting its use to the specific context for which it is admissible. For instance, evidence may be admissible for the purpose of proving a defendant's motive but may not be admissible to prove the defendant's character. In such cases, Rule 105 allows the court to admit the evidence for the limited purpose of proving motive and instruct the jury to consider it only within that context.

The rule is especially important in cases involving multiple parties or complex legal issues, where evidence might be admissible against one party but not against another, or admissible for one legal issue but not for another. Without the protections provided by Rule 105, there is a significant risk that the jury might improperly use evidence in a way that could unfairly prejudice one of the parties.

Timely Request Requirement

Rule 105 specifies that the court's duty to provide a limiting instruction is triggered by a timely request from a party. This requirement places the onus on the parties to recognize when evidence is being admitted for a limited purpose and to promptly request an appropriate limiting instruction from the court.

A timely request typically means that the request is made at the time the evidence is introduced or shortly thereafter. If a party fails to make a timely request, they may waive their right to a limiting instruction, and the evidence may be considered by the jury without restriction. This highlights the importance of vigilance on the part of attorneys in recognizing when evidence requires a limiting instruction to avoid potential misuse by the jury.

The Court's Obligation to Provide Limiting Instructions

When a timely request is made, Rule 105 mandates that the court must restrict the evidence to its proper scope and instruct the jury accordingly. This instruction is intended to guide the jury in understanding the specific purpose for which the evidence is admitted and to prevent them from considering it for any improper or prejudicial purpose.

The court's limiting instruction should be clear, specific, and tailored to the evidence in question. The instruction should explain to the jury the exact purpose for which the evidence is being admitted and explicitly state that the evidence should not be considered for any other purpose. For example, if evidence of prior bad acts is admitted solely for the purpose of establishing intent, the court should instruct the jury that they may consider the evidence only for determining intent and not for assessing the defendant's character.

Ensuring Compliance with Limiting Instructions

While Rule 105 empowers the court to provide limiting instructions, it is ultimately the jury's responsibility to comply with these instructions. The assumption underlying Rule 105 is that juries will follow the court's instructions and consider the evidence only for its proper purpose. However, there is ongoing debate within the legal community about the effectiveness of limiting instructions, with some arguing that juries may have difficulty compartmentalizing evidence and adhering strictly to the limitations imposed by the court.

Despite these concerns, Rule 105 remains a critical tool for safeguarding the fairness of the trial process. It ensures that evidence is used in a manner consistent with the rules of evidence and the principles of due process, and it provides a mechanism for parties to protect their rights when potentially prejudicial evidence is admitted.

Interplay with Other Rules of Evidence

Rule 105 often works in conjunction with other rules of evidence, particularly those that address the admissibility of evidence for specific purposes. For example, Rule 404(b) allows evidence of prior bad acts to be admitted for purposes such as proving motive, intent, or identity, but not for proving character. In such cases, Rule 105 provides the mechanism for limiting the use of that evidence to the permissible purpose and instructing the jury accordingly.

Similarly, Rule 403, which allows the exclusion of evidence if its probative value is substantially outweighed by the risk of unfair prejudice, may also interact with Rule 105. In some cases, the court may decide to admit evidence despite the risk of prejudice, provided that a proper limiting instruction is given to mitigate that risk.

Practical Implications of Rule 105

Rule 105 has significant practical implications for trial practice, particularly in how attorneys and judges handle evidence that is admissible for limited purposes. Understanding and effectively utilizing Rule 105 is essential for ensuring that evidence is properly managed and that the jury is appropriately guided in its consideration of the evidence.

Strategic Use of Limiting Instructions

For trial attorneys, the strategic use of limiting instructions is a critical aspect of trial practice. When potentially prejudicial evidence is admitted, an attorney must be prepared to request a limiting instruction to protect their client's interests. This requires a deep understanding of the rules of evidence and the ability to anticipate how the jury might misuse certain evidence if not properly instructed.

Attorneys must also be mindful of the timing of their requests for limiting instructions. A request that is made too late may be deemed untimely, resulting in the waiver of the right to a limiting instruction. Conversely, a well-timed request can help to ensure that the evidence is considered only for its intended purpose, thereby minimizing the risk of unfair prejudice.

Crafting Effective Limiting Instructions

For judges, crafting effective limiting instructions is a critical component of managing the trial process. Limiting instructions must be clear, concise, and specific to the evidence in question. Judges must ensure that the instructions are understandable to the jury and that they accurately reflect the limited purpose for which the evidence is admitted.

In some cases, judges may need to revisit or reinforce limiting instructions during the trial, particularly if there is a risk that the jury may forget or disregard the limitations. This might involve repeating the instruction at relevant points during the trial or including it in the final jury instructions before deliberations.

Addressing Potential Jury Confusion

One of the challenges associated with Rule 105 is the potential for jury confusion. Juries may struggle to understand why certain evidence is admissible for one purpose but not for another, or they may have difficulty compartmentalizing their consideration of the evidence. Attorneys and judges must work together to ensure that the jury understands the reasons for the limitation and the importance of adhering to the court's instructions.

In some cases, attorneys may choose to reinforce the limiting instruction during their closing arguments, reminding the jury of the specific purpose for which the evidence was admitted and cautioning them against considering it for any improper purpose.

Appellate Review of Limiting Instructions

Limiting instructions are often subject to appellate review, particularly in cases where a party argues that the jury failed to adhere to the limitations imposed by the court or that the limiting instruction was inadequate. On appeal, courts will generally presume that juries follow the instructions given by the trial court, but this presumption can be challenged if there is evidence to the contrary.

Appellate courts may also review the adequacy of the limiting instruction itself, examining whether it was clear, accurate, and sufficient to mitigate the risk of prejudice. If an appellate court finds that a limiting instruction was deficient or that the jury likely misused the evidence, it may order a new trial or other appropriate relief.

Rule 106 - Remainder of or Related Writings or Recorded Statements

Text of Rule 106

Rule 106. Remainder of or Related Writings or Recorded Statements
If a party introduces all or part of a writing or recorded statement, an adverse party may require the introduction, at that time, of any other part—or any other writing or recorded statement—that in fairness ought to be considered at the same time.

Introduction to Rule 106

Rule 106 of the Federal Rules of Evidence, often referred to as the "rule of completeness," addresses the admissibility of additional parts of a writing or recorded statement when a party introduces a portion of that writing or statement into evidence. This rule is designed to prevent misleading impressions that might arise if a statement is introduced out of context. By ensuring that the entirety of relevant portions of a document or recorded statement is considered, Rule 106 upholds the principles of fairness and accuracy in the judicial process. This chapter provides a detailed analysis of Rule 106, exploring its text, application, and the broader implications it has for the administration of evidence.

Analysis of Rule 106

Rule 106 embodies the principle that evidence should be presented in a manner that allows the fact-finder to understand the context of the information being considered. This rule is particularly important in cases where selective presentation of evidence could create a misleading or incomplete picture of the facts. Rule 106 ensures that when a portion of a document or recorded statement is introduced, any other part of that document or statement that is necessary to provide a full and accurate understanding of the matter can also be introduced by the opposing party.

The Rule of Completeness

The primary purpose of Rule 106 is to implement the "rule of completeness," which is a common law principle designed to protect against the distortion of meaning that can occur when parts of a document or statement are presented without context. The rule allows the adverse party to introduce additional evidence that provides context, thereby preventing the jury or judge from being misled by an incomplete or selective presentation.

For example, if a party introduces a portion of a recorded conversation that appears to be an admission of guilt, Rule 106 allows the opposing party to introduce other parts of the conversation that may explain, qualify, or negate the apparent admission. This ensures that the fact-finder receives a complete and balanced view of the evidence.

Timing of Introduction

Rule 106 specifies that the additional parts of the writing or recorded statement must be introduced "at that time," meaning contemporaneously with the portion introduced by the initial party. This requirement is crucial because it ensures that the fact-finder considers the complete context of the evidence as it is being presented, rather than having to piece together different parts of the evidence at a later stage in the trial.

The timing requirement also serves to maintain the coherence of the evidence as it is presented to the jury or judge. By requiring that the related parts of the writing or statement be introduced simultaneously, Rule 106 minimizes the risk of confusion and helps to ensure that the evidence is evaluated in its proper context.

Scope of Rule 106

Rule 106 applies specifically to writings and recorded statements. It does not, by its terms, extend to oral statements or other forms of evidence. However, courts have occasionally applied the principle underlying Rule 106 more broadly to ensure fairness in the presentation of other types of evidence. The rule applies to any writing or recorded statement that is introduced, whether it is a document, a letter, an email, a transcript of a conversation, or any other form of recorded communication.

The rule also allows for the introduction of "any other writing or recorded statement" that in fairness ought to be considered at the same time. This means that if a related document or recording is necessary to provide context to the part introduced, the opposing party may require that the related document or recording be introduced as well. This provision ensures that the context is not artificially limited to the specific document or recording that the initial party has chosen to introduce.

Fairness as the Guiding Principle

The key standard under Rule 106 is fairness. The rule is designed to ensure that evidence is presented in a way that is fair to both parties and that does not mislead the fact-finder. The determination of what constitutes fairness in a particular case is left to the discretion of the trial judge, who must consider whether the additional parts of the writing or recorded statement are necessary to avoid creating a misleading impression.

Fairness might require the introduction of additional material if the initial portion introduced is misleading, incomplete, or taken out of context in a way that could distort its meaning. For example, if a document contains both incriminating and exculpatory statements, fairness would require that both types of statements be presented together to provide a balanced view.

Discretion of the Court

While Rule 106 provides a mechanism for ensuring completeness, the trial judge retains discretion over the application of the rule. The judge must determine whether the additional portions of the writing or recorded statement are necessary to provide context and whether they meet the requirements of relevance and admissibility under other rules of evidence.

The judge may also need to balance the need for completeness against other considerations, such as the risk of prejudice or the potential for confusion. In some cases, the judge might decide that introducing additional material would be unnecessary or would unduly complicate the proceedings. In making these determinations, the judge must carefully weigh the interests of fairness and accuracy against the need to manage the trial efficiently.

Interplay with Other Rules of Evidence

Rule 106 interacts with other rules of evidence, particularly those governing relevance (Rule 401), prejudice (Rule 403), and hearsay (Rules 801–805). For instance, while Rule 106 might allow the introduction of additional parts of a document to provide context, those parts must still satisfy the requirements of relevance under Rule 401 and must not be excluded under Rule 403 for being unduly prejudicial, confusing, or misleading.

In addition, if the additional parts of a writing or recorded statement contain hearsay, the court must determine whether they fall within an exception to the hearsay rule. Rule 106 does not automatically render all parts of a document or statement admissible; they must still be subject to the same evidentiary standards that apply to other evidence.

Practical Implications of Rule 106

Rule 106 has significant practical implications for both trial strategy and the administration of justice. Understanding how to effectively invoke Rule 106 can be critical for attorneys seeking to protect their clients from the misuse of evidence or to ensure that the evidence is presented in its full context.

Strategic Use of Rule 106

For trial attorneys, Rule 106 can be a powerful tool for preventing the opposing party from presenting evidence in a misleading or incomplete manner. Attorneys must be vigilant in identifying situations where only part of a writing or recorded statement is being introduced and must be prepared to request that the remainder or related parts be introduced contemporaneously.

Attorneys should also consider how Rule 106 might be used proactively in their own case strategy. For example, when introducing a document or recording that could be seen as damaging, an attorney might preemptively introduce the complete context to mitigate any negative impact and to present a more balanced view to the jury or judge.

Timing and Objections

The timing of a Rule 106 request is crucial. A request that is made after the jury has already heard the incomplete evidence may be less effective, as the initial impression may have already influenced the fact-finder. Therefore, attorneys should be prepared to make timely objections and requests under Rule 106 as soon as the partial evidence is introduced.

In some cases, opposing counsel might object to the introduction of additional material under Rule 106, arguing that it is irrelevant, prejudicial, or inadmissible for other reasons. Attorneys should be prepared to argue why the additional material is necessary for completeness and why it should be admitted under the rule of fairness.

Crafting a Complete Record

When invoking Rule 106, it is important for attorneys to ensure that the record is complete and clear. This means providing a clear explanation of why the additional material is necessary for fairness and ensuring that the judge's ruling on the request is fully documented. A well-developed record can be crucial if the issue is later raised on appeal.

Appellate Review

On appeal, courts may review the trial court's application of Rule 106 to determine whether the exclusion of additional material led to an unfair or misleading presentation of the evidence. Appellate courts generally give deference to the trial judge's discretion, but they will consider whether the exclusion of material under Rule 106 affected the fairness of the trial or the accuracy of the fact-finder's decision.

If an appellate court finds that the trial court improperly excluded material that should have been admitted under Rule 106, it may order a new trial or other appropriate relief. Therefore, it is essential for trial attorneys to ensure that Rule 106 is properly invoked and applied during the trial.

ARTICLE II. JUDICIAL NOTICE

Rule 201 - Judicial Notice of Adjudicative Facts

Text of Rule 201

Rule 201. Judicial Notice of Adjudicative Facts

(a) **Scope.** This rule governs judicial notice of an adjudicative fact only, not a legislative fact.

(b) **Kinds of Facts That May Be Judicially Noticed.** The court may judicially notice a fact that is not subject to reasonable dispute because it: (1) is generally known within the trial court's territorial jurisdiction; or (2) can be accurately and readily determined from sources whose accuracy cannot reasonably be questioned.

(c) **Taking Notice.** The court: (1) may take judicial notice on its own; or (2) must take judicial notice if a party requests it and the court is supplied with the necessary information.

(d) **Timing.** The court may take judicial notice at any stage of the proceeding.

(e) **Opportunity to Be Heard.** On timely request, a party is entitled to be heard on the propriety of taking judicial notice and the nature of the fact to be noticed. If the court takes judicial notice before notifying a party, the party, on request, is still entitled to be heard.

(f) **Instructing the Jury.** In a civil case, the court must instruct the jury to accept the noticed fact as conclusive. In a criminal case, the court must instruct the jury that it may or may not accept the noticed fact as conclusive.

Introduction to Rule 201

Rule 201 of the Federal Rules of Evidence governs the judicial notice of adjudicative facts—those facts that pertain directly to the parties involved in a particular legal proceeding and are significant to the outcome of the case. Judicial notice is a legal doctrine that allows a court to recognize and accept certain facts as true without requiring formal proof. This rule streamlines the litigation process by allowing courts to bypass the need for evidence on matters that are indisputable or widely known. Rule 201 outlines the types of facts that may be judicially noticed, the procedures for taking notice, and the implications of judicial notice for both the court and the parties involved. This chapter provides a comprehensive analysis of Rule 201, exploring its text, application, and the broader implications it has for the administration of justice.

Analysis of Rule 201

Rule 201 establishes the framework for the judicial notice of adjudicative facts within federal courts. This rule plays a crucial role in the judicial process by allowing courts to recognize certain facts as true without requiring formal proof, thus expediting proceedings and focusing the trial on genuinely disputed issues. Each subsection of Rule 201 addresses specific aspects of how judicial notice should be applied, ensuring that the process is both fair and efficient.

Scope of Rule 201 (Rule 201(a))

The first subsection of Rule 201 clarifies that the rule applies exclusively to adjudicative facts, distinguishing these from legislative facts. Adjudicative facts are those facts that relate directly to the matters at issue in the case—facts that help the court or jury understand what happened between the parties involved.

Adjudicative vs. Legislative Facts

Adjudicative facts are specific to the case and involve the who, what, where, when, and how of the events in question.

For example, an adjudicative fact might be the date on which a particular contract was signed or the weather conditions at the time of an alleged crime.

In contrast, legislative facts are broader, more general facts that relate to the development of law and policy rather than to the specifics of the case. These facts inform the court's understanding of the context or framework within which the law operates but are not directly related to the dispute between the parties. Rule 201 explicitly states that it governs only adjudicative facts, leaving legislative facts outside its scope.

Kinds of Facts That May Be Judicially Noticed (Rule 201(b))

Rule 201(b) specifies the types of facts that may be judicially noticed, focusing on those that are not subject to reasonable dispute. This subsection provides two categories of facts that can be judicially noticed:

1. **Facts Generally Known Within the Court's Jurisdiction (Rule 201(b)(1))**

A court may take judicial notice of facts that are generally known within its territorial jurisdiction. These are facts that are so well established and widely recognized within the jurisdiction that they cannot reasonably be disputed. For example, a court might take judicial notice that a certain city is the capital of a state or that a specific date was a federal holiday.

2. **Facts That Can Be Accurately and Readily Determined (Rule 201(b)(2))**

The second category includes facts that can be accurately and readily determined from sources whose accuracy cannot reasonably be questioned. This category covers facts that, while not generally known, can be verified through reliable and authoritative sources. Examples might include historical dates, official records, or scientific data published by reputable institutions.

Taking Judicial Notice (Rule 201(c))

Rule 201(c) outlines the procedures for taking judicial notice, providing the court with the discretion to do so either on its own initiative or at the request of a party.

1. **Court-Initiated Judicial Notice (Rule 201(c)(1))**

The rule allows a court to take judicial notice on its own accord. This provision gives the court the flexibility to recognize facts that are clearly established and undisputed without waiting for a party to request judicial notice. This can help streamline the proceedings by eliminating the need to present evidence on matters that are already clear.

2. **Party-Initiated Judicial Notice (Rule 201(c)(2))**

Alternatively, a party may request judicial notice of a fact. If a party makes such a request and provides the court with the necessary information to verify the fact, the court is obligated to take judicial notice. This ensures that parties have the opportunity to expedite the proceedings by formally recognizing certain facts as established without the need for evidence.

Timing of Judicial Notice (Rule 201(d))

Rule 201(d) states that the court may take judicial notice at any stage of the proceeding, including during the trial, on a motion for summary judgment, or even on appeal. The flexibility in timing allows the court to efficiently manage the case by acknowledging certain facts as established whenever it becomes relevant or necessary to do so. This provision helps to prevent unnecessary delays and ensures that the judicial notice process can be adapted to the needs of the case.

Opportunity to Be Heard (Rule 201(e))

One of the key aspects of Rule 201 is the requirement that parties be given an opportunity to be heard on the propriety of taking judicial notice. If a party believes that a fact should not be judicially noticed or that it is not the type of fact that qualifies under Rule 201, they may request a hearing to present their arguments.

1. **Timely Request for a Hearing**

A party must make a timely request to be heard, which typically means making the request as soon as they become aware that judicial notice might be taken. If the court takes judicial notice without prior notice to the parties, the party may still request a hearing to challenge the decision.

2. **Ensuring Fairness in the Judicial Process**

This provision ensures that the process of taking judicial notice remains fair and that both parties have the opportunity to contest the recognition of certain facts if they believe it is improper or could prejudice their case. The right to be heard is fundamental to due process and helps to maintain the integrity of the judicial process.

Instructing the Jury (Rule 201(f))

Rule 201(f) distinguishes between civil and criminal cases in terms of how judicially noticed facts are treated by the jury.

1. **Civil Cases**

In civil cases, the court must instruct the jury to accept the judicially noticed fact as conclusive. This means that the fact is deemed to be true for the purposes of the case, and the jury is not permitted to question or disregard it. This provision reinforces the idea that judicial notice is a way of establishing facts beyond dispute, thereby streamlining the trial process.

2. **Criminal Cases**

In criminal cases, the court must instruct the jury that it may, but is not required to, accept the judicially noticed fact as conclusive. This distinction recognizes the higher stakes involved in criminal trials, where the defendant's liberty is at issue. The rule provides a safeguard for defendants by allowing the jury to exercise its discretion in determining whether to accept the judicially noticed fact, thereby protecting the defendant's right to a fair trial.

Practical Implications of Rule 201

Rule 201 has significant practical implications for both trial strategy and the administration of justice. The rule allows for the efficient resolution of certain factual issues, thereby focusing the trial on genuinely disputed matters. However, it also requires careful consideration to ensure that judicial notice is applied appropriately and fairly.

Strategic Use of Judicial Notice

For trial attorneys, understanding when and how to request judicial notice can be a valuable strategic tool. By obtaining judicial notice of certain facts, attorneys can streamline their case, avoid unnecessary presentation of evidence, and focus the trial on the key issues in dispute.

However, attorneys must also be vigilant in monitoring the court's use of judicial notice to ensure that it does not unfairly prejudice their case. If a fact is judicially noticed that should have been subject to evidence and cross-examination, the party must promptly request a hearing to challenge the decision.

Judicial Discretion and Fairness

Judges must exercise their discretion carefully when taking judicial notice, particularly in criminal cases where the consequences of accepting certain facts as true can be severe. The requirement that the jury in a criminal case be instructed that they may choose whether or not to accept a judicially noticed fact reflects the need to protect the defendant's rights and ensure a fair trial.

Judges must also ensure that the process of taking judicial notice is transparent and that parties are given the opportunity to be heard. This helps to maintain the integrity of the judicial process and ensures that the use of judicial notice does not undermine the fairness of the proceedings.

ARTICLE III. PRESUMPTIONS IN CIVIL CASES

Rule 301 - Presumptions in Civil Cases Generally

Text of Rule 301

Rule 301. Presumptions in Civil Cases Generally
In a civil case, unless a federal statute or these rules provide otherwise, the party against whom a presumption is directed has the burden of producing evidence to rebut the presumption. But this rule does not shift the burden of persuasion, which remains on the party who had it originally.

Introduction to Rule 301

Rule 301 of the Federal Rules of Evidence governs the operation and effect of presumptions in civil cases. A presumption is a legal inference or assumption that a court makes about a fact in the absence of conclusive evidence to the contrary. Presumptions play a significant role in the burden of proof and the dynamics of litigation by shifting the burden of production to the opposing party. Rule 301 specifically addresses how these presumptions function in federal civil litigation, providing guidance on their application and the consequences for both parties. This chapter provides a detailed analysis of Rule 301, exploring its text, interpretation, and the broader implications for civil litigation.

Analysis of Rule 301

Rule 301 establishes a critical aspect of civil litigation by defining how presumptions affect the burden of production while maintaining the original burden of persuasion. This rule ensures that presumptions serve their intended purpose—facilitating the resolution of disputes by simplifying the evidentiary process—without unfairly tipping the scales in favor of one party.

The Concept of Presumptions in Civil Litigation

Presumptions are legal constructs that allow courts to assume a fact is true until evidence is presented to rebut it. They are typically created by law to address situations where certain facts are likely to be true based on common experience or policy considerations. For example, there is a presumption that a letter properly addressed, stamped, and mailed was received by the addressee. Presumptions are designed to streamline the litigation process by allowing courts to infer certain facts without requiring the party benefiting from the presumption to produce direct evidence of those facts.

The Burden of Production vs. the Burden of Persuasion

Rule 301 distinguishes between two types of burdens in civil litigation: the burden of production and the burden of persuasion.

1.   Burden of Production

The burden of production refers to a party's obligation to produce sufficient evidence to support a particular fact or issue. When a presumption is applied, Rule 301 shifts the burden of production to the party against whom the presumption is directed. This means that the party must present evidence that could reasonably rebut the presumed fact. If the party fails to produce such evidence, the presumption stands, and the court or jury may treat the presumed fact as established.

2.   Burden of Persuasion

The burden of persuasion, on the other hand, refers to the obligation of a party to convince the fact-finder (judge or jury) of the truth of a particular issue. Rule 301 clarifies that while the burden of production may shift due to a presumption, the burden of persuasion remains with the party who initially bore it. This means that even if the opposing party produces evidence to rebut the presumption, the original party retains the responsibility of ultimately persuading the fact-finder of the truth of the matter.

Operation of Presumptions Under Rule 301

Under Rule 301, when a presumption arises in a civil case, the party against whom it is directed must respond by producing evidence to counter the presumption. The rule does not require this party to disprove the presumed fact conclusively; rather, they must produce enough evidence to allow a reasonable fact-finder to conclude that the presumed fact may not be true. If the party successfully rebuts the presumption by producing such evidence, the presumption is effectively neutralized, and the case proceeds as if the presumption had never existed.

However, if the party fails to rebut the presumption, the court may instruct the jury that they should find the presumed fact to be true, unless they are persuaded otherwise by the totality of the evidence presented.

The Impact of Rule 301 on Litigation Strategy

Rule 301 has a significant impact on litigation strategy, particularly in how parties approach the presentation of evidence. A party benefiting from a presumption may use it as a strategic tool to compel the opposing party to come forward with evidence. This can shift the focus of the trial and potentially expose weaknesses in the opposing party's case.

Conversely, the party against whom a presumption is directed must be prepared to respond effectively. This may involve presenting direct evidence to counter the presumption or challenging the validity of the presumption itself. The ability to neutralize a presumption can be crucial in influencing the outcome of the case.

Relationship Between Rule 301 and Other Rules or Statutes

Rule 301 applies unless a federal statute or other rule provides otherwise. This means that certain statutes or specific rules of evidence may establish different procedures or requirements for presumptions in particular contexts. For example, some statutes may impose a more stringent burden of proof on the party against whom the presumption is directed, or they may create irrebuttable presumptions that cannot be challenged.

It is important for practitioners to be aware of any statutory or rule-based exceptions that might apply to the presumptions in their case. Understanding these exceptions can be critical in formulating an effective litigation strategy and ensuring that presumptions are handled appropriately within the context of the applicable law.

Judicial Discretion in Applying Rule 301

While Rule 301 sets the framework for the operation of presumptions in civil cases, judges have discretion in how they apply the rule. This includes decisions about whether a presumption applies in the first place, how the burden of production should shift, and what instructions should be given to the jury. Judges may also consider the specific facts and circumstances of the case in determining whether the presumption should have its usual effect or whether an exception should apply.

Judicial discretion ensures that Rule 301 is applied in a way that is fair and appropriate to the particular case, balancing the interests of both parties and promoting the overall goals of the judicial process.

Practical Implications of Rule 301

Rule 301 has important practical implications for civil litigation, influencing how attorneys approach the presentation of evidence and the overall strategy of their case. Understanding the operation of presumptions under Rule 301 is essential for effectively managing the dynamics of the trial and ensuring that the burden of proof is appropriately addressed.

Strategic Use of Presumptions

For attorneys, the strategic use of presumptions can be a powerful tool in civil litigation. By invoking a presumption, an attorney can shift the burden of production to the opposing party, forcing them to address a particular fact or issue. This can be particularly advantageous in cases where the opposing party is unlikely to have sufficient evidence to rebut the presumption.

Attorneys must also be prepared to counter presumptions that arise against their clients. This may involve presenting evidence that directly contradicts the presumed fact, challenging the basis of the presumption, or demonstrating that the presumption does not apply under the specific facts of the case.

Jury Instructions and the Role of the Judge

Judges play a crucial role in managing presumptions under Rule 301, particularly in how they instruct the jury. When a presumption is at issue, the judge must carefully craft jury instructions that explain the effect of the presumption, the burden of production, and the burden of persuasion. These instructions must be clear and accurate to ensure that the jury understands how to properly evaluate the evidence and the impact of the presumption.

In some cases, the judge may also need to provide additional guidance to the jury if the presumption is rebutted, explaining how the jury should consider the evidence in light of the presumption and any rebuttal evidence.

Appellate Review of Presumptions

Appellate courts often review the application of presumptions under Rule 301, particularly in cases where the operation of the presumption may have affected the outcome of the trial. Appellate review may focus on whether the trial court correctly applied the presumption, whether the burden of production was properly shifted, and whether the jury was appropriately instructed.

If an appellate court finds that a presumption was improperly applied or that the jury instructions were inadequate, it may order a new trial or other appropriate relief. This highlights the importance of properly managing presumptions during the trial to avoid potential errors on appeal.

Interaction with State Laws and Federal Statutes

While Rule 301 governs presumptions in federal civil cases, attorneys must also be aware of how state laws or federal statutes might interact with or modify the rule. In cases where state law provides the rule of decision, state presumptions may apply, and these may operate differently than presumptions under Rule 301.

Similarly, certain federal statutes may create specific presumptions that override or modify the general rules established by Rule 301. Attorneys must carefully research and understand the relevant legal framework to ensure that they are applying the correct presumptions in their case.

Rule 302 - Applying State Law to Presumptions in Civil Cases

Text of Rule 302

Rule 302. Applying State Law to Presumptions in Civil Cases

In a civil case, state law governs the effect of a presumption regarding a claim or defense for which state law supplies the rule of decision.

Introduction to Rule 302

Rule 302 of the Federal Rules of Evidence addresses the application of state law to presumptions in civil cases where state law provides the rule of decision. This rule plays a critical role in determining how presumptions operate in federal courts when state law is applicable, particularly in diversity jurisdiction cases where federal courts must apply state substantive law. Rule 302 ensures that the interplay between federal procedural rules and state substantive law is managed in a way that respects both the federal system and the principles of federalism. This chapter provides a detailed analysis of Rule 302, exploring its text, interpretation, and implications for civil litigation.

Analysis of Rule 302

Rule 302 provides clear guidance on the application of state law to presumptions in civil cases where state law is the rule of decision. This rule is essential in the context of the Erie doctrine, which requires federal courts sitting in diversity to apply state substantive law while following federal procedural rules. Rule 302 ensures that state law presumptions, which are often rooted in substantive law, are applied appropriately in federal court.

The Erie Doctrine and Its Implications

The Erie doctrine, derived from the landmark Supreme Court decision in *Erie Railroad Co. v. Tompkins*, 304 U.S. 64 (1938), mandates that federal courts sitting in diversity jurisdiction must apply state substantive law and federal procedural law. This doctrine is grounded in principles of federalism and the need to prevent forum shopping by ensuring that the outcome of a case does not depend on whether it is heard in state or federal court.

Substantive vs. Procedural Law

Under the Erie doctrine, determining whether a particular rule is substantive or procedural is crucial because it dictates whether federal or state law applies. Substantive law includes rules that affect the rights and obligations of the parties, while procedural law governs the process by which the case is adjudicated. Presumptions often straddle the line between substantive and procedural law, as they can affect both the burden of proof and the outcome of the case.

Application of State Law Presumptions in Federal Court

Rule 302 specifically addresses the application of state law presumptions in federal civil cases. When state law provides the rule of decision—meaning the law that determines the substantive rights and obligations of the parties—state law also governs the effect of any presumption related to a claim or defense.

Types of Presumptions Governed by State Law

State law presumptions can vary widely, ranging from presumptions that shift the burden of production to those that shift the burden of persuasion. Some state presumptions are conclusive, meaning they cannot be rebutted, while others are rebuttable. Rule 302 ensures that these state law presumptions are applied in federal court in the same manner they would be in state court, preserving the substantive rights of the parties.

For example, if state law provides a presumption of negligence based on the violation of a safety statute, Rule 302 would require the federal court to apply that presumption in the same way a state court would, including any effects on the burden of production or persuasion.

The Role of the Federal Court

The federal court's role under Rule 302 is to faithfully apply state law presumptions as they relate to the claims or defenses governed by state law. This may involve interpreting state statutes or common law to determine how the presumption operates and ensuring that the presumption is applied consistently with state court decisions.

The application of Rule 302 may require the federal court to engage in a detailed analysis of state law, including reviewing state statutes, case law, and other relevant legal authorities to understand how the presumption should be applied. In cases where state law is unclear or where there is a conflict between different state court decisions, the federal court may need to predict how the state's highest court would resolve the issue.

Federalism and the Uniformity of Law

Rule 302 reflects the balance between federalism and the need for uniformity in the application of the law. By requiring federal courts to apply state law presumptions in cases where state law provides the rule of decision, Rule 302 respects the principles of federalism and ensures that state substantive law is given full effect in federal court.

At the same time, Rule 302 maintains the uniform application of federal procedural law, as required by the Federal Rules of Evidence. This balance helps to prevent forum shopping and ensures that the outcome of a case does not depend on whether it is heard in state or federal court, thereby promoting fairness and consistency in the judicial process.

Interaction with Other Federal Rules of Evidence

Rule 302 interacts with other Federal Rules of Evidence, particularly those governing the burden of proof, relevance, and admissibility of evidence. While Rule 302 requires the application of state law presumptions, other rules of evidence, such as Rule 301 (which governs the general effect of presumptions in civil cases), continue to apply unless superseded by Rule 302.

For instance, if a state law presumption shifts the burden of persuasion, Rule 302 would require the federal court to apply that presumption in the same way a state court would. However, if the presumption only shifts the burden of production, Rule 301 would still govern the operation of that presumption unless state law provides otherwise.

Challenges and Considerations in Applying Rule 302

Applying Rule 302 can present challenges, particularly in cases where state law is complex or unsettled. Federal courts must carefully navigate these issues to ensure that state law presumptions are applied correctly and consistently. This may involve resolving ambiguities in state law or reconciling conflicting interpretations from different state courts.

In some cases, federal courts may need to certify questions to the state's highest court to obtain authoritative guidance on how a particular presumption should be applied. This process ensures that the federal court's application of state law is accurate and reflects the current state of the law.

Practical Implications of Rule 302

Rule 302 has significant practical implications for civil litigation in federal court, particularly in cases involving state law claims or defenses. Understanding how Rule 302 operates is essential for attorneys and judges, as it influences the application of presumptions and the overall strategy of the case.

Strategic Considerations for Attorneys

For attorneys, Rule 302 highlights the importance of thoroughly understanding the relevant state law when litigating in federal court. This includes being aware of any presumptions that may apply to the claims or defenses at issue and understanding how those presumptions operate under state law.

Attorneys must also be prepared to argue for the application of state law presumptions in federal court, including providing the court with the necessary legal authorities and evidence to support their position. Conversely, attorneys may need to challenge the application of certain presumptions if they believe that the presumption is not supported by state law or that it conflicts with federal procedural rules.

Judicial Application of Rule 302

Judges must carefully apply Rule 302 to ensure that state law presumptions are given full effect in federal court. This requires a deep understanding of the relevant state law and the ability to interpret and apply that law in the context of the case. Judges must also be mindful of the potential for conflicts between state and federal law and be prepared to address those conflicts in a way that respects both the principles of federalism and the requirements of the Federal Rules of Evidence.

Appellate Review

Appellate courts often review the application of Rule 302, particularly in cases where the federal court's interpretation of state law is challenged. Appellate review may focus on whether the federal court correctly applied the state law presumption, whether the presumption was appropriately recognized as substantive rather than procedural, and whether the application of the presumption affected the outcome of the case.

If an appellate court finds that the federal court misapplied Rule 302, it may order a new trial or other appropriate relief. This underscores the importance of correctly applying state law presumptions in federal court to avoid potential errors on appeal.

ARTICLE IV. RELEVANCE AND ITS LIMITS

Rule 401 - Test for Relevant Evidence

Text of Rule 401

> **Rule 401. Test for Relevant Evidence**
>
> Evidence is relevant if: (a) it has any tendency to make a fact more or less probable than it would be without the evidence; and (b) the fact is of consequence in determining the action.

Introduction to Rule 401

Rule 401 of the Federal Rules of Evidence provides the foundational definition of relevant evidence, a concept that lies at the heart of the evidentiary framework governing both civil and criminal litigation in federal courts. The rule establishes a two-part test for determining the relevance of evidence, which is a prerequisite for its admissibility. Evidence that fails to meet the standard of relevance is generally inadmissible, while evidence that satisfies the test may still be subject to exclusion under other rules. This chapter offers a detailed analysis of Rule 401, exploring its text, application, and broader implications for the administration of justice.

Analysis of Rule 401

Rule 401 establishes a straightforward yet essential test for determining whether evidence is relevant in the context of a legal proceeding. The rule's definition of relevance is broad, allowing for the inclusion of a wide range of evidence, provided it meets the two-part test set forth in the rule.

The Two-Part Test for Relevance

Rule 401's test for relevance consists of two key components:

1. **Tendency to Make a Fact More or Less Probable (Rule 401(a))**

The first part of the test examines whether the evidence has "any tendency" to make a fact more or less probable than it would be without the evidence. This standard is deliberately low, reflecting the understanding that relevance is a threshold issue. The evidence need not conclusively prove or disprove a fact; rather, it need only affect the likelihood that a fact is true or untrue to some degree.

This broad standard allows for the admission of evidence that may have a relatively minor influence on the fact-finder's determination of a fact, provided it contributes to the overall understanding of the case. For example, in a breach of contract case, an email from a party indicating hesitation to fulfill the contract might have a tendency to make it more probable that the party anticipated not performing their contractual obligations, even if it does not definitively establish breach.

2. **Fact of Consequence in Determining the Action (Rule 401(b))**

The second part of the test requires that the fact made more or less probable by the evidence be "of consequence in determining the action." This means that the fact must be material to the issues in the case—i.e., it must relate to a fact that is significant under the substantive law governing the case. A fact is "of consequence" if it has a legitimate bearing on the case's outcome, such as a fact that is part of a claim, defense, or element of a cause of action.

The requirement that the fact be of consequence ensures that the court's inquiry remains focused on facts that matter to the resolution of the case, preventing the introduction of evidence that is irrelevant or tangential to the main issues. For example, in a personal injury case, evidence of the defendant's prior unrelated accidents might not be of consequence unless it is relevant to an issue like the defendant's knowledge of a hazardous condition or habit of carelessness.

Broad Scope of Relevance

Rule 401 is intentionally broad in its scope, allowing for the inclusion of evidence that may indirectly or circumstantially relate to a material fact. This broad definition of relevance reflects the principle that the fact-finder should have access to all evidence that might help in the accurate determination of the facts in dispute. By adopting a low threshold for relevance, Rule 401 ensures that the fact-finder is not deprived of evidence that could contribute to a more complete understanding of the case.

However, the broad definition of relevance under Rule 401 does not mean that all relevant evidence is admissible. Even if evidence is deemed relevant under Rule 401, it may still be excluded under other rules, such as Rule 403, which allows the exclusion of relevant evidence if its probative value is substantially outweighed by the risk of unfair prejudice, confusion, or waste of time.

The Role of the Judge in Determining Relevance

The determination of relevance under Rule 401 is generally made by the judge as a preliminary matter. The judge's role is to apply the two-part test to decide whether the evidence has any tendency to make a fact of consequence more or less probable. This decision is often made in the context of an objection raised by one of the parties, where the judge must evaluate the proffered evidence and rule on its admissibility.

The judge's discretion in applying Rule 401 is broad, and appellate courts typically give deference to the trial judge's determinations of relevance. This deference recognizes the trial judge's familiarity with the specifics of the case and the importance of judicial efficiency in managing the flow of evidence.

Interplay with Other Rules of Evidence

Rule 401 serves as the gateway for the admissibility of evidence, but it must be understood in conjunction with other rules of evidence that further refine or limit the admission of relevant evidence. For example:

*   **Rule 402** states that relevant evidence is generally admissible unless otherwise excluded by the

Constitution, a federal statute, another rule of evidence, or other rules prescribed by the Supreme Court.

- **Rule 403** allows the exclusion of relevant evidence if its probative value is substantially outweighed by the risk of unfair prejudice, confusion, or delay.

- **Rules 404 to 415** govern the admissibility of evidence related to character, other crimes, or acts, which may be relevant under Rule 401 but subject to additional limitations.

By setting the threshold for relevance, Rule 401 establishes the starting point for the analysis of admissibility, with other rules providing additional criteria and safeguards.

Policy Considerations Underlying Rule 401

The broad definition of relevance in Rule 401 is grounded in the policy of ensuring that trials are based on a full and fair consideration of the evidence. The rule is designed to allow the fact-finder to see the "whole picture," rather than a fragmented or incomplete view of the facts. This approach promotes the accurate determination of facts and helps to ensure that justice is served.

However, the rule also reflects a balance between inclusiveness and the need to prevent trials from becoming bogged down by evidence that is only marginally relevant or likely to distract the fact-finder from the main issues. This balance is achieved by the combination of Rule 401's broad definition of relevance with the safeguards provided by other rules that govern the exclusion of evidence.

Practical Implications of Rule 401

Rule 401 has significant practical implications for both trial strategy and the administration of justice. Understanding the rule's broad definition of relevance is essential for attorneys, judges, and litigants as they navigate the evidentiary landscape of a trial.

Strategic Use of Relevant Evidence

For attorneys, Rule 401 provides a powerful tool for introducing evidence that supports their case theory. By emphasizing the low threshold for relevance, attorneys can argue for the admission of a wide range of evidence, including circumstantial evidence, that might help to establish a fact of consequence. This can be particularly useful in cases where direct evidence is limited or unavailable.

Attorneys must also be prepared to challenge the relevance of evidence introduced by the opposing party, particularly if that evidence has only a tenuous connection to the issues in

the case. By raising objections based on relevance, attorneys can help to keep the trial focused on the key facts and avoid the introduction of evidence that might confuse or mislead the fact-finder.

Judicial Management of Evidence

Judges play a critical role in managing the relevance of evidence during a trial. By applying the two-part test of Rule 401, judges ensure that the evidence presented to the fact-finder is pertinent to the issues at hand. This judicial gatekeeping helps to streamline the trial process, prevent the introduction of extraneous or confusing evidence, and protect the fairness of the proceedings.

Judges must also be mindful of the interplay between Rule 401 and other rules of evidence, particularly Rule 403. Even if evidence is relevant under Rule 401, judges have the discretion to exclude it if they determine that its probative value is outweighed by the potential for prejudice or other negative effects. This requires careful consideration of the specific circumstances of each case.

Appellate Review of Relevance Determinations

Appellate courts typically review relevance determinations for abuse of discretion, meaning they give deference to the trial judge's decision unless it was clearly unreasonable or arbitrary. This standard of review reflects the understanding that the trial judge is in the best position to evaluate the relevance of evidence in the context of the case.

However, appellate courts may overturn a trial judge's relevance determination if it resulted in the exclusion of critical evidence or the admission of highly prejudicial evidence that affected the outcome of the trial. This underscores the importance of careful and reasoned decision-making by trial judges when applying Rule 401.

Relevance in Specific Types of Cases

The application of Rule 401 can vary depending on the type of case and the specific legal issues involved. For example, in criminal cases, the relevance of evidence related to the defendant's prior conduct may be subject to additional scrutiny under rules governing character evidence. In civil cases, the relevance of certain types of evidence, such as financial records or expert testimony, may depend on the specific claims or defenses at issue.

Attorneys and judges must be attuned to the specific context of the case when applying Rule 401, ensuring that the evidence presented is both relevant and appropriate under the circumstances.

Rule 402 - General Admissibility of Relevant Evidence

Rule 402. General Admissibility of Relevant Evidence
Relevant evidence is admissible unless any of the following provides otherwise:
• the United States Constitution;
• a federal statute;
• these rules; or
• other rules prescribed by the Supreme Court.
Irrelevant evidence is not admissible.

Introduction to Rule 402

Rule 402 of the Federal Rules of Evidence establishes the fundamental principle that relevant evidence is generally admissible in federal courts, while irrelevant evidence is not. This rule reflects the core evidentiary standard that only evidence which has a bearing on the issues in a case should be considered by the fact-finder. However, Rule 402 also acknowledges that there are exceptions to this principle, where even relevant evidence may be excluded due to overriding legal rules, policies, or constitutional concerns. This chapter provides a detailed analysis of Rule 402, exploring its text, interpretation, and broader implications for the administration of justice.

Analysis of Rule 402

Rule 402 operates as the gateway through which evidence must pass to be admitted in federal court. It underscores the presumption in favor of admitting relevant evidence, while simultaneously recognizing that certain legal and constitutional considerations may necessitate the exclusion of such evidence. The rule also clearly states that irrelevant evidence is inadmissible, reinforcing the principle that the court's focus should remain on facts that are material to the case.

General Admissibility of Relevant Evidence

The first clause of Rule 402 sets forth the general rule that relevant evidence is admissible. This principle is rooted in the belief that the fact-finder should have access to all information that could reasonably assist in determining the truth of the matters in dispute. By allowing relevant evidence to be admitted, Rule 402 ensures that the judicial process is informed by a comprehensive and accurate presentation of the facts.

Relevance as a Threshold Requirement

Relevance, as defined by Rule 401, is a threshold requirement for admissibility under Rule 402. Evidence must first meet the standard of relevance, meaning it must have any tendency to make a fact of consequence more or less probable than it would be without the evidence. Once evidence is deemed relevant, Rule 402 presumes its admissibility unless specific legal grounds for exclusion apply.

Exceptions to the General Rule of Admissibility

While Rule 402 favors the admission of relevant evidence, it also provides for several key exceptions where such evidence may be excluded. These exceptions are grounded in overarching legal principles and policies that sometimes outweigh the benefits of admitting relevant evidence.

1. The United States Constitution

The Constitution serves as the supreme law of the land, and its provisions may require the exclusion of certain evidence, even if it is relevant. For example, evidence obtained in violation of the Fourth Amendment's protection against unreasonable searches and seizures may be excluded under the exclusionary rule. Similarly, the Fifth Amendment's protection against self-incrimination may prevent the admission of coerced confessions. Rule 402 recognizes the paramount importance of constitutional rights and ensures that they are upheld in the evidentiary process.

2. Federal Statutes

Federal statutes may also provide grounds for the exclusion of relevant evidence. For instance, the Federal Rules of Evidence themselves are grounded in statutory authority, and specific statutes may set forth rules that limit or exclude the admissibility of certain types of evidence. Examples include statutes that protect privileged communications, such as attorney-client communications, or those that impose confidentiality requirements, such as the Health Insurance Portability and Accountability Act (HIPAA), which protects the privacy of medical records.

3. These Rules (Federal Rules of Evidence)

The Federal Rules of Evidence contain specific provisions that may require the exclusion of relevant evidence. For example, Rule 403 allows the exclusion of relevant evidence if its probative value is substantially outweighed by the risk of unfair prejudice, confusion, or delay. Other rules, such as those governing hearsay (Rules 801–807), character evidence (Rules 404–405), and privileges (Rule 501), also impose limitations on the admissibility of relevant evidence. Rule 402 ensures that these specific rules are applied appropriately, maintaining the integrity of the judicial process.

4. Other Rules Prescribed by the Supreme Court

The Supreme Court may prescribe additional rules that govern the admissibility of evidence in federal courts. These rules, which may arise from the Court's inherent authority or its rule-making powers, can impose further limitations on the admission of relevant evidence. Rule 402 acknowledges the Supreme Court's role in shaping evidentiary standards and ensures that any such rules are given effect.

Exclusion of Irrelevant Evidence

The second clause of Rule 402 provides that irrelevant evidence is not admissible. This straightforward rule reflects the principle that the court's focus should be on matters that are pertinent to the resolution of the case. Irrelevant evidence, by definition, does not have any tendency to make a fact of consequence more or less probable, and its admission would only serve to confuse or distract the fact-finder.

By excluding irrelevant evidence, Rule 402 helps to streamline the trial process, ensuring that the fact-finder's attention is directed to the facts that truly matter. This exclusion also serves to protect the efficiency and fairness of the proceedings, preventing the introduction of evidence that could needlessly complicate or prolong the trial.

The Role of Judicial Discretion

While Rule 402 establishes clear principles regarding the admissibility of relevant and irrelevant evidence, the application of these principles often involves the exercise of judicial discretion. Judges must determine whether evidence is relevant, and if so, whether it should be admitted or excluded based on the exceptions outlined in the rule.

Judicial discretion plays a particularly important role in cases where the relevance of evidence is marginal or where competing legal principles must be balanced. For example, a judge may need to decide whether the probative value of relevant evidence is outweighed by the potential for unfair prejudice under Rule 403. In such cases, the judge's role is to ensure that the trial remains focused on the key issues and that the evidence presented is both relevant and fair.

Interplay with Other Rules of Evidence

Rule 402 serves as the foundational rule for the admissibility of evidence, but it must be read in conjunction with other rules that further refine or limit the admission of evidence. For example:

- **Rule 403** addresses situations where the exclusion of relevant evidence may be warranted due to concerns about prejudice, confusion, or delay.

- **Rules 404–415** impose specific limitations on the admissibility of character evidence, prior acts, and similar issues that may be relevant under Rule 402 but are subject to additional scrutiny.

- **Rules 501–502** govern the recognition and application of privileges, which may exclude otherwise relevant evidence.

By setting the general standard for admissibility, Rule 402 provides the framework within which these other rules operate, ensuring that the admission of evidence is governed by both relevance and broader legal principles.

Practical Implications of Rule 402

Rule 402 has significant practical implications for the conduct of trials and the overall administration of justice. Understanding how Rule 402 operates is essential for attorneys, judges, and litigants as they navigate the evidentiary process.

Strategic Considerations for Attorneys

For attorneys, Rule 402 provides the basis for arguing for or against the admissibility of evidence. When seeking to admit evidence, attorneys must first establish its relevance under Rule 401 and then argue for its admissibility under Rule 402. Conversely, when challenging the admissibility of evidence, attorneys may invoke the exceptions outlined in Rule 402, such as constitutional protections, statutory exclusions, or specific rules of evidence that limit the use of certain types of evidence.

Attorneys must also be prepared to respond to the potential exclusion of relevant evidence by demonstrating its probative value and addressing any concerns that might warrant its exclusion. This involves a careful analysis of the facts, the applicable law, and the specific circumstances of the case.

Judicial Management of Evidence

Judges play a critical role in applying Rule 402 and managing the admission of evidence during a trial. By carefully evaluating the relevance of evidence and considering any applicable exceptions, judges ensure that the trial remains focused on the key issues and that the evidence presented is both pertinent and fair.

Judges must also balance the need for a comprehensive presentation of the facts with the need to protect the rights of the parties and the integrity of the judicial process. This may involve making difficult decisions about whether to admit or exclude certain evidence, particularly in cases where constitutional rights or other significant legal principles are at stake.

Appellate Review of Admissibility Decisions

Appellate courts often review decisions made under Rule 402, particularly in cases where the exclusion or admission of evidence is contested. Appellate review may focus on whether the trial court correctly applied the standard of relevance, whether the evidence was properly excluded or admitted under the exceptions outlined in Rule 402, and whether any errors affected the outcome of the trial.

Appellate courts typically give deference to the trial judge's decisions on the admissibility of evidence, recognizing the trial judge's familiarity with the case and the importance of judicial discretion. However, appellate courts may overturn decisions that are clearly erroneous or that reflect a misunderstanding of the law.

Rule 403 - Excluding Relevant Evidence for Prejudice, Confusion, Waste of Time, or Other Reasons

Rule 403. Excluding Relevant Evidence for Prejudice, Confusion, Waste of Time, or Other Reasons
The court may exclude relevant evidence if its probative value is substantially outweighed by a danger of one or more of the following:
• unfair prejudice,
• confusing the issues,
• misleading the jury,
• undue delay,
• wasting time, or
• needlessly presenting cumulative evidence.

Introduction to Rule 403

Rule 403 of the Federal Rules of Evidence serves as a critical safeguard in the evidentiary process by providing courts with the discretion to exclude relevant evidence under certain circumstances. While Rule 401 and Rule 402 establish that relevant evidence is generally admissible, Rule 403 introduces a balancing test that allows courts to exclude evidence if its probative value is substantially outweighed by the risk of unfair prejudice, confusion, misleading the jury, undue delay, wasting time, or needlessly presenting cumulative evidence. This rule is essential for ensuring that trials remain fair, focused, and efficient. This chapter provides a detailed analysis of Rule 403, exploring its text, application, and broader implications for the administration of justice.

Analysis of Rule 403

Rule 403 empowers judges with the discretion to exclude evidence that, while relevant, may negatively impact the fairness or efficiency of the trial. The rule's balancing test requires courts to weigh the probative value of the evidence against the potential risks associated with its admission. This balancing act is fundamental to the court's role in ensuring that the evidence presented to the jury is both helpful and fair.

The Balancing Test

The core of Rule 403 is its balancing test, which requires courts to evaluate whether the probative value of the evidence is substantially outweighed by the dangers listed in the rule. The phrase "substantially outweighed" indicates that exclusion under Rule 403 is not appropriate merely because the evidence poses some risk; rather, the risk must significantly outweigh the evidence's value.

1. **Probative Value**

Probative value refers to the extent to which evidence makes a fact of consequence more or less probable. The greater the probative value, the more likely the evidence is to be admitted, as it directly contributes to the fact-finder's understanding of the issues at hand. In assessing probative value, courts consider factors such as the importance of the evidence to the party's case, the extent to which it supports or refutes a key issue, and the availability of alternative evidence.

2. **Dangers Considered in the Balancing Test**

   o **Unfair Prejudice:** Unfair prejudice refers to the risk that evidence might induce the fact-finder to make a decision based on emotion, bias, or an improper basis, rather than on the factual evidence presented. Evidence is considered unfairly prejudicial if it has the potential to inflame the passions of the jury or to lead them to make a decision that is not based on the merits of the case. For example, graphic photographs in a criminal case might be excluded if their emotional impact could cause the jury to convict based on sympathy or horror rather than the evidence.

   o **Confusing the Issues:** Evidence may be excluded if it has the potential to confuse the issues or to distract the jury from the main questions they need to resolve. This often occurs when evidence is complex, technical, or unrelated to the central issues in the case. If the jury might struggle to understand the relevance of the evidence or might be led to focus on a peripheral issue, the court may decide to exclude it.

   o **Misleading the Jury:** Evidence that might mislead the jury, either because it is presented out of context or because it suggests a false narrative, can also be excluded under Rule 403. This is particularly important in cases where evidence, while technically accurate, might lead the jury to draw incorrect or unjustified inferences.

- ○ **Undue Delay and Waste of Time:** Courts are concerned with the efficient administration of justice, and evidence that could cause undue delay or waste time may be excluded. This consideration is especially relevant in cases where the evidence would require extensive additional testimony, cross-examination, or explanation, which might prolong the trial unnecessarily.

- ○ **Needlessly Presenting Cumulative Evidence:** Rule 403 allows for the exclusion of evidence that is merely cumulative—meaning it repeats information already provided by other evidence. While cumulative evidence may still be relevant, its repetitive nature can unnecessarily lengthen the trial and burden the jury with redundant information.

Judicial Discretion Under Rule 403

Rule 403 grants judges significant discretion in applying the balancing test. This discretion allows judges to tailor the evidentiary process to the specific needs and circumstances of each case, ensuring that the trial remains fair and efficient. Because the application of Rule 403 is highly contextual, judges must carefully consider the unique aspects of the case, including the nature of the evidence, the issues at stake, and the potential impact on the jury.

Appellate courts typically review decisions under Rule 403 for abuse of discretion, giving considerable deference to the trial judge's judgment. This reflects the understanding that the trial judge is in the best position to assess the nuances of the case and the potential effects of the evidence on the jury.

Application of Rule 403 in Various Contexts

Rule 403 is applied across a wide range of contexts, each of which may present unique challenges in balancing probative value against potential risks.

1. Criminal Cases

In criminal cases, Rule 403 is often invoked to exclude evidence that might unfairly prejudice the defendant, such as evidence of prior bad acts or highly inflammatory material. For example, evidence of a defendant's past criminal history might be excluded if it could lead the jury to assume the defendant's guilt based on past behavior rather than the evidence presented in the current case. Similarly, graphic crime scene photographs might be excluded if they are deemed more likely to provoke an emotional response than to provide substantive insight into the case.

2. Civil Cases

In civil cases, Rule 403 is frequently used to exclude evidence that could confuse the issues or cause undue delay. For instance, in a complex contract dispute, highly technical expert testimony might be excluded if it risks confusing the jury about the central issues or if it introduces concepts that are tangential to the main dispute. Additionally, evidence that is cumulative or that has limited probative value relative to the

time required to present it might be excluded to streamline the proceedings.

3. Evidentiary Hearings and Pre-Trial Motions

Rule 403 also plays a role in evidentiary hearings and pre-trial motions, where judges may need to decide whether to admit or exclude evidence before the trial begins. These decisions can shape the scope of the trial, influencing which issues will be presented to the jury and how the evidence will be framed. Judges must use Rule 403 to ensure that the trial remains focused on the key issues and that the evidence presented is both relevant and fair.

Interaction with Other Rules of Evidence

Rule 403 interacts with various other rules of evidence that govern specific types of evidence or issues of admissibility. For example:

- **Rule 404** restricts the use of character evidence, but even if character evidence is deemed relevant under Rule 404, it may still be excluded under Rule 403 if it poses a substantial risk of unfair prejudice.

- **Rule 609** allows the impeachment of witnesses with prior convictions, but Rule 403 can be invoked to exclude such evidence if its prejudicial effect substantially outweighs its probative value.

- **Rules 801–807** govern hearsay evidence, and even if an out-of-court statement meets a hearsay exception, Rule 403 may still exclude it if its admission would lead to unfair prejudice, confusion, or other issues.

By applying Rule 403 in conjunction with these other rules, courts can maintain a fair and balanced trial process.

Policy Considerations Underlying Rule 403

The policy considerations underlying Rule 403 are rooted in the principles of fairness, efficiency, and the integrity of the judicial process. The rule reflects a recognition that not all relevant evidence should be admitted, particularly when its admission could compromise the fairness of the trial or distract from the central issues.

By giving judges the discretion to exclude evidence that poses significant risks, Rule 403 helps to ensure that trials are conducted in a manner that respects the rights of the parties, protects the jury from undue influence, and promotes the accurate determination of the facts.

Practical Implications of Rule 403

Rule 403 has significant practical implications for trial strategy, the conduct of judges, and the overall administration of justice. Understanding how to apply and argue Rule 403 is essential for attorneys, judges, and litigants.

Strategic Considerations for Attorneys

For attorneys, Rule 403 is a crucial tool for shaping the evidentiary landscape of a trial. When seeking to exclude evidence, attorneys must carefully argue that the potential risks—such as unfair prejudice or confusion—substantially outweigh the probative value of the evidence. This requires a nuanced understanding of the evidence's impact on the jury and the ability to articulate why its admission would be detrimental to a fair trial.

Conversely, when seeking to admit evidence that might be challenged under Rule 403, attorneys must be prepared to defend its probative value and demonstrate that any potential risks are minimal or manageable. This may involve proposing limiting instructions or other safeguards to mitigate the risk of unfair prejudice or confusion.

Judicial Management of Rule 403

Judges play a central role in applying Rule 403 and managing the evidentiary process during a trial. By carefully balancing the probative value of evidence against its potential risks, judges ensure that the trial remains focused, fair, and efficient. This requires judges to be vigilant in assessing the impact of evidence and to exercise their discretion in a manner that protects the integrity of the judicial process.

Judges must also be prepared to provide clear explanations for their Rule 403 rulings, particularly in cases where the exclusion or admission of evidence is likely to be contentious. This helps to ensure that the parties understand the basis for the court's decisions and that the record is clear for any potential appellate review.

Appellate Review of Rule 403 Decisions

Appellate courts typically review Rule 403 decisions for abuse of discretion, meaning they defer to the trial judge's judgment unless it was clearly unreasonable or arbitrary. This standard of review reflects the understanding that trial judges are best positioned to assess the nuances of the evidence and the dynamics of the trial.

However, appellate courts may overturn a Rule 403 decision if they find that the trial judge misapplied the balancing test or failed to consider relevant factors. This underscores the importance of a careful and reasoned application of Rule 403 at the trial level.

Rule 403 in Specific Contexts

The application of Rule 403 can vary depending on the context of the case, the nature of the evidence, and the specific legal issues involved. For example, in cases involving sensitive issues such as sexual misconduct or racial discrimination, the potential for unfair prejudice may be particularly high, requiring a careful and nuanced application of Rule 403.

Attorneys and judges must be attuned to the specific challenges presented by each case and be prepared to address the unique considerations that may arise under Rule 403.

Rule 404 - Character Evidence; Other Crimes, Wrongs, or Acts

Rule 404. Character Evidence; Other Crimes, Wrongs, or Acts

(a) **Character Evidence.** (1) **Prohibited Uses.** Evidence of a person's character or character trait is not admissible to prove that on a particular occasion the person acted in accordance with the character or trait. (2) **Exceptions for a Defendant or Victim in a Criminal Case.** The following exceptions apply in a criminal case: (A) a defendant may offer evidence of the defendant's pertinent trait, and if the evidence is admitted, the prosecutor may offer evidence to rebut it; (B) subject to the limitations in Rule 412, a defendant may offer evidence of an alleged victim's pertinent trait, and if the evidence is admitted, the prosecutor may: (i) offer evidence to rebut it; and (ii) offer evidence of the defendant's same trait; and (C) in a homicide case, the prosecutor may offer evidence of the alleged victim's trait of peacefulness to rebut evidence that the victim was the first aggressor. (3) **Exceptions for a Witness.** Evidence of a witness's character may be admitted under Rules 607, 608, and 609.

(b) **Other Crimes, Wrongs, or Acts.** (1) **Prohibited Uses.** Evidence of a crime, wrong, or other act is not admissible to prove a person's character in order to show that on a particular occasion the person acted in accordance with the character. (2) **Permitted Uses; Notice in a Criminal Case.** This evidence may be admissible for another purpose, such as proving motive, opportunity, intent, preparation, plan, knowledge, identity, absence of mistake, or lack of accident. On request by a defendant in a criminal case, the prosecutor must: (A) provide reasonable notice of the general nature of any such evidence that the prosecutor intends to offer at trial; and (B) do so before trial—or during trial if the court, for good cause, excuses lack of pretrial notice.

Introduction to Rule 404

Rule 404 of the Federal Rules of Evidence addresses the admissibility of character evidence and evidence of other crimes, wrongs, or acts in both civil and criminal cases. This rule reflects the principle that evidence of a person's character or past actions should not be used to suggest that the person acted in conformity with that character or those actions on a particular occasion. Rule 404 is designed to prevent unfair prejudice, ensuring that trials focus on the facts relevant to the specific issues in dispute rather than on a party's general character or prior conduct. This chapter provides a detailed analysis of Rule 404, exploring its text, interpretation, and broader implications for the administration of justice.

Analysis of Rule 404

Rule 404 is divided into two main sections: Rule 404(a) addresses character evidence, while Rule 404(b) deals with evidence of other crimes, wrongs, or acts. Both sections are grounded in the principle that the admissibility of such evidence should be carefully controlled to prevent unfair prejudice and to ensure that the trial remains focused on the relevant issues.

Rule 404(a) - Character Evidence

Rule 404(a) governs the admissibility of character evidence, generally prohibiting the use of such evidence to prove that a person acted in conformity with their character on a specific occasion. The rule reflects the understanding that character evidence can be highly prejudicial, as it may lead the fact-finder to judge a person not based on the specific facts of the case but on a generalized view of their character.

Prohibited Uses (Rule 404(a)(1))

Rule 404(a)(1) explicitly prohibits the use of character evidence to prove that a person acted in accordance with that character or character trait on a particular occasion. For example, evidence that a defendant in a criminal case has a reputation for being dishonest would generally not be admissible to suggest that the defendant committed a theft simply because of that character trait. This prohibition aims to ensure that the trial focuses on the specific facts and evidence relevant to the alleged offense or issue at hand.

Exceptions for a Defendant or Victim in a Criminal Case (Rule 404(a)(2))

While Rule 404(a)(1) sets a general prohibition, Rule 404(a)(2) provides specific exceptions for criminal cases:

1. **Defendant's Pertinent Trait (Rule 404(a)(2)(A))**

A defendant in a criminal case may offer evidence of their own pertinent character trait. If the defendant introduces such evidence, the prosecutor is allowed to rebut it with evidence to the contrary. For instance, if a defendant accused of assault offers evidence that they have a peaceful character, the prosecution may introduce evidence to rebut this claim.

2. **Victim's Pertinent Trait (Rule 404(a)(2)(B))**

Subject to the limitations of Rule 412 (which generally governs the admissibility of evidence regarding a victim's sexual behavior or predisposition), a defendant may offer evidence of an alleged victim's pertinent character trait. If the court admits this evidence, the prosecutor may rebut it with evidence of the same trait in the defendant. For example, in a case of self-defense, a defendant might offer evidence of the victim's violent character to support their claim that the victim was the aggressor. The prosecution could then introduce evidence of the defendant's own violent character to counter this claim.

3. **Homicide Cases (Rule 404(a)(2)(C))**

In a homicide case, if the defendant introduces evidence suggesting that the victim was the first aggressor, the prosecutor may offer evidence of the victim's peaceful character to rebut the claim. This exception recognizes the particular relevance of the victim's character in cases where the defendant argues self-defense in response to an alleged attack by the victim.

Exceptions for a Witness (Rule 404(a)(3))

Rule 404(a)(3) provides that character evidence related to a witness may be admissible under Rules 607, 608, and 609. These rules govern the impeachment of witnesses, allowing evidence of a witness's character for truthfulness or untruthfulness to be considered in assessing their credibility. For example, evidence that a witness has previously been convicted of a crime involving dishonesty may be admissible to challenge their credibility on the stand.

Rule 404(b) - Other Crimes, Wrongs, or Acts

Rule 404(b) addresses the admissibility of evidence related to other crimes, wrongs, or acts committed by a person. Like character evidence, such evidence is generally inadmissible to prove that a person acted in conformity with past behavior. However, Rule 404(b) provides exceptions where this type of evidence may be admitted for other purposes.

Prohibited Uses (Rule 404(b)(1))

Rule 404(b)(1) prohibits the use of evidence of a crime, wrong, or other act to prove a person's character in order to show that they acted in accordance with that character on a particular occasion. This reflects the same concern about unfair prejudice that underlies the prohibition on character evidence: juries might give undue weight to past misconduct and assume guilt based on a person's history rather than the facts of the current case.

Permitted Uses (Rule 404(b)(2))

Rule 404(b)(2) outlines specific circumstances under which evidence of other crimes, wrongs, or acts may be admissible for purposes other than proving character. These include:

- **Motive:** Evidence that shows a motive for the crime or act in question. For example, evidence that a defendant committed a prior similar crime might be admissible to show that they had a motive to commit the current crime.

- **Opportunity:** Evidence that demonstrates the defendant had the opportunity to commit the crime. For instance, a prior act that placed the defendant at the scene of the crime could be relevant to show they had the opportunity to commit the offense.

- **Intent:** Evidence that helps establish the defendant's intent to commit the crime. If a defendant has committed similar acts in the past, this may be relevant to proving that their actions were intentional rather than accidental.

- **Preparation and Plan:** Evidence showing that the defendant had a plan or preparation that connects the prior act to the current offense. For example, if a defendant previously prepared in a similar way before committing a crime, this could be used to show a pattern of behavior.

- **Knowledge:** Evidence indicating that the defendant had knowledge relevant to the crime. For instance, evidence of prior illegal conduct could demonstrate that the defendant knew how to carry out the crime in question.

- **Identity:** Evidence that helps establish the defendant's identity as the perpetrator. For example, if a distinctive method or signature was used in both the prior act and the current crime, this could be relevant to identifying the defendant.

- **Absence of Mistake or Lack of Accident:** Evidence that refutes claims that the act was a mistake or accident. For instance, if a defendant previously engaged in similar conduct, this could be used to argue that the current act was not accidental.

Notice Requirement in Criminal Cases

Rule 404(b)(2) imposes a notice requirement on the prosecution in criminal cases. Upon request by the defendant, the prosecutor must provide reasonable notice of the general nature of any evidence of other crimes, wrongs, or acts that they intend to introduce at trial. This notice must be given before the trial begins, although the court may allow notice during the trial if good cause is shown. This requirement ensures that the defendant has an opportunity to prepare a defense against such evidence and helps prevent surprise or unfair prejudice.

Practical Implications of Rule 404

Rule 404 has significant practical implications for the conduct of trials, the preparation of cases, and the overall administration of justice. Understanding the rule's limitations and exceptions is essential for both prosecutors and defense attorneys in criminal cases, as well as for litigants in civil cases.

Strategic Use of Character Evidence and Other Acts

For attorneys, Rule 404 requires careful consideration when deciding whether to introduce character evidence or evidence of other crimes, wrongs, or acts. In criminal cases, the decision to introduce evidence of a defendant's character trait or a victim's character can be a double-edged sword, as it opens the door for the prosecution to introduce rebuttal evidence. Attorneys must weigh the potential benefits of such evidence against the risks of inviting damaging rebuttal evidence.

Similarly, when dealing with evidence of other crimes or acts, attorneys must be prepared to argue for or against its admissibility based on the specific exceptions outlined in Rule 404(b)(2). Prosecutors may seek to introduce such evidence to establish motive, intent, or identity, while defense attorneys must be vigilant in challenging its admissibility, particularly if it risks prejudicing the jury against the defendant based on past behavior.

Judicial Management of Rule 404 Evidence

Judges play a crucial role in applying Rule 404, as they must determine whether the evidence falls within the prohibited uses or qualifies for one of the exceptions. This requires a careful balancing of the evidence's probative value against the potential for unfair prejudice, confusion, or waste of time. Judges must also ensure that the notice requirements are met in criminal cases, providing the defense with adequate time to prepare a response.

Judges may also need to provide limiting instructions to the jury, explaining how they should consider the evidence of other crimes, wrongs, or acts. Such instructions are essential for ensuring that the jury understands the limited purpose of the evidence and does not use it to make improper inferences about the defendant's character.

Appellate Review of Rule 404 Decisions

Appellate courts often review decisions made under Rule 404, particularly when the admissibility of character evidence or other acts evidence is contested. Appellate review typically focuses on whether the trial court correctly applied the rule's prohibitions and exceptions, as well as whether the admission of such evidence resulted in unfair prejudice that affected the outcome of the trial.

If an appellate court finds that evidence was improperly admitted under Rule 404, it may order a new trial or other appropriate relief. This underscores the importance of a careful and reasoned application of Rule 404 at the trial level.

Rule 404 in Specific Types of Cases

The application of Rule 404 can vary depending on the type of case and the specific issues involved. For example, in cases involving allegations of sexual misconduct, Rule 412 imposes additional restrictions on the admissibility of evidence regarding the victim's character or past sexual behavior. In such cases, attorneys must navigate both Rule 404 and Rule 412 to ensure that their evidence is admissible and that they are adequately protecting their client's rights.

In civil cases, Rule 404 is often invoked in disputes where a party's character or prior conduct is at issue, such as in defamation cases or cases involving claims of fraud or misrepresentation. Attorneys must be prepared to argue for or against the admissibility of character evidence based on the specific facts and legal issues in the case.

Rule 405 - Methods of Proving Character

Rule 405. Methods of Proving Character
(a) **By Reputation or Opinion.** When evidence of a person's character or character trait is admissible, it may be proved by testimony about the person's reputation or by testimony in the form of an opinion. On cross-examination of the character witness, the court may allow an inquiry into relevant specific instances of the person's conduct.
(b) **By Specific Instances of Conduct.** When a person's character or character trait is an essential element of a charge, claim, or defense, the character or trait may also be proved by relevant specific instances of the person's conduct.

Introduction to Rule 405

Rule 405 of the Federal Rules of Evidence establishes the methods by which character may be proven in both civil and criminal cases. Building upon the principles set forth in Rule 404, which limits the use of character evidence, Rule 405 outlines the specific ways in which character evidence can be introduced when it is admissible under the exceptions provided in Rule 404. The rule provides for two primary methods of proving character: by reputation or opinion, and by specific instances of conduct. This chapter provides a detailed analysis of Rule 405, exploring its text, application, and the broader implications for the administration of justice.

Analysis of Rule 405

Rule 405 sets out the permissible methods for proving character when character evidence is allowed under the Federal Rules of Evidence. The rule distinguishes between general character evidence that can be presented by reputation or opinion and specific instances of conduct that are permissible only under certain circumstances. The rule reflects a careful balance between the need to allow relevant character evidence and the need to protect against unfair prejudice, confusion, and unnecessary invasions of privacy.

Rule 405(a) - Proving Character by Reputation or Opinion

Under Rule 405(a), when character evidence is admissible, it may be proved by testimony about a person's reputation or by testimony in the form of an opinion. This provision allows parties to introduce general character evidence through witnesses who are familiar with the person's reputation in the community or who have formed an opinion about the person's character based on their interactions or observations.

Reputation Testimony

Reputation testimony involves a witness testifying about the general perception of a person's character within a relevant community. This type of evidence is often used when the character of the person is a matter of public knowledge, such as in cases where the person is well-known in a particular social, business, or professional community. The reputation testimony must be based on the collective view of the community rather than the personal opinion of the witness. For example, in a criminal case where the defendant claims to have a reputation for honesty, a witness might testify that the defendant is generally known in their community as an honest person.

Opinion Testimony

Opinion testimony allows a witness to express a personal opinion about a person's character. This testimony is based on the witness's direct knowledge or experience with the person. Opinion testimony is particularly useful in cases where the witness has had significant interactions with the person and can speak to their character traits based on firsthand observations. For example, a long-time colleague might testify that, in their opinion, the defendant is a peaceful and nonviolent person.

Cross-Examination and Specific Instances of Conduct

On cross-examination of a character witness who has provided reputation or opinion testimony, Rule 405(a) allows the court to permit inquiry into specific instances of the person's conduct that are relevant to the character trait at issue. This provision serves as a safeguard against the introduction of misleading or incomplete character evidence by allowing the opposing party to challenge the credibility of the character witness's testimony.

For example, if a witness testifies that the defendant has a reputation for honesty, the prosecution may cross-examine the witness about specific instances in which the defendant allegedly acted dishonestly. The purpose of such cross-examination is to test the accuracy and reliability of the witness's testimony, as well as to provide the fact-finder with a more complete picture of the person's character.

Rule 405(b) - Proving Character by Specific Instances of Conduct

Rule 405(b) provides that specific instances of a person's conduct may be used to prove character when the person's character or character trait is an essential element of a charge, claim, or defense. This provision allows for a more detailed and focused examination of character when character itself is directly at issue in the case.

Character as an Essential Element

Character is considered an essential element of a charge, claim, or defense when the law requires that character be proved as part of the legal standard or burden of proof. For example, in a defamation case where the plaintiff's reputation for honesty is directly in question, specific instances of the plaintiff's conduct may be introduced to prove or disprove that reputation. Similarly, in a criminal case where the defendant asserts a defense of entrapment, the prosecution might introduce evidence of the defendant's prior conduct to show that they were predisposed to commit the crime, thereby rebutting the defense.

Use of Specific Instances in Court

When specific instances of conduct are admissible under Rule 405(b), they must be directly relevant to the character trait at issue and must be presented in a manner that is consistent with the other rules of evidence. This includes considerations of relevance under Rule 401 and the potential for unfair prejudice under Rule 403. The introduction of specific instances of conduct allows the fact-finder to consider concrete examples of the person's behavior, providing a more nuanced and detailed understanding of the character trait in question.

For instance, in a case where a defendant claims to have acted in self-defense, evidence of the victim's prior violent conduct might be admissible to support the defendant's claim that the victim was the aggressor. However, the court must carefully evaluate such evidence to ensure that it is genuinely relevant to the case and that its probative value outweighs any potential for unfair prejudice.

Judicial Discretion in Applying Rule 405

Rule 405 grants judges significant discretion in determining the admissibility of character evidence and the appropriate method of proof. This discretion is essential for managing the potential risks associated with character evidence, including the risk of unfair prejudice, confusion, and the undue consumption of time. Judges must carefully consider the context of the case, the nature of the character evidence being offered, and the potential impact on the fact-finder's decision-making process.

In exercising their discretion, judges may limit the scope of cross-examination or the introduction of specific instances of conduct to ensure that the trial remains focused on the relevant issues. Judges may also provide limiting instructions to the jury, explaining how they should consider the character evidence and cautioning them against using it to make improper inferences about the person's behavior on a specific occasion.

Interplay with Other Rules of Evidence

Rule 405 must be understood in the context of other rules of evidence that govern the admissibility and use of character evidence. For example:

- **Rule 404** establishes the general prohibitions and exceptions for the use of character evidence, setting the stage for when Rule 405's methods of proof may be applied.

- **Rule 406** allows for the admissibility of evidence regarding a person's habit or routine practice, which is distinct from character evidence and may be proved by specific instances of conduct.

- **Rules 607, 608, and 609** govern the impeachment of witnesses, including the use of character evidence related to truthfulness or untruthfulness, which may be introduced through reputation, opinion, or specific instances of conduct.

By providing the methods for proving character, Rule 405 complements these other rules, ensuring that character evidence is presented in a manner that is consistent with the overall goals of the Federal Rules of Evidence.

Practical Implications of Rule 405

Rule 405 has significant practical implications for trial strategy, the conduct of judges, and the overall administration of justice. Understanding the methods of proving character under Rule 405 is essential for attorneys, judges, and litigants as they navigate the evidentiary process.

Strategic Considerations for Attorneys

For attorneys, Rule 405 provides important guidance on how to introduce character evidence in a way that is both effective and admissible. When character evidence is admissible under Rule 404, attorneys must decide whether to introduce it through reputation or opinion testimony or through specific instances of conduct. This decision will depend on the nature of the case, the availability of witnesses, and the potential impact of the evidence on the jury.

Attorneys must also be prepared for cross-examination of their character witnesses, particularly if they have introduced evidence of reputation or opinion. By anticipating potential challenges and preparing their witnesses to respond to inquiries about specific instances of conduct, attorneys can help ensure that their character evidence is persuasive and credible.

Judicial Management of Rule 405 Evidence

Judges play a critical role in managing the introduction of character evidence under Rule 405. By carefully applying the rule's provisions, judges ensure that the evidence presented is relevant, fair, and consistent with the overall goals of the trial. This may involve making determinations about the admissibility of specific instances of conduct, limiting the scope of cross-examination, or providing instructions to the jury on how to evaluate the character evidence.

Judges must also be vigilant in balancing the probative value of character evidence against the potential for unfair prejudice, confusion, or waste of time. This requires a careful consideration of the specific facts and circumstances of the case, as well as an understanding of the broader legal principles that underlie the rules of evidence.

Appellate Review of Rule 405 Decisions

Appellate courts often review decisions made under Rule 405, particularly when the admissibility of character evidence is contested. Appellate review typically focuses on whether the trial court correctly applied the methods of proof outlined in Rule 405 and whether the admission or exclusion of such evidence affected the outcome of the trial.

If an appellate court finds that the trial court improperly admitted or excluded character evidence under Rule 405, it may order a new trial or other appropriate relief. This underscores the importance of a careful and reasoned application of Rule 405 at the trial level.

Rule 405 in Specific Types of Cases

The application of Rule 405 can vary depending on the type of case and the specific issues involved. In criminal cases, the decision to introduce character evidence is often a critical part of the defense strategy, particularly when the defendant's character is a key issue in the case. In civil cases, character evidence may be relevant in disputes involving defamation, custody, or other issues where the character of a party is directly at issue.

Rule 406 - Habit; Routine Practice

Text of Rule 406

Rule 406. Habit; Routine Practice
Evidence of a person's habit or an organization's routine practice may be admitted to prove that on a particular occasion the person or organization acted in accordance with the habit or routine practice. The court may admit this evidence regardless of whether it is corroborated or whether there was an eyewitness.

Introduction to Rule 406

Rule 406 of the Federal Rules of Evidence governs the admissibility of evidence related to a person's habit or an organization's routine practice. Unlike character evidence, which is generally inadmissible to prove that a person acted in conformity with a character trait on a particular occasion, evidence of habit or routine practice is admissible to demonstrate that a person or organization acted in accordance with that habit or routine practice in specific circumstances. This rule reflects the understanding that habits and routine practices are reliable predictors of behavior, and as such, they are relevant to proving conduct in particular instances. This chapter provides a detailed analysis of Rule 406, exploring its text, application, and broader implications for the administration of justice.

Analysis of Rule 406

Rule 406 permits the introduction of evidence related to a person's habit or an organization's routine practice to demonstrate that they likely acted in accordance with that habit or practice on a specific occasion. The rule's recognition of habit and routine practice as reliable indicators of behavior distinguishes it from the general rules regarding character evidence, which typically prohibits such inferences due to the potential for unfair prejudice.

Definition of Habit and Routine Practice

Rule 406 does not explicitly define "habit" or "routine practice," but these terms have well-established meanings in legal contexts.

1. Habit

A habit refers to a person's regular response to a specific situation, characterized by a repetitive, semi-automatic behavior pattern. Habits are more specific and consistent than general character traits, involving particular actions taken in specific contexts. For example, a person's habit of always locking their car doors when leaving the vehicle can be distinguished from a broader character trait such as general carefulness or attentiveness. Habit evidence is admissible because it is seen as a reliable indicator of behavior in similar situations.

2. Routine Practice

Routine practice refers to the regular, systematic way an organization or entity conducts its operations. This might include standardized procedures or protocols that are consistently followed in specific circumstances. For example, a company's routine practice of conducting safety inspections every morning before opening to the public can be used to infer that the inspections were conducted on a particular day. Routine practices, like habits, are considered reliable and can be used to predict behavior or actions on specific occasions.

Admissibility of Habit and Routine Practice Evidence

Rule 406 allows for the admission of habit and routine practice evidence without the need for corroboration or eyewitness testimony. This provision underscores the reliability of such evidence in predicting behavior and ensures that the absence of direct observation does not preclude its admissibility.

Proving Habit

Habit evidence can be introduced through testimony that details the person's regular behavior in specific circumstances. For example, a coworker might testify that they regularly observed the defendant double-checking that all machinery was turned off before leaving work. This testimony can be used to support an argument that the defendant likely performed this action on the occasion in question.

The regularity and specificity of the behavior are key factors in establishing habit. The more frequent and consistent the behavior, the stronger the inference that the person acted in accordance with the habit on a particular occasion.

Proving Routine Practice

Routine practice can be proven through evidence that demonstrates the consistent implementation of a particular procedure or protocol within an organization. This might involve testimony from employees, documentation of the organization's procedures, or other evidence showing that the routine practice was regularly followed.

For example, in a case involving a slip-and-fall incident at a store, the store's routine practice of cleaning the floors every hour could be introduced to suggest that the floors were likely cleaned before the plaintiff's fall. The routine nature of the practice supports the inference that it was followed on the day in question, even if there is no direct evidence of cleaning that day.

Judicial Discretion in Applying Rule 406

Judges have discretion in determining whether evidence qualifies as habit or routine practice under Rule 406. This discretion involves assessing the regularity, specificity, and context of the behavior or practice in question. Judges must ensure that the evidence genuinely reflects a habit or routine practice rather than a one-time or sporadic action, which would not carry the same predictive value.

Judges must also consider whether the introduction of habit or routine practice evidence might cause confusion, prejudice, or waste of time, as governed by Rule 403. Even when habit or routine practice evidence is admissible under Rule 406, judges may exclude it if its probative value is substantially outweighed by the risks outlined in Rule 403.

Interaction with Other Rules of Evidence

Rule 406 must be considered in conjunction with other rules of evidence that govern the admissibility of evidence and the evaluation of its probative value.

- **Rule 401** defines relevance, establishing the baseline for what evidence can be considered by the court. Habit and routine practice evidence must be relevant to the issues in the case to be admissible under Rule 406.

- **Rule 403** allows for the exclusion of relevant evidence if its probative value is substantially outweighed by the potential for unfair prejudice, confusion, or delay. Judges may apply Rule 403 to exclude habit or routine practice evidence if it poses such risks.

- **Rule 404** generally prohibits the use of character evidence to prove that a person acted in accordance with that character on a particular occasion. However, Rule 406 serves as an exception to Rule 404 by allowing habit evidence, which is viewed as a more specific and reliable predictor of behavior than general character traits.

By allowing habit and routine practice evidence, Rule 406 operates within the broader framework of the Federal Rules of Evidence to ensure that reliable and relevant evidence is presented while safeguarding against potential abuses.

Practical Implications of Rule 406

Rule 406 has important practical implications for both the preparation and presentation of cases in federal court. Attorneys, judges, and litigants must understand how to effectively use and evaluate habit and routine practice evidence to support their arguments and ensure a fair trial.

Strategic Use of Habit and Routine Practice Evidence

For attorneys, Rule 406 provides a valuable tool for establishing behavior patterns that are relevant to the issues in a case. By introducing evidence of habit or routine practice, attorneys can strengthen their arguments about how a party likely acted in specific circumstances. This is particularly useful in cases where direct evidence of the party's actions on the occasion in question is unavailable or limited.

When preparing to introduce habit or routine practice evidence, attorneys must ensure that the behavior or practice in question is sufficiently regular and specific to qualify under Rule 406. They should be prepared to present testimony or documentation that clearly demonstrates the consistency of

the behavior or practice. Additionally, attorneys must anticipate and address any potential challenges to the admissibility of this evidence, particularly under Rule 403.

Judicial Management of Rule 406 Evidence

Judges play a critical role in managing the introduction of habit and routine practice evidence under Rule 406. By carefully evaluating the evidence's relevance, reliability, and potential impact on the trial, judges ensure that the evidence admitted under Rule 406 contributes to a fair and accurate resolution of the case.

Judges must also provide clear instructions to the jury regarding how to evaluate habit and routine practice evidence. This may involve explaining the difference between habit evidence and character evidence, emphasizing that habit evidence is admissible because it is a reliable predictor of behavior in specific situations.

Appellate Review of Rule 406 Decisions

Appellate courts review decisions regarding the admissibility of habit and routine practice evidence under Rule 406 for abuse of discretion. This standard of review recognizes the trial judge's broad discretion in assessing the relevance and reliability of evidence, as well as the need to balance probative value against potential risks.

If an appellate court finds that a trial judge improperly admitted or excluded habit or routine practice evidence, it may order a new trial or other appropriate relief. This underscores the importance of a careful and reasoned application of Rule 406 at the trial level.

Rule 406 in Specific Types of Cases

The application of Rule 406 can vary depending on the type of case and the specific legal issues involved. In personal injury cases, for example, habit evidence may be used to establish that a party regularly engaged in a particular safety practice or that they consistently neglected a safety protocol. In commercial litigation, routine practice evidence may be introduced to demonstrate that a business followed a standard procedure in its dealings with customers or clients.

Attorneys and judges must be attuned to the specific challenges and opportunities presented by Rule 406 in each case. By effectively using and evaluating habit and routine practice evidence, they can help ensure that the trial remains focused on the relevant facts and that the fact-finder is provided with reliable evidence to guide their decision-making.

Rule 407 - Subsequent Remedial Measures

Text of Rule 407

Rule 407. Subsequent Remedial Measures
When measures are taken that would have made an earlier injury or harm less likely to occur, evidence of the subsequent measures is not admissible to prove:
• negligence;
• culpable conduct;
• a defect in a product or its design; or
• a need for a warning or instruction.
But the court may admit this evidence for another purpose, such as impeachment or—if disputed—proving ownership, control, or the feasibility of precautionary measures.

Introduction to Rule 407

Rule 407 of the Federal Rules of Evidence addresses the admissibility of evidence related to subsequent remedial measures—actions taken after an event that are intended to prevent future occurrences of a similar nature. The rule generally prohibits the introduction of such evidence when offered to prove negligence, culpable conduct, a defect in a product or its design, or a need for a warning or instruction. The underlying rationale is to encourage individuals and organizations to take remedial actions without fear that those actions will be used against them in litigation. This chapter provides a detailed analysis of Rule 407, exploring its text, interpretation, and broader implications for the administration of justice.

Analysis of Rule 407

Rule 407 embodies the principle that evidence of subsequent remedial measures should not be used to establish a party's liability in a legal proceeding. The rule's primary aim is to encourage responsible behavior by ensuring that parties can take corrective actions without those actions being interpreted as admissions of fault or negligence.

General Prohibition on the Use of Subsequent Remedial Measures

The core of Rule 407 is its prohibition on using evidence of subsequent remedial measures to prove negligence, culpable conduct, a defect in a product or its design, or a need for a warning or instruction. This prohibition applies to actions taken after an incident that would have reduced the likelihood of the harm occurring had they been implemented earlier.

1. Negligence and Culpable Conduct

Evidence of subsequent remedial measures is not admissible to establish that a party was negligent or engaged in culpable conduct. For example, if a company repairs a faulty machine after an accident, evidence of that repair cannot be introduced to show that the company was negligent in maintaining the machine prior to the accident. The rationale is that admitting such evidence could deter parties from making safety improvements for fear that these improvements might be used as evidence of prior negligence.

2. Defect in a Product or Its Design

Similarly, evidence of design changes or product recalls made after an incident is generally inadmissible to prove that the product was defective at the time of the incident. For example, if a manufacturer redesigns a product to eliminate a safety hazard, that redesign cannot be used to argue that the original design was defective.

3. Need for a Warning or Instruction

If a party adds warnings or instructions to a product or a procedure after an incident, that action cannot be used to argue that the original lack of warnings or instructions constituted negligence. The prohibition encourages parties to enhance safety measures without the concern that such actions might be construed as an admission of prior fault.

Exceptions to the General Prohibition

While Rule 407 broadly prohibits the use of subsequent remedial measures to prove liability, it also recognizes certain exceptions where such evidence may be admissible for other purposes.

1. Impeachment

Evidence of subsequent remedial measures may be admitted for impeachment purposes if a party's testimony or evidence suggests that no remedial measures were necessary or feasible. For instance, if a defendant argues that a particular safety feature was unnecessary or impossible to implement, evidence that they later implemented the feature might be admissible to challenge the credibility of that argument.

2. Ownership or Control

If the ownership or control of the property or product involved in the incident is disputed, evidence of subsequent remedial measures may be used to prove ownership or control. For example, if a defendant denies owning a property where an accident occurred, evidence that they later made repairs or improvements to that property could be admissible to prove ownership.

3. Feasibility of Precautionary Measures

When the feasibility of a precautionary measure is in dispute, evidence of subsequent remedial measures may be introduced to demonstrate that the measure was indeed feasible. For instance, if a defendant claims that a safety modification was not feasible, evidence that they later made the modification could be used to counter that claim.

These exceptions are designed to ensure that Rule 407 does not unduly limit the introduction of relevant and probative evidence, particularly in situations where the evidence serves a purpose other than establishing liability.

Judicial Discretion in Applying Rule 407

Judges have considerable discretion in determining whether evidence of subsequent remedial measures should be admitted under Rule 407. This discretion involves assessing whether the evidence is being offered for a permissible purpose under the exceptions to the rule and whether its probative value outweighs any potential for unfair prejudice or confusion.

Judges must also ensure that evidence admitted under an exception to Rule 407 is not used improperly by the jury to infer negligence or culpable conduct. This may involve providing limiting instructions to the jury, clarifying the specific purpose for which the evidence is being introduced and cautioning against using it to draw inferences about liability.

Interaction with Other Rules of Evidence

Rule 407 must be understood in conjunction with other rules of evidence that govern the admissibility of evidence and the evaluation of its probative value.

- **Rule 401** defines relevance, establishing the baseline for what evidence can be considered by the court. Evidence of subsequent remedial measures must be relevant to an issue in the case, such as ownership or feasibility, to be admissible under an exception to Rule 407.

- **Rule 403** allows for the exclusion of relevant evidence if its probative value is substantially outweighed by the potential for unfair prejudice, confusion, or delay. Even if evidence of subsequent remedial measures is admissible under an exception, judges may exclude it under Rule 403 if it poses such risks.

- **Rule 404** governs character evidence and the prohibition on using prior or subsequent actions to prove character, which aligns with the principles underlying Rule 407's general prohibition on subsequent remedial measures.

By operating within the broader framework of the Federal Rules of Evidence, Rule 407 ensures that evidence is presented in a manner that is both relevant and fair, while also encouraging remedial actions that enhance safety and prevent harm.

Practical Implications of Rule 407

Rule 407 has significant practical implications for trial strategy, the conduct of judges, and the overall administration of justice. Understanding how to navigate the rule's prohibitions and exceptions is essential for attorneys, judges, and litigants as they prepare and present their cases.

Strategic Considerations for Attorneys

For attorneys, Rule 407 requires careful consideration when deciding whether to introduce evidence of subsequent remedial measures. If the evidence is being offered to prove liability, attorneys must be aware that it will likely be excluded under Rule 407. However, if the evidence serves a different purpose—such as impeachment, proving ownership, or demonstrating feasibility—attorneys must be prepared to argue for its admissibility under one of the rule's exceptions.

Attorneys should also anticipate challenges to the admissibility of subsequent remedial measures and be prepared to defend their relevance and probative value. This might involve demonstrating that the evidence is directly related to a disputed issue in the case and that it is necessary for a fair resolution of that issue.

Judicial Management of Rule 407 Evidence

Judges play a critical role in managing the introduction of evidence under Rule 407. By carefully applying the rule's provisions and considering the specific context of each case, judges ensure that the trial remains focused on the relevant issues and that the evidence presented is both fair and probative.

Judges must also be vigilant in providing appropriate jury instructions when evidence of subsequent remedial measures is admitted under an exception. These instructions are essential for ensuring that the jury understands the limited purpose of the evidence and does not use it to infer negligence or culpable conduct.

Appellate Review of Rule 407 Decisions

Appellate courts review decisions regarding the admissibility of evidence under Rule 407 for abuse of discretion. This standard of review reflects the trial judge's broad discretion in assessing the relevance, admissibility, and potential impact of evidence.

If an appellate court finds that a trial judge improperly admitted or excluded evidence of subsequent remedial measures, it may order a new trial or other appropriate relief. This underscores the importance of a careful and reasoned application of Rule 407 at the trial level.

Rule 407 in Specific Types of Cases

The application of Rule 407 can vary depending on the type of case and the specific legal issues involved. In personal injury cases, for example, subsequent remedial measures often play a critical role in determining whether a party was negligent or whether a product was defective. Attorneys and judges must be particularly mindful of Rule 407's provisions in such cases to ensure that the evidence presented is both relevant and fair.

In product liability cases, the rule's prohibition on using subsequent remedial measures to prove a defect in a product or its design is particularly significant. Manufacturers and other defendants may take remedial actions to improve product safety without fear that these actions will be used against them as evidence of a defect.

Rule 408 - Compromise Offers and Negotiations

Rule 408. Compromise Offers and Negotiations

(a) **Prohibited Uses.** Evidence of the following is not admissible—on behalf of any party—either to prove or disprove the validity or amount of a disputed claim or to impeach by a prior inconsistent statement or a contradiction: (1) furnishing, promising, or offering—or accepting, promising to accept, or offering to accept—a valuable consideration in compromising or attempting to compromise the claim; and (2) conduct or a statement made during compromise negotiations about the claim—except when offered in a criminal case and when the negotiations related to a claim by a public office in the exercise of its regulatory, investigative, or enforcement authority.

(b) **Exceptions.** The court may admit this evidence for another purpose, such as proving a witness's bias or prejudice, negating a contention of undue delay, or proving an effort to obstruct a criminal investigation or prosecution.

Introduction to Rule 408

Rule 408 of the Federal Rules of Evidence addresses the admissibility of evidence related to compromise offers and negotiations. The rule generally prohibits the introduction of such evidence to prove or disprove the validity or amount of a disputed claim or to impeach by a prior inconsistent statement or a contradiction. The purpose of Rule 408 is to promote the settlement of disputes by allowing parties to engage in candid negotiations without fear that their statements or offers will be used against them in court. This chapter provides a detailed analysis of Rule 408, exploring its text, interpretation, and broader implications for the administration of justice.

Analysis of Rule 408

Rule 408 reflects the principle that the legal system should encourage the settlement of disputes without litigation. By protecting the confidentiality of settlement negotiations, the rule fosters open and honest communication between parties, which is essential for achieving amicable resolutions. At the same time, Rule 408 recognizes that there are certain situations where evidence of compromise negotiations may be relevant and admissible for purposes other than proving or disproving a claim.

Prohibited Uses of Compromise Offers and Negotiations

Rule 408(a) sets forth the general prohibition against using evidence of compromise offers and negotiations to prove or disprove the validity or amount of a disputed claim or to impeach a party through prior inconsistent statements made during such negotiations.

1. **Offers and Promises of Compromise (Rule 408(a)(1))**

The first category of prohibited evidence under Rule 408(a)(1) includes offers, promises, or attempts to compromise a disputed claim. This encompasses any valuable consideration offered or exchanged during settlement discussions, such as monetary payments, promises to perform or refrain from certain actions, or other concessions made in an effort to resolve the dispute. For example, if a party offers to pay a certain amount to settle a lawsuit, that offer cannot be introduced as evidence to prove liability or the amount of damages at trial.

2. **Conduct or Statements During Negotiations (Rule 408(a)(2))**

The second category of prohibited evidence under Rule 408(a)(2) includes conduct or statements made during compromise negotiations. This covers a wide range of communications, including admissions of liability, acknowledgments of fault, or statements about the strength or weakness of a claim. The rule protects these communications to encourage parties to speak freely during settlement discussions, without the fear that their words will be used against them in court. For instance, if a defendant acknowledges during negotiations that their product might have had a defect, that statement cannot be used as evidence to prove the defect at trial.

Exceptions to the Prohibition

While Rule 408 broadly prohibits the use of compromise offers and negotiations for certain purposes, it also recognizes exceptions where such evidence may be admissible for other purposes.

1. **Proving Bias or Prejudice**

One exception allows the introduction of evidence from compromise negotiations to prove a witness's bias or prejudice. For example, if a witness has a financial interest in the outcome of a case due to a prior settlement offer, that fact may be relevant to assessing the witness's credibility. In such cases, Rule 408 does not bar the use of evidence from the negotiations to demonstrate bias or prejudice.

2. **Negating a Contention of Undue Delay**

Another exception permits the use of evidence from compromise negotiations to counter an argument that a party unduly delayed bringing a claim or taking action. For instance, if a party argues that the opposing side delayed filing a lawsuit, evidence that the parties were engaged in ongoing settlement discussions during that time may be admissible to explain the delay.

3. **Proving an Effort to Obstruct a Criminal Investigation or Prosecution**

Rule 408 also allows the admission of evidence from compromise negotiations when it is offered to prove an effort to obstruct a criminal investigation or prosecution. For example, if a party attempted to bribe a government official during settlement discussions to avoid criminal charges, that conduct may be admissible as evidence of obstruction.

4. **Criminal Cases Involving Public Authorities**

Rule 408(a)(2) contains a specific provision allowing statements made during negotiations related to a claim by a public office or agency in the exercise of its regulatory, investigative, or enforcement authority to be used in a subsequent criminal case. This exception recognizes the public interest in prosecuting criminal conduct and allows the government to use evidence from settlement negotiations when pursuing criminal charges.

Judicial Discretion in Applying Rule 408

Judges have considerable discretion in determining whether evidence from compromise negotiations should be admitted under Rule 408. This discretion involves assessing the purpose for which the evidence is being offered and whether it falls within one of the rule's exceptions. Judges must also consider whether admitting the evidence would serve the interests of justice without undermining the policy goals of Rule 408.

In some cases, judges may need to provide limiting instructions to the jury, clarifying the specific purpose for which the evidence is being admitted and cautioning the jury against using it to infer liability or the amount of damages.

Interaction with Other Rules of Evidence

Rule 408 must be considered in conjunction with other rules of evidence that govern the admissibility and use of evidence in legal proceedings.

- **Rule 401** defines relevance, establishing the baseline for what evidence can be considered by the court. Evidence from compromise negotiations must be relevant to an issue in the case to be admissible under an exception to Rule 408.

- **Rule 403** allows for the exclusion of relevant evidence if its probative value is substantially outweighed by the potential for unfair prejudice, confusion, or delay. Even if evidence from compromise negotiations is admissible under an exception, judges may exclude it under Rule 403 if it poses such risks.

- **Rule 404** governs character evidence and the prohibition on using prior actions to prove character, which aligns with the principles underlying Rule 408's general prohibition on using compromise offers to prove liability.

By operating within the broader framework of the Federal Rules of Evidence, Rule 408 ensures that evidence from compromise negotiations is used appropriately and that parties are encouraged to engage in settlement discussions without fear of prejudice.

Practical Implications of Rule 408

Rule 408 has significant practical implications for trial strategy, the conduct of judges, and the overall administration of justice. Understanding how to navigate the rule's prohibitions and exceptions is essential for attorneys, judges, and litigants as they prepare and present their cases.

Strategic Considerations for Attorneys

For attorneys, Rule 408 requires careful consideration when deciding whether to introduce evidence related to compromise offers and negotiations. If the evidence is being offered to prove liability or the amount of damages, attorneys must recognize that it will likely be excluded under Rule 408. However, if the evidence serves a different purpose—such as proving bias, countering an argument of undue delay, or demonstrating obstruction—attorneys must be prepared to argue for its admissibility under one of the rule's exceptions.

Attorneys should also be mindful of the potential impact of Rule 408 on settlement negotiations. Knowing that offers and statements made during negotiations are generally protected can encourage more open and productive discussions, which may lead to successful settlements without the need for litigation.

Judicial Management of Rule 408 Evidence

Judges play a critical role in managing the introduction of evidence under Rule 408. By carefully applying the rule's provisions and considering the specific context of each case, judges ensure that the trial remains focused on the relevant issues and that the evidence presented is both fair and probative.

Judges must also be vigilant in providing appropriate jury instructions when evidence from compromise negotiations is admitted under an exception. These instructions are essential for ensuring that the jury understands the limited purpose of the evidence and does not use it to infer liability or the amount of damages.

Appellate Review of Rule 408 Decisions

Appellate courts review decisions regarding the admissibility of evidence under Rule 408 for abuse of discretion. This standard of review reflects the trial judge's broad discretion in assessing the relevance, admissibility, and potential impact of evidence.

If an appellate court finds that a trial judge improperly admitted or excluded evidence from compromise negotiations, it may order a new trial or other appropriate relief. This underscores the importance of a careful and reasoned application of Rule 408 at the trial level.

Rule 408 in Specific Types of Cases

The application of Rule 408 can vary depending on the type of case and the specific legal issues involved. In civil cases, where settlement negotiations are common, Rule 408 plays a crucial role in protecting the confidentiality of those discussions and encouraging parties to reach amicable resolutions. In criminal cases, the exceptions to Rule 408 may allow the introduction of evidence from settlement negotiations, particularly when there is a public interest in prosecuting criminal conduct.

Attorneys and judges must be attuned to the specific challenges and opportunities presented by Rule 408 in each case. By effectively using and evaluating evidence from compromise negotiations, they can help ensure that the trial remains focused on the relevant facts and that the fact-finder is provided with reliable evidence to guide their decision-making.

Rule 409 - Offers to Pay Medical and Similar Expenses

Rule 409. Offers to Pay Medical and Similar Expenses
Evidence of furnishing, promising to pay, or offering to pay medical, hospital, or similar expenses resulting from an injury is not admissible to prove liability for the injury.

Introduction to Rule 409

Rule 409 of the Federal Rules of Evidence addresses the admissibility of evidence related to offers to pay medical, hospital, or similar expenses following an injury. The rule generally prohibits the introduction of such evidence to prove liability for the injury. This provision reflects the principle that acts of kindness or compassion, such as offering to pay someone's medical expenses, should not be interpreted as admissions of fault or responsibility. By protecting these offers from being used as evidence of liability, Rule 409 encourages individuals and organizations to assist injured parties without the fear that their generosity will be used against them in litigation. This chapter provides a detailed analysis of Rule 409, exploring its text, interpretation, and broader implications for the administration of justice.

Analysis of Rule 409

Rule 409 provides a specific exclusion for evidence related to the payment or offer of payment of medical, hospital, or similar expenses. The rule's exclusion is narrowly tailored to address situations where a party attempts to introduce such evidence to establish liability for an injury. The primary objective of Rule 409 is to promote acts of goodwill and humanitarian gestures by ensuring that they cannot be used as admissions of liability in court.

General Prohibition on the Use of Offers to Pay Medical Expenses

The central provision of Rule 409 is its prohibition on the admissibility of evidence concerning offers to pay medical, hospital, or similar expenses to prove liability for an injury. This rule applies to various forms of financial assistance, including direct payments, promises to pay, and offers to cover medical costs.

1. Furnishing, Promising to Pay, or Offering to Pay

Rule 409 covers a wide range of scenarios, including:

- **Furnishing:** Directly providing payment for medical, hospital, or similar expenses.

- **Promising to Pay:** Making a commitment or assurance to cover these expenses in the future.

- **Offering to Pay:** Proposing to pay for these expenses, even if the offer is not accepted or acted upon.

For example, if a defendant offers to pay for the plaintiff's medical bills following an accident, that offer cannot be introduced as evidence to suggest that the defendant admits liability for the accident. The rule ensures that such offers are seen as acts of compassion rather than as implicit acknowledgments of fault.

2. Medical, Hospital, or Similar Expenses

The term "medical, hospital, or similar expenses" is broad and includes any costs associated with medical treatment, hospitalization, rehabilitation, and other healthcare-related services. The rule's scope covers both physical and mental health expenses incurred as a result of an injury. For instance, offers to pay for physical therapy, psychological counseling, or prescription medications would fall within the ambit of Rule 409.

Scope of the Exclusion

The exclusion under Rule 409 is specifically limited to using offers to pay medical and similar expenses as evidence of liability. The rule does not preclude the use of such evidence for other purposes, provided it is relevant and admissible under other rules of evidence. For example, if a party's motive or intent is at issue in a case, evidence of an offer to pay medical expenses might be relevant for purposes other than proving liability, such as demonstrating a party's concern for the well-being of the injured person.

Distinction from Other Rules of Evidence

Rule 409 is distinct from other rules of evidence that address similar issues, such as Rule 408, which deals with compromise offers and negotiations, and Rule 411, which pertains to liability insurance. While these rules share the common goal of encouraging certain behaviors without the risk of legal consequences, they address different contexts and types of evidence.

1. Comparison with Rule 408

Rule 408 generally excludes evidence of settlement offers and negotiations from being used to prove liability. However, Rule 409 is more narrowly focused on offers to pay medical expenses and does not require the existence of a disputed claim, as Rule 408 does. Rule 409 applies even in situations where there is no formal dispute or negotiation, making it applicable in a broader range of circumstances.

2. Comparison with Rule 411

Rule 411 excludes evidence that a person was or was not insured against liability from being used to prove negligence or wrongful conduct. While Rule 409 and Rule 411 both serve to prevent the unfair use of certain types of evidence, Rule 409 specifically addresses the context of offers to pay medical expenses, whereas Rule 411 deals with the existence of liability insurance.

Judicial Discretion in Applying Rule 409

Judges have discretion in determining whether evidence related to offers to pay medical expenses should be excluded under Rule 409. This discretion involves assessing the relevance and purpose for which the evidence is being offered. Judges must ensure that the evidence is not being used to infer liability, in line with the rule's prohibitions.

In cases where such evidence is deemed admissible for purposes other than proving liability, judges may provide limiting instructions to the jury. These instructions are crucial to ensure that the jury understands the specific purpose for which the evidence is being considered and does not misuse it to draw improper conclusions about liability.

Practical Implications of Rule 409

Rule 409 has significant practical implications for both legal strategy and the broader administration of justice. Understanding the scope and application of this rule is essential for attorneys, judges, and litigants as they navigate the evidentiary landscape of a trial.

Strategic Considerations for Attorneys

For attorneys, Rule 409 requires careful consideration when deciding how to handle evidence related to offers to pay medical expenses. If an attorney seeks to introduce such evidence to prove liability, they must recognize that it will likely be excluded under Rule 409. However, if the evidence is relevant for another purpose, such as demonstrating a party's intent or state of mind, attorneys must be prepared to argue for its admissibility under the appropriate evidentiary rules.

Attorneys should also advise their clients about the implications of Rule 409 during the course of a dispute. Clients should be made aware that offering to pay medical expenses does not constitute an admission of liability and that such offers are protected under Rule 409.

Judicial Management of Rule 409 Evidence

Judges play a critical role in managing the introduction of evidence related to offers to pay medical expenses. By carefully applying Rule 409, judges ensure that the trial remains focused on the relevant issues and that the evidence presented is both fair and probative.

Judges must also be vigilant in providing appropriate jury instructions when evidence is admitted for a purpose other than proving liability. These instructions are essential for ensuring that the jury understands the limited scope of the evidence and does not use it to infer fault or responsibility for the injury.

Appellate Review of Rule 409 Decisions

Appellate courts review decisions regarding the admissibility of evidence under Rule 409 for abuse of discretion. This standard of review recognizes the trial judge's broad discretion in assessing the relevance and admissibility of evidence. If an appellate court finds that a trial judge improperly admitted or excluded evidence related to offers to pay medical expenses, it may order a new trial or other appropriate relief.

Rule 409 in Specific Types of Cases

The application of Rule 409 can vary depending on the type of case and the specific legal issues involved. In personal injury cases, where offers to pay medical expenses are common, Rule 409 plays a crucial role in protecting the parties' efforts to provide assistance without the fear of legal repercussions. In such cases, attorneys and judges must be particularly mindful of Rule 409's provisions to ensure that the evidence is used appropriately and that the trial remains fair.

In cases involving potential liability, Rule 409 may also influence the parties' strategies in settlement negotiations and dispute resolution. Understanding the protection offered by Rule 409 can encourage parties to engage in acts of goodwill, knowing that their offers to pay medical expenses will not be used against them in court.

Rule 410 - Pleas, Plea Discussions, and Related Statements

Text of Rule 410

Rule 410. Pleas, Plea Discussions, and Related Statements

(a) **Prohibited Uses.** In a civil or criminal case, evidence of the following is not admissible against the defendant who made the plea or participated in the plea discussions: (1) a guilty plea that was later withdrawn; (2) a nolo contendere plea; (3) a statement made during a proceeding on either of those pleas under Federal Rule of Criminal Procedure 11 or a comparable state procedure; or (4) a statement made during plea discussions with an attorney for the prosecuting authority if the discussions did not result in a guilty plea or they resulted in a later-withdrawn guilty plea.

(b) **Exceptions.** The court may admit a statement described in Rule 410(a)(3) or (4): (1) in any proceeding in which another statement made during the same plea or plea discussions has been introduced, if in fairness the statements ought to be considered together; or (2) in a criminal proceeding for perjury or false statement, if the defendant made the statement under oath, on the record, and with counsel present.

Introduction to Rule 410

Rule 410 of the Federal Rules of Evidence governs the admissibility of evidence related to pleas, plea discussions, and related statements in both civil and criminal cases. The rule generally prohibits the use of certain types of evidence against a defendant who was involved in plea negotiations or who has entered a plea that was later withdrawn. The underlying policy of Rule 410 is to encourage open and honest plea negotiations by ensuring that defendants can engage in such discussions without fear that their statements or offers will be used against them if the negotiations fail or the plea is withdrawn. This chapter provides a detailed analysis of Rule 410, exploring its text, interpretation, and broader implications for the administration of justice.

Analysis of Rule 410

Rule 410 provides critical protections for defendants engaged in plea negotiations, reflecting the legal system's commitment to promoting fair and effective resolution of criminal cases through negotiated pleas. The rule carefully balances the interests of encouraging plea discussions with the need to preserve the integrity of the judicial process, particularly in cases involving perjury or false statements.

Prohibited Uses of Pleas and Related Statements

Rule 410(a) establishes the general prohibition against using certain types of evidence against a defendant who participated in plea negotiations. This prohibition is intended to create a safe environment for plea discussions, where defendants can negotiate in good faith without the risk that their statements will be used against them if the negotiations fail.

1. Withdrawn Guilty Pleas (Rule 410(a)(1))

Evidence of a guilty plea that was later withdrawn is not admissible against the defendant. The rationale for this prohibition is that a withdrawn plea reflects a change of mind, often influenced by new legal advice or reconsideration of the consequences. Admitting such a plea as evidence of guilt would undermine the defendant's right to reconsider their position and could unfairly prejudice the fact-finder against them.

For example, if a defendant initially pleads guilty to a charge but later withdraws the plea, the fact that they once pleaded guilty cannot be introduced as evidence of their guilt at trial.

2. Nolo Contendere Pleas (Rule 410(a)(2))

A plea of nolo contendere, or "no contest," is also protected under Rule 410. A nolo contendere plea allows a defendant to accept conviction without admitting guilt, and it cannot be used against the defendant in any subsequent civil or criminal proceeding to establish liability or fault. This protection ensures that defendants can enter such pleas without fear that their decision will be used against them in other contexts.

For instance, if a defendant pleads nolo contendere to a criminal charge, that plea cannot be used as evidence in a related civil lawsuit.

3. Statements Made During Plea Proceedings (Rule 410(a)(3))

Statements made during a proceeding on a withdrawn guilty plea or a nolo contendere plea under Federal Rule of Criminal Procedure 11, or a comparable state procedure, are also inadmissible against the defendant. This protection extends to any statements the defendant makes in court as part of the plea process, recognizing that these statements are often made in the context of negotiated agreements rather than as independent admissions of guilt.

4. Statements Made During Plea Discussions (Rule 410(a)(4))

Rule 410 also excludes statements made during plea discussions with an attorney for the prosecuting authority if the discussions did not result in a guilty plea or resulted in a later-withdrawn guilty plea. This provision is crucial for maintaining the integrity of plea negotiations, as it ensures that defendants can engage in candid discussions with prosecutors without worrying that their statements will be used against them if negotiations break down.

For example, if a defendant discusses potential plea terms with a prosecutor but the negotiations do not result in a plea agreement, any statements made during those discussions cannot be introduced as evidence of guilt at trial.

Exceptions to the Prohibition

While Rule 410 broadly prohibits the use of plea-related evidence against a defendant, it also recognizes certain exceptions where such evidence may be admissible.

1. Statements Considered Together (Rule 410(b)(1))

The first exception allows the admission of statements made during plea discussions if another statement from the same discussions has been introduced and fairness requires that the statements be considered together. This exception prevents one party from presenting a misleading or incomplete account of the plea discussions by selectively introducing only part of the conversation. If the defense introduces a statement made during plea discussions to support their case, the prosecution may be allowed to introduce additional statements from the same discussions to provide context and ensure a fair representation of what was said.

2. Perjury or False Statement Proceedings (Rule 410(b)(2))

The second exception permits the use of statements made during plea discussions in criminal proceedings for perjury or false statements, provided the defendant made the statements under oath, on the record, and with counsel present. This exception reflects the legal system's interest in upholding the integrity of judicial proceedings and ensuring that defendants who commit perjury during plea discussions can be held accountable.

For instance, if a defendant lies under oath during a plea hearing, the statements they made can be used as evidence in a subsequent prosecution for perjury.

Judicial Discretion in Applying Rule 410

Judges have discretion in determining whether evidence related to plea negotiations should be excluded under Rule 410. This discretion involves assessing whether the evidence falls within the prohibitions set forth in the rule and whether any of the exceptions apply. Judges must also consider whether admitting the evidence would serve the interests of justice without undermining the policy goals of Rule 410.

In cases where evidence from plea negotiations is deemed admissible under an exception, judges may need to provide limiting instructions to the jury. These instructions are crucial for ensuring that the jury understands the specific purpose for which the evidence is being introduced and does not misuse it to draw improper inferences about the defendant's guilt.

Interaction with Other Rules of Evidence

Rule 410 operates within the broader context of the Federal Rules of Evidence, particularly in conjunction with other rules that govern the admissibility and use of evidence.

- **Rule 401** defines relevance, establishing the baseline for what evidence can be considered by the court. Evidence from plea negotiations must be relevant to an issue in the case to be admissible under an exception to Rule 410.

- **Rule 403** allows for the exclusion of relevant evidence if its probative value is substantially outweighed by the potential for unfair prejudice, confusion, or delay. Even if evidence from plea negotiations is admissible under an exception, judges may exclude it under Rule 403 if it poses such risks.

- **Rule 404** governs character evidence and the prohibition on using prior actions to prove character, which aligns with the principles underlying Rule 410's general prohibition on using plea-related evidence to prove guilt.

By operating within this framework, Rule 410 ensures that evidence from plea negotiations is used appropriately and that defendants are not unfairly prejudiced by their participation in plea discussions.

Practical Implications of Rule 410

Rule 410 has significant practical implications for both legal strategy and the broader administration of justice. Understanding the scope and application of this rule is essential for attorneys, judges, and defendants as they navigate the plea negotiation process and prepare for trial.

Strategic Considerations for Attorneys

For attorneys, Rule 410 provides important protections that must be carefully considered during plea negotiations. Defense attorneys can advise their clients with confidence that their statements made during plea discussions will generally not be admissible against them if negotiations fail. This protection encourages defendants to engage in plea negotiations and consider settlement options without fear that their discussions will later be used as evidence of guilt.

However, attorneys must also be aware of the exceptions to Rule 410 and be prepared to argue for or against the admissibility of evidence depending on the circumstances of the case. For example, if the defense introduces statements from plea discussions, the prosecution may seek to admit additional statements under the fairness exception. Defense attorneys must be vigilant in ensuring that any such evidence is appropriately limited and does not unfairly prejudice their client.

Rule 411 - Liability Insurance

Text of Rule 411

Rule 411. Liability Insurance

Evidence that a person was or was not insured against liability is not admissible to prove whether the person acted negligently or otherwise wrongfully. But the court may admit this evidence for another purpose, such as proving a witness's bias or prejudice or proving agency, ownership, or control.

Introduction to Rule 411

Rule 411 of the Federal Rules of Evidence addresses the admissibility of evidence regarding a person's liability insurance. The rule generally prohibits the introduction of evidence that a person was or was not insured against liability to prove whether the person acted negligently or otherwise wrongfully. The underlying rationale for Rule 411 is to prevent the fact-finder from being influenced by considerations that are not directly related to the determination of fault, such as the existence or absence of insurance coverage. This chapter provides a detailed analysis of Rule 411, exploring its text, interpretation, and broader implications for the administration of justice.

Analysis of Rule 411

Rule 411 is designed to exclude evidence of liability insurance from being used to establish a party's fault in civil and criminal cases. The rule reflects the concern that knowledge of a party's insurance status could improperly influence the jury's decision-making, leading to unfair prejudice or the assumption that a party is either more or less likely to have been negligent or at fault based on their insurance coverage.

General Prohibition on the Use of Liability Insurance

The primary provision of Rule 411 prohibits the introduction of evidence that a person was or was not insured against liability to prove whether that person acted negligently or wrongfully. This rule applies broadly to any attempt to use liability insurance as evidence of fault.

1. Negligence and Wrongful Conduct

Rule 411 specifically bars the use of insurance evidence to prove negligence or other wrongful conduct. For instance, if a defendant in a personal injury case is insured, the plaintiff cannot introduce evidence of the defendant's insurance coverage to suggest that the defendant was negligent. Similarly, the absence of insurance cannot be used to imply that a person was more careful or less likely to engage in wrongful conduct.

The rationale for this prohibition is that insurance coverage is not directly relevant to whether a person acted negligently or wrongfully. Introducing such evidence could lead the jury to make decisions based on the presence or absence of insurance rather than on the facts of the case and the applicable legal standards.

Exceptions to the General Prohibition

While Rule 411 broadly excludes evidence of liability insurance to prove fault, it also recognizes certain exceptions where such evidence may be admissible for other purposes.

1. Proving Bias or Prejudice

One exception allows the introduction of insurance evidence to show a witness's bias or prejudice. For example, if a witness is an employee of an insurance company that stands to gain or lose depending on the outcome of the case, evidence of the witness's connection to the insurer may be admissible to demonstrate potential bias. This helps the fact-finder assess the credibility of the witness and the weight to give their testimony.

2. Proving Agency, Ownership, or Control

Another exception permits the use of insurance evidence to establish agency, ownership, or control. For instance, if there is a dispute over who owned a vehicle involved in an accident, evidence that a particular person or entity insured the vehicle may be relevant to proving ownership or control. This type of evidence can help clarify the relationships between the parties and the subject matter of the litigation.

3. Other Legitimate Purposes

Although Rule 411 explicitly mentions bias, prejudice, agency, ownership, and control as exceptions, the rule is not limited to these examples. Courts have the discretion to admit insurance evidence for other legitimate purposes, provided that the evidence is relevant and its probative value outweighs the risk of unfair prejudice under Rule 403.

For example, evidence of insurance might be relevant in a case where the defendant claims that they could not have afforded certain safety measures, but it turns out they were insured for such risks. In such a situation, the insurance evidence could be used to rebut the defendant's claim, without suggesting that the insurance coverage itself implies fault.

Judicial Discretion in Applying Rule 411

Judges have considerable discretion in determining whether evidence related to liability insurance should be admitted under Rule 411. This discretion involves assessing the relevance of the insurance evidence to the issues at hand and evaluating whether the probative value of the evidence outweighs the potential for unfair prejudice.

When considering the admissibility of insurance evidence under one of the exceptions, judges must carefully weigh the evidence's potential impact on the jury. If the risk of prejudice or confusion is too great, the judge may exclude the evidence under Rule 403, even if it is otherwise admissible under Rule 411.

Judges may also provide limiting instructions to the jury when admitting insurance evidence under an exception. These instructions are critical to ensuring that the jury understands the specific purpose for which the evidence is being introduced and does not misuse it to draw improper inferences about the defendant's liability.

Interaction with Other Rules of Evidence

Rule 411 operates within the broader context of the Federal Rules of Evidence, particularly in conjunction with other rules that govern the admissibility and use of evidence.

- **Rule 401** defines relevance, establishing the baseline for what evidence can be considered by the court. Evidence of liability insurance must be relevant to an issue in the case to be admissible under an exception to Rule 411.

- **Rule 403** allows for the exclusion of relevant evidence if its probative value is substantially outweighed by the potential for unfair prejudice, confusion, or delay. Even if insurance evidence is admissible under an exception, judges may exclude it under Rule 403 if it poses such risks.

- **Rule 404** governs character evidence and the prohibition on using prior actions to prove character, which aligns with the principles underlying Rule 411's general prohibition on using insurance evidence to prove fault.

By operating within this framework, Rule 411 ensures that evidence of liability insurance is used appropriately and that parties are not unfairly prejudiced by the introduction of such evidence.

Practical Implications of Rule 411

Rule 411 has significant practical implications for both legal strategy and the broader administration of justice. Understanding the scope and application of this rule is essential for attorneys, judges, and litigants as they prepare and present their cases.

Strategic Considerations for Attorneys

For attorneys, Rule 411 requires careful consideration when deciding whether to introduce evidence related to liability insurance. If an attorney seeks to introduce such evidence to prove negligence or wrongful conduct, they must recognize that it will likely be excluded under Rule 411. However, if the evidence is relevant for another purpose—such as proving bias, ownership, or control—attorneys must be prepared to argue for its admissibility under one of the rule's exceptions.

Attorneys should also be mindful of the potential impact of Rule 411 on the jury's perceptions. Introducing insurance evidence, even for a permissible purpose, carries the risk that the jury may improperly infer that the insured party is more likely to be liable simply because they are insured. To mitigate this risk, attorneys should work closely with the court to ensure that appropriate limiting instructions are provided to the jury.

Judicial Management of Rule 411 Evidence

Judges play a critical role in managing the introduction of evidence related to liability insurance. By carefully applying Rule 411, judges ensure that the trial remains focused on the relevant issues and that the evidence presented is both fair and probative.

Judges must also be vigilant in providing appropriate jury instructions when evidence of liability insurance is admitted under an exception. These instructions are essential for ensuring that the jury understands the limited purpose of the evidence and does not use it to infer fault or responsibility for the injury.

Appellate Review of Rule 411 Decisions

Appellate courts review decisions regarding the admissibility of evidence under Rule 411 for abuse of discretion. This standard of review recognizes the trial judge's broad discretion in assessing the relevance and admissibility of evidence. If an appellate court finds that a trial judge improperly admitted or excluded evidence related to liability insurance, it may order a new trial or other appropriate relief.

Rule 411 in Specific Types of Cases

The application of Rule 411 can vary depending on the type of case and the specific legal issues involved. In personal injury cases, where liability insurance is often present, Rule 411 plays a crucial role in ensuring that the jury's decision is based on the facts and applicable legal standards, rather than on the existence or absence of insurance coverage.

In commercial and corporate litigation, where issues of agency, ownership, and control are frequently contested, Rule 411's exceptions may become particularly relevant. Attorneys and judges must be particularly mindful of Rule 411's provisions in such cases to ensure that the evidence is used appropriately and that the trial remains fair.

Rule 412 - Sex-Offense Cases: The Victim's Sexual Behavior or Predisposition

---

Rule 412. Sex-Offense Cases: The Victim's Sexual Behavior or Predisposition

(a) **Prohibited Uses.** The following evidence is not admissible in a civil or criminal proceeding involving alleged sexual misconduct: (1) evidence offered to prove that a victim engaged in other sexual behavior; or (2) evidence offered to prove a victim's sexual predisposition.

(b) **Exceptions.** (1) **Criminal Cases.** The court may admit the following evidence in a criminal case: (A) evidence of specific instances of a victim's sexual behavior, if offered to prove that someone other than the defendant was the source of semen, injury, or other physical evidence; (B) evidence of specific instances of a victim's sexual behavior with respect to the person accused of the sexual misconduct, if offered by the defendant to prove consent or if offered by the prosecutor; and (C) evidence whose exclusion would violate the defendant's constitutional rights. (2) **Civil Cases.** In a civil case, the court may admit evidence offered to prove a victim's sexual behavior or sexual predisposition if its probative value substantially outweighs the danger of harm to any victim and of unfair prejudice to any party. The court may admit evidence of a victim's reputation only if the victim has placed it in controversy.

(c) **Procedure to Determine Admissibility.** (1) **Motion.** If a party intends to offer evidence under Rule 412(b), the party must: (A) file a motion that specifically describes the evidence and states the purpose for which it is to be offered; (B) do so at least 14 days before trial unless the court, for good cause, sets a different time; (C) serve the motion on all parties; and (D) notify the victim or, when appropriate, the victim's guardian or representative. (2) **Hearing.** Before admitting evidence under this rule, the court must conduct an in camera hearing and give the victim and parties a right to attend and be heard. Unless the court orders otherwise, the motion, related materials, and the record of the hearing must be and remain sealed.

Introduction to Rule 412

Rule 412 of the Federal Rules of Evidence, commonly known as the "Rape Shield Law," governs the admissibility of evidence related to a victim's sexual behavior or predisposition in sex-offense cases. The rule is designed to protect victims of sexual misconduct from invasive and irrelevant inquiries into their sexual history, thereby encouraging victims to come forward and testify without fear of being publicly humiliated or having their private lives unjustly scrutinized. Rule 412 reflects the legal system's commitment to balancing the rights of the accused with the need to protect victims from unfair prejudice. This chapter provides a detailed analysis of Rule 412, exploring its text, interpretation, and broader implications for the administration of justice.

Analysis of Rule 412

Rule 412 serves as a critical protective measure in cases involving alleged sexual misconduct. The rule strictly limits the admissibility of evidence related to a victim's past sexual behavior or sexual predisposition, recognizing that such evidence is often irrelevant to the issues at hand and can lead to significant prejudice, humiliation, and deterrence of victims from participating in the judicial process.

General Prohibition on the Use of Evidence Related to Sexual Behavior or Predisposition

Rule 412(a) establishes a general prohibition against the introduction of evidence concerning a victim's sexual behavior or predisposition in both civil and criminal cases involving alleged sexual misconduct.

1. **Sexual Behavior (Rule 412(a)(1))**

Evidence offered to prove that a victim engaged in other sexual behavior is inadmissible under Rule 412(a)(1). This includes evidence of the victim's past sexual activities, sexual practices, or any conduct that could be construed as sexual in nature. The rule is grounded in the understanding that such evidence is typically irrelevant to the issues of consent, guilt, or liability and serves only to unfairly bias the fact-finder against the victim.

For example, in a criminal case involving allegations of sexual assault, evidence that the victim had consensual sexual relations with other individuals before the alleged assault would generally be inadmissible to suggest that the victim consented to the defendant's actions.

2. **Sexual Predisposition (Rule 412(a)(2))**

Rule 412(a)(2) also prohibits the introduction of evidence aimed at proving a victim's sexual predisposition. This category includes evidence related to the victim's reputation for promiscuity, sexual orientation, or any other characteristic that might be used to imply a sexual nature or inclination. The exclusion of such evidence is intended to prevent the victim from being unfairly judged based on stereotypes or societal biases about sexual behavior.

For instance, evidence that the victim frequently attends social gatherings or parties where sexual activity might occur would not be admissible to suggest that the victim was more likely to have consented to the alleged sexual conduct.

Exceptions to the General Prohibition

While Rule 412 broadly excludes evidence related to a victim's sexual behavior or predisposition, it recognizes certain limited exceptions where such evidence may be admissible.

1. **Exceptions in Criminal Cases (Rule 412(b)(1))**

Rule 412(b)(1) outlines specific exceptions that apply in criminal cases:

- ○ **Evidence of Alternative Source of Physical Evidence (Rule 412(b)(1)(A))**

The court may admit evidence of specific instances of a victim's sexual behavior if it is offered to prove that someone other than the defendant was the source of semen, injury, or other physical evidence. This exception is critical in situations where the presence of physical evidence could be misinterpreted as implicating the defendant when it might actually be attributable to another person.

For example, if semen is found on the victim's body, the defendant may introduce evidence that the victim had consensual sexual intercourse with another individual around the time of the alleged assault to suggest that the semen might have come from that other individual.

- ○ **Evidence of Sexual Behavior with the Accused (Rule 412(b)(1)(B))**

The court may also admit evidence of specific instances of a victim's sexual behavior with respect to the person accused of the sexual misconduct if offered by the defendant to prove consent or if offered by the prosecution. This exception acknowledges that prior sexual interactions between the victim and the accused might be relevant to the issue of consent in certain cases.

For instance, if the defendant and the victim had an ongoing sexual relationship, the defendant might introduce evidence of their past consensual encounters to support a claim that the victim consented to the sexual activity in question.

- ○ **Evidence Necessary to Protect Constitutional Rights (Rule 412(b)(1)(C))**

The rule allows for the admission of evidence when its exclusion would violate the defendant's constitutional rights, such as the right to confront witnesses or to present a complete defense. This exception ensures that Rule 412 does not infringe upon the defendant's fundamental legal protections.

For example, if excluding evidence related to the victim's sexual history would prevent the defendant from effectively cross-examining the victim or challenging the credibility of the prosecution's case, the court may admit the evidence to safeguard the defendant's constitutional rights.

2. **Exceptions in Civil Cases (Rule 412(b)(2))**

Rule 412(b)(2) provides a different standard for civil cases, where the court may admit evidence of a victim's sexual behavior or predisposition if its probative value substantially outweighs the danger of harm to the victim and of unfair prejudice to any party. This balancing test is more stringent than the typical Rule 403 analysis, reflecting the special sensitivity of the issues involved in sex-offense cases.

In civil cases, evidence of a victim's reputation may only be admitted if the victim has placed it in controversy, such as by making claims about their sexual character or behavior. This provision ensures that victims are not unfairly subjected to scrutiny of their private lives unless they themselves have made those issues relevant to the case.

For example, in a civil lawsuit alleging sexual harassment, if the victim has testified about their sexual conservatism as part of their claim, the defendant might be allowed to introduce evidence challenging that assertion, but only if the court finds that the probative value of the evidence substantially outweighs the potential harm and prejudice.

Procedure to Determine Admissibility

Rule 412(c) sets forth a specific procedure that must be followed to determine the admissibility of evidence covered by the rule.

1. **Motion Requirement (Rule 412(c)(1))**

A party intending to offer evidence under one of the exceptions in Rule 412(b) must file a motion that specifically describes the evidence and states the purpose for which it is to be offered. The motion must be filed at least 14 days before trial, unless the court sets a different deadline for good cause. This procedural requirement ensures that the court has adequate time to consider the motion and that all parties are properly notified.

The motion must also be served on all parties and, where appropriate, the victim or the victim's guardian or representative. This notice provision allows the victim to be aware of and respond to the motion, ensuring that their interests are represented in the proceedings.

2. **In Camera Hearing (Rule 412(c)(2))**

Before admitting evidence under Rule 412, the court is required to conduct an in camera hearing, which is a private hearing held outside the presence of the jury. During this hearing, the court hears arguments from both parties and considers the evidence in question. The victim and the parties have the right to attend and be heard at the hearing.

The in camera hearing procedure is designed to protect the victim's privacy and to ensure that the court carefully considers the admissibility of the evidence without undue influence from the jury or public. The motion, related materials, and the record of the hearing are generally sealed to maintain confidentiality, unless the court orders otherwise.

Practical Implications of Rule 412

Rule 412 has significant practical implications for the conduct of trials, the protection of victims, and the overall administration of justice. Understanding the scope and application of this rule is essential for attorneys, judges, and litigants in sex-offense cases.

Strategic Considerations for Attorneys

For attorneys, Rule 412 requires careful consideration when deciding whether to introduce evidence related to a victim's sexual behavior or predisposition. Defense attorneys must be particularly cautious in assessing whether such evidence is admissible under one of the rule's exceptions and must be prepared to file a detailed motion and argue for the evidence's relevance and necessity.

Prosecutors, on the other hand, should be vigilant in protecting the victim's privacy and ensuring that inadmissible evidence is excluded from the trial. They must be prepared to challenge any attempt by the defense to introduce evidence that violates Rule 412 and to argue for the application of the rule's protections.

Judicial Management of Rule 412 Evidence

Judges play a crucial role in managing the introduction of evidence under Rule 412. By carefully applying the rule's provisions and conducting in camera hearings, judges ensure that the trial remains focused on the relevant issues and that the evidence presented is both fair and probative.

Judges must also be vigilant in providing appropriate jury instructions when evidence is admitted under an exception to Rule 412. These instructions are essential for ensuring that the jury understands the limited purpose for which the evidence is being introduced and does not misuse it to draw improper inferences about the victim's character or credibility.

Appellate Review of Rule 412 Decisions

Appellate courts review decisions regarding the admissibility of evidence under Rule 412 for abuse of discretion. This standard of review recognizes the trial judge's broad discretion in assessing the relevance and admissibility of evidence. If an appellate court finds that a trial judge improperly admitted or excluded evidence related to a victim's sexual behavior or predisposition, it may order a new trial or other appropriate relief.

Rule 412 in Specific Types of Cases

The application of Rule 412 can vary depending on the type of case and the specific legal issues involved. In criminal cases involving sexual assault or rape, Rule 412's protections are particularly important in safeguarding the victim's dignity and encouraging the reporting and prosecution of such offenses.

In civil cases, where the standard for admitting evidence under Rule 412 is somewhat more flexible, courts must carefully balance the probative value of the evidence against the potential harm and prejudice to the victim. This balancing test is critical in ensuring that the victim's rights are protected while also allowing for the fair resolution of the case.

Rule 413 - Similar Crimes in Sexual-Assault Cases

Rule 413. Similar Crimes in Sexual-Assault Cases
(a) **Permitted Uses.** In a criminal case in which a defendant is accused of a sexual assault, the court may admit evidence that the defendant committed any other sexual assault. The evidence may be considered on any matter to which it is relevant.
(b) **Disclosure to the Defendant.** If the prosecutor intends to offer this evidence, the prosecutor must disclose it to the defendant, including witnesses' statements or a summary of the expected testimony. The prosecutor must do so at least 15 days before trial or at a later time that the court allows for good cause.
(c) **Definition of "Sexual Assault."** In this rule and Rule 415, "sexual assault" means a crime under federal law or under state law involving: (1) any conduct prohibited by 18 U.S.C. chapter 109A; (2) contact, without consent, between any part of the defendant's body—or an object—and another person's genitals or anus; (3) contact, without consent, between the defendant's genitals or anus and any part of another person's body; (4) deriving sexual pleasure or gratification from inflicting death, bodily injury, or physical pain on another person; or (5) an attempt or conspiracy to engage in conduct described in subparagraphs (1)–(4).

Introduction to Rule 413

Rule 413 of the Federal Rules of Evidence addresses the admissibility of evidence regarding a defendant's commission of other sexual assaults in cases where they are currently accused of sexual assault. Unlike the general rule against propensity evidence, which prohibits using a defendant's past actions to prove their character or to suggest they acted in accordance with that character on a particular occasion, Rule 413 provides a specific exception in the context of sexual-assault cases. The rule allows the introduction of evidence that the defendant committed other sexual assaults, thereby permitting the jury to consider the defendant's past behavior as relevant to the charges they currently face. This chapter provides a detailed analysis of Rule 413, exploring its text, interpretation, and broader implications for the administration of justice.

Analysis of Rule 413

Rule 413 creates a significant exception to the general rule against admitting propensity evidence. By allowing evidence of similar past crimes in sexual-assault cases, the rule acknowledges the unique challenges in prosecuting such offenses, where issues of consent and the credibility of the victim and defendant are often central. Rule 413 is designed to provide the fact-finder with a fuller understanding of the defendant's behavior patterns, potentially making it easier to establish guilt in cases where the evidence might otherwise be limited to the testimony of the victim and the defendant.

Permitted Uses of Evidence Under Rule 413

Rule 413(a) authorizes the admission of evidence that the defendant committed other sexual assaults in cases where they are currently charged with a sexual assault. The rule permits this evidence to be considered on any matter to which it is relevant, including the defendant's propensity to commit sexual assaults.

1. Relevance of Prior Sexual Assaults

Under Rule 413, prior sexual assaults committed by the defendant can be introduced to demonstrate a pattern of behavior, which may be relevant to establishing the defendant's intent, modus operandi, or lack of mistake. The rule allows the jury to consider the defendant's past actions as part of the context in evaluating the current charges, which

can be particularly persuasive in cases where the prosecution's evidence relies heavily on the testimony of the victim.

For example, if a defendant is accused of sexually assaulting a victim in a manner similar to previous incidents for which they were also accused or convicted, evidence of those prior incidents may be admissible to suggest that the defendant has a propensity to engage in such conduct.

2. Scope of Admissibility

The evidence of prior sexual assaults admitted under Rule 413 is not limited to prior convictions. It may include allegations that did not result in a conviction, provided that the court determines the evidence to be relevant and reliable. The rule's broad scope reflects the understanding that evidence of other sexual assaults can be highly probative, even if the prior incidents did not result in legal proceedings or a conviction.

However, the admissibility of such evidence remains subject to Rule 403, which allows for the exclusion of evidence if its probative value is substantially outweighed by the risk of unfair prejudice, confusion, or other concerns. Thus, while Rule 413 permits the admission of prior sexual assaults, the court must still ensure that the evidence is used in a manner that is fair and does not unduly prejudice the defendant.

Disclosure Requirements

Rule 413(b) imposes a disclosure obligation on the prosecution. If the prosecutor intends to introduce evidence of the defendant's prior sexual assaults, they must disclose this evidence to the defendant at least 15 days before trial, unless the court permits a later disclosure for good cause.

1. Content of the Disclosure

The disclosure must include the evidence itself, such as prior witness statements or a summary of the expected testimony. This requirement is intended to provide the defendant with sufficient time to prepare a defense against the evidence and to challenge its admissibility or reliability.

2. Timing of the Disclosure

The 15-day minimum notice period is designed to ensure fairness in the proceedings, giving the defense adequate time to investigate the prior allegations, gather counter-evidence, or develop arguments for excluding the evidence under Rule 403. In exceptional circumstances, the court may allow the prosecution to disclose the evidence later, but this is typically reserved for cases where the evidence was not available earlier or where there are other compelling reasons.

Definition of "Sexual Assault" Under Rule 413

Rule 413(c) defines what constitutes "sexual assault" for the purposes of the rule. This definition is critical in determining what kinds of prior conduct can be introduced under Rule 413.

1. **Federal and State Crimes**

The definition of "sexual assault" includes any crime under federal law or state law that involves sexual misconduct, particularly those covered under 18 U.S.C. chapter 109A. This includes a wide range of offenses, such as aggravated sexual abuse, sexual abuse, and abusive sexual contact.

2. **Non-Consensual Contact**

The rule also encompasses any non-consensual sexual contact between any part of the defendant's body or an object and the victim's genitals or anus, or between the defendant's genitals or anus and any part of the victim's body. This broad inclusion ensures that a wide array of sexual misconduct can be considered under Rule 413.

3. **Sexual Pleasure from Inflicting Harm**

Additionally, Rule 413 covers conduct where the defendant derives sexual pleasure or gratification from inflicting death, bodily injury, or physical pain on another person. This includes more extreme forms of sexual assault, ensuring that the rule applies to a broad spectrum of criminal behavior.

4. **Attempts and Conspiracies**

The rule also includes attempts or conspiracies to engage in the prohibited conduct, recognizing that the intent to commit a sexual assault is relevant to establishing a pattern of behavior, even if the assault was not completed.

Judicial Discretion in Applying Rule 413

Judges have significant discretion in determining the admissibility of evidence under Rule 413. While the rule permits the introduction of prior sexual assaults, the judge must still assess the relevance and probative value of the evidence in each case.

1. **Balancing Probative Value and Prejudice**

Even if the evidence falls within the definition of "sexual assault" and is relevant, the court must still consider whether its probative value is substantially outweighed by the danger of unfair prejudice, as provided by Rule 403. The judge must ensure that the evidence does not lead to unfair bias against the defendant or distract the jury from the specific charges at hand.

2. **Limiting Instructions**

When admitting evidence under Rule 413, judges may issue limiting instructions to the jury, explaining how the evidence

should be considered. For example, the jury may be instructed to consider the prior assaults only as evidence of the defendant's propensity to commit sexual assaults, and not as definitive proof of guilt in the current case. These instructions are essential to prevent the jury from misusing the evidence and to maintain the fairness of the trial.

Interaction with Other Rules of Evidence

Rule 413 must be understood in the context of the broader framework of the Federal Rules of Evidence, particularly in conjunction with other rules that govern the admissibility of evidence.

- **Rule 401** defines relevance, establishing the baseline for what evidence can be considered by the court. Evidence of prior sexual assaults must be relevant to the issues in the case to be admissible under Rule 413.

- **Rule 403** allows for the exclusion of relevant evidence if its probative value is substantially outweighed by the potential for unfair prejudice, confusion, or delay. This rule provides an important check on the broad admissibility of evidence under Rule 413.

- **Rule 404(b)** typically restricts the use of other crimes, wrongs, or acts to prove character or propensity, but Rule 413 provides a specific exception to this general prohibition in the context of sexual-assault cases.

By operating within this framework, Rule 413 ensures that evidence of prior sexual assaults is used appropriately and that defendants are not unfairly prejudiced by the introduction of such evidence.

Practical Implications of Rule 413

Rule 413 has significant practical implications for both legal strategy and the broader administration of justice. Understanding the scope and application of this rule is essential for attorneys, judges, and defendants as they navigate sexual-assault cases.

Strategic Considerations for Attorneys

For prosecutors, Rule 413 provides a powerful tool for establishing a defendant's propensity to commit sexual assaults. However, prosecutors must be diligent in disclosing the evidence to the defense in a timely manner and in ensuring that the evidence is both relevant and reliable.

For defense attorneys, Rule 413 presents significant challenges, as it allows for the introduction of potentially prejudicial evidence that might sway the jury. Defense counsel must be prepared to challenge the admissibility of such evidence under Rule 403 and to argue that its probative value is outweighed by the risk of unfair prejudice. Defense attorneys should also be vigilant in cross-examining witnesses and presenting counter-evidence to mitigate the impact of prior sexual assault evidence.

Judicial Management of Rule 413 Evidence

Judges play a critical role in managing the introduction of evidence under Rule 413. By carefully applying the rule's provisions and conducting thorough analyses under Rule 403, judges ensure that the trial remains focused on the relevant issues and that the evidence presented is both fair and probative.

Judges must also be vigilant in providing appropriate jury instructions when evidence of prior sexual assaults is admitted. These instructions are essential for ensuring that the jury understands the specific purpose for which the evidence is being introduced and does not misuse it to draw improper inferences about the defendant's character or guilt.

Appellate Review of Rule 413 Decisions

Appellate courts review decisions regarding the admissibility of evidence under Rule 413 for abuse of discretion. This standard of review recognizes the trial judge's broad discretion in assessing the relevance and admissibility of evidence. If an appellate court finds that a trial judge improperly admitted or excluded evidence of prior sexual assaults, it may order a new trial or other appropriate relief.

Rule 413 in Specific Types of Cases

The application of Rule 413 can vary depending on the type of case and the specific legal issues involved. In criminal cases involving sexual assault, Rule 413's provisions are particularly impactful, as they allow the prosecution to introduce evidence that might otherwise be excluded under general rules prohibiting propensity evidence.

In cases involving serial offenders or patterns of sexual misconduct, Rule 413's provisions can be crucial in establishing the defendant's behavior patterns and in persuading the jury of the defendant's guilt. However, courts must be cautious in applying the rule to ensure that the defendant's right to a fair trial is preserved.

Rule 414 - Similar Crimes in Child-Molestation Cases

Rule 414. Similar Crimes in Child-Molestation Cases

(a) **Permitted Uses.** In a criminal case in which a defendant is accused of child molestation, the court may admit evidence that the defendant committed any other child molestation. The evidence may be considered on any matter to which it is relevant.

(b) **Disclosure to the Defendant.** If the prosecutor intends to offer this evidence, the prosecutor must disclose it to the defendant, including witnesses' statements or a summary of the expected testimony. The prosecutor must do so at least 15 days before trial or at a later time that the court allows for good cause.

(c) **Definition of "Child" and "Child Molestation."** In this rule and Rule 415: (1) "child" means a person below the age of 14; and (2) "child molestation" means a crime under federal law or under state law involving: (A) any conduct prohibited by 18 U.S.C. chapter 109A and committed with a child; (B) any conduct prohibited by 18 U.S.C. chapter 110; (C) contact between any part of the defendant's body—or an object—and a child's genitals or anus; (D) contact between the defendant's genitals or anus and any part of a child's body; (E) deriving sexual pleasure or gratification from inflicting death, bodily injury, or physical pain on a child; or (F) an attempt or conspiracy to engage in conduct described in subparagraphs (A)–(E).

Introduction to Rule 414

Rule 414 of the Federal Rules of Evidence governs the admissibility of evidence related to a defendant's commission of other offenses of child molestation in cases where they are currently accused of child molestation. This rule, like Rule 413, creates an exception to the general prohibition against using evidence of prior bad acts to prove a defendant's propensity to commit the crime charged. Rule 414 reflects a recognition of the serious and often repetitive nature of child molestation offenses and aims to provide the fact-finder with relevant information about the defendant's history that might be crucial to the case. This chapter provides a detailed analysis of Rule 414, exploring its text, interpretation, and broader implications for the administration of justice.

Analysis of Rule 414

Rule 414 provides a specific and powerful exception to the general rule against admitting evidence of a defendant's prior bad acts to show their propensity to commit a crime. In the context of child-molestation cases, the rule allows evidence of the defendant's prior offenses of child molestation to be admitted and considered by the jury. This exception reflects the belief that prior acts of child molestation are particularly probative of the defendant's likelihood to engage in similar behavior again, given the repetitive nature of such offenses.

Permitted Uses of Evidence Under Rule 414

Rule 414(a) allows for the admission of evidence that the defendant committed other offenses of child molestation in a criminal case where the defendant is currently accused of child molestation. The rule provides that such evidence may be considered on any matter to which it is relevant, effectively allowing the jury to use the defendant's past behavior to infer a propensity to commit the charged offense.

1. Relevance of Prior Child Molestation

Under Rule 414, prior acts of child molestation by the defendant can be introduced to establish a pattern of behavior, which may be relevant to the jury's determination of the defendant's intent, motive, or modus operandi. The rule permits the jury to consider the defendant's previous conduct as indicative of their propensity to commit similar crimes, which can be especially critical in cases where the evidence

might otherwise be limited to the testimony of the victim and the defendant.

For example, if a defendant is accused of sexually abusing a child in a manner similar to previous incidents for which they were also accused or convicted, evidence of those prior incidents may be admitted to suggest that the defendant has a pattern or propensity to engage in such conduct.

2. Scope of Admissibility

The evidence of prior child molestation admitted under Rule 414 is not limited to prior convictions. It may include allegations that did not result in a conviction, as long as the court determines that the evidence is relevant and reliable. This broad scope reflects the understanding that evidence of prior child molestation can be highly probative, even if the prior incidents did not result in formal legal action.

However, like all evidence admitted under the Federal Rules of Evidence, the admissibility of such evidence remains subject to Rule 403, which allows for the exclusion of evidence if its probative value is substantially outweighed by the risk of unfair prejudice, confusion, or other concerns. Therefore, while Rule 414 permits the introduction of prior child-molestation evidence, the court must still ensure that its admission does not lead to an unfair trial.

Disclosure Requirements

Rule 414(b) requires that the prosecution disclose to the defendant any evidence of prior child molestation that they intend to introduce at trial. This disclosure must occur at least 15 days before the trial, unless the court permits a later disclosure for good cause.

1. Content of the Disclosure

The disclosure must include the evidence itself, such as witness statements or a summary of the expected testimony. This requirement is intended to provide the defendant with sufficient time to prepare a defense against the evidence, to investigate the allegations, and to challenge the evidence's admissibility or reliability.

2. Timing of the Disclosure

The 15-day minimum notice period is designed to ensure fairness in the proceedings, allowing the defense adequate time to prepare for the introduction of such potentially prejudicial evidence. In exceptional circumstances, the court may allow the prosecution to disclose the evidence later, but this typically requires a showing of good cause, such as new evidence becoming available shortly before trial.

Definition of "Child" and "Child Molestation" Under Rule 414

Rule 414(c) provides specific definitions for the terms "child" and "child molestation" as they apply within the context of this rule and Rule 415.

1. Definition of "Child"

Under Rule 414(c)(1), a "child" is defined as a person below the age of 14. This definition ensures that the rule applies specifically to offenses involving young children, who are considered particularly vulnerable to sexual exploitation and abuse.

2. Definition of "Child Molestation"

Rule 414(c)(2) defines "child molestation" as encompassing a broad range of criminal conduct under both federal and state law. The definition includes:

- **Conduct Prohibited by Federal Law:** This includes crimes under 18 U.S.C. chapter 109A, which covers sexual abuse offenses, and chapter 110, which addresses sexual exploitation and other abuse of children.

- **Non-Consensual Sexual Contact:** The rule includes any non-consensual contact between any part of the defendant's body—or an object—and a child's genitals or anus, as well as contact between the defendant's genitals or anus and any part of a child's body.

- **Sexual Pleasure from Inflicting Harm:** The definition also covers cases where the defendant derives sexual pleasure or gratification from inflicting death, bodily injury, or physical pain on a child.

- **Attempts and Conspiracies:** The rule includes attempts or conspiracies to engage in the prohibited conduct, recognizing that the intent to commit such offenses is relevant to establishing a pattern of behavior, even if the offenses were not completed.

Judicial Discretion in Applying Rule 414

Judges have considerable discretion in determining the admissibility of evidence under Rule 414. While the rule permits the introduction of prior child-molestation evidence, judges must carefully assess the relevance and probative value of the evidence in each case.

1. Balancing Probative Value and Prejudice

Even if the evidence falls within the definition of "child molestation" and is relevant, the court must still consider whether its probative value is substantially outweighed by the danger of unfair prejudice, as provided by Rule 403. Judges must ensure that the evidence does not unfairly bias the jury against the defendant or distract from the specific charges at hand.

2. Limiting Instructions

When admitting evidence under Rule 414, judges may issue limiting instructions to the jury, explaining how the evidence should be considered. For example, the jury may be instructed to consider the prior offenses only as evidence of the defendant's propensity to commit child molestation and not as definitive proof of guilt in the current case. These instructions are essential to prevent the jury from misusing the evidence and to maintain the fairness of the trial.

Interaction with Other Rules of Evidence

Rule 414 must be understood in the context of the broader framework of the Federal Rules of Evidence, particularly in conjunction with other rules that govern the admissibility of evidence.

- **Rule 401** defines relevance, establishing the baseline for what evidence can be considered by the court. Evidence of prior child molestation must be relevant to the issues in the case to be admissible under Rule 414.

- **Rule 403** allows for the exclusion of relevant evidence if its probative value is substantially outweighed by the potential for unfair prejudice, confusion, or delay. This rule provides an important check on the broad admissibility of evidence under Rule 414.

- **Rule 404(b)** generally restricts the use of other crimes, wrongs, or acts to prove character or propensity, but Rule 414 provides a specific exception to this general prohibition in the context of child-molestation cases.

By operating within this framework, Rule 414 ensures that evidence of prior child molestation is used appropriately and that defendants are not unfairly prejudiced by the introduction of such evidence.

Practical Implications of Rule 414

Rule 414 has significant practical implications for both legal strategy and the broader administration of justice. Understanding the scope and application of this rule is essential for attorneys, judges, and defendants as they navigate child-molestation cases.

Strategic Considerations for Attorneys

For prosecutors, Rule 414 provides a powerful tool for establishing a defendant's propensity to commit child molestation. However, prosecutors must be diligent in disclosing the evidence to the defense in a timely manner and ensuring that the evidence is both relevant and reliable.

For defense attorneys, Rule 414 presents significant challenges, as it allows for the introduction of potentially prejudicial evidence that might sway the jury. Defense counsel must be prepared to challenge the admissibility of such evidence under Rule 403 and to argue that its probative value is outweighed by the risk of unfair prejudice. Defense attorneys should also be vigilant in cross-examining witnesses and presenting counter-evidence to mitigate the impact of prior child-molestation evidence.

Judicial Management of Rule 414 Evidence

Judges play a critical role in managing the introduction of evidence under Rule 414. By carefully applying the rule's provisions and conducting thorough analyses under Rule 403, judges ensure that the trial remains focused on the relevant issues and that the evidence presented is both fair and probative.

Judges must also be vigilant in providing appropriate jury instructions when evidence of prior child molestation is admitted. These instructions are essential for ensuring that the jury understands the specific purpose for which the evidence is being introduced and does not misuse it to draw improper inferences about the defendant's character or guilt.

Appellate Review of Rule 414 Decisions

Appellate courts review decisions regarding the admissibility of evidence under Rule 414 for abuse of discretion. This standard of review recognizes the trial judge's broad discretion in assessing the relevance and admissibility of evidence. If an appellate court finds that a trial judge improperly admitted or excluded evidence of prior child molestation, it may order a new trial or other appropriate relief.

Rule 414 in Specific Types of Cases

The application of Rule 414 can vary depending on the type of case and the specific legal issues involved. In criminal cases involving child molestation, Rule 414's provisions are particularly impactful, as they allow the prosecution to introduce evidence that might otherwise be excluded under general rules prohibiting propensity evidence.

In cases involving serial offenders or patterns of sexual misconduct involving children, Rule 414's provisions can be crucial in establishing the defendant's behavior patterns and in persuading the jury of the defendant's guilt. However, courts must be cautious in applying the rule to ensure that the defendant's right to a fair trial is preserved.

Rule 415 - Similar Acts in Civil Cases Involving Sexual Assault or Child Molestation

Text of Rule 415

Rule 415. Similar Acts in Civil Cases Involving Sexual Assault or Child Molestation
(a) **Permitted Uses.** In a civil case involving a claim for relief based on a party's alleged sexual assault or child molestation, the court may admit evidence that the party committed any other sexual assault or child molestation. The evidence may be considered as provided in Rules 413 and 414.
(b) **Disclosure to the Opponent.** If a party intends to offer this evidence, the party must disclose it to the opponent, including witnesses' statements or a summary of the expected testimony. The party must do so at least 15 days before trial or at a later time that the court allows for good cause.
(c) **Effect on Other Rules.** This rule does not limit the admission or consideration of evidence under any other rule.

Introduction to Rule 415

Rule 415 of the Federal Rules of Evidence addresses the admissibility of evidence regarding a defendant's commission of similar acts in civil cases involving allegations of sexual assault or child molestation. This rule allows evidence of the defendant's prior acts of sexual assault or child molestation to be admitted, similar to the exceptions provided in Rules 413 and 414 for criminal cases. Rule 415 recognizes the unique nature of sexual misconduct and child molestation, where patterns of behavior are often critical in establishing the defendant's liability. This chapter provides a detailed analysis of Rule 415, exploring its text, interpretation, and broader implications for the administration of justice in civil cases.

Analysis of Rule 415

Rule 415 permits the introduction of evidence regarding similar acts of sexual assault or child molestation in civil cases. This rule mirrors the approach taken in criminal cases under Rules 413 and 414, allowing the fact-finder to consider a party's past behavior as relevant to the claims at issue in the civil case. The rule acknowledges that patterns of sexual misconduct or child molestation may be particularly probative in civil cases, where liability often hinges on the credibility of the parties and the existence of a consistent pattern of behavior.

Permitted Uses of Evidence Under Rule 415

Rule 415(a) allows for the admission of evidence that a party committed other acts of sexual assault or child molestation in civil cases involving similar claims. The rule provides that such evidence may be considered in the same manner as under Rules 413 and 414, which govern criminal cases.

1. Relevance of Prior Acts

Under Rule 415, prior acts of sexual assault or child molestation committed by the defendant can be introduced to establish a pattern of behavior that is relevant to the civil claims at issue. The rule allows the jury to consider the defendant's past conduct as indicative of their propensity to engage in similar acts, which can be crucial in establishing liability in cases where the evidence may otherwise be limited.

For example, in a civil lawsuit alleging sexual assault, evidence that the defendant has previously committed similar acts may be admitted to suggest that the defendant has a propensity for such behavior, thereby supporting the plaintiff's claims.

2. Scope of Admissibility

The evidence of prior acts admitted under Rule 415 is not limited to prior convictions or formal charges. It may include allegations of similar acts that did not result in legal proceedings, provided that the court determines the evidence to be relevant and reliable. This broad scope reflects the understanding that evidence of prior similar acts can be highly probative in establishing liability in civil cases, even if the prior incidents did not result in a conviction or formal legal action.

However, the admissibility of such evidence remains subject to Rule 403, which allows for the exclusion of evidence if its probative value is substantially outweighed by the risk of unfair prejudice, confusion, or other concerns. Thus, while Rule 415 permits the introduction of prior acts evidence, the court must still ensure that its admission does not lead to an unfair trial.

Disclosure Requirements

Rule 415(b) requires that the party intending to introduce evidence of similar acts of sexual assault or child molestation must disclose this evidence to the opposing party at least 15 days before trial, unless the court permits a later disclosure for good cause.

1. Content of the Disclosure

The disclosure must include the evidence itself, such as witness statements or a summary of the expected testimony. This requirement is intended to provide the opposing party with sufficient time to prepare a defense against the evidence, to investigate the allegations, and to challenge the evidence's admissibility or reliability.

2. Timing of the Disclosure

The 15-day minimum notice period is designed to ensure fairness in the proceedings, allowing the opposing party adequate time to prepare for the introduction of potentially prejudicial evidence. In exceptional circumstances, the court may allow the disclosing party to provide the evidence later, but this typically requires a showing of good cause, such as new evidence becoming available shortly before trial.

Effect on Other Rules

Rule 415(c) clarifies that the rule does not limit the admission or consideration of evidence under any other rule of evidence. This means that even if evidence is not admissible under Rule 415, it may still be admitted under other relevant rules if it meets the criteria for admissibility.

1. Interplay with Other Rules of Evidence

Rule 415 operates within the broader context of the Federal Rules of Evidence, particularly in conjunction with other rules that govern the admissibility of evidence. For example, Rule 404(b) allows for the admission of evidence of other crimes, wrongs, or acts for purposes other than proving character, such as to establish motive, opportunity, or intent. If evidence of prior similar acts is not admissible under Rule 415, it may still be considered under Rule 404(b) if it is relevant to a non-propensity issue in the case.

2. Rule 403 Considerations

As with Rules 413 and 414, evidence admitted under Rule 415 is subject to the balancing test of Rule 403. This test allows the court to exclude evidence if its probative value is substantially outweighed by the risk of unfair prejudice, confusion, or undue delay. Judges must carefully apply this test to ensure that the evidence admitted under Rule 415 does not result in an unfair trial or improperly influence the jury.

Definition of "Sexual Assault" and "Child Molestation" Under Rule 415

While Rule 415 does not itself define "sexual assault" and "child molestation," it incorporates the definitions provided in Rules 413 and 414.

1. Sexual Assault

As defined in Rule 413, "sexual assault" includes any crime under federal or state law involving non-consensual sexual contact, sexual acts involving force or the threat of force, and other forms of sexual violence. This broad definition ensures that a wide range of conduct can be considered under Rule 415.

2. Child Molestation

As defined in Rule 414, "child molestation" includes any crime involving sexual misconduct with a child under the age of 14, including acts such as sexual contact, exploitation, and other forms of sexual abuse. This definition is similarly broad, ensuring that Rule 415 applies to a wide range of offenses involving children.

Judicial Discretion in Applying Rule 415

Judges have significant discretion in determining the admissibility of evidence under Rule 415. While the rule permits the introduction of prior acts of sexual assault or child molestation, judges must carefully assess the relevance and probative value of the evidence in each case.

1. Balancing Probative Value and Prejudice

Even if the evidence falls within the definitions of "sexual assault" or "child molestation" and is relevant, the court must still consider whether its probative value is substantially outweighed by the danger of unfair prejudice, as provided by Rule 403. Judges must ensure that the evidence does not unfairly bias the jury against the defendant or distract from the specific issues at hand.

2. Limiting Instructions

When admitting evidence under Rule 415, judges may issue limiting instructions to the jury, explaining how the evidence should be considered. For example, the jury may be instructed to consider the prior acts only as evidence of the defendant's propensity to commit similar acts and not as definitive proof of liability in the current case. These instructions are essential to prevent the jury from misusing the evidence and to maintain the fairness of the trial.

Practical Implications of Rule 415

Rule 415 has significant practical implications for both legal strategy and the broader administration of justice in civil cases. Understanding the scope and application of this rule is essential for attorneys, judges, and parties involved in civil litigation involving allegations of sexual assault or child molestation.

Strategic Considerations for Attorneys

For plaintiffs, Rule 415 provides a powerful tool for establishing a defendant's propensity to commit sexual assault or child molestation. However, plaintiffs must be diligent in disclosing the evidence to the defense in a timely manner and in ensuring that the evidence is both relevant and reliable.

For defendants, Rule 415 presents significant challenges, as it allows for the introduction of potentially prejudicial evidence that might sway the jury. Defense counsel must be prepared to challenge the admissibility of such evidence under Rule 403 and to argue that its probative value is outweighed by the risk of unfair prejudice. Defense attorneys should also be vigilant in cross-examining witnesses and presenting counter-evidence to mitigate the impact of prior acts evidence.

Judicial Management of Rule 415 Evidence

Judges play a critical role in managing the introduction of evidence under Rule 415. By carefully applying the rule's provisions and conducting thorough analyses under Rule 403, judges ensure that the trial remains focused on the relevant issues and that the evidence presented is both fair and probative.

Judges must also be vigilant in providing appropriate jury instructions when evidence of prior acts is admitted under Rule 415. These instructions are essential for ensuring that the jury understands the specific purpose for which the evidence is being introduced and does not misuse it to draw improper inferences about the defendant's liability.

Appellate Review of Rule 415 Decisions

Appellate courts review decisions regarding the admissibility of evidence under Rule 415 for abuse of discretion. This standard of review recognizes the trial judge's broad discretion in assessing the relevance and admissibility of evidence. If an appellate court finds that a trial judge improperly admitted or excluded evidence of prior acts, it may order a new trial or other appropriate relief.

Rule 415 in Specific Types of Cases

The application of Rule 415 can vary depending on the type of case and the specific legal issues involved. In civil cases involving allegations of sexual assault or child molestation, Rule 415's provisions are particularly impactful, as they allow the plaintiff to introduce evidence that might otherwise be excluded under general rules prohibiting propensity evidence.

In cases involving patterns of sexual misconduct or child molestation, Rule 415's provisions can be crucial in establishing the defendant's behavior patterns and in persuading the jury of the defendant's liability. However, courts must be cautious in applying the rule to ensure that the defendant's right to a fair trial is preserved.

ARTICLE V. PRIVILEGES

Rule 501 - Privilege in General

Text of Rule 501

Rule 501. Privilege in General
The common law—as interpreted by United States courts in the light of reason and experience—governs a claim of privilege unless any of the following provides otherwise:
• the United States Constitution;
• a federal statute; or
• rules prescribed by the Supreme Court.
But in a civil case, state law governs privilege regarding a claim or defense for which state law supplies the rule of decision.

Introduction to Rule 501

Rule 501 of the Federal Rules of Evidence addresses the law governing privileges in the context of federal court proceedings. Privileges serve as exceptions to the general rule that all relevant evidence is admissible. They are designed to protect certain confidential communications or relationships from being disclosed in legal proceedings, recognizing that the public interest in preserving these confidences outweighs the need for full disclosure. Rule 501 grants federal courts the flexibility to develop and apply privilege rules based on the common law, as interpreted by judicial precedent, except where federal statutes or the Constitution provide otherwise. This chapter provides a detailed analysis of Rule 501, exploring its text, interpretation, and broader implications for the administration of justice.

Analysis of Rule 501

Rule 501 establishes the framework for determining when a privilege may be asserted in federal court. Unlike other rules of evidence that provide specific guidelines, Rule 501 is deliberately open-ended, allowing federal courts to develop privilege rules based on common law principles, constitutional mandates, federal statutes, and the Supreme Court's rules. The rule reflects a balance between the need for flexible, context-sensitive privilege determinations and the importance of protecting certain communications and relationships.

Common Law Privileges

Under Rule 501, federal courts rely on common law principles to determine the existence and scope of privileges, as interpreted through judicial precedent and shaped by reason and experience.

1. **Development of Privileges in Common Law**

The common law approach allows federal courts to recognize and adapt privileges to meet evolving societal needs and values. For example, the attorney-client privilege, one of the most established privileges in common law, protects confidential communications between a lawyer and their client made for the purpose of seeking or providing legal advice. This privilege is rooted in the recognition that effective

legal representation depends on full and frank communication between attorneys and their clients.

Other commonly recognized privileges under the common law include the spousal privilege, which protects confidential communications between spouses; the psychotherapist-patient privilege, which safeguards communications between a patient and their therapist; and the clergy-penitent privilege, which covers confidential communications made to a clergy member in their professional capacity as a spiritual advisor.

These privileges, while well-established, are not absolute. Courts may limit or even deny the application of a privilege in certain circumstances, particularly where the need for disclosure outweighs the interests protected by the privilege. For example, the crime-fraud exception to the attorney-client privilege allows the disclosure of communications made in furtherance of a crime or fraud, recognizing that the privilege cannot be used to shield unlawful conduct.

2. **Judicial Interpretation and Flexibility**

Rule 501's reliance on common law provides federal courts with significant flexibility in interpreting and applying privileges. This flexibility allows courts to consider the specific facts and circumstances of each case, ensuring that privilege rules are applied in a manner that is both fair and consistent with the underlying principles of justice.

For instance, courts have occasionally recognized new privileges or extended existing ones in response to changing societal norms or legal needs. The recognition of the psychotherapist-patient privilege, for example, emerged as courts increasingly acknowledged the importance of mental health treatment and the need to protect the confidentiality of therapeutic communications.

Constitutional and Statutory Privileges

In addition to common law privileges, Rule 501 recognizes that certain privileges may be grounded in the United States Constitution or established by federal statute.

1. **Constitutional Privileges**

The Constitution provides the basis for certain privileges that are fundamental to the protection of individual rights. For example, the Fifth Amendment privilege against self-incrimination allows individuals to refuse to testify against themselves in criminal proceedings, safeguarding the right to avoid compelled self-incrimination.

Another constitutional privilege is the executive privilege, which allows the President and other high-level executive branch officials to withhold information from Congress, the courts, and the public in certain circumstances. This privilege is based on the need to protect the confidentiality of executive branch communications and to ensure the effective functioning of the government.

Constitutional privileges are generally non-negotiable and are afforded a high degree of protection by the courts. However, they are not absolute and may be subject to limitations or exceptions based on competing legal or public policy interests.

2. **Statutory Privileges**

Congress has the authority to create privileges through federal statutes, which can either codify common law privileges or establish new ones. For example, the federal physician-patient privilege, as set forth in some specific contexts by statute, protects the confidentiality of medical information shared between a patient and their doctor.

Statutory privileges may also be created to address particular legal issues or to protect certain types of information from disclosure. For instance, the Privacy Act of 1974 restricts the disclosure of personal information held by federal agencies, thereby establishing a statutory privilege that serves to protect individual privacy.

Federal statutes can also limit or override common law privileges in specific contexts. For example, certain federal statutes related to national security or law enforcement may restrict the application of privileges in cases involving terrorism, espionage, or other matters of national importance.

State Law Privileges in Civil Cases

Rule 501 also provides that in civil cases where state law supplies the rule of decision, state law governs the determination of privileges. This provision recognizes the federalist structure of the United States legal system, where state laws often play a significant role in civil litigation.

1. **Application of State Privilege Laws**

In civil cases involving claims or defenses that are governed by state law, federal courts are required to apply the privilege rules as defined by the relevant state. This ensures that the legal standards for privilege remain consistent with the substantive law that governs the case.

For example, in a diversity jurisdiction case involving a state law claim for medical malpractice, the federal court would apply the state's physician-patient privilege rather than any federal privilege or common law rule. This approach respects the states' authority to regulate the legal relationships and confidentiality interests within their jurisdiction.

2. **Variability Among States**

State privilege laws can vary significantly, reflecting the diverse legal traditions and public policy considerations across different jurisdictions. As a result, the application of privilege rules in civil cases may differ depending on the state law that governs the case. Federal courts must therefore carefully analyze the relevant state law to determine the applicable privilege standards.

In some instances, conflicts may arise between state and federal privilege laws, particularly when state law is more restrictive or expansive than the common law or federal statutes. In such cases, federal courts must balance the need to respect state law with the federal interests at stake, often leading to complex legal analyses and potential challenges on appeal.

Judicial Discretion and the Evolution of Privilege Law

Rule 501 grants federal judges considerable discretion in developing and applying privilege rules. This discretion is essential for ensuring that privilege law remains adaptable to the changing needs of society and the legal system.

1. **Role of Judicial Discretion**

Judicial discretion under Rule 501 allows courts to consider the specific circumstances of each case, including the nature of the confidential relationship, the importance of the evidence, and the potential harm from disclosure. This case-by-case approach ensures that privilege determinations are tailored to the facts, promoting fairness and justice.

For example, courts may recognize a qualified privilege in cases where the need for confidentiality is significant, but the interests in disclosure are also compelling. In such cases, the court may permit the disclosure of privileged information under certain conditions, such as limiting the scope of disclosure or issuing protective orders to minimize harm.

2. **Evolution of Privilege Law**

The flexible framework of Rule 501 allows privilege law to evolve in response to societal changes, technological advancements, and new legal challenges. Courts have the ability to extend existing privileges to new contexts or recognize new privileges when warranted by reason and experience.

For instance, as communication technologies have evolved, courts have had to address issues related to the confidentiality of electronic communications, such as emails and text messages. In some cases, courts have extended existing privileges, such as the attorney-client privilege, to cover these new forms of communication, recognizing their importance in modern legal practice.

Additionally, as societal attitudes toward certain relationships or professions change, courts may adjust the scope of privileges to reflect contemporary values. For example, as mental health has gained greater recognition as a critical component of overall well-being, courts have increasingly recognized the importance of protecting the confidentiality of communications between patients and mental health professionals.

Rule 502 - Attorney-Client Privilege and Work Product; Limitations on Waiver

Text of Rule 502

Rule 502. Attorney-Client Privilege and Work Product; Limitations on Waiver
(a) Disclosure Made in a Federal Proceeding or to a Federal Office or Agency; Scope of a Waiver. When the disclosure is made in a federal proceeding or to a federal office or agency and waives the attorney-client privilege or work-product protection, the waiver extends to an undisclosed communication or information in a federal or state proceeding only if: (1) the waiver is intentional; (2) the disclosed and undisclosed communications or information concern the same subject matter; and (3) they ought in fairness to be considered together.
(b) Inadvertent Disclosure. When made in a federal proceeding or to a federal office or agency, the disclosure does not operate as a waiver in a federal or state proceeding if: (1) the disclosure is inadvertent; (2) the holder of the privilege or protection took reasonable steps to prevent disclosure; and (3) the holder promptly took reasonable steps to rectify the error, including (if applicable) following Federal Rule of Civil Procedure 26(b)(5)(B).
(c) Disclosure Made in a State Proceeding. When the disclosure is made in a state proceeding and is not the subject of a state-court order concerning waiver, the disclosure does not operate as a waiver in a federal proceeding if the disclosure: (1) would not be a waiver under this rule if it had been made in a federal proceeding; or (2) is not a waiver under the law of the state where the disclosure occurred.
(d) Controlling Effect of a Court Order. A federal court may order that the privilege or protection is not waived by disclosure connected with the litigation pending before the court—in which event the disclosure is also not a waiver in any other federal or state proceeding.
(e) Controlling Effect of a Party Agreement. An agreement on the effect of disclosure between the parties to the litigation is binding only on the parties to the agreement, unless it is incorporated into a court order.
(f) Controlling Effect of This Rule. Notwithstanding Rules 101 and 1101, this rule applies to state proceedings and to federal court–annexed and federal court–mandated arbitration proceedings, in the circumstances set out in the rule. And notwithstanding Rule 501, this rule applies even if state law provides the rule of decision.

Introduction to Rule 502

Rule 502 of the Federal Rules of Evidence addresses the attorney-client privilege and the work product doctrine, specifically focusing on the limitations on the waiver of these protections. The rule is designed to provide clarity and uniformity in the handling of inadvertent disclosures of privileged or protected materials, particularly in the context of large-scale document productions and electronic discovery. By setting clear guidelines on when a waiver occurs and the extent of such a waiver, Rule 502 seeks to protect the confidentiality of privileged communications and attorney work product while promoting fairness and efficiency in legal proceedings. This chapter provides a detailed analysis of Rule 502, exploring its text, interpretation, and broader implications for the administration of justice.

Analysis of Rule 502

Rule 502 establishes comprehensive guidelines for determining when the attorney-client privilege or work product protection is waived and the extent of such a waiver. The rule is particularly important in the context of modern discovery practices, where the volume of documents and electronic communications involved in litigation has significantly increased the risk of inadvertent disclosures. Rule 502 aims to balance the need to protect privileged and protected materials with the practical realities of legal practice, providing clear standards for both intentional and inadvertent waivers.

Scope of Waiver in Federal Proceedings (Rule 502(a))

Rule 502(a) addresses the circumstances under which a waiver of attorney-client privilege or work product protection in a federal proceeding extends to undisclosed communications or information. The rule sets forth three conditions that must be met for a waiver to extend beyond the disclosed material.

1. Intentional Waiver

The waiver must be intentional for it to extend to other, undisclosed communications or information. This means that the holder of the privilege or protection must have knowingly and voluntarily disclosed the privileged or protected material. An intentional waiver may occur, for example, when a party decides to use privileged communications as evidence to support their case.

2. Same Subject Matter

The disclosed and undisclosed communications or information must concern the same subject matter. This requirement ensures that the waiver is limited to information that is directly related to the disclosed material, preventing a broad or indiscriminate waiver of privilege. The purpose is to maintain fairness by allowing the opposing party to examine related communications or information, while preventing the use of selective disclosures to gain an unfair advantage.

For instance, if a party discloses part of a privileged legal opinion on a specific issue, the waiver may extend to other parts of the legal opinion that address the same issue, but not to unrelated matters.

3. Fairness Consideration

The court must determine that the disclosed and undisclosed communications or information ought in fairness to be considered together. This requirement allows the court to consider the specific context of the disclosure and ensure that the waiver does not result in an unfair or misleading presentation of the evidence. The fairness consideration helps to prevent a party from using selective disclosures to mislead the court or opposing party.

Inadvertent Disclosure (Rule 502(b))

Rule 502(b) provides a framework for determining whether an inadvertent disclosure of privileged or protected material constitutes a waiver. The rule aims to protect parties from the harsh consequences of an unintentional mistake, particularly in the context of large-scale document productions.

1. Inadvertent Disclosure

The rule applies when the disclosure is inadvertent, meaning that it was unintentional or accidental. Inadvertent disclosures commonly occur during large-scale document reviews or electronic discovery, where the sheer volume of material increases the likelihood of mistakes.

2. Reasonable Steps to Prevent Disclosure

The holder of the privilege or protection must have taken reasonable steps to prevent the disclosure. This requirement encourages parties to implement robust document review and production processes to minimize the risk of inadvertent disclosures. Reasonable steps may include using advanced search tools, conducting thorough privilege reviews, and employing safeguards such as privilege logs.

Courts will consider what constitutes "reasonable steps" based on the specific circumstances, including the volume of documents, the complexity of the review process, and the resources available to the party.

3. Prompt Rectification of the Error

The holder of the privilege or protection must promptly take reasonable steps to rectify the error upon discovering the inadvertent disclosure. This may involve notifying the opposing party of the mistake, requesting the return or destruction of the inadvertently disclosed material, and following procedures outlined in Federal Rule of Civil Procedure 26(b)(5)(B), which governs the handling of inadvertently produced privileged materials during discovery.

Prompt action is critical in preserving the privilege or protection and mitigating the impact of the disclosure. Courts will evaluate the timeliness and effectiveness of the corrective measures taken by the party.

Disclosure Made in a State Proceeding (Rule 502(c))

Rule 502(c) addresses the impact of disclosures made in state proceedings on subsequent federal proceedings. The rule provides that a disclosure made in a state proceeding does not constitute a waiver in a federal proceeding if the disclosure would not have been a waiver under Rule 502 if made in a federal proceeding, or if it is not a waiver under the law of the state where the disclosure occurred.

1. Non-Waiver Under Federal Standards

If the disclosure would not have resulted in a waiver under Rule 502 had it occurred in a federal proceeding, then it does not operate as a waiver in a federal proceeding. This provision ensures consistency in the application of privilege rules across different jurisdictions, protecting parties from unintended waivers when state and federal standards differ.

2. State Law Governing Waiver

If the disclosure is not a waiver under the law of the state where it occurred, it does not constitute a waiver in a federal proceeding. This provision respects the autonomy of state privilege laws while ensuring that federal courts do not undermine state law protections in subsequent federal litigation.

Controlling Effect of Court Orders and Party Agreements

Rules 502(d) and 502(e) recognize the ability of federal courts and parties to establish specific terms governing the effect of disclosures on privilege or protection.

1. Court Orders (Rule 502(d))

Rule 502(d) allows a federal court to issue an order stating that a disclosure connected with the litigation pending before the court does not constitute a waiver in any other federal or state proceeding. Such orders provide certainty and protection against waiver, particularly in complex cases involving extensive discovery. A court order under Rule 502(d) can override the default waiver rules and ensure that inadvertent or even intentional disclosures do not result in unintended waivers of privilege or protection.

For example, a court may issue a non-waiver order that protects all privileged communications disclosed during discovery, thereby allowing parties to engage in more open and efficient discovery without the risk of waiving privilege.

2. Party Agreements (Rule 502(e))

Rule 502(e) allows parties to agree on the effect of disclosures between themselves. However, such agreements are binding only on the parties to the agreement unless incorporated into a court order. This provision encourages parties to negotiate and establish clear terms for handling privileged or protected materials, particularly in the context of large-scale or complex litigation.

An agreement under Rule 502(e) might specify that certain types of disclosures will not constitute a waiver of privilege or protection, providing the parties with a level of control over the waiver process. If the agreement is incorporated into a court order, it gains broader effect and can protect against waiver in other proceedings.

Controlling Effect of Rule 502 (Rule 502(f))

Rule 502(f) establishes the applicability of Rule 502 to state proceedings, federal court-annexed arbitration, and federal court-mandated arbitration. This provision ensures that the protections and limitations on waiver established by Rule 502 apply broadly, even in cases where state law provides the rule of decision or where arbitration is involved.

1. Applicability to State Proceedings

Rule 502(f) clarifies that the rule applies to state proceedings, ensuring that federal standards for waiver and privilege are respected even when state law might otherwise govern the substantive issues in the case. This promotes consistency in the application of privilege rules across jurisdictions and helps prevent unintended waivers that could undermine the parties' legal rights.

2. Applicability to Arbitration

The rule also applies to federal court-annexed and federal court-mandated arbitration proceedings. This ensures that the same protections against waiver apply in arbitration as in traditional court proceedings, recognizing the increasing importance of arbitration in resolving legal disputes.

Judicial Discretion and the Interpretation of Rule 502

Rule 502 grants federal judges considerable discretion in interpreting and applying the limitations on waiver. This discretion is essential for ensuring that the rule's protections are applied fairly and consistently, taking into account the specific circumstances of each case.

1. Role of Judicial Discretion

Judges have the authority to determine whether a disclosure constitutes a waiver of privilege or protection, considering factors such as the intent of the party, the steps taken to prevent and rectify the disclosure, and the overall fairness of the waiver. This case-by-case approach allows courts to tailor their decisions to the unique facts of each case, promoting justice and fairness in the legal process.

2. Evolving Standards and Judicial Interpretation

As legal practices and technologies evolve, courts may develop new interpretations of Rule 502, particularly in the context of electronic discovery and large-scale document productions. Judges must stay informed about the latest developments in legal technology and discovery practices to effectively apply the rule's provisions and protect the interests of the parties involved.

Practical Implications of Rule 502

Rule 502 has significant practical implications for attorneys, judges, and litigants in both civil and criminal cases. Understanding the scope and application of Rule 502 is essential for effectively navigating legal proceedings and protecting clients' interests.

Strategic Considerations for Attorneys

For attorneys, Rule 502 requires careful consideration when managing privileged or protected materials during discovery and litigation. Attorneys must implement robust procedures to prevent inadvertent disclosures and to promptly address any errors that do occur.

1. Preventing Inadvertent Disclosures

Attorneys should establish comprehensive document review processes, use advanced search tools, and create privilege logs to minimize the risk of inadvertent disclosures. Training

legal teams and using technology-assisted review (TAR) can also enhance the accuracy and efficiency of privilege reviews.

2. Responding to Inadvertent Disclosures

If an inadvertent disclosure occurs, attorneys must act quickly to rectify the situation, including notifying the opposing party, requesting the return or destruction of the disclosed materials, and following the procedures outlined in Rule 26(b)(5)(B). Prompt and effective action is critical to preserving the privilege or protection and preventing broader waiver.

Judicial Management of Rule 502 Issues

Judges play a critical role in managing disputes related to waiver of privilege under Rule 502. By carefully applying the rule's provisions and considering the specific facts of each case, judges ensure that the rule's protections are applied fairly and that the legal process remains efficient and just.

1. Issuing Non-Waiver Orders

Judges can issue non-waiver orders under Rule 502(d) to provide certainty and protection against waiver in complex cases. These orders can facilitate more open and efficient discovery by allowing parties to share privileged information without the fear of waiver.

2. Resolving Disputes Over Waiver

When disputes arise over whether a waiver has occurred, judges must carefully analyze the intent of the disclosing party, the steps taken to prevent and rectify the disclosure, and the fairness of extending the waiver to undisclosed materials. This analysis ensures that waiver decisions are based on a thorough consideration of the relevant factors and that the parties' legal rights are protected.

Impact on Discovery and Litigation Strategy

Rule 502 has a significant impact on discovery and litigation strategy, particularly in cases involving large volumes of documents and electronic communications. Understanding the rule's provisions allows attorneys to navigate the discovery process more effectively and to protect their clients' interests.

1. Negotiating Protective Orders and Agreements

Attorneys should consider negotiating protective orders and agreements under Rule 502(d) and (e) to establish clear terms for handling privileged or protected materials. These agreements can provide additional security against waiver and help to streamline the discovery process.

2. Managing Electronic Discovery

In the context of electronic discovery, Rule 502's protections are particularly important. Attorneys must be vigilant in managing e-discovery to prevent inadvertent disclosures, including using technology-assisted review, conducting thorough privilege reviews, and promptly addressing any errors.

ARTICLE VI. WITNESSES

Rule 601 - Competency to Testify in General

Text of Rule 601

Rule 601. Competency to Testify in General

Every person is competent to be a witness unless these rules provide otherwise. But in a civil case, state law governs the witness's competency regarding a claim or defense for which state law supplies the rule of decision.

Introduction to Rule 601

Rule 601 of the Federal Rules of Evidence governs the competency of witnesses to testify in legal proceedings. Competency refers to the legal qualifications a witness must possess to give testimony in court. The rule adopts a broad and inclusive approach, presuming that all persons are competent to testify unless the rules of evidence or other legal principles provide otherwise. This presumption reflects the modern view that questions about a witness's credibility or the weight of their testimony should be determined by the fact-finder rather than by preemptive exclusions based on competency. This chapter provides a detailed analysis of Rule 601, exploring its text, interpretation, and broader implications for the administration of justice.

Analysis of Rule 601

Rule 601 establishes a general presumption of competency, meaning that virtually all individuals are considered capable of testifying in legal proceedings. This inclusive approach underscores the principle that the ability to testify should not be restricted by rigid legal standards but should instead be subject to evaluation by the fact-finder, who can consider the credibility and reliability of the testimony.

General Presumption of Competency

Under Rule 601, the default position is that every person is competent to be a witness. This broad presumption reflects the evolution of evidentiary rules away from categorical exclusions based on specific characteristics or conditions, such as age, mental capacity, or criminal history, toward a more flexible and inclusive standard.

1. Rationale for the General Presumption

The rationale behind this general presumption is that courts should not preclude testimony based on assumptions about a person's ability to perceive, remember, or communicate. Instead, the fact-finder—typically the jury in a jury trial, or the judge in a bench trial—should have the opportunity to hear the testimony and assess its credibility. This approach ensures that potentially valuable testimony is not excluded from the outset and that the fact-finder has access to all relevant information when making decisions.

For example, a child witness may be deemed competent to testify, even if they are very young, as long as they have the ability to understand the importance of telling the truth and can communicate their observations. Similarly, a witness with a mental disability might be allowed to testify if they are capable of understanding and responding to questions about the events in question.

2. Evaluation of Credibility and Weight

The competency of a witness under Rule 601 does not imply that their testimony is necessarily credible or reliable. Rather, it means that the witness is legally permitted to testify. The credibility and weight of the testimony are determined by the fact-finder, who considers various factors such as the witness's demeanor, consistency, ability to recall events, and potential biases.

For instance, the testimony of a witness with a history of dishonesty or a significant cognitive impairment may be viewed with skepticism, but it is the role of the fact-finder to assess the impact of these factors on the overall credibility of the witness and the reliability of their testimony.

Exceptions to the General Presumption of Competency

While Rule 601 sets a broad presumption of competency, it also acknowledges that there may be exceptions based on other rules of evidence or specific legal principles. These exceptions are designed to address situations where a witness's testimony may be inherently unreliable or where public policy concerns justify excluding certain categories of witnesses.

1. Competency Rules Provided by the Federal Rules of Evidence

Certain rules within the Federal Rules of Evidence address specific situations where a witness's competency might be limited or excluded. For example:

- **Rule 602** requires that a witness have personal knowledge of the matter about which they are testifying. A witness who lacks personal knowledge is not competent to testify on that matter, as their testimony would be based on speculation or hearsay rather than firsthand experience.

- **Rule 603** requires that witnesses take an oath or affirmation to testify truthfully, which serves as a fundamental prerequisite for competency. A witness who refuses or is unable to take the oath or affirmation may be deemed incompetent to testify.

- **Rule 605** disqualifies judges from testifying as witnesses in cases over which they are presiding, ensuring that the judge remains an impartial arbiter rather than a participant in the case.

- ○ **Rule 606** addresses the competency of jurors to testify in certain situations, particularly regarding matters occurring during deliberations or the validity of the verdict. This rule helps maintain the confidentiality and integrity of the jury's deliberative process.

2. **Competency in Civil Cases Governed by State Law**

In civil cases, Rule 601 provides that state law governs the competency of witnesses when state law supplies the rule of decision for a particular claim or defense. This provision reflects the federal system's respect for state sovereignty and the recognition that state laws may establish specific competency standards in certain types of cases.

For example, in a civil lawsuit based on a state law tort claim, the state's rules regarding the competency of witnesses will apply. This might include specific provisions addressing the competency of minors, persons with mental disabilities, or individuals with a direct financial interest in the outcome of the case.

The application of state law in these cases ensures consistency with the underlying substantive law and respects the states' authority to regulate the qualifications of witnesses within their jurisdiction.

Judicial Discretion and the Application of Rule 601

Judges have considerable discretion in determining the competency of witnesses under Rule 601. This discretion is essential for ensuring that the rule is applied fairly and appropriately, taking into account the specific circumstances of each case.

1. **Judicial Assessment of Competency**

When a party challenges a witness's competency, the judge must assess whether the witness meets the basic requirements for competency, such as the ability to understand the oath or affirmation and the ability to perceive, recall, and communicate relevant facts. The judge's assessment may involve questioning the witness, reviewing evidence related to the witness's capacity, and considering arguments from both parties.

For instance, if a party argues that a witness is incompetent due to mental incapacity, the judge may consider medical evidence, expert testimony, or observations of the witness's behavior to determine whether the witness is capable of providing reliable testimony.

2. **Case-by-Case Determinations**

Competency determinations under Rule 601 are highly fact-specific and must be made on a case-by-case basis. This approach allows judges to consider the unique characteristics of each witness and the context of the testimony, ensuring that the rule is applied in a manner that is both just and equitable.

For example, in cases involving child witnesses, the judge may evaluate the child's ability to understand the difference between truth and falsehood, their ability to recall events accurately, and their susceptibility to suggestion. Based on these factors, the judge can make an informed decision about whether the child is competent to testify.

Implications of Rule 601 for Legal Practice

Rule 601 has significant implications for attorneys, judges, and litigants in both civil and criminal cases. Understanding the scope and application of Rule 601 is essential for effectively navigating legal proceedings and ensuring that witness testimony is appropriately evaluated.

1. **Strategic Considerations for Attorneys**

Attorneys must be aware of the broad presumption of competency under Rule 601 and be prepared to challenge or defend the competency of witnesses when necessary. This may involve gathering evidence to support a claim of incompetency, such as medical records or expert testimony, or countering such claims by demonstrating the witness's ability to provide reliable testimony.

For example, in a criminal case, the defense attorney might challenge the competency of a key prosecution witness based on their mental health history, arguing that the witness's testimony is unreliable. Conversely, the prosecutor might defend the witness's competency by presenting evidence of their capacity to understand and communicate relevant facts.

2. **Evaluating the Credibility and Weight of Testimony**

While Rule 601 establishes the competency of witnesses, attorneys must also focus on evaluating and challenging the credibility and weight of the testimony. This involves cross-examination, presenting contradictory evidence, and highlighting any factors that may affect the witness's reliability, such as bias, memory lapses, or inconsistencies in their account.

For instance, if a witness is deemed competent but has a history of dishonesty, the opposing attorney may use this information to undermine the witness's credibility and persuade the fact-finder to give less weight to their testimony.

3. **Judicial Management of Competency Issues**

Judges play a critical role in managing competency issues under Rule 601. By carefully assessing the competency of witnesses and ensuring that only reliable testimony is presented, judges help maintain the integrity of the legal process and protect the rights of all parties involved.

Judges must also be prepared to provide clear instructions to the jury regarding the evaluation of witness testimony, particularly when there are questions about the witness's competency. These instructions can help the jury understand the factors that may affect the reliability of the testimony and guide them in making informed decisions.

Rule 602 - Need for Personal Knowledge

Rule 602. Need for Personal Knowledge

A witness may testify to a matter only if evidence is introduced sufficient to support a finding that the witness has personal knowledge of the matter. Evidence to prove personal knowledge may consist of the witness's own testimony. This rule does not apply to a witness's expert testimony under Rule 703.

Introduction to Rule 602

Rule 602 of the Federal Rules of Evidence establishes the requirement that a witness must have personal knowledge of the matter about which they are testifying. This rule is fundamental to ensuring that the testimony presented in court is based on the witness's own observations or experiences, rather than on speculation, hearsay, or assumptions. By requiring personal knowledge, Rule 602 upholds the integrity of the fact-finding process and ensures that the evidence considered by the jury or judge is reliable and relevant. This chapter provides a detailed analysis of Rule 602, exploring its text, interpretation, and broader implications for the administration of justice.

Analysis of Rule 602

Rule 602 serves as a critical safeguard in the evidentiary process by ensuring that only testimony based on direct, personal knowledge is admitted into evidence. This requirement helps to exclude unreliable testimony that could mislead the fact-finder and distort the truth-seeking function of the trial.

The Requirement of Personal Knowledge

Under Rule 602, a witness is permitted to testify about a matter only if there is sufficient evidence to support a finding that the witness has personal knowledge of the matter. Personal knowledge refers to the witness's direct perception of the events or facts in question, obtained through their senses (e.g., seeing, hearing, touching).

1. **Direct Perception as a Basis for Testimony**

Personal knowledge must arise from the witness's direct experience or observation of the event or fact to which they are testifying. This means that the witness must have seen, heard, or otherwise directly perceived the matter they are discussing in their testimony.

For example, if a witness testifies that they saw a car accident occur at a specific intersection, their testimony is based on personal knowledge because they directly observed the accident. Conversely, if a witness testifies about what they heard another person say about the accident, their testimony would not be based on personal knowledge but rather on hearsay, unless it falls under an exception to the hearsay rule.

2. **Exclusion of Speculative or Secondhand Information**

Rule 602 is designed to prevent the admission of speculative testimony or testimony based on secondhand information. Speculative testimony occurs when a witness offers an opinion or conclusion not grounded in their direct perception. Such testimony is unreliable because it is based on assumptions rather than actual experience.

For instance, if a witness testifies that they "believe" a person must have been speeding based on the noise of the car but did not actually see the car's speedometer or observe the car's movement, their testimony would likely be considered speculative and excluded under Rule 602.

Similarly, testimony based on what the witness was told by others, rather than what they personally observed, is excluded under Rule 602 unless it meets an exception under the hearsay rules.

Establishing Personal Knowledge

To comply with Rule 602, the party offering the testimony must provide evidence sufficient to support a finding that the witness has the requisite personal knowledge. This requirement is typically met through the witness's own testimony, where they explain how they acquired their knowledge of the facts in question.

1. **Testimony of the Witness**

The most common way to establish personal knowledge is through the testimony of the witness themselves. The witness might be asked to describe the circumstances under which they observed or experienced the events they are testifying about.

For example, a witness might testify, "I was standing on the corner of Main Street and 5th Avenue when I saw the red car run the stop sign." This statement establishes that the witness was physically present and directly observed the event, thereby satisfying the personal knowledge requirement.

2. **Corroborating Evidence**

In some cases, corroborating evidence might be introduced to further establish the witness's personal knowledge. This could include physical evidence, documents, or testimony from other witnesses that confirms the witness's presence or ability to observe the events in question.

For instance, if there is a question about whether a witness was actually at the scene of an event, surveillance footage or other witnesses who saw the person at the scene might be introduced to corroborate the witness's testimony.

Exceptions and Special Considerations

While Rule 602 sets a strict standard for the requirement of personal knowledge, there are specific exceptions and considerations that modify its application in certain contexts.

1. **Expert Testimony (Rule 703)**

Rule 602 does not apply to expert witnesses testifying under Rule 703. Experts are permitted to offer opinions based on information that they did not personally observe, as long as that information is of a type reasonably relied upon by experts in the particular field. This reflects the understanding that expert testimony often involves interpreting data, facts, or evidence that the expert did not personally perceive but that falls within their professional expertise.

For example, a forensic accountant might testify about the financial condition of a company based on their analysis of financial records, even though they did not personally generate or observe all the transactions. This testimony is admissible because it is based on the expert's specialized knowledge and the information typically relied upon by professionals in that field.

2. Lay Opinion Testimony

While Rule 602 requires personal knowledge, lay witnesses are sometimes allowed to offer opinions or inferences based on their personal observations, as long as those opinions are rationally based on their perception and are helpful to understanding the witness's testimony or determining a fact in issue, as governed by Rule 701.

For example, a lay witness might testify, "The driver seemed drunk because I saw them swerving across the lanes and struggling to keep their balance when they got out of the car." This opinion is based on the witness's direct observations and is thus permissible under Rule 701 in conjunction with Rule 602.

3. Situations Involving Memory and Recollection

Rule 602 requires that a witness have present recollection of the events to which they are testifying. If a witness cannot recall an event at the time of testimony, their testimony may be limited or excluded unless it can be refreshed under Rule 612, which allows a witness to use a writing or other item to refresh their memory.

For example, if a witness cannot recall specific details of an event, they might be allowed to review notes they took at the time of the event to refresh their memory before testifying. Once their memory is refreshed, they can testify based on their renewed personal knowledge.

Judicial Discretion in Applying Rule 602

Judges have discretion in determining whether a witness's testimony meets the personal knowledge requirement of Rule 602. This discretion is crucial for ensuring that testimony is reliable and that the fact-finder is presented with evidence that is based on the witness's direct experience.

1. Assessing Sufficiency of Evidence for Personal Knowledge

Judges must assess whether the evidence introduced to support a finding of personal knowledge is sufficient. This might involve evaluating the witness's testimony about how they acquired their knowledge, considering any corroborating evidence, and determining whether the witness's testimony is grounded in their direct perception of the events.

For example, if a witness claims to have seen an event but was physically far away or had an obstructed view, the judge might consider whether the witness's testimony is sufficiently reliable to be admitted under Rule 602.

2. Exclusion of Testimony for Lack of Personal Knowledge

If the judge determines that a witness lacks personal knowledge of the matter they are testifying about, the testimony may be excluded under Rule 602. This helps prevent the introduction of unreliable or irrelevant testimony that could confuse or mislead the fact-finder.

For instance, if a witness is asked to testify about a conversation they did not hear directly but only learned about through another person, the judge may exclude the testimony for lack of personal knowledge unless an applicable hearsay exception applies.

Implications of Rule 602 for Legal Practice

Rule 602 has significant implications for attorneys, judges, and litigants in both civil and criminal cases. Understanding the scope and application of Rule 602 is essential for effectively presenting and challenging witness testimony.

1. Strategic Considerations for Attorneys

Attorneys must carefully assess whether their witnesses have the necessary personal knowledge to testify about specific matters. This involves preparing witnesses to explain how they acquired their knowledge and ensuring that their testimony is based on direct observations or experiences.

For example, in preparing a witness, an attorney might review the events the witness will testify about, helping the witness to recall specific details that establish their personal knowledge. The attorney might also gather corroborating evidence to support the witness's testimony.

2. Challenging Testimony for Lack of Personal Knowledge

When cross-examining witnesses, attorneys may challenge the basis of the witness's testimony by questioning whether the witness actually has personal knowledge of the events or facts they are discussing. This can be an effective strategy for undermining the credibility of the testimony and persuading the judge or jury to give it less weight.

For instance, an attorney might ask a witness to clarify their position at the time of an event or to describe what they actually saw or heard. If the witness's testimony appears to be based on assumptions or hearsay, the attorney can argue for its exclusion under Rule 602.

3. Judicial Management of Personal Knowledge Issues

Judges play a key role in managing issues related to personal knowledge under Rule 602. By carefully evaluating the sufficiency of the evidence supporting personal knowledge, judges ensure that only reliable testimony is admitted and that the fact-finder is presented with a clear and accurate account of the events.

Judges may also provide instructions to the jury about the importance of personal knowledge in evaluating witness testimony, helping the jury understand the basis for the testimony and guiding them in determining its credibility and relevance.

Rule 603 - Oath or Affirmation to Testify Truthfully

Rule 603. Oath or Affirmation to Testify Truthfully
Before testifying, a witness must give an oath or affirmation to testify truthfully. It must be in a form designed to impress that duty on the witness's conscience.

Introduction to Rule 603

Rule 603 of the Federal Rules of Evidence addresses the requirement that every witness must take an oath or affirmation to testify truthfully before giving testimony in court. This rule is fundamental to the integrity of the judicial process, as it underscores the seriousness of the obligation to provide truthful testimony. The oath or affirmation serves as a solemn promise by the witness to tell the truth, and it is intended to impress upon the witness the moral and legal consequences of giving false testimony. This chapter provides a detailed analysis of Rule 603, exploring its text, interpretation, and broader implications for the administration of justice.

Analysis of Rule 603

Rule 603 establishes the requirement that every witness must take an oath or affirmation before providing testimony in legal proceedings. This rule reflects the importance of ensuring that all testimony presented in court is given under a binding commitment to truthfulness, thereby promoting the accuracy and reliability of the fact-finding process.

The Purpose of the Oath or Affirmation

The primary purpose of the oath or affirmation is to impress upon the witness the solemn duty to tell the truth while testifying. This requirement serves both a moral and a legal function: it reminds the witness of the ethical obligation to be truthful and subjects the witness to potential penalties for perjury if they knowingly provide false testimony.

1. Moral and Ethical Responsibility

The oath or affirmation is intended to invoke the witness's moral and ethical responsibility to be honest. By taking an oath or affirmation, the witness acknowledges the seriousness of their role in the judicial process and the potential consequences of misleading the court.

The requirement is designed to make the witness aware that their testimony could significantly impact the outcome of the case, the lives of the parties involved, and the administration of justice. Therefore, the oath or affirmation serves as a reminder that the witness's words carry weight and must be truthful.

2. Legal Consequences of False Testimony

Beyond the moral implications, the oath or affirmation has legal significance. A witness who knowingly provides false testimony after taking an oath or affirmation is subject to prosecution for perjury, a serious criminal offense. This legal consequence underscores the binding nature of the oath or affirmation and serves as a deterrent against dishonesty.

Perjury is a crime punishable by fines and imprisonment, reflecting the importance that the legal system places on truthful testimony. The possibility of facing such penalties reinforces the obligation of the witness to adhere strictly to the truth.

Form and Administration of the Oath or Affirmation

Rule 603 does not prescribe a specific form for the oath or affirmation, allowing flexibility in its administration. The rule requires only that the form used be designed to impress the duty of truthfulness on the witness's conscience. This flexibility allows courts to accommodate different beliefs and practices while ensuring that all witnesses understand their obligation to testify truthfully.

1. Traditional Oath

The traditional oath, often administered with the witness raising their right hand and placing their left hand on a religious text (such as the Bible), typically involves the witness swearing to tell the truth, the whole truth, and nothing but the truth. This form of the oath is deeply rooted in the history of the legal system and is still commonly used in many courts.

The language of the traditional oath is designed to cover all aspects of the testimony, emphasizing the witness's obligation to provide a complete and truthful account of the facts as they know them.

2. Affirmation

For witnesses who have religious objections to taking an oath or who prefer not to swear on a religious text, Rule 603 permits an affirmation instead. An affirmation is a solemn declaration to tell the truth without invoking a religious context, making it suitable for individuals of different faiths or those who do not subscribe to religious beliefs.

The language of an affirmation might be as simple as, "I affirm that I will tell the truth," and it carries the same legal weight as an oath. Courts are required to respect the witness's preference for an affirmation and to ensure that the form used is equally effective in impressing the duty of truthfulness on the witness.

3. Adaptations for Special Circumstances

Rule 603 allows for adaptations in the form of the oath or affirmation to accommodate special circumstances, such as witnesses with disabilities, children, or individuals with limited language proficiency. In such cases, the court may modify the procedure to ensure that the witness understands the significance of the oath or affirmation and their obligation to tell the truth.

For example, a child witness might be asked to promise to tell the truth in language that is simple and understandable to them, or a witness who is hearing-impaired might take the oath or affirmation through sign language.

Judicial Discretion in Administering the Oath or Affirmation

Judges have discretion in determining how the oath or affirmation is administered, provided that the form used effectively communicates the importance of truthfulness to the witness. This discretion is essential for ensuring that the oath or affirmation is meaningful and appropriate for the individual witness and the circumstances of the case.

1. Tailoring the Oath or Affirmation

Judges may tailor the administration of the oath or affirmation to meet the needs of the witness and to ensure that the witness comprehends the significance of the process. This might involve simplifying the language for a child witness, allowing a witness to hold a different religious text or no text at all, or using alternative methods of communication for witnesses with disabilities.

The goal is to ensure that the witness is fully aware of their obligation to tell the truth and understands the consequences of providing false testimony.

2. Ensuring Comprehension

Judges are responsible for ensuring that the witness comprehends the meaning and importance of the oath or affirmation. If there is any doubt about the witness's understanding, the judge may take additional steps to clarify the process and reinforce the duty to testify truthfully.

For instance, before administering the oath or affirmation, the judge might ask the witness if they understand what it means to tell the truth and whether they are willing to commit to doing so. This can be particularly important in cases involving young children, individuals with cognitive impairments, or witnesses with limited proficiency in the language used in court.

Consequences of Failing to Take the Oath or Affirmation

Rule 603 requires that every witness take an oath or affirmation before testifying. If a witness refuses to take the oath or affirmation, they may be disqualified from providing testimony. This requirement is fundamental to ensuring that all testimony presented in court is given under a binding commitment to truthfulness.

1. Refusal to Take the Oath or Affirmation

A witness who refuses to take the oath or affirmation may be barred from testifying, as their testimony would not be subject to the legal and moral obligations imposed by the rule. This ensures that the court does not hear testimony from individuals who are not bound by a commitment to tell the truth.

In some cases, the refusal to take the oath or affirmation may raise concerns about the witness's willingness to be truthful or their understanding of the seriousness of the legal proceedings. The judge may inquire into the reasons for the refusal and determine whether any accommodations can be made to address the witness's concerns.

2. Implications for Testimony and Legal Proceedings

The failure to administer the oath or affirmation, or to do so in a manner that impresses upon the witness the duty to testify truthfully, can have significant implications for the validity of the testimony and the outcome of the case. Testimony given without an oath or affirmation may be challenged or excluded, and any resulting verdict or judgment could be subject to appeal or reversal.

For example, if it is discovered that a key witness testified without taking an oath or affirmation, the opposing party might argue that the testimony should be excluded or that a mistrial should be declared. Courts must therefore ensure that the requirements of Rule 603 are strictly followed to preserve the integrity of the legal process.

Implications of Rule 603 for Legal Practice

Rule 603 has important implications for attorneys, judges, and litigants in both civil and criminal cases. Understanding the scope and application of Rule 603 is essential for ensuring that witness testimony is properly admitted and that the legal process is conducted with integrity.

1. Strategic Considerations for Attorneys

Attorneys must be aware of the requirements of Rule 603 and ensure that their witnesses are prepared to take the oath or affirmation. This may involve discussing the process with the witness beforehand, addressing any concerns they may have about the oath or affirmation, and ensuring that they understand the importance of telling the truth.

For instance, if a witness has religious or ethical objections to taking an oath, the attorney should inform the court in advance and request that the witness be allowed to take an affirmation instead. This proactive approach helps avoid delays or disruptions during the testimony.

2. Challenging the Testimony Based on Oath or Affirmation Issues

If there are concerns about whether a witness has properly taken the oath or affirmation, attorneys may raise objections or challenge the admissibility of the testimony. This might occur if the oath or affirmation was administered incorrectly, if the witness did not understand its significance, or if the witness refused to take the oath or affirmation.

For example, an attorney might object to the testimony of a witness who was not sworn in, arguing that the testimony should be excluded because it was not given under the required commitment to truthfulness.

3. Judicial Management of the Oath or Affirmation Process

Judges play a key role in managing the administration of the oath or affirmation and ensuring that it is done in accordance with Rule 603. This includes tailoring the process to meet the needs of the witness, ensuring that the witness understands the obligation to tell the truth, and addressing any issues that arise during the testimony.

Judges must also be vigilant in ensuring that all witnesses are properly sworn in before testifying, as failure to do so can undermine the validity of the testimony and the outcome of the case. By adhering to the requirements of Rule 603, judges help maintain the integrity of the judicial process and protect the rights of all parties involved.

Rule 604 - Interpreter

Text of Rule 604

Rule 604. Interpreter
An interpreter must be qualified and must give an oath or affirmation to make a true translation.

Introduction to Rule 604

Rule 604 of the Federal Rules of Evidence addresses the use of interpreters in legal proceedings. The rule ensures that witnesses or parties who do not speak or understand English, or who have hearing or speech impairments, can effectively participate in the judicial process through the use of an interpreter. The interpreter's role is to facilitate accurate communication between the court, the parties, and the witness, ensuring that language barriers do not impede the fair administration of justice. Rule 604 establishes the qualifications and obligations of interpreters, emphasizing the importance of accuracy, impartiality, and adherence to ethical standards. This chapter provides a detailed analysis of Rule 604, exploring its text, interpretation, and broader implications for the administration of justice.

Analysis of Rule 604

Rule 604 sets forth the requirements for the use of interpreters in legal proceedings. The rule mandates that interpreters must be both qualified and sworn to provide accurate translations, thereby ensuring that all parties involved in the proceeding can understand and participate fully, regardless of language or communication barriers.

Qualifications of Interpreters

The first requirement under Rule 604 is that the interpreter must be qualified. This means that the interpreter must possess the necessary skills, knowledge, and proficiency to accurately translate the spoken or signed language of the witness or party into English, and vice versa.

1. Skills and Proficiency

An interpreter must have a strong command of both the source language (the language being translated) and the target language (typically English in U.S. courts). This includes not only fluency in the languages but also an understanding of legal terminology and concepts. The interpreter must be able to convey both the literal meaning and the nuances of the testimony, ensuring that the translation accurately reflects the original statements.

For example, an interpreter in a legal proceeding must be able to accurately translate legal terms, idiomatic expressions, and culturally specific references that may arise during testimony. This requires both linguistic skill and familiarity with legal procedures and terminology.

2. Certification and Experience

While Rule 604 does not explicitly require interpreters to be certified, many courts prefer or require the use of certified interpreters, especially in complex or high-stakes cases. Certification typically involves passing a rigorous examination that tests the interpreter's proficiency in both languages and their knowledge of legal terminology and procedures.

In addition to certification, courts may also consider an interpreter's experience and track record in legal settings. Experienced interpreters are often more adept at handling the pressures of courtroom proceedings and are better equipped to manage the challenges of translating live testimony.

3. Assessment of Qualifications

The court is responsible for assessing the qualifications of the interpreter. This may involve reviewing the interpreter's credentials, experience, and any relevant certifications. In some cases, the court may also conduct a voir dire examination of the interpreter to ensure that they are qualified to perform the task.

For example, before allowing an interpreter to serve in a trial, the judge might ask the interpreter about their training, certification, experience in legal settings, and familiarity with the specific languages involved in the case. The judge's assessment ensures that the interpreter is capable of providing accurate and reliable translations.

Oath or Affirmation of Accuracy

The second requirement under Rule 604 is that the interpreter must take an oath or affirmation to make a true translation. This requirement serves to underscore the importance of accuracy in translation and to bind the interpreter to a standard of truthfulness and impartiality.

1. Purpose of the Oath or Affirmation

The oath or affirmation emphasizes the interpreter's duty to provide a faithful and accurate translation of the testimony or statements made by the witness or party. It serves as a formal declaration that the interpreter will perform their duties with integrity, avoiding any alterations, omissions, or additions that could distort the original meaning.

By taking the oath or affirmation, the interpreter acknowledges their responsibility to the court and the legal process, as well as the potential consequences of failing to provide an accurate translation, which could include perjury charges or other legal sanctions.

2. Administration of the Oath or Affirmation

The oath or affirmation is typically administered by the judge before the interpreter begins their duties. The standard language for the oath may vary, but it generally requires the interpreter to swear or affirm that they will translate accurately and truthfully.

For example, the oath might be phrased as, "Do you solemnly swear (or affirm) that you will accurately and truthfully translate the questions and answers to the best of your ability, so help you God (or under penalty of perjury)?" This oath reinforces the interpreter's commitment to providing a true and faithful translation.

Ethical Considerations and Impartiality

Rule 604 implicitly requires that interpreters adhere to high ethical standards, including impartiality, confidentiality, and the avoidance of conflicts of interest. These ethical considerations are crucial to ensuring that the interpreter's role is performed in a manner that upholds the integrity of the legal process.

1. Impartiality

Interpreters must remain impartial throughout the proceedings, translating the testimony or statements without injecting their own opinions, biases, or interpretations. Impartiality is essential to maintaining the fairness of the trial and ensuring that all parties receive an accurate representation of the testimony.

For instance, an interpreter who has a personal relationship with one of the parties or a financial interest in the outcome of the case may be disqualified to avoid any appearance of bias. The court must be vigilant in ensuring that interpreters maintain their neutrality and do not favor one side over the other.

2. Confidentiality

Interpreters are often privy to sensitive information during legal proceedings, and they are bound by confidentiality requirements to protect this information. Confidentiality ensures that the interpreter does not disclose any information learned during the course of their duties, whether it is related to the case or the private matters of the parties involved.

For example, an interpreter translating attorney-client communications during a deposition or trial must maintain strict confidentiality, as these communications are privileged and protected by law.

3. Avoidance of Conflicts of Interest

Interpreters must avoid situations where their impartiality or ethical obligations might be compromised. This includes avoiding conflicts of interest, such as interpreting in cases where they have a personal or financial stake, or where they have previously provided services to one of the parties in a way that could affect their neutrality.

Before accepting an assignment, interpreters should disclose any potential conflicts of interest to the court, and the court should take appropriate measures to address these concerns, which may include appointing a different interpreter.

Judicial Discretion in Appointing and Evaluating Interpreters

Judges have significant discretion in appointing and evaluating interpreters under Rule 604. This discretion is critical for ensuring that interpreters meet the necessary qualifications and adhere to the required ethical standards.

1. Appointment of Interpreters

Judges are responsible for appointing interpreters when needed in a legal proceeding. The decision to appoint an interpreter typically arises when a party or witness does not speak or understand English, or when they have a hearing or speech impairment that necessitates the use of a sign language interpreter.

In appointing an interpreter, the judge must consider the qualifications, experience, and potential biases of the candidates. The judge may seek input from the parties involved or rely on court administration procedures to select a qualified interpreter.

2. Evaluation of Interpreter Performance

Judges must also monitor the performance of interpreters during the proceedings to ensure that they are providing accurate and impartial translations. If issues arise, such as difficulties in communication, apparent inaccuracies, or concerns about the interpreter's neutrality, the judge may take steps to address these problems.

For example, if a party objects to the accuracy of an interpretation, the judge may allow for a review or challenge of the translation, or may appoint a different interpreter if necessary. The judge's oversight helps to maintain the fairness and integrity of the trial.

Implications of Rule 604 for Legal Practice

Rule 604 has significant implications for attorneys, judges, and litigants in both civil and criminal cases. Understanding the requirements and application of Rule 604 is essential for ensuring that all participants in a legal proceeding can effectively communicate and that their rights are protected.

1. Strategic Considerations for Attorneys

Attorneys must be aware of the need for interpreters when representing clients or questioning witnesses who do not speak English or who have communication impairments. This involves requesting the appointment of a qualified interpreter in advance of the proceeding and ensuring that the interpreter is competent and impartial.

For example, if an attorney is representing a non-English-speaking client, they should file a motion to appoint an interpreter early in the case and work with the court to ensure that the interpreter is certified and capable of accurately translating legal concepts.

2. Challenging the Qualifications or Performance of an Interpreter

If there are concerns about an interpreter's qualifications or the accuracy of their translations, attorneys may raise objections or request a voir dire examination of the interpreter. This is particularly important if there is reason to believe that the interpreter's performance could affect the fairness of the trial.

For instance, if an attorney believes that an interpreter is not accurately conveying a witness's testimony, they might ask the court to pause the proceedings and address the issue, potentially requesting the appointment of a different interpreter.

3. Ensuring Effective Communication

Attorneys and judges must work together to ensure that interpreters are used effectively in the courtroom. This includes speaking clearly and at a pace that allows the interpreter to keep up, providing interpreters with access to relevant case materials in advance, and addressing any communication challenges that arise during the testimony.

Rule 605 - Judge's Competency as a Witness

Text of Rule 605

Rule 605. Judge's Competency as a Witness
The presiding judge may not testify as a witness at the trial. A party need not object to preserve the issue.

Introduction to Rule 605

Rule 605 of the Federal Rules of Evidence addresses the issue of whether a judge presiding over a case may serve as a witness in that same proceeding. The rule categorically prohibits judges from testifying as witnesses in cases over which they are presiding. This prohibition reflects the need to maintain the impartiality, integrity, and public perception of the judiciary, as well as the fundamental principle that a judge should not participate in a case in any capacity other than as an impartial adjudicator. This chapter provides a detailed analysis of Rule 605, exploring its text, interpretation, and broader implications for the administration of justice.

Analysis of Rule 605

Rule 605 establishes a clear and absolute prohibition against a judge serving as a witness in the trial over which they are presiding. This rule is designed to preserve the impartiality of the judicial process, prevent conflicts of interest, and uphold the public's confidence in the fairness of the judiciary.

Prohibition Against Testimony by the Presiding Judge

The core principle of Rule 605 is that a judge who is presiding over a trial may not testify as a witness in that trial. This prohibition is absolute, meaning that no exceptions or circumstances permit the presiding judge to serve as a witness in the case.

1. Impartiality and the Role of the Judge

The role of a judge is to serve as an impartial arbiter of the law, ensuring that the trial is conducted fairly and that the rights of all parties are respected. Testifying as a witness would compromise this role, as it would involve the judge in the proceedings in a manner that is incompatible with judicial impartiality.

For example, if a judge were to testify about facts relevant to the case, it could give the appearance that the judge is biased or has a vested interest in the outcome of the trial. Such a situation could undermine the fairness of the trial and erode public confidence in the judicial system.

2. Avoidance of Conflicts of Interest

By prohibiting judges from testifying, Rule 605 also prevents potential conflicts of interest. A judge who testifies in a case over which they are presiding would be placed in the untenable position of serving as both a witness and the decision-maker, which could lead to a conflict between their duties as a judge and their personal involvement in the case.

This conflict could manifest in various ways, such as the judge giving undue weight to their own testimony or making rulings that favor their perspective as a witness. Rule 605 eliminates this risk by ensuring that the judge remains a neutral party throughout the proceedings.

No Objection Required to Preserve the Issue

Another important aspect of Rule 605 is that it does not require a party to object to the judge's testimony to preserve the issue for appeal or review. This provision recognizes the fundamental nature of the prohibition and ensures that the rights of the parties are protected without placing the burden on them to challenge the judge's participation as a witness.

1. Automatic Preservation of the Issue

The rule's provision that no objection is required means that, even if a judge were to testify without an objection from the parties, the issue of the judge's competency as a witness would still be preserved for review. This automatic preservation underscores the severity of the violation and the potential impact on the fairness of the trial.

For example, if a judge were to provide testimony during the trial and no party objected at that moment, the appellate court could still address the issue on appeal and potentially reverse the judgment or order a new trial based on the judge's improper testimony.

2. Judicial Responsibility

The responsibility to adhere to Rule 605 falls squarely on the judge. Judges must be aware of this rule and refrain from participating as witnesses in cases they are presiding over. If a situation arises where the judge has relevant information that could be considered as testimony, the judge must either recuse themselves from the case or ensure that another judge handles the matter.

This responsibility emphasizes the importance of judicial self-regulation and the ethical standards that judges are expected to uphold. Judges must be vigilant in maintaining their impartiality and avoiding any actions that could compromise the integrity of the judicial process.

Potential Issues and Remedies

Although Rule 605 clearly prohibits a judge from testifying as a witness, there are potential issues that could arise if this rule is violated. The rule's absolute nature provides a framework for addressing such violations and ensuring that the trial's fairness is maintained.

1. Remedies for Violation of Rule 605

If a judge improperly testifies in a case they are presiding over, the primary remedy is to seek an appeal of the judgment or to request a mistrial. The appellate court would likely consider the judge's testimony a fundamental error, given the potential for prejudice and the violation of the rule.

For example, an appellate court might vacate a judgment and remand the case for a new trial before a different judge, ensuring that the trial is conducted in accordance with the principles of fairness and impartiality.

2. Judge's Recusal

If a judge becomes aware that their testimony might be relevant to a case they are presiding over, the appropriate course of action is for the judge to recuse themselves from the case. Recusal allows the case to proceed before another judge, who can maintain the necessary impartiality.

Recusal is particularly important in situations where the judge's testimony involves critical facts or issues central to the case. By stepping aside, the judge protects the integrity of the proceedings and ensures that the parties receive a fair trial.

Judicial Discretion and Interpretation of Rule 605

While Rule 605 is an absolute prohibition, judges must still exercise discretion in interpreting and applying the rule in cases where issues related to the judge's potential testimony arise. This discretion is critical for ensuring that the rule is applied consistently and fairly.

1. Interpreting the Scope of Rule 605

Judges must interpret the scope of Rule 605 in situations where their actions or statements outside of the courtroom could be construed as testimony. For example, if a judge makes an offhand comment about the facts of a case during a hearing, it might raise concerns about whether that comment constitutes testimony.

In such cases, the judge must carefully consider whether their actions are consistent with the role of an impartial arbiter or whether they have crossed the line into providing testimony. Judges must err on the side of caution to avoid any appearance of impropriety.

2. Addressing Potential Conflicts

If a potential conflict arises under Rule 605, judges must take proactive steps to address the issue, such as disclosing the potential conflict to the parties and seeking their input on how to proceed. In some cases, the judge may need to step aside to ensure that the trial remains fair and impartial.

This proactive approach helps to maintain public confidence in the judiciary and ensures that the trial process is conducted in a manner that upholds the principles of justice and fairness.

Implications of Rule 605 for Legal Practice

Rule 605 has significant implications for attorneys, judges, and litigants in both civil and criminal cases. Understanding the scope and application of Rule 605 is essential for ensuring that the trial process remains fair and that the judiciary maintains its role as an impartial arbiter.

1. Strategic Considerations for Attorneys

Attorneys must be aware of Rule 605 and be prepared to address any situations where a judge might improperly testify. This includes raising concerns if the judge's actions suggest a potential violation of the rule and ensuring that the issue is preserved for appeal if necessary.

For example, if an attorney becomes aware that the judge has relevant information about the case that could be construed as testimony, they should consider filing a motion for recusal or taking other steps to protect their client's right to a fair trial.

2. Judicial Awareness and Responsibility

Judges must be vigilant in upholding Rule 605 and ensuring that they do not place themselves in a position where they might be called upon to testify. This requires a clear understanding of the boundaries of their role and a commitment to maintaining impartiality throughout the trial.

Judges must also be prepared to take appropriate action, such as recusal, if they find themselves in a situation where their testimony could become an issue. By doing so, they help preserve the integrity of the judicial process and protect the rights of all parties involved.

Rule 606 - Juror's Competency as a Witness

Text of Rule 606

Rule 606. Juror's Competency as a Witness
(a) **At the Trial.** A juror may not testify as a witness before the other jurors at the trial. If a juror is called to testify, the court must give a party an opportunity to object outside the jury's presence.
(b) **During an Inquiry into the Validity of a Verdict or Indictment. (1) Prohibited Testimony or Other Evidence.** During an inquiry into the validity of a verdict or indictment, a juror may not testify about any statement made or incident that occurred during the jury's deliberations; the effect of anything on that juror's or another juror's vote; or any juror's mental processes concerning the verdict or indictment. The court may not receive a juror's affidavit or evidence of a juror's statement on these matters. (2) **Exceptions.** A juror may testify about whether: (A) extraneous prejudicial information was improperly brought to the jury's attention; (B) an outside influence was improperly brought to bear on any juror; or (C) a mistake was made in entering the verdict on the verdict form.

Introduction to Rule 606

Rule 606 of the Federal Rules of Evidence addresses the circumstances under which a juror may testify as a witness. The rule is designed to maintain the integrity and finality of jury deliberations by limiting the situations in which a juror's testimony can be used to challenge a verdict. Rule 606 distinguishes between a juror's competency to testify during the trial itself and after the verdict has been rendered. The rule reflects the legal system's strong interest in protecting the confidentiality of jury deliberations, ensuring that verdicts are based on the collective judgment of the jurors rather than on extraneous or improper influences. This chapter provides a detailed analysis of Rule 606, exploring its text, interpretation, and broader implications for the administration of justice.

Analysis of Rule 606

Rule 606 plays a crucial role in balancing the need to protect the confidentiality and integrity of jury deliberations with the need to ensure that verdicts are free from external influences and errors. The rule is divided into two main sections, each dealing with different aspects of a juror's competency to testify.

Juror's Competency to Testify During the Trial (Rule 606(a))

Rule 606(a) provides that a juror may not testify as a witness before the other jurors during the trial. This rule is designed to prevent any disruption of the trial process and to ensure that the jurors' role remains focused on evaluating the evidence presented rather than participating in the case as witnesses.

1. **Rationale for the Prohibition**

The prohibition against juror testimony during the trial is rooted in the principle that jurors must remain impartial and uninvolved in the evidence-gathering process. Allowing a juror to testify could lead to bias, confusion, or undue influence on the other jurors, thereby compromising the fairness of the trial.

For example, if a juror were permitted to testify about a fact they personally observed outside the courtroom, this could introduce extraneous information into the deliberations, which is not subject to cross-examination or the rules of evidence. Such a scenario would undermine the integrity of the trial and the adversarial process.

2. **Procedure for Handling Objections**

If a juror is called to testify, Rule 606(a) requires that the court give the parties an opportunity to object outside the presence of the jury. This procedure ensures that any issues related to the juror's potential testimony can be addressed without influencing the other jurors or affecting the deliberative process.

For instance, if a party attempts to call a juror as a witness, the court would hold a hearing outside the presence of the jury to consider the objection. The judge would then decide whether the juror's testimony is necessary and appropriate, taking into account the potential impact on the fairness of the trial.

Juror's Competency to Testify During an Inquiry into the Validity of a Verdict or Indictment (Rule 606(b))

Rule 606(b) governs the circumstances under which a juror may testify during an inquiry into the validity of a verdict or indictment. This section of the rule is designed to protect the finality of verdicts and the secrecy of jury deliberations, while also allowing for certain exceptions in cases of misconduct or external influence.

1. **General Prohibition on Juror Testimony**

Rule 606(b)(1) establishes a general prohibition against juror testimony regarding the internal processes of the jury's deliberations. Specifically, a juror may not testify about:

- o Any statement made or incident that occurred during deliberations;

- o The effect of anything on the juror's or another juror's vote; or

- o Any juror's mental processes concerning the verdict or indictment.

This prohibition is intended to preserve the sanctity of the jury room and to prevent post-verdict challenges based on the subjective thoughts or feelings of individual jurors. The rule ensures that the deliberative process remains confidential and that jurors can engage in open and frank discussions without fear of later scrutiny or recrimination.

For example, if a juror changes their vote during deliberations due to the persuasive arguments of another juror, Rule 606(b) prohibits the first juror from later testifying about the reasons for their change of mind or the influence of the discussions on their decision.

2. **Exceptions to the Prohibition**

Rule 606(b)(2) provides three specific exceptions to the general prohibition, allowing a juror to testify in certain circumstances where the integrity of the verdict may be in question.

- ○ **Extraneous Prejudicial Information (Rule 606(b)(2)(A))**

A juror may testify about whether extraneous prejudicial information was improperly brought to the jury's attention. This exception addresses situations where information not presented at trial, such as media reports or other outside information, has influenced the jury's decision.

For example, if a juror reads a newspaper article about the case during the trial and shares this information with the other jurors during deliberations, this could be considered extraneous prejudicial information. Under Rule 606(b)(2)(A), a juror could testify about the introduction of this information as grounds for challenging the verdict.

- ○ **Outside Influence (Rule 606(b)(2)(B))**

A juror may testify about whether any outside influence was improperly brought to bear on any juror. This exception is concerned with external pressures or attempts to influence the jury's decision, such as bribery, threats, or other forms of coercion.

For instance, if a juror receives a threatening message from someone outside the court instructing them to vote a certain way, this would constitute an outside influence. A juror could testify about the existence of such an influence as a basis for challenging the validity of the verdict.

- ○ **Mistake in Entering the Verdict (Rule 606(b)(2)(C))**

A juror may testify about whether there was a mistake in entering the verdict on the verdict form. This exception allows for correction of clerical or administrative errors that do not involve the substantive deliberations of the jury.

For example, if the jury unanimously agrees on a verdict of "not guilty" but accidentally records a "guilty" verdict on the form, a juror may testify to correct this error. This exception ensures that the recorded verdict accurately reflects the jury's true decision.

Judicial Discretion and Interpretation of Rule 606

Judges have considerable discretion in interpreting and applying Rule 606, particularly when determining whether a situation falls within the exceptions to the general prohibition on juror testimony. This discretion is essential for maintaining the balance between protecting the integrity of the jury deliberations and addressing legitimate concerns about the fairness of the verdict.

1. **Assessing the Applicability of Exceptions**

Judges must carefully assess whether a particular situation qualifies for one of the exceptions under Rule 606(b)(2). This involves evaluating the nature of the information or influence in question and determining whether it meets the criteria established by the rule.

For example, if a party alleges that extraneous prejudicial information influenced the jury, the judge must decide whether the information was truly external to the trial and whether it had a prejudicial impact on the jury's decision. This assessment requires a nuanced understanding of the rule and the ability to apply it to the specific facts of the case.

2. **Maintaining the Confidentiality of Deliberations**

Even when an exception applies, judges must be careful to protect the confidentiality of the jury's deliberations to the greatest extent possible. This may involve limiting the scope of the juror's testimony to the specific issue at hand and avoiding inquiries into the juror's mental processes or the content of deliberations beyond what is necessary to resolve the issue.

For instance, if a juror testifies about an outside influence, the judge might restrict the testimony to the fact of the influence itself without delving into how it affected the juror's thoughts or votes during deliberations. This approach helps preserve the confidentiality of the deliberative process while addressing the potential impact of the external influence.

Implications of Rule 606 for Legal Practice

Rule 606 has significant implications for attorneys, judges, and litigants in both civil and criminal cases. Understanding the scope and application of Rule 606 is essential for effectively navigating post-verdict challenges and ensuring that jury deliberations are protected while still addressing potential misconduct or errors.

1. **Strategic Considerations for Attorneys**

Attorneys must be aware of the limitations imposed by Rule 606 when considering whether to challenge a verdict based on juror testimony. This involves carefully evaluating whether the situation falls within one of the exceptions and determining the best approach for presenting the issue to the court.

For example, if an attorney suspects that a juror was exposed to extraneous prejudicial information, they must gather evidence to support the claim and be prepared to argue that the information meets the criteria for an exception under Rule 606(b)(2). This requires a thorough understanding of the rule and the ability to present a compelling case to the judge.

2. **Judicial Management of Post-Verdict Inquiries**

Judges play a critical role in managing post-verdict inquiries under Rule 606. This includes determining whether to allow juror testimony, setting boundaries for the scope of the inquiry, and ensuring that the integrity of the jury's deliberations is maintained.

Judges must also be prepared to make difficult decisions about whether a verdict should be set aside or a new trial ordered based on the evidence presented. These decisions require a careful balancing of the need to correct any potential misconduct or errors with the importance of upholding the finality and confidentiality of the jury's decision-making process.

Rule 607 - Who May Impeach a Witness

Rule 607. Who May Impeach a Witness

Any party, including the party that called the witness, may attack the witness's credibility.

Introduction to Rule 607

Rule 607 of the Federal Rules of Evidence addresses the issue of who is permitted to impeach a witness during a legal proceeding. Impeachment refers to the process of challenging the credibility of a witness, typically by presenting evidence that contradicts the witness's testimony, exposes inconsistencies, or demonstrates bias, interest, or a lack of truthfulness. The rule establishes that any party, including the party that called the witness, may impeach the witness. This provision reflects a modern and pragmatic approach to ensuring that the fact-finder receives accurate and reliable testimony, even if it requires discrediting one's own witness. This chapter provides a detailed analysis of Rule 607, exploring its text, interpretation, and broader implications for the administration of justice.

Analysis of Rule 607

Rule 607 establishes a broad and inclusive rule for the impeachment of witnesses, allowing any party in a legal proceeding to challenge the credibility of a witness, regardless of which party called the witness to testify. This rule reflects the principle that the search for truth is paramount and that all relevant evidence should be considered, even if it undermines the testimony of one's own witness.

Historical Context and the Evolution of Rule 607

Historically, under common law, parties were generally prohibited from impeaching their own witnesses. This restriction was based on the idea that a party vouched for the credibility of any witness it called and should not be allowed to discredit its own evidence. However, this approach often led to situations where the truth was obscured, as parties were unable to challenge false or misleading testimony from their own witnesses.

1. Abolition of the Common Law Rule

Rule 607 represents a significant departure from the common law rule, reflecting the modern understanding that the ultimate goal of a trial is to discover the truth. By allowing any party to impeach any witness, including their own, Rule 607 removes the artificial barriers that could prevent the fact-finder from considering all relevant information.

For example, if a party calls a witness expecting favorable testimony but the witness gives testimony that is inconsistent with prior statements, Rule 607 allows the calling party to impeach the witness by presenting evidence of the inconsistency, thereby helping to clarify the truth.

2. Justification for the Rule

The justification for Rule 607 lies in the recognition that witnesses may be unreliable, mistaken, or even dishonest, regardless of which party called them to testify. Allowing any party to impeach any witness ensures that the fact-finder is not misled by inaccurate or unreliable testimony. This approach promotes a more thorough and accurate fact-finding process.

For instance, a prosecutor in a criminal trial may need to impeach a witness who, after being called to testify, unexpectedly recants their prior testimony or makes statements that are inconsistent with the prosecution's case. Rule 607 permits the prosecutor to challenge the credibility of that witness, thereby helping to prevent the introduction of false or misleading evidence.

Methods of Impeachment Under Rule 607

While Rule 607 establishes who may impeach a witness, it does not specify the methods of impeachment. However, the methods typically used to impeach a witness are governed by other rules within the Federal Rules of Evidence. Common methods of impeachment include:

1. Contradictory Evidence

A party may impeach a witness by introducing evidence that directly contradicts the witness's testimony. This could involve presenting other witnesses, documents, or physical evidence that shows the witness's testimony to be false or inaccurate.

For example, if a witness testifies that they were at a certain location at a specific time, the opposing party might introduce surveillance footage or cell phone records that place the witness at a different location, thereby impeaching the witness's credibility.

2. Prior Inconsistent Statements

A witness's credibility can be impeached by showing that they have made prior statements that are inconsistent with their current testimony. This method is particularly effective in highlighting discrepancies and casting doubt on the reliability of the witness's testimony.

For instance, if a witness testifies in court that they did not see the defendant at the scene of a crime, but previously told police that they did see the defendant there, the prior inconsistent statement can be introduced to impeach the witness.

3. Bias or Interest

A witness may be impeached by showing that they have a bias, interest, or motive to testify in a certain way. Bias or interest might arise from a personal relationship with one of the parties, financial incentives, or other factors that could influence the witness's testimony.

For example, if a witness is a close friend of the defendant and has a personal interest in the outcome of the trial, the opposing party may introduce evidence of this relationship to suggest that the witness's testimony may be biased.

4. Character for Untruthfulness

A witness's credibility can also be challenged by presenting evidence of their character for untruthfulness. This might include evidence of prior dishonest conduct, such as previous instances of lying, fraud, or perjury.

For instance, if a witness has been convicted of fraud in the past, this evidence may be introduced to suggest that the witness has a propensity for dishonesty, thereby impeaching their credibility.

5. Incapacity

Impeachment may also involve showing that a witness lacks the capacity to accurately perceive, remember, or communicate about the events in question. This could include evidence of mental illness, intoxication, or other factors that affect the witness's ability to provide reliable testimony.

For example, if a witness was heavily intoxicated at the time they claim to have observed certain events, the opposing party may introduce evidence of the intoxication to impeach the witness's capacity to recall those events accurately.

Strategic Use of Rule 607 in Legal Practice

Rule 607 provides attorneys with a powerful tool to challenge the credibility of witnesses, including their own, as part of their overall trial strategy. Understanding how and when to use impeachment effectively is crucial for presenting a persuasive case.

1. Impeaching One's Own Witness

One of the most significant aspects of Rule 607 is that it allows a party to impeach its own witness. This can be a critical strategy when a witness provides unexpected or unfavorable testimony that could undermine the party's case.

For example, if a defense attorney calls a witness expecting them to provide an alibi for the defendant, but the witness instead gives testimony that suggests the defendant was at the scene of the crime, the attorney may impeach the witness by introducing prior statements or other evidence that contradicts the witness's testimony.

This approach allows the attorney to minimize the damage caused by the witness's testimony and to maintain the credibility of their overall case.

2. Preemptive Impeachment

In some cases, attorneys may use impeachment preemptively to address potential issues with a witness's credibility before the opposing party has an opportunity to do so. By acknowledging and addressing weaknesses in a witness's testimony upfront, the attorney can control the narrative and reduce the impact of the impeachment.

For example, if an attorney knows that a witness has made prior inconsistent statements, they might introduce those statements during direct examination and allow the witness to explain the inconsistencies. This preemptive approach can mitigate the effectiveness of the opposing party's impeachment efforts.

3. Cross-Examination and Impeachment

Cross-examination is a primary tool for impeaching a witness. During cross-examination, the attorney may question the witness about prior inconsistent statements, biases, or other factors that could affect their credibility. Effective cross-examination requires careful preparation and a strategic approach to questioning.

For instance, an attorney might carefully lead a witness through a series of questions designed to expose inconsistencies in their testimony or to highlight their bias or interest in the outcome of the case. The goal is to undermine the witness's credibility in the eyes of the jury or judge.

Judicial Discretion in Impeachment

Judges have discretion in managing the impeachment process and ensuring that it is conducted fairly and in accordance with the rules of evidence. This discretion includes determining the admissibility of impeachment evidence and controlling the scope of cross-examination.

1. Admissibility of Impeachment Evidence

Judges must decide whether the evidence presented for impeachment purposes is admissible under the relevant rules of evidence. This may involve balancing the probative value of the evidence against its potential for unfair prejudice, confusion, or delay, as governed by Rule 403.

For example, if an attorney seeks to introduce evidence of a witness's prior criminal conviction to impeach their character for truthfulness, the judge must determine whether the evidence is relevant and whether its probative value outweighs any potential prejudice to the witness or the party that called them.

2. Controlling the Scope of Impeachment

Judges also have the authority to control the scope of impeachment, ensuring that it remains focused on relevant issues and does not devolve into a personal attack on the witness. This includes limiting cross-examination to matters that are directly related to the witness's credibility and excluding extraneous or inflammatory evidence.

For instance, if an attorney attempts to impeach a witness by questioning them about unrelated personal matters, the judge may intervene to limit the questioning and keep the focus on the issues that are relevant to the witness's testimony.

Implications of Rule 607 for Legal Practice

Rule 607 has significant implications for attorneys, judges, and litigants in both civil and criminal cases. Understanding the scope and application of Rule 607 is essential for effectively managing witness testimony and ensuring that the fact-finder receives a complete and accurate picture of the evidence.

1. Strategic Considerations for Attorneys

Attorneys must be prepared to use Rule 607 strategically to challenge the credibility of witnesses, including their own, when necessary. This requires careful planning and preparation, as well as the ability to adapt to unexpected developments during the trial.

For example, an attorney might prepare for the possibility that a key witness could provide unfavorable testimony by gathering impeachment evidence in advance, such as prior inconsistent statements or evidence of bias. This preparation allows the attorney to respond quickly and effectively if the witness's testimony turns out to be problematic.

2. Ensuring Fairness in Impeachment

While Rule 607 allows for broad impeachment of witnesses, attorneys must also be mindful of the need to conduct impeachment in a manner that is fair and respectful. This includes avoiding overly aggressive or hostile questioning and ensuring that the impeachment process does not unfairly prejudice the witness or the party that called them.

Judges play a key role in overseeing the impeachment process and ensuring that it is conducted in accordance with the rules of evidence and the principles of fairness. By maintaining control over the proceedings, judges help to protect the rights of all parties and ensure that the trial remains focused on the search for truth.

Rule 608 - A Witness's Character for Truthfulness or Untruthfulness

Text of Rule 608

Rule 608. A Witness's Character for Truthfulness or Untruthfulness
(a) Reputation or Opinion Evidence. A witness's credibility may be attacked or supported by testimony about the witness's reputation for having a character for truthfulness or untruthfulness, or by testimony in the form of an opinion about that character. But evidence of truthful character is admissible only after the witness's character for truthfulness has been attacked.
(b) Specific Instances of Conduct. Except for a criminal conviction under Rule 609, extrinsic evidence is not admissible to prove specific instances of a witness's conduct in order to attack or support the witness's character for truthfulness. But the court may, on cross-examination, allow them to be inquired into if they are probative of the character for truthfulness or untruthfulness of: (1) the witness; or (2) another witness whose character the witness being cross-examined has testified about.

Introduction to Rule 608

Rule 608 of the Federal Rules of Evidence governs the admissibility of evidence concerning a witness's character for truthfulness or untruthfulness. The rule is central to the process of impeaching or bolstering a witness's credibility. It provides specific guidelines on when and how a witness's character for truthfulness or untruthfulness can be introduced in court, either through reputation or opinion evidence or by inquiry into specific instances of conduct. This rule balances the need to assess the credibility of witnesses against the risk of unfair prejudice, confusion, or distraction that might arise from delving into a witness's character. This chapter provides a detailed analysis of Rule 608, exploring its text, interpretation, and broader implications for the administration of justice.

Analysis of Rule 608

Rule 608 is a crucial rule for determining when and how evidence related to a witness's character for truthfulness or untruthfulness can be introduced. The rule is designed to provide a structured approach to assessing a witness's credibility while preventing trials from becoming mired in collateral issues related to the witness's character.

Reputation or Opinion Evidence (Rule 608(a))

Rule 608(a) allows a witness's credibility to be attacked or supported through testimony about their reputation for truthfulness or untruthfulness or through opinion testimony about their character. However, the rule imposes limitations to ensure that such evidence is used appropriately and does not lead to unfair prejudice or confusion.

1. Reputation Evidence

Reputation evidence involves testimony regarding the general reputation of the witness in the community for truthfulness or untruthfulness. This type of evidence is based on the collective judgment of those who know the witness and have observed their behavior over time.

For example, if a witness has a reputation in their community for being dishonest, another witness who is familiar with that reputation might testify to it in court. This testimony would be relevant to assessing the credibility of the witness whose truthfulness is in question.

However, reputation evidence must be based on a sufficiently broad and consistent perception of the witness's character, rather than isolated incidents or opinions. The witness testifying about reputation must have a substantial familiarity with the subject's reputation within a relevant community.

2. Opinion Evidence

Opinion evidence involves testimony from a witness who has a personal opinion about the truthfulness or untruthfulness of another witness's character. This type of evidence allows the testifying witness to express their own judgment, based on their interactions with or observations of the subject witness.

For example, a close colleague of a witness might testify that, in their opinion, the witness is generally truthful or untruthful based on their experiences working together. The court must evaluate the foundation for the opinion to ensure that it is based on sufficient knowledge and relevant experience.

3. Timing and Conditions for Admission

Rule 608(a) allows evidence of a witness's truthful character to be introduced only after the witness's character for truthfulness has been attacked. This limitation prevents parties from preemptively bolstering a witness's credibility before there has been any challenge to it.

For example, if the opposing party has introduced evidence suggesting that a witness is untruthful, the party that called the witness may respond by introducing reputation or opinion evidence of the witness's truthful character. This rule ensures that evidence of good character is used to rebut specific challenges, rather than as a general means of enhancing the witness's credibility.

The attack on a witness's character for truthfulness can occur through various means, including direct evidence of untruthfulness, impeachment with prior inconsistent statements, or evidence of bias. Once such an attack has been made, the door is opened for the introduction of evidence to support the witness's character for truthfulness.

Specific Instances of Conduct (Rule 608(b))

Rule 608(b) addresses the admissibility of specific instances of conduct to attack or support a witness's character for truthfulness. The rule generally prohibits the use of extrinsic evidence to prove specific instances of a witness's conduct, with some exceptions for cross-examination.

1. Prohibition on Extrinsic Evidence

Under Rule 608(b), extrinsic evidence—evidence other than the witness's own testimony—is not admissible to prove specific instances of a witness's conduct in order to attack or support their character for truthfulness. This prohibition is intended to prevent trials from becoming bogged down in collateral issues that distract from the main questions of fact.

For example, if a witness is alleged to have lied on a prior occasion, the opposing party cannot introduce documents or other witnesses solely to prove that the witness lied in the past. Instead, such specific instances of conduct can only be explored through cross-examination, and the evidence must come from the witness's own responses.

The rule against extrinsic evidence helps maintain the focus of the trial on the issues at hand and prevents the undue consumption of time on matters that are not directly relevant to the case.

2. Cross-Examination on Specific Instances

While extrinsic evidence is generally prohibited, Rule 608(b) allows for specific instances of conduct to be inquired into during cross-examination if they are probative of the witness's character for truthfulness or untruthfulness. This applies to both the witness being cross-examined and other witnesses whose character the witness has testified about.

For example, during cross-examination, an attorney might ask a witness, "Isn't it true that you lied on your job application last year?" If the witness admits to the conduct, this admission can be used to impeach the witness's character for truthfulness. However, if the witness denies the conduct, the cross-examiner cannot introduce extrinsic evidence to prove the lie.

The decision to allow such inquiry during cross-examination is at the discretion of the court, which must consider whether the probative value of the specific instance of conduct outweighs the potential for unfair prejudice, confusion, or delay.

3. Limitations and Judicial Discretion

The court has significant discretion in determining whether to allow cross-examination on specific instances of conduct. Judges must carefully balance the probative value of the evidence against the risk of unfair prejudice, confusion, or the introduction of collateral issues.

For example, if the alleged conduct is only marginally relevant to the witness's character for truthfulness or if it is likely to inflame the jury, the judge may exclude the inquiry. The judge's role is to ensure that the focus remains on the key issues of the case and that the jury is not distracted by extraneous matters.

Additionally, the court must consider the potential impact on the witness's dignity and privacy, particularly when the specific instances of conduct involve sensitive or personal matters. The judge's discretion is critical in maintaining the fairness and integrity of the proceedings.

Interplay with Other Rules of Evidence

Rule 608 interacts with other rules of evidence, particularly those governing impeachment, character evidence, and the admissibility of prior criminal convictions.

1. Interaction with Rule 609 (Impeachment by Evidence of a Criminal Conviction)

Rule 609 governs the admissibility of evidence related to a witness's prior criminal convictions for the purpose of impeaching their character for truthfulness. Unlike Rule 608(b), Rule 609 allows for the introduction of extrinsic evidence of certain criminal convictions to challenge a witness's credibility.

For example, if a witness has been convicted of a crime involving dishonesty or a false statement, Rule 609 may permit the introduction of that conviction as extrinsic evidence to impeach the witness's character for truthfulness. This differs from the general prohibition on extrinsic evidence in Rule 608(b), highlighting the specific allowance made for criminal convictions.

2. Interaction with Rule 404 (Character Evidence)

Rule 404 generally prohibits the use of character evidence to prove that a person acted in conformity with that character on a particular occasion. However, Rule 608 provides an exception to this general prohibition by allowing the introduction of evidence related to a witness's character for truthfulness or untruthfulness.

For instance, while Rule 404 might prevent the introduction of character evidence to suggest that a person is generally dishonest and therefore likely committed a specific act of dishonesty, Rule 608 allows for the introduction of character evidence to assess the credibility of a witness's testimony.

This interplay between the rules reflects the careful balancing required in the admissibility of character evidence, ensuring that it is used appropriately and only in ways that contribute to the fairness and accuracy of the fact-finding process.

Strategic Considerations for Attorneys

Rule 608 provides attorneys with tools to challenge or support a witness's credibility based on their character for truthfulness or untruthfulness. Understanding how to use these tools effectively is essential for constructing a persuasive case.

1. Impeaching a Witness's Character for Truthfulness

When impeaching a witness's character for truthfulness, attorneys must carefully select the most effective method, whether it be through reputation or opinion evidence, or through cross-examination on specific instances of conduct. The choice depends on the nature of the case, the witness's background, and the available evidence.

For example, if an attorney has strong evidence that a witness has a poor reputation for truthfulness in the community, they may choose to introduce reputation evidence through a qualified witness. Alternatively, if there are known instances where the witness lied in a similar context, cross-examination may be the most effective approach.

2. Bolstering a Witness's Credibility

If a witness's character for truthfulness has been attacked, the attorney who called the witness may introduce evidence of the witness's truthful character to rehabilitate their credibility. This requires careful timing and strategic use of Rule 608(a), ensuring that the evidence presented is compelling and relevant.

For instance, if the opposing party has questioned a witness's honesty by highlighting prior inconsistent statements, the calling party might respond by introducing testimony from a respected colleague who can vouch for the witness's general reputation for truthfulness.

3. Avoiding Overreach and Collateral Issues

Attorneys must be cautious not to overreach when using Rule 608, particularly when exploring specific instances of conduct. Cross-examination should be focused and relevant, avoiding unnecessary forays into collateral issues that could confuse the jury or prejudice the witness.

For example, while it might be tempting to question a witness about every instance of dishonest behavior in their past, such an approach could backfire by overwhelming the jury with irrelevant details or by appearing overly aggressive. The goal is to present a clear and compelling case that effectively challenges or supports the witness's credibility without distracting from the main issues.

Judicial Discretion and the Application of Rule 608

Judges have significant discretion in applying Rule 608, particularly in determining the admissibility of reputation or opinion evidence and in controlling cross-examination on specific instances of conduct.

1. Evaluating Probative Value vs. Prejudice

Judges must evaluate the probative value of evidence related to a witness's character for truthfulness against the potential for unfair prejudice, confusion, or the introduction of collateral issues. This balancing act is critical for ensuring that the trial remains focused and that the fact-finder receives reliable and relevant evidence.

For example, if the probative value of a specific instance of conduct is minimal compared to the risk of prejudicing the jury, the judge may exclude the inquiry to maintain the fairness and integrity of the trial.

2. Maintaining Control of the Proceedings

Judges must also maintain control over the proceedings, particularly during cross-examination, to ensure that the questioning remains relevant and appropriate. This includes preventing cross-examiners from delving into irrelevant or excessively personal matters that could distract from the key issues or unfairly damage the witness's reputation.

For instance, if a cross-examiner begins questioning a witness about personal matters unrelated to their character for truthfulness, the judge may intervene to redirect the examination or to exclude the line of questioning altogether.

Rule 609 - Impeachment by Evidence of a Criminal Conviction

Text of Rule 609

Rule 609. Impeachment by Evidence of a Criminal Conviction

(a) **In General.** The following rules apply to attacking a witness's character for truthfulness by evidence of a criminal conviction: (1) for a crime that, in the convicting jurisdiction, was punishable by death or by imprisonment for more than one year, the evidence: (A) must be admitted, subject to Rule 403, in a civil case or in a criminal case in which the witness is not a defendant; and (B) must be admitted in a criminal case in which the witness is a defendant, if the probative value of the evidence outweighs its prejudicial effect to that defendant; and (2) for any crime regardless of the punishment, the evidence must be admitted if the court can readily determine that establishing the elements of the crime required proving—or the witness's admitting—a dishonest act or false statement.

(b) **Limit on Using the Evidence After 10 Years.** This subdivision (b) applies if more than 10 years have passed since the witness's conviction or release from confinement for it, whichever is later. Evidence of the conviction is admissible only if: (1) its probative value, supported by specific facts and circumstances, substantially outweighs its prejudicial effect; and (2) the proponent gives an adverse party reasonable written notice of the intent to use it so that the party has a fair opportunity to contest its use.

(c) **Effect of a Pardon, Annulment, or Certificate of Rehabilitation.** Evidence of a conviction is not admissible if: (1) the conviction has been the subject of a pardon, annulment, certificate of rehabilitation, or other equivalent procedure based on a finding that the person has been rehabilitated, and the person has not been convicted of a later crime punishable by death or by imprisonment for more than one year; or (2) the conviction has been the subject of a pardon, annulment, or other equivalent procedure based on a finding of innocence.

(d) **Juvenile Adjudications.** Evidence of a juvenile adjudication is admissible under this rule only if: (1) it is offered in a criminal case; (2) the adjudication was of a witness other than the defendant; (3) an adult's conviction for that offense would be admissible to attack the adult's credibility; and (4) admitting the evidence is necessary to fairly determine guilt or innocence.

(e) **Pendency of an Appeal.** A conviction that satisfies this rule is admissible even if an appeal is pending. Evidence of the pendency is also admissible.

Introduction to Rule 609

Rule 609 of the Federal Rules of Evidence governs the use of evidence related to a witness's prior criminal convictions for the purpose of impeaching their credibility. The rule strikes a balance between allowing the fact-finder to consider relevant information about a witness's character for truthfulness and protecting the witness from unfair prejudice due to past criminal behavior. Rule 609 establishes specific guidelines for when and how evidence of a criminal conviction can be introduced, depending on the nature of the crime, the time elapsed since the conviction, and whether the witness is the defendant in a criminal case. This chapter provides a detailed analysis of Rule 609, exploring its text, interpretation, and broader implications for the administration of justice.

Analysis of Rule 609

Rule 609 provides a comprehensive framework for determining when evidence of a witness's prior criminal convictions may be used to impeach their credibility. The rule is structured to address different types of crimes and circumstances, balancing the probative value of such evidence against the potential for unfair prejudice.

Impeachment by Conviction of a Crime Punishable by Death or Imprisonment for More Than One Year (Rule 609(a)(1))

Rule 609(a)(1) distinguishes between convictions for crimes punishable by death or imprisonment for more than one year and other types of convictions. This distinction reflects the notion that serious crimes are more likely to reflect on a witness's character for truthfulness.

1. Non-Defendant Witnesses in Civil and Criminal Cases

For witnesses who are not defendants in a criminal case, evidence of a conviction for a crime punishable by death or imprisonment for more than one year must be admitted, subject to the balancing test of Rule 403. Rule 403 allows the court to exclude evidence if its probative value is substantially outweighed by the danger of unfair prejudice, confusion, or delay.

For example, if a witness in a civil case has a prior conviction for a felony, the court will admit evidence of that conviction unless it determines that the potential prejudice to the witness outweighs its relevance to their character for truthfulness. The balancing test ensures that the evidence is used appropriately and does not unfairly harm the witness or distort the fact-finding process.

2. Defendants in Criminal Cases

When the witness is the defendant in a criminal case, Rule 609(a)(1)(B) imposes a stricter standard. The court must determine that the probative value of the conviction evidence outweighs its prejudicial effect to the defendant before admitting it. This heightened standard recognizes the significant risk that the jury might improperly infer guilt from the defendant's prior criminal record.

For instance, if a defendant in a criminal trial has a prior felony conviction, the prosecution may seek to introduce this evidence to impeach the defendant's credibility. However, the court must carefully weigh the probative value of the conviction against the risk that the jury will use it to infer that the defendant has a criminal disposition and is therefore more likely to have committed the crime charged.

Impeachment by Conviction of a Crime Involving Dishonesty or False Statement (Rule 609(a)(2))

Rule 609(a)(2) mandates the admission of evidence of any conviction, regardless of the punishment, if the crime involved dishonesty or a false statement. Crimes involving dishonesty or false statements are considered directly relevant to a witness's character for truthfulness and are therefore automatically admissible for impeachment purposes.

1. Types of Crimes Involving Dishonesty or False Statements

Crimes that fall under this category typically involve deceit, fraud, or falsification. Examples include perjury, fraud, embezzlement, and forgery. The reasoning is that such crimes directly reflect on the witness's propensity to lie or deceive, making them particularly relevant to the witness's credibility.

For example, if a witness has a prior conviction for perjury, this conviction would be admissible under Rule 609(a)(2) because it involves making false statements under oath, which is directly relevant to the witness's truthfulness.

2. Automatic Admission

Unlike convictions under Rule 609(a)(1), which are subject to balancing under Rule 403 or a more stringent standard for criminal defendants, convictions involving dishonesty or false statements must be admitted without any balancing test. This reflects the high probative value of such evidence in assessing a witness's credibility.

Limitations on Using the Evidence After 10 Years (Rule 609(b))

Rule 609(b) imposes additional restrictions on the use of convictions that are more than ten years old. The rationale behind this limitation is that older convictions are less likely to be relevant to a witness's current character for truthfulness and are more likely to lead to unfair prejudice.

1. Balancing Test for Older Convictions

Evidence of a conviction that is more than ten years old is admissible only if its probative value, supported by specific facts and circumstances, substantially outweighs its prejudicial effect. This is a higher standard than the typical Rule 403 balancing test, reflecting the increased potential for prejudice due to the passage of time.

For example, if a witness was convicted of a crime involving dishonesty 15 years ago, the party seeking to introduce this evidence must demonstrate that it is still highly probative of the witness's current credibility. The court will then weigh this probative value against the potential prejudice to the witness and decide whether to admit the evidence.

2. Notice Requirement

Rule 609(b) also requires the proponent of the evidence to provide reasonable written notice to the adverse party of their intent to use the conviction. This notice requirement ensures that the opposing party has a fair opportunity to contest the admissibility of the evidence and to prepare an appropriate response.

For instance, if the prosecution in a criminal case intends to use a defendant's decades-old conviction for impeachment, it must notify the defense well in advance so that the defense can challenge the admissibility of the evidence or prepare to mitigate its impact.

Effect of a Pardon, Annulment, or Certificate of Rehabilitation (Rule 609(c))

Rule 609(c) addresses the admissibility of convictions that have been pardoned, annulled, or otherwise rehabilitated. The rule generally prohibits the use of such convictions for impeachment, recognizing that the legal system has formally acknowledged the individual's rehabilitation or innocence.

1. Convictions Based on Rehabilitation

Evidence of a conviction that has been pardoned, annulled, or subject to a certificate of rehabilitation based on a finding of rehabilitation is not admissible if the person has not been subsequently convicted of a crime punishable by death or imprisonment for more than one year. This provision reflects the idea that the legal system has recognized the individual's rehabilitation and that the conviction should no longer be held against them.

For example, if a witness was convicted of a felony but later received a pardon based on rehabilitation, that conviction cannot be used to impeach their credibility unless they have since committed another serious crime.

2. Convictions Based on Innocence

Evidence of a conviction that has been pardoned, annulled, or otherwise invalidated based on a finding of innocence is also inadmissible. This provision underscores the principle that a conviction wrongfully imposed should not be used to undermine a witness's credibility.

For instance, if a witness was wrongfully convicted and later exonerated through a pardon or annulment, that conviction cannot be used to impeach their credibility in any legal proceeding.

Juvenile Adjudications (Rule 609(d))

Rule 609(d) sets forth specific conditions under which juvenile adjudications may be used for impeachment. The rule generally restricts the use of juvenile adjudications, reflecting the legal system's emphasis on rehabilitation rather than punishment for minors.

1. Conditions for Admissibility

Evidence of a juvenile adjudication is admissible under Rule 609 only if:

- It is offered in a criminal case;
- The adjudication was of a witness other than the defendant;
- An adult's conviction for that offense would be admissible to attack the adult's credibility; and
- Admitting the evidence is necessary to fairly determine guilt or innocence.

These stringent conditions ensure that juvenile adjudications are used only when they are directly relevant to the credibility of a witness in a criminal case and when their exclusion would compromise the fairness of the trial.

For example, if a witness in a criminal trial was adjudicated delinquent for a crime involving dishonesty as a juvenile, and the defense argues that this is critical to assessing the witness's credibility, the court may admit the adjudication if it meets all the conditions of Rule 609(d).

2. Emphasis on Fairness

The rule's emphasis on fairness reflects the legal system's recognition that juvenile adjudications should generally be protected from public scrutiny to promote rehabilitation. However, when such evidence is crucial to determining the truth in a criminal case, the rule allows for its use under controlled conditions.

Pendency of an Appeal (Rule 609(e))

Rule 609(e) provides that a conviction is admissible for impeachment purposes even if an appeal is pending. The rule also allows evidence of the pendency of the appeal to be introduced.

1. Admissibility Despite Pending Appeal

The admissibility of a conviction despite a pending appeal reflects the principle that a conviction is considered final for the purposes of impeachment until it is overturned. This ensures that the fact-finder has access to relevant information about a witness's credibility, even if the conviction is still under review.

For example, if a witness was recently convicted of a felony and has filed an appeal, the opposing party can still introduce evidence of the conviction to impeach the witness's credibility. However, the court may also allow the witness or the party that called the witness to introduce evidence that the conviction is under appeal, which may affect the weight the jury gives to the impeachment evidence.

2. Consideration of the Appeal

The ability to introduce evidence of the pendency of an appeal allows the jury or judge to consider the possibility that the conviction might be overturned. This ensures that the fact-finder has a complete picture of the witness's legal status and can appropriately weigh the impeachment evidence.

For instance, if a witness's conviction is on appeal and there are significant questions about the validity of the conviction, the jury may decide to give less weight to the impeachment evidence, recognizing that the conviction could be reversed.

Judicial Discretion in Applying Rule 609

Judges have significant discretion in applying Rule 609, particularly in balancing the probative value of a conviction against its potential prejudicial effect. This discretion is essential for ensuring that the rule is applied fairly and in a manner that promotes justice.

1. Balancing Probative Value and Prejudice

Judges must carefully balance the probative value of a criminal conviction against the potential for unfair prejudice, especially when the witness is the defendant in a criminal case. This balancing test is crucial for protecting the defendant's right to a fair trial while allowing the jury to consider relevant information about credibility.

For example, if a defendant has a prior conviction for a non-violent felony that is only marginally relevant to their character for truthfulness, the judge may exclude the evidence if its admission would likely lead the jury to make an improper inference about the defendant's guilt in the current case.

2. Controlling the Scope of Impeachment

Judges also have the authority to control the scope of impeachment by limiting the details of the conviction that can be introduced. This may involve allowing the jury to hear only the fact of the conviction and its nature, without delving into the specific facts of the prior crime, to prevent undue prejudice.

For instance, in a case where a witness has a prior conviction for fraud, the judge might permit the jury to hear that the witness was convicted of a crime involving dishonesty but may prohibit detailed testimony about the specific fraudulent acts committed to avoid inflaming the jury.

Strategic Considerations for Attorneys

Rule 609 provides attorneys with a powerful tool for challenging a witness's credibility, but its use requires careful strategic consideration.

1. Deciding When to Use Conviction Evidence

Attorneys must weigh the benefits and risks of introducing evidence of a prior conviction. While such evidence can be highly effective in undermining a witness's credibility, it also carries the risk of creating unfair prejudice or distracting the jury from the main issues of the case.

For example, in a criminal case, the defense might choose to introduce evidence of a key prosecution witness's prior conviction for perjury to challenge the witness's credibility. However, the defense must consider whether this strategy could backfire by opening the door to the prosecution introducing the defendant's prior convictions.

2. Preparing for the Impact of Conviction Evidence

When a party expects that their witness's prior conviction will be introduced, they must prepare to mitigate the impact. This might involve addressing the conviction during direct examination, explaining its context, or introducing evidence of the witness's rehabilitation.

For instance, if a defendant in a criminal case is expected to be impeached with a prior conviction, the defense attorney might preemptively introduce the conviction during direct examination and provide a narrative that minimizes its impact, such as by highlighting the defendant's efforts to reform since the conviction.

Rule 610 - Religious Beliefs or Opinions

Rule 610. Religious Beliefs or Opinions
Evidence of a witness's religious beliefs or opinions is not admissible to attack or support the witness's credibility.

Introduction to Rule 610

Rule 610 of the Federal Rules of Evidence addresses the admissibility of evidence related to a witness's religious beliefs or opinions in legal proceedings. The rule establishes that evidence of a witness's religious beliefs or opinions is not admissible to attack or support the witness's credibility. This rule reflects the principle that an individual's religious beliefs or practices should not be used as a basis for assessing their truthfulness, thereby protecting the freedom of religion and ensuring that trials are conducted fairly and without prejudice. This chapter provides a detailed analysis of Rule 610, exploring its text, interpretation, and broader implications for the administration of justice.

Analysis of Rule 610

Rule 610 serves as a safeguard against the misuse of religious beliefs or opinions in the courtroom, ensuring that witnesses are not judged based on their religious affiliations or practices. The rule aligns with broader constitutional principles, including the First Amendment's guarantee of religious freedom, and seeks to prevent bias and discrimination in the legal process.

Prohibition on Using Religious Beliefs or Opinions to Assess Credibility

The core principle of Rule 610 is that evidence of a witness's religious beliefs or opinions cannot be introduced to attack or support their credibility. This prohibition is absolute, meaning that such evidence is inadmissible regardless of the context in which it is offered.

1. Rationale for the Prohibition

The rationale behind Rule 610 is that religious beliefs are deeply personal and often reflect an individual's moral and ethical convictions rather than their propensity for truthfulness. Allowing such beliefs to be scrutinized in court could lead to unfair prejudice and discrimination, as jurors or judges might be influenced by their own biases or assumptions about certain religions.

For example, if a witness is a member of a minority religion that is viewed with suspicion or misunderstanding by the general public, introducing evidence of their religious beliefs could unfairly influence the jury's perception of their credibility. Rule 610 prevents this by ensuring that religious beliefs are kept out of the assessment of a witness's truthfulness.

2. Protection of Religious Freedom

Rule 610 also serves to protect religious freedom by ensuring that individuals are not compelled to disclose or defend their religious beliefs in a legal setting where those beliefs are irrelevant to the issues at hand. This protection is in line with the First Amendment's guarantee of freedom of religion, which prohibits the government from interfering with an individual's religious practices or from favoring one religion over another.

For instance, if a witness is asked about their religious beliefs during cross-examination, the opposing attorney can object to the question under Rule 610, ensuring that the witness's religious practices are not used against them in assessing their credibility.

Scope and Application of Rule 610

While Rule 610 broadly prohibits the use of religious beliefs or opinions to attack or support credibility, it is important to understand the specific contexts in which this rule applies and the types of evidence it excludes.

1. Types of Prohibited Evidence

Rule 610 covers all forms of evidence related to a witness's religious beliefs or opinions, including direct testimony, documents, and other exhibits. This includes evidence that a witness belongs to a particular religious group, practices certain religious rituals, adheres to specific religious doctrines, or holds particular religious convictions.

For example, evidence that a witness is a devout member of a particular church, regularly attends religious services, or subscribes to specific religious teachings would all be inadmissible under Rule 610 if offered to attack or support the witness's credibility.

2. Context of Application

The prohibition applies in both civil and criminal cases and is relevant during all stages of the trial where witness credibility is at issue, including during direct examination, cross-examination, and the presentation of rebuttal evidence. Rule 610 is designed to ensure that the trial remains focused on the relevant facts and issues rather than being diverted by irrelevant and potentially prejudicial considerations related to religion.

For example, during cross-examination, an attorney might attempt to suggest that a witness's religious beliefs make them more or less likely to tell the truth. Rule 610 bars such a line of questioning, ensuring that the examination remains focused on relevant issues rather than the witness's personal religious views.

Exceptions and Clarifications

While Rule 610 imposes a broad prohibition on the use of religious beliefs or opinions to assess credibility, there are certain situations where religious beliefs may become relevant for other purposes. It is important to distinguish these situations from those covered by Rule 610.

1. Religious Beliefs and the Truthfulness Oath

One potential area of confusion arises from the role of religious beliefs in the administration of the oath or affirmation to testify truthfully, as required by Rule 603. Witnesses often take an oath on a religious text or make an affirmation that is consistent with their religious beliefs. However, this practice is distinct from using religious beliefs to assess credibility and does not fall within the scope of Rule 610.

For example, if a witness takes an oath on a Bible or another religious text, this action is not considered evidence of their religious beliefs for the purposes of assessing their credibility under Rule 610. The oath is simply a formal procedure to impress upon the witness the importance of telling the truth, and it does not introduce the witness's religious beliefs into the trial as a factor for consideration.

2. Relevance of Religious Beliefs for Other Legal Issues

There may be rare situations where a witness's religious beliefs are directly relevant to a legal issue in the case, such as when the beliefs form part of the factual background or are related to the conduct at issue. In such cases, Rule 610 does not bar the introduction of evidence related to those beliefs, provided that the evidence is not used to attack or support the witness's credibility.

For instance, in a case involving religious discrimination, the religious beliefs of the parties may be central to the claims or defenses, and evidence related to those beliefs may be admissible. However, even in such cases, Rule 610 would still prohibit using that evidence to assess the witness's truthfulness or credibility.

Judicial Discretion and Enforcement of Rule 610

Judges play a crucial role in enforcing Rule 610 and ensuring that evidence related to religious beliefs or opinions is not improperly introduced to assess credibility. Judicial discretion is essential for maintaining the fairness and impartiality of the trial.

1. Exclusion of Improper Evidence

Judges must be vigilant in excluding any evidence or questioning that violates Rule 610. This includes preventing attorneys from introducing evidence of religious beliefs during examination or from making arguments that appeal to the jury's biases regarding religion.

For example, if an attorney attempts to suggest that a witness's religious beliefs make them inherently more or less trustworthy, the judge should sustain an objection based on Rule 610 and instruct the jury to disregard any such implications.

2. Jury Instructions

In cases where there is a risk that the jury may be influenced by improper considerations related to a witness's religion, judges may provide specific instructions to the jury to ensure that they do not consider religious beliefs or opinions when assessing credibility. These instructions reinforce the principle that religious views are irrelevant to the determination of truthfulness and should not factor into the jury's deliberations.

For instance, a judge might instruct the jury that they must not consider any evidence or suggestions related to the religious beliefs of the witnesses when deciding the case, emphasizing that all witnesses are to be evaluated solely based on the evidence and their testimony.

Strategic Considerations for Attorneys

Attorneys must be mindful of Rule 610 when preparing for trial, particularly in cases where religion might be a sensitive or relevant issue. Understanding how to navigate this rule is essential for ensuring that the trial remains focused on the relevant issues and that the rights of all parties are protected.

1. Avoiding Inadmissible Evidence

Attorneys must carefully avoid introducing any evidence or questioning that could be construed as using religious beliefs to attack or support a witness's credibility. This requires a thorough understanding of Rule 610 and careful preparation to ensure that all examination strategies comply with the rule.

For example, when preparing cross-examination questions, an attorney should avoid any inquiries that might indirectly suggest that a witness's religious beliefs influence their truthfulness. Instead, the attorney should focus on other, permissible methods of impeachment, such as prior inconsistent statements or bias.

2. Responding to Violations of Rule 610

If opposing counsel attempts to introduce evidence or questioning that violates Rule 610, the attorney must be prepared to object promptly and effectively. This includes citing Rule 610 and requesting that the judge exclude the improper evidence or line of questioning.

For instance, if the opposing counsel asks a witness about their religious practices in a way that implies it affects their credibility, the attorney should immediately object based on Rule 610 and ask the judge to instruct the jury to disregard the question.

Rule 611 - Mode and Order of Examining Witnesses and Presenting Evidence

> **Rule 611. Mode and Order of Examining Witnesses and Presenting Evidence**
>
> (a) **Control by the Court; Purposes.** The court should exercise reasonable control over the mode and order of examining witnesses and presenting evidence so as to: (1) make those procedures effective for determining the truth; (2) avoid wasting time; and (3) protect witnesses from harassment or undue embarrassment.
>
> (b) **Scope of Cross-Examination.** Cross-examination should not go beyond the subject matter of the direct examination and matters affecting the witness's credibility. The court may allow inquiry into additional matters as if on direct examination.
>
> (c) **Leading Questions.** Leading questions should not be used on direct examination except as necessary to develop the witness's testimony. Ordinarily, the court should allow leading questions: (1) on cross-examination; and (2) when a party calls a hostile witness, an adverse party, or a witness identified with an adverse party.

Introduction to Rule 611

Rule 611 of the Federal Rules of Evidence governs the mode and order of examining witnesses and presenting evidence in court. The rule is designed to give trial judges broad discretion to manage the presentation of evidence and the examination of witnesses in a manner that ensures fairness, efficiency, and the ascertainment of truth. Rule 611 provides guidelines on controlling the examination of witnesses, the use of leading questions, and the order in which evidence is presented. This chapter provides a detailed analysis of Rule 611, exploring its text, interpretation, and broader implications for the administration of justice.

Analysis of Rule 611

Rule 611 establishes a framework that allows trial judges to manage the presentation of evidence and the examination of witnesses in a way that promotes the efficiency and integrity of the trial process. The rule provides general principles that guide the mode and order of examination and empowers judges to make decisions that ensure a fair and orderly trial.

Control by the Court (Rule 611(a))

Rule 611(a) grants judges the authority to exercise reasonable control over the mode and order of examining witnesses and presenting evidence. This control is essential for maintaining the fairness and efficiency of the trial, as well as for protecting the rights of witnesses and parties.

1. **Purposes of Judicial Control**

Rule 611(a) outlines three primary purposes for judicial control over the examination of witnesses and the presentation of evidence:

- **Effective Determination of the Truth (Rule 611(a)(1))**

The primary goal of controlling the mode and order of examination is to ensure that the procedures used are effective for determining the truth. This involves allowing the judge to manage the presentation of evidence in a way that clarifies the issues for the jury or judge, prevents confusion, and ensures that the fact-finder has access to all relevant information.

For example, a judge may require that witnesses testify in a particular sequence or that evidence be presented in a certain order to create a coherent narrative that aids in the understanding of the case.

- **Avoiding Wasting Time (Rule 611(a)(2))**

Another key purpose of judicial control under Rule 611(a) is to avoid wasting time. This includes preventing repetitive, irrelevant, or unnecessarily lengthy testimony and ensuring that the trial proceeds efficiently. By exercising control over the mode and order of examination, the judge can streamline the proceedings and focus on the essential issues.

For instance, if an attorney repeatedly asks the same question or dwells on minor points that are not in dispute, the judge may intervene to redirect the examination and move the trial forward.

- **Protecting Witnesses from Harassment or Undue Embarrassment (Rule 611(a)(3))**

Rule 611(a) also empowers judges to protect witnesses from harassment or undue embarrassment during examination. This protection is particularly important for vulnerable witnesses, such as children, victims of crime, or individuals with limited legal experience, who may be intimidated or distressed by aggressive questioning.

For example, if a cross-examiner adopts an overly confrontational or harassing tone, the judge may step in to moderate the questioning and ensure that the witness is treated with respect and dignity.

2. **Judicial Discretion in Implementing Rule 611(a)**

Judges have broad discretion under Rule 611(a) to determine how best to achieve the purposes outlined in the rule. This discretion allows judges to tailor the examination process to the specific needs of each case, taking into account factors such as the complexity of the issues, the number of witnesses, and the nature of the evidence.

For instance, in a complex case with multiple expert witnesses, a judge might impose time limits on testimony or require that witnesses present their evidence in a structured manner to ensure that the trial remains focused and comprehensible.

Scope of Cross-Examination (Rule 611(b))

Rule 611(b) governs the scope of cross-examination, establishing general guidelines for how far cross-examination may go beyond the topics covered in direct examination. The rule reflects the principle that cross-examination should be both relevant and focused, while also allowing flexibility in certain circumstances.

1. Limiting Cross-Examination to the Subject Matter of Direct Examination

Under Rule 611(b), cross-examination is generally limited to the subject matter of the direct examination and matters affecting the witness's credibility. This limitation is intended to keep the cross-examination relevant to the issues raised during direct examination and to prevent the introduction of new, unrelated topics that could confuse the fact-finder.

For example, if a witness testifies on direct examination about the events they observed at a crime scene, the cross-examination should focus on those events and any factors that might affect the witness's credibility, such as inconsistencies in their account or potential biases.

2. Inquiring into Additional Matters

While Rule 611(b) limits the scope of cross-examination, it also provides the court with discretion to allow inquiry into additional matters as if on direct examination. This means that, if appropriate, the court may permit the cross-examiner to explore new topics that were not covered in direct examination, effectively treating the cross-examination as a form of direct examination.

For instance, if a cross-examiner believes that a witness has relevant information about an issue not addressed during direct examination, the judge may allow questioning on that issue, provided it is relevant and probative.

This flexibility ensures that the cross-examination can be thorough and that all relevant information is brought before the court, even if it extends beyond the initial scope of direct examination.

Leading Questions (Rule 611(c))

Rule 611(c) addresses the use of leading questions during witness examination. Leading questions are those that suggest the desired answer, often by including the answer within the question itself. The rule sets out specific guidelines for when leading questions are permissible and when they should be avoided.

1. Prohibition on Leading Questions During Direct Examination

As a general rule, leading questions should not be used during direct examination, except as necessary to develop the witness's testimony. This prohibition is based on the concern that leading questions can unduly influence the witness's responses, potentially skewing the evidence presented.

For example, instead of asking a witness, "The car was blue, wasn't it?" (a leading question), the attorney should ask, "What color was the car?" This open-ended question allows the witness to provide their own recollection without being guided toward a particular answer.

However, Rule 611(c) recognizes that there are situations where leading questions may be necessary to develop the witness's testimony, such as when the witness is struggling to recall details or when the testimony involves complex or technical matters.

2. Permissibility of Leading Questions on Cross-Examination

Leading questions are generally allowed during cross-examination. The rationale for this allowance is that cross-examination is often adversarial in nature, with the goal of testing the credibility and accuracy of the witness's testimony. Leading questions can be an effective tool for challenging a witness's statements and uncovering inconsistencies.

For instance, during cross-examination, an attorney might ask, "Isn't it true that you didn't see the defendant clearly?" to challenge the witness's earlier testimony. This leading question is designed to elicit a specific response that may undermine the witness's credibility.

The use of leading questions in cross-examination helps ensure that the witness's testimony is rigorously tested and that any weaknesses or contradictions are exposed.

3. Leading Questions with Hostile Witnesses or Adverse Parties

Rule 611(c) also allows leading questions when a party calls a hostile witness, an adverse party, or a witness identified with an adverse party. In these situations, leading questions are permitted because the witness's interests are likely to be aligned with the opposing party, and the examining attorney may need to use leading questions to effectively elicit testimony.

For example, if a plaintiff calls the defendant as a witness in a civil case, the plaintiff's attorney may use leading questions to control the narrative and extract admissions or contradictions from the defendant.

This provision ensures that the examining attorney has the tools necessary to obtain useful testimony from witnesses who may be reluctant or biased against the party calling them.

Judicial Discretion and the Application of Rule 611

Judges have significant discretion in applying Rule 611, particularly in determining the mode and order of examining witnesses, controlling the use of leading questions, and managing the scope of cross-examination. This discretion is essential for maintaining the fairness and efficiency of the trial process.

1. Managing the Examination Process

Judges are responsible for managing the examination of witnesses in a way that achieves the objectives outlined in Rule 611(a). This includes making decisions about the order in which witnesses testify, the timing and duration of examinations, and the admissibility of certain types of questions.

For instance, if a witness's testimony is becoming repetitive or irrelevant, the judge may direct the attorney to move on to new topics or to conclude the examination. Similarly, if an attorney is using leading questions inappropriately during direct examination, the judge may instruct the attorney to rephrase the questions in a non-leading manner.

The judge's role in managing the examination process helps ensure that the trial remains focused on the relevant issues and that the fact-finder is presented with clear and reliable evidence.

2. Ensuring Fairness and Protecting Witnesses

Judges also have a duty to ensure that the examination of witnesses is conducted fairly and without harassment or undue embarrassment. This includes intervening when questioning becomes overly aggressive, disrespectful, or invasive, particularly with vulnerable witnesses.

For example, if an attorney's cross-examination of a witness becomes confrontational to the point of intimidating the witness, the judge may step in to moderate the tone of the questioning and protect the witness's dignity.

By exercising this discretion, judges help maintain the integrity of the trial process and protect the rights of all participants.

Strategic Considerations for Attorneys

Rule 611 provides attorneys with guidelines and opportunities for effectively managing witness examinations and presenting evidence. Understanding how to navigate these guidelines is crucial for building a strong case and ensuring that the evidence is presented in the most favorable light.

1. Planning Direct and Cross-Examinations

Attorneys must carefully plan their direct and cross-examinations, taking into account the limitations on leading questions and the scope of cross-examination. Effective planning involves crafting open-ended questions for direct examination that allow the witness to provide detailed and credible testimony, while also preparing leading questions for cross-examination that challenge the witness's statements and expose inconsistencies.

For example, during direct examination, an attorney might ask a series of questions designed to gradually build the witness's narrative, while on cross-examination, the attorney might focus on pinpointing specific areas where the witness's testimony can be challenged.

2. Adapting to Judicial Control

Attorneys must also be prepared to adapt to the judge's control over the examination process. This includes being flexible in responding to judicial directives regarding the order of witness testimony, the use of leading questions, and the management of time during examination.

For instance, if a judge imposes time limits on witness examination, the attorney must prioritize the most critical questions and ensure that the key points are made within the allotted time.

3. Using Leading Questions Strategically

The strategic use of leading questions can be a powerful tool, particularly during cross-examination or when dealing with hostile or adverse witnesses. Attorneys should be mindful of when and how to use leading questions to maximize their impact, while also being aware of the limitations imposed by Rule 611(c).

For example, in a situation where the attorney is cross-examining a witness who has provided damaging testimony on direct examination, carefully crafted leading questions can be used to highlight inconsistencies or to suggest alternative interpretations of the facts.

Rule 612 - Writing Used to Refresh a Witness's Memory

Text of Rule 612

Rule 612. Writing Used to Refresh a Witness's Memory
(a) **Scope.** This rule gives an adverse party certain options when a witness uses a writing to refresh memory: (1) while testifying; or (2) before testifying, if the court decides that justice requires the party to have those options.
(b) **Adverse Party's Options; Deleting Unrelated Matter.** Unless 18 U.S.C. § 3500 provides otherwise in a criminal case, an adverse party is entitled to have the writing produced at the hearing, to inspect it, to cross-examine the witness about it, and to introduce in evidence any portion that relates to the witness's testimony. If the producing party claims that the writing includes unrelated matter, the court must examine the writing in camera, delete any unrelated portion, and order that the rest be delivered to the adverse party. Any portion deleted over objection must be preserved for the record.
(c) **Failure to Produce or Deliver the Writing.** If a writing is not produced or is not delivered as ordered, the court may issue any appropriate order. But if the prosecution does not comply in a criminal case, the court must strike the witness's testimony or—if justice so requires—declare a mistrial.

Introduction to Rule 612

Rule 612 of the Federal Rules of Evidence governs the use of writings to refresh a witness's memory during testimony. This rule allows a witness to use a document or other writing to jog their memory when they are unable to recall certain facts during testimony. Rule 612 ensures that the fact-finder has access to accurate and complete information by allowing witnesses to refresh their recollection while maintaining safeguards to prevent the improper use of such materials. This chapter provides a detailed analysis of Rule 612, exploring its text, interpretation, and broader implications for the administration of justice.

Analysis of Rule 612

Rule 612 provides a framework for using writings to refresh a witness's memory, balancing the need for accurate testimony with the rights of the opposing party to scrutinize the materials used. The rule covers the scope of its application, the rights of the adverse party, and the consequences of failing to comply with its provisions.

Scope of Rule 612 (Rule 612(a))

Rule 612(a) defines the scope of the rule, specifying when and how a witness may use a writing to refresh their memory. The rule applies in two situations: when a witness uses a writing to refresh their memory while testifying and when a witness uses a writing to refresh their memory before testifying, if the court deems it necessary for justice.

1. **Refreshing Memory While Testifying**

The most common scenario under Rule 612 is when a witness uses a writing to refresh their memory during their testimony. This occurs when a witness, while on the stand, struggles to recall specific details and is permitted to consult a document to help them remember the facts accurately.

For example, a witness in a contract dispute might have difficulty recalling the exact terms of the contract. The attorney may provide the witness with a copy of the contract to refresh their memory. After reviewing the document, the witness can then testify based on their refreshed recollection.

2. **Refreshing Memory Before Testifying**

Rule 612 also allows for the use of writings to refresh a witness's memory before they testify, though this is less common and requires judicial discretion. If the court decides that justice requires it, the adverse party may be granted access to the writing used to refresh the witness's memory prior to their testimony. This provision ensures that the witness's testimony is not unfairly influenced by undisclosed materials.

For instance, if a witness reviews notes or a report before taking the stand and their testimony appears unusually precise or detailed, the opposing party might request access to the materials reviewed. The court must then decide whether to allow this access based on considerations of fairness and the interests of justice.

Adverse Party's Options and Rights (Rule 612(b))

Rule 612(b) outlines the rights of the adverse party when a writing is used to refresh a witness's memory. These rights are crucial for maintaining the transparency and fairness of the trial process, ensuring that the opposing party can challenge the credibility and reliability of the refreshed testimony.

1. **Inspection and Use of the Writing**

When a writing is used to refresh a witness's memory, the adverse party is entitled to have the writing produced at the hearing. This allows the opposing party to inspect the document, cross-examine the witness about it, and introduce any relevant portions into evidence.

For example, if a witness consults a business ledger to refresh their memory about financial transactions, the adverse party has the right to examine the ledger, question the witness about its contents, and use parts of the ledger to challenge the witness's testimony or to support their own case.

This provision ensures that the witness's testimony is subject to full scrutiny and that the opposing party has an opportunity to test the accuracy and completeness of the refreshed recollection.

2. In Camera Review and Deletion of Unrelated Matter

If the writing contains information that is unrelated to the witness's testimony, the producing party may request that the court examine the document in camera (privately) to delete the irrelevant portions before delivering the rest to the adverse party. The court must carefully review the writing, delete any unrelated material, and ensure that the relevant portions are provided to the opposing party.

For example, if a witness reviews a lengthy report that contains both relevant information and sensitive personal data unrelated to the case, the court may remove the personal data before allowing the opposing party to see the document.

Any portion deleted over objection must be preserved for the record, allowing for appellate review if necessary. This process protects sensitive or irrelevant information while ensuring that the opposing party has access to the material that influenced the witness's testimony.

Consequences of Failing to Produce or Deliver the Writing (Rule 612(c))

Rule 612(c) addresses the consequences if the party using the writing fails to produce it or deliver it as ordered by the court. This section underscores the importance of compliance with Rule 612 and provides remedies to ensure that the trial proceeds fairly.

1. Appropriate Court Orders

If a party fails to produce or deliver the writing as required, the court has the discretion to issue any appropriate order. This might include sanctions, instructions to the jury, or other measures designed to address the non-compliance and to mitigate any prejudice caused to the opposing party.

For instance, if a party refuses to provide the writing used to refresh a witness's memory, the court might order that certain portions of the witness's testimony be disregarded or that the jury be instructed to consider the refusal when assessing the credibility of the witness.

2. Striking Testimony or Declaring a Mistrial in Criminal Cases

In criminal cases, if the prosecution fails to comply with Rule 612, the court is required to strike the witness's testimony or, if justice demands, declare a mistrial. This strict approach reflects the heightened importance of protecting the defendant's rights in criminal proceedings, where the consequences of non-compliance could be particularly severe.

For example, if a key prosecution witness in a criminal trial uses a report to refresh their memory and the prosecution refuses to provide the report to the defense, the court may strike the witness's testimony entirely. In extreme cases, where the refusal significantly impacts the fairness of the trial, the court might declare a mistrial.

Judicial Discretion in Applying Rule 612

Judges have significant discretion in applying Rule 612, particularly in deciding when justice requires access to writings used before testimony, determining what constitutes unrelated material in a writing, and imposing appropriate remedies for non-compliance.

1. Determining Justice Requirements

Judges must assess whether allowing the adverse party access to writings used before testimony is necessary to ensure a fair trial. This involves considering the potential impact of the writing on the witness's testimony, the relevance of the material, and the need for transparency in the proceedings.

For example, if a witness's testimony appears unusually detailed or rehearsed, the judge may decide that justice requires the adverse party to inspect the writing used to refresh the witness's memory beforehand. This decision helps prevent the improper influence of undisclosed materials on the testimony.

2. Managing In Camera Reviews

Judges are responsible for conducting in camera reviews of writings to determine what portions, if any, should be deleted before the document is provided to the adverse party. This process requires a careful balance between protecting irrelevant or sensitive information and ensuring that the opposing party has access to all relevant material.

For instance, if a document contains privileged information or details that are unrelated to the case, the judge must decide how to redact those portions while preserving the integrity of the witness's testimony and the rights of the adverse party.

3. Imposing Remedies for Non-Compliance

When a party fails to comply with Rule 612, judges must decide on the appropriate remedy. This could range from issuing a warning or imposing sanctions to striking testimony or declaring a mistrial. The chosen remedy must be proportionate to the severity of the non-compliance and its impact on the fairness of the trial.

For example, in a civil case, the judge might instruct the jury to consider the party's refusal to produce the writing when evaluating the credibility of the witness. In a criminal case, more severe measures, such as striking the testimony or declaring a mistrial, might be necessary to protect the defendant's rights.

Strategic Considerations for Attorneys

Rule 612 provides attorneys with both opportunities and challenges in managing witness testimony and the use of writings to refresh memory. Understanding how to navigate this rule is essential for effectively presenting or challenging evidence in court.

1. Using Writings to Refresh Memory

Attorneys should carefully consider when and how to use writings to refresh a witness's memory. While this technique can be valuable for ensuring accurate testimony, it also opens the door for the opposing party to inspect the writing and potentially use it to challenge the witness's credibility.

For example, before using a writing to refresh a witness's memory, an attorney should review the document to ensure that it does not contain any information that could be harmful or that could be used against the witness during cross-examination.

2. Challenging the Use of Writings by Opposing Counsel

When the opposing party uses a writing to refresh a witness's memory, the attorney must be prepared to assert their rights under Rule 612. This includes requesting access to the writing, scrutinizing its contents for inconsistencies or inaccuracies, and using relevant portions to challenge the witness's testimony.

For instance, if the opposing counsel uses a document to refresh a witness's memory, the attorney should request the document's production, review it for any discrepancies with the witness's testimony, and consider whether any portions of the document should be introduced as evidence.

3. Preparing for In Camera Reviews

Attorneys should be prepared for the possibility that the court will conduct an in camera review of a writing used to refresh a witness's memory. This may involve arguing for or against the inclusion of certain portions of the document and ensuring that any deletions are appropriately justified.

For example, if a document contains sensitive or privileged information, the attorney may need to persuade the court that these portions should be redacted before the document is provided to the opposing party.

Rule 613 - Witness's Prior Statement

Rule 613. Witness's Prior Statement
(a) **Showing or Disclosing the Statement During Examination.** When examining a witness about the witness's prior statement, a party need not show it or disclose its contents to the witness. But the party must, on request, show it or disclose its contents to an adverse party's attorney.
(b) **Extrinsic Evidence of a Prior Inconsistent Statement.** Extrinsic evidence of a witness's prior inconsistent statement is admissible only if the witness is given an opportunity to explain or deny the statement and an adverse party is given an opportunity to examine the witness about it, or if justice so requires. This subdivision (b) does not apply to an opposing party's statement under Rule 801(d)(2).

Introduction to Rule 613

Rule 613 of the Federal Rules of Evidence governs the use of a witness's prior statements during legal proceedings. This rule provides a structured approach for introducing and using a witness's prior statements to challenge or corroborate their testimony in court. Rule 613 ensures that the process of confronting a witness with their earlier statements is both fair and transparent, thereby upholding the integrity of the fact-finding process. This chapter provides a detailed analysis of Rule 613, exploring its text, interpretation, and broader implications for the administration of justice.

Analysis of Rule 613

Rule 613 provides a framework for the use of prior statements made by a witness during testimony, particularly focusing on prior inconsistent statements. The rule is designed to allow parties to challenge the credibility of a witness while ensuring that the process is conducted fairly.

Showing or Disclosing the Statement During Examination (Rule 613(a))

Rule 613(a) addresses the procedure for examining a witness about their prior statement. This provision sets out the rules for when and how a prior statement can be introduced during examination, focusing on the requirements for disclosure to the witness and the opposing party.

1. **No Obligation to Show or Disclose to the Witness**

Under Rule 613(a), when a party examines a witness about their prior statement, the examining party is not required to show the statement or disclose its contents to the witness during the examination. This allows the examining attorney to question the witness about the prior statement without immediately revealing the document or recording on which the examination is based.

For example, an attorney might ask a witness, "Did you previously state that you were not present at the scene?" without showing the witness the document where the statement was recorded. This approach can help the attorney assess the witness's credibility by observing their reaction and responses without giving the witness an opportunity to tailor their answers to the document.

2. **Obligation to Disclose to the Opposing Party**

While Rule 613(a) permits an attorney to withhold the statement from the witness during examination, it also requires that the attorney disclose the statement's contents to the opposing party's attorney upon request. This requirement ensures that the opposing party is fully informed and has an opportunity to prepare a response or challenge the use of the prior statement.

For instance, if the opposing attorney requests to see the prior statement during the examination, the examining attorney must provide it. This transparency helps maintain the fairness of the trial and allows the opposing party to effectively cross-examine the witness or address the implications of the prior statement.

Extrinsic Evidence of a Prior Inconsistent Statement (Rule 613(b))

Rule 613(b) governs the use of extrinsic evidence to prove a witness's prior inconsistent statement. This provision establishes conditions under which such evidence can be introduced, focusing on the need to give the witness an opportunity to explain or deny the statement and allowing the opposing party to respond.

1. **Conditions for Admissibility of Extrinsic Evidence**

Extrinsic evidence of a prior inconsistent statement is admissible only if two conditions are met: (1) the witness must be given an opportunity to explain or deny the statement, and (2) the opposing party must be given an opportunity to examine the witness about the statement. These conditions ensure that the witness's credibility is fairly challenged and that the fact-finder has access to all relevant information.

For example, if a witness testified in court that they saw the defendant at the scene of the crime, but previously stated in a deposition that they did not see the defendant, the attorney can introduce the deposition as extrinsic evidence. However, before doing so, the witness must be given a chance to explain the discrepancy, such as by asking, "Did you not previously testify in your deposition that you did not see the defendant at the scene?"

This procedure helps ensure that the witness's testimony is rigorously tested while giving the witness an opportunity to clarify or correct any inconsistencies.

2. **Exceptions to the Rule**

Rule 613(b) includes an exception for opposing party statements under Rule 801(d)(2), which deals with admissions by a party-opponent. This exception means that when the prior inconsistent statement is an admission by an opposing party, the need to give the witness an opportunity to explain or deny the statement does not apply.

For example, if a defendant in a criminal case made a prior statement to the police that contradicts their testimony in court, this statement can be introduced without the requirement to give the defendant an opportunity to explain or deny it, as it falls under the exception for party-opponent admissions.

Judicial Discretion in Applying Rule 613

Judges have significant discretion in applying Rule 613, particularly in determining whether the conditions for admitting extrinsic evidence of a prior inconsistent statement have been met and in ensuring that the process of confronting a witness with prior statements is conducted fairly.

1. **Ensuring Fairness and Adequate Opportunity**

Judges must ensure that the witness is given a fair opportunity to explain or deny the prior inconsistent statement and that the opposing party has an adequate chance to examine the witness about it. This involves monitoring the examination process to ensure that it adheres to the procedural requirements of Rule 613 and that neither party is unfairly disadvantaged.

For example, if an attorney introduces extrinsic evidence of a prior inconsistent statement without first giving the witness an opportunity to explain or deny it, the judge may intervene, requiring the attorney to follow the proper procedure before the evidence is admitted.

2. **Balancing Probative Value and Prejudice**

Judges also have the discretion to balance the probative value of the prior inconsistent statement against the potential for unfair prejudice. This balancing act is essential for ensuring that the evidence introduced does not unduly influence the fact-finder or distract from the central issues of the case.

For instance, if a prior inconsistent statement is only marginally relevant or is likely to cause undue prejudice, the judge may decide to exclude the extrinsic evidence, ensuring that the trial remains focused on the key facts and that the witness is not unfairly discredited.

Strategic Considerations for Attorneys

Rule 613 provides attorneys with a valuable tool for challenging the credibility of witnesses by using their prior statements. Understanding how to effectively apply this rule is crucial for constructing a persuasive case and for defending against challenges to witness credibility.

1. **Timing and Presentation of Prior Inconsistent Statements**

Attorneys must carefully consider the timing and presentation of prior inconsistent statements. This involves deciding when to confront a witness with their prior statement—whether during direct examination, cross-examination, or rebuttal—and how to do so in a manner that maximizes the impact on the witness's credibility.

For example, during cross-examination, an attorney might choose to confront a witness with a prior inconsistent statement at a moment when the witness's credibility is already in question, thereby increasing the likelihood that the fact-finder will view the inconsistency as significant.

2. **Preparation for Witness Explanations**

Attorneys must also be prepared for the witness to offer explanations or denials of prior inconsistent statements. This requires anticipating possible justifications for the inconsistency and preparing follow-up questions or additional evidence to challenge the witness's explanation.

For instance, if a witness explains a prior inconsistent statement by claiming they were confused or misremembered, the attorney might introduce other evidence that contradicts the witness's current testimony, thereby reinforcing the inconsistency and undermining the witness's credibility.

3. **Defending Against Use of Prior Statements**

When defending against the use of a witness's prior statements, attorneys must be vigilant in ensuring that the procedural requirements of Rule 613 are followed. This includes objecting if the opposing party fails to give the witness an opportunity to explain or deny the prior statement or if the introduction of extrinsic evidence does not comply with the rule.

For example, if the opposing counsel introduces extrinsic evidence of a prior inconsistent statement without following the proper procedure, the defense attorney should object and request that the evidence be excluded or that the witness be given an opportunity to address the inconsistency.

Rule 614 - Court's Calling or Examining a Witness

Rule 614. Court's Calling or Examining a Witness
(a) **Calling.** The court may call a witness on its own or at a party's request. Each party is entitled to cross-examine the witness.
(b) **Examining.** The court may examine a witness regardless of who calls the witness.
(c) **Objections.** A party may object to the court's calling or examining a witness either at that time or at the next opportunity when the jury is not present.

Introduction to Rule 614

Rule 614 of the Federal Rules of Evidence governs the authority of the court to call and examine witnesses during a trial. This rule acknowledges the court's active role in the fact-finding process, permitting judges to take direct action in the examination of witnesses when necessary to ensure that the truth is ascertained and that justice is served. Rule 614 provides the legal framework within which a judge may call or question witnesses, and it also outlines the rights of the parties to object to such actions. This chapter provides a detailed analysis of Rule 614, exploring its text, interpretation, and broader implications for the administration of justice.

Analysis of Rule 614

Rule 614 provides the court with the authority to call and examine witnesses, reflecting the judge's role as an active participant in the trial process. This rule balances the court's duty to ensure a fair and thorough fact-finding process with the parties' rights to present their cases and to object to judicial interventions when necessary.

Court's Authority to Call a Witness (Rule 614(a))

Rule 614(a) grants the court the power to call witnesses on its own initiative or at the request of a party. This provision reflects the court's role in ensuring that all relevant evidence is presented and that the fact-finder has the information necessary to make an informed decision.

1. Court's Initiative in Calling Witnesses

The rule allows the court to call a witness independently, even if neither party has requested that the witness testify. This power is rooted in the court's responsibility to ensure that justice is served by thoroughly exploring all relevant facts, especially in cases where the testimony of a particular witness may be crucial to understanding the issues at hand.

For example, in a complex civil case where neither party has called a key expert witness whose testimony could clarify a critical issue, the judge may decide to call the expert witness themselves to provide the court with the necessary information.

2. Calling a Witness at a Party's Request

Rule 614(a) also allows the court to call a witness at the request of a party. This provision ensures that the court can assist in situations where a party may have difficulty securing the attendance of a necessary witness or when the court deems the testimony to be essential to the interests of justice.

For instance, if a party requests that the court call a witness who is reluctant to testify or who is crucial to the case but has not been subpoenaed by either side, the court may grant the request and call the witness to testify.

3. Right to Cross-Examine

When the court calls a witness under Rule 614(a), both parties are entitled to cross-examine the witness. This right is fundamental to the adversarial process, ensuring that the testimony elicited by the court can be challenged and tested for accuracy, consistency, and credibility.

For example, if a judge calls a witness to clarify a specific factual issue, both the plaintiff and the defendant have the right to question the witness after the court's examination, allowing them to explore any potential biases, inconsistencies, or gaps in the testimony.

Court's Authority to Examine a Witness (Rule 614(b))

Rule 614(b) allows the court to examine any witness, regardless of which party called the witness to testify. This provision emphasizes the judge's role in actively managing the trial and ensuring that all relevant evidence is fully explored.

1. Judicial Examination of Witnesses

The rule permits the court to ask questions of any witness during the trial. This can occur when the judge believes that additional information is needed, that the witness's testimony requires clarification, or that certain aspects of the case have not been adequately covered by the parties' examinations.

For example, during a witness's testimony, a judge might intervene to ask a clarifying question if the witness's response is ambiguous or if the testimony appears to conflict with other evidence. This intervention helps to ensure that the fact-finder has a clear and accurate understanding of the witness's statements.

2. Ensuring Neutrality and Fairness

While Rule 614(b) empowers the court to examine witnesses, it also imposes a duty on judges to maintain neutrality and fairness. The judge's questions should be aimed at eliciting relevant information and should not be used to advocate for one side or to suggest the judge's own views on the case.

For instance, a judge might ask a witness to clarify a timeline of events or to explain technical terms that are important for the jury's understanding. However, the judge must avoid asking leading questions or making statements that could be perceived as showing bias toward one party.

Objections to the Court's Actions (Rule 614(c))

Rule 614(c) provides parties with the right to object to the court's actions in calling or examining a witness. This provision ensures that parties can protect their rights and the fairness of the proceedings, particularly if they believe the court's intervention may prejudice the case.

1. Timing of Objections

Rule 614(c) allows a party to object to the court's calling or examining a witness either at the time the action occurs or at the next opportunity when the jury is not present. This flexibility is crucial because it allows attorneys to raise objections without the risk of influencing the jury improperly or highlighting a potentially prejudicial issue in front of them.

For example, if a judge asks a series of questions that an attorney believes are leading or biased, the attorney might choose to wait until the jury is excused before raising an objection. This approach allows the issue to be addressed without drawing undue attention to the judge's actions in the jury's eyes.

2. Grounds for Objection

Parties may object to the court's actions on various grounds, such as if the judge's questions appear to be leading, argumentative, or otherwise suggestive of the judge's opinion on the case. Objections may also be raised if the court's examination delves into matters beyond the scope of the issues at trial or if the questioning is perceived as unfairly influencing the witness.

For example, if a judge questions a witness in a manner that seems to imply disbelief or skepticism about the witness's testimony, the attorney for the party that called the witness might object on the grounds that the judge's questions could unfairly influence the jury's perception of the witness's credibility.

3. Judicial Response to Objections

When an objection is raised under Rule 614(c), the judge must consider the merits of the objection and decide whether to sustain it. If the objection is sustained, the judge may take steps to mitigate any potential prejudice, such as instructing the jury to disregard the judge's questions or refraining from further questioning on the matter.

For instance, if an objection is sustained, the judge might clarify to the jury that they should not infer any conclusions from the judge's questions and should base their decisions solely on the evidence presented by the parties.

Judicial Discretion and the Application of Rule 614

Judges have significant discretion in applying Rule 614, particularly in deciding when and how to call or examine witnesses. This discretion is essential for ensuring that the trial is conducted in a manner that is both efficient and fair, while also protecting the rights of the parties.

1. Balancing Judicial Involvement and Impartiality

Judges must balance their active involvement in calling or examining witnesses with their duty to remain impartial. While Rule 614 empowers judges to take a more active role in the fact-finding process, they must be careful not to overstep their bounds or to give the appearance of taking sides.

For example, a judge who notices that a key issue has not been adequately addressed by the parties might decide to ask a few clarifying questions. However, the judge must ensure that these questions are neutral and that they do not suggest any conclusions about the merits of the case.

2. Managing the Courtroom

The ability to call or examine witnesses under Rule 614 also allows judges to manage the courtroom more effectively. This includes addressing gaps in the evidence, clarifying complex issues, and ensuring that the testimony presented is coherent and understandable to the jury.

For instance, in a case involving highly technical testimony, a judge might ask questions to break down the information into simpler terms that the jury can more easily understand. This helps to ensure that the fact-finder is fully informed and that the trial proceeds smoothly.

Strategic Considerations for Attorneys

Rule 614 presents both opportunities and challenges for attorneys. Understanding how to navigate the court's involvement in calling or examining witnesses is essential for effectively representing a client's interests.

1. Responding to the Court's Examination

Attorneys must be prepared to respond strategically when the court decides to examine a witness. This includes being ready to object if the judge's questions are leading or prejudicial and being prepared to follow up on the court's questions with their own to clarify or reinforce the testimony.

For example, if a judge's questions inadvertently introduce ambiguity into a witness's testimony, the attorney might use their follow-up questions to clarify the witness's statements and to mitigate any potential confusion caused by the court's examination.

2. Requesting the Court to Call a Witness

In certain situations, it may be advantageous for an attorney to request that the court call a particular witness. This can be a strategic move when the witness's testimony is crucial but might not be forthcoming through the standard procedures, or when the attorney believes that the judge's involvement could lend additional weight to the witness's testimony.

For example, in a case where a key witness is hesitant to testify, an attorney might request that the judge call the witness to ensure that the testimony is heard and to alleviate any concerns the witness might have about being called by one of the parties.

3. Preparing for Objections

Attorneys should also be prepared to object to the court's examination of witnesses when appropriate. This requires a deep understanding of the boundaries of judicial questioning and the ability to quickly assess whether the judge's involvement is affecting the fairness of the trial.

For instance, if a judge's questions seem to favor one party's version of events, the opposing attorney should be ready to object and to articulate clearly the reasons why the questioning is problematic, all while maintaining respect for the court's authority.

Rule 615 - Excluding Witnesses from the Courtroom; Preventing an Excluded Witness's Access to Trial Testimony

Text of Rule 615

Rule 615. Excluding Witnesses
At a party's request, the court must order witnesses excluded so that they cannot hear other witnesses' testimony. Or the court may do so on its own. But this rule does not authorize excluding:
(a) a party who is a natural person;
(b) an officer or employee of a party that is not a natural person, after being designated as the party's representative by its attorney;
(c) a person whose presence a party shows to be essential to presenting the party's claim or defense; or
(d) a person authorized by statute to be present.

Introduction to Rule 615

Rule 615 of the Federal Rules of Evidence governs the exclusion of witnesses from the courtroom during the testimony of other witnesses. This rule, often referred to as the "Rule on Witnesses" or the "Sequestration Rule," is designed to prevent witnesses from being influenced by the testimony of others and to ensure that each witness provides an independent and uninfluenced account of the events in question. Rule 615 also addresses the prevention of an excluded witness's access to trial testimony, ensuring that the integrity of the witness's testimony is preserved. This chapter provides a detailed analysis of Rule 615, exploring its text, interpretation, and broader implications for the administration of justice.

Analysis of Rule 615

Rule 615 provides a clear and mandatory procedure for excluding witnesses from the courtroom during the testimony of others, with specific exceptions. This rule is essential for maintaining the integrity of the fact-finding process by preventing witnesses from tailoring their testimony based on what they have heard from other witnesses.

Mandatory Exclusion of Witnesses (Rule 615)

Rule 615 mandates that the court must exclude witnesses from the courtroom at the request of any party or on the court's own initiative. This exclusion is intended to prevent witnesses from being influenced by the testimony of others, thereby ensuring that each witness's testimony is based solely on their own recollection of events.

1. **Party's Request or Court's Initiative**

The rule specifies that either party in a case may request the exclusion of witnesses, and if such a request is made, the court is obligated to grant it. Additionally, the court has the discretion to order the exclusion of witnesses on its own initiative, even if no party has made a request. This flexibility allows the court to take proactive measures to preserve the integrity of the trial.

For example, in a criminal trial, the prosecution might request the exclusion of all witnesses except the defendant to prevent them from hearing each other's testimony. The court, recognizing the importance of independent testimony, would then exclude the witnesses from the courtroom until it is their turn to testify.

2. **Purpose of Exclusion**

The primary purpose of excluding witnesses is to prevent them from being influenced by the testimony of others. This practice, known as sequestration, is crucial in avoiding the potential for witnesses to align their testimonies or to alter their accounts based on what they hear from other witnesses. It helps ensure that each witness's testimony is authentic, based on their own memory and perception, and not colored by the influence of others.

For instance, if multiple witnesses observed the same event, excluding them from the courtroom ensures that each witness provides an independent account, rather than modifying their testimony to match or differ from what they hear from others.

Exceptions to Exclusion (Rule 615(a)–(d))

While Rule 615 mandates the exclusion of witnesses, it also provides specific exceptions to this requirement. These exceptions recognize situations where the presence of certain individuals is necessary or legally mandated, even if they are also witnesses.

1. **Natural Person Parties (Rule 615(a))**

Rule 615(a) exempts parties who are natural persons from exclusion. This means that a party to the case, whether plaintiff or defendant, cannot be excluded from the courtroom during the testimony of other witnesses. The rationale for this exception is that a party has a fundamental right to be present at their own trial and to hear all the testimony presented.

For example, in a personal injury lawsuit, the plaintiff, as a natural person and a party to the case, cannot be excluded from the courtroom while other witnesses testify. The plaintiff has the right to be present and to hear all the evidence presented.

2. Designated Representatives (Rule 615(b))

Rule 615(b) allows an officer or employee of a party that is not a natural person (such as a corporation or government agency) to remain in the courtroom after being designated as the party's representative by its attorney. This exception ensures that a party that is not a natural person is still represented in the courtroom and can participate fully in the trial process.

For instance, in a corporate lawsuit, a company's attorney might designate the CEO or another high-ranking employee as the company's representative. This individual, despite being a potential witness, would be allowed to remain in the courtroom throughout the trial.

3. Essential Persons (Rule 615(c))

Rule 615(c) provides an exception for persons whose presence a party shows to be essential to presenting their claim or defense. This exception recognizes that, in some cases, a witness's presence in the courtroom is necessary for the party's ability to effectively present their case, such as when a witness is needed to provide technical expertise or to assist in cross-examining other witnesses.

For example, in a complex medical malpractice case, an attorney might argue that a medical expert's presence is essential to assist in understanding the testimony of other expert witnesses. If the court agrees, the medical expert would not be excluded under Rule 615(c).

4. Persons Authorized by Statute (Rule 615(d))

Rule 615(d) exempts individuals who are authorized by statute to be present during the trial. This provision recognizes that certain statutes may grant specific individuals the right to remain in the courtroom, even if they are also witnesses, overriding the general rule of exclusion.

For instance, in certain cases involving child witnesses, a statute might allow a parent or guardian to remain in the courtroom to provide emotional support, even if that parent or guardian is also a witness in the case.

Enforcement and Challenges Related to Rule 615

The enforcement of Rule 615 involves ensuring that excluded witnesses do not have access to the testimony of other witnesses, whether in person or through other means. This section explores how courts manage this process and the potential challenges that can arise.

1. Preventing Access to Testimony

When a witness is excluded under Rule 615, the court must take steps to ensure that the witness does not gain access to the testimony of other witnesses indirectly, such as through discussions with others or by reading transcripts. This is critical to preserving the integrity of the exclusion and ensuring that the witness's testimony remains independent.

For example, the court might instruct excluded witnesses to avoid discussing the case with anyone until after they have testified, and to refrain from reading any media reports or trial transcripts. Attorneys and parties involved in the case are also prohibited from sharing such information with excluded witnesses.

2. Addressing Violations of Rule 615

If a witness who has been excluded under Rule 615 gains access to the testimony of other witnesses, whether intentionally or inadvertently, the court must address the violation. The remedies for such violations can include striking the witness's testimony, instructing the jury to disregard the testimony, or, in extreme cases, declaring a mistrial.

For instance, if it is discovered that an excluded witness discussed the testimony of another witness with someone who was present in the courtroom, the opposing party might move to have the witness's testimony stricken from the record. The court would then consider the severity of the violation and determine the appropriate remedy.

3. Objections and Requests for Exclusion

Attorneys must be proactive in raising objections if they believe that a witness should be excluded under Rule 615 or if they suspect that an excluded witness has gained access to other testimony. The timing and manner of these objections can be crucial, as failing to raise an objection in a timely manner could result in a waiver of the issue on appeal.

For example, if an attorney learns that an excluded witness has been discussing the trial with someone who has been in the courtroom, the attorney should immediately bring this to the court's attention and request appropriate relief, such as exclusion of the witness's testimony or a mistrial.

Judicial Discretion in Applying Rule 615

Judges have significant discretion in applying Rule 615, particularly in determining whether a person falls within one of the exceptions and in managing the logistics of excluding witnesses and preventing access to testimony.

1. Interpreting the Exceptions

Judges must carefully interpret and apply the exceptions outlined in Rule 615, considering the specific circumstances of each case. This involves balancing the need to exclude witnesses with the rights of parties to have essential persons present in the courtroom.

For example, if a party argues that a particular expert witness is essential to their case under Rule 615(c), the judge must assess whether the witness's presence is genuinely necessary and whether it might unfairly influence the testimony of other witnesses.

2. Managing Sequestration

Judges are also responsible for managing the sequestration of witnesses, including issuing instructions to ensure that excluded witnesses do not access the testimony of others. This might involve coordinating with court staff to monitor who enters and exits the courtroom and ensuring that all parties understand and comply with the exclusion order.

For instance, a judge might instruct court officers to ensure that excluded witnesses do not enter the courtroom until it is their turn to testify and to monitor any interactions between witnesses outside the courtroom to prevent discussions about the trial.

Strategic Considerations for Attorneys

Rule 615 presents strategic opportunities and challenges for attorneys in managing the testimony of witnesses and ensuring that the trial proceeds fairly.

1. Deciding When to Request Exclusion

Attorneys must decide when it is advantageous to request the exclusion of witnesses under Rule 615. This decision often depends on the nature of the testimony, the number of witnesses, and the potential for one witness's testimony to influence another's.

For example, in a case involving multiple eyewitnesses to an event, an attorney might request the exclusion of all witnesses to prevent them from aligning their testimonies or from being influenced by the testimony of others.

2. Managing the Exclusion Process

Once witnesses are excluded, attorneys must be vigilant in ensuring that the exclusion order is followed. This includes advising their clients and witnesses on the rules of exclusion, monitoring the actions of excluded witnesses, and being prepared to raise objections if there is any indication that an excluded witness has accessed other testimony.

For instance, if an attorney suspects that an excluded witness has been speaking with other witnesses about the trial, the attorney should investigate the matter and, if necessary, bring it to the court's attention to protect the integrity of the trial.

3. Handling Exceptions

Attorneys should be prepared to argue for or against exceptions to Rule 615, depending on their strategic goals. This might involve demonstrating why a particular witness is essential to the case under Rule 615(c) or opposing such a designation by the opposing party.

For example, if the opposing party seeks to keep an expert witness in the courtroom under the exception in Rule 615(c), the attorney might argue that the expert's presence is not truly essential and that their testimony could be influenced by hearing the testimony of other witnesses.

ARTICLE VII. OPINIONS AND EXPERT TESTIMONY

Rule 701 - Opinion Testimony by Lay Witnesses

Text of Rule 701

Rule 701. Opinion Testimony by Lay Witnesses
If a witness is not testifying as an expert, testimony in the form of an opinion is limited to one that is:
(a) **rationally based on the witness's perception**;
(b) **helpful to clearly understanding the witness's testimony or to determining a fact in issue**; and
(c) **not based on scientific, technical, or other specialized knowledge within the scope of Rule 702**.

Introduction to Rule 701

Rule 701 of the Federal Rules of Evidence governs the admissibility of opinion testimony by lay witnesses. Unlike expert witnesses, who may provide opinions based on specialized knowledge, training, or experience, lay witnesses are limited in the scope of their opinion testimony. Rule 701 is designed to ensure that lay opinions are based on the witness's personal knowledge and perceptions, and that such opinions are helpful to the fact-finder in understanding the witness's testimony or determining a fact in issue. This chapter provides a detailed analysis of Rule 701, exploring its text, interpretation, and broader implications for the administration of justice.

Analysis of Rule 701

Rule 701 sets clear boundaries for lay witness opinion testimony, ensuring that such testimony is both relevant and reliable without encroaching upon the domain of expert testimony. The rule's three prongs—rational basis, helpfulness, and exclusion of specialized knowledge—serve as a guide for determining the admissibility of lay opinions in court.

Rational Basis on the Witness's Perception (Rule 701(a))

The first requirement under Rule 701 is that the opinion must be rationally based on the witness's perception. This means that the opinion must stem directly from the witness's personal observations and experiences, rather than from speculation, hearsay, or information acquired secondhand.

1. Personal Knowledge Requirement

The opinion must be grounded in the witness's firsthand experience of the events in question. This ensures that the testimony is reliable and directly related to the witness's own sensory perceptions—what they saw, heard, smelled, touched, or otherwise personally experienced.

For example, a lay witness who observed a car accident may testify that, in their opinion, the driver appeared to be speeding based on their observation of the car's speed relative to other vehicles. This opinion is admissible because it is based on the witness's direct perception of the event.

2. Exclusion of Speculation

Rule 701(a) prohibits opinions based on speculation or conjecture. The witness must have a factual basis for their opinion, derived from their own observations, rather than drawing conclusions without adequate grounds.

For instance, if a witness speculates that someone was angry simply because they were quiet, without observing any specific angry behavior, such an opinion would likely be excluded under Rule 701(a) because it lacks a rational basis rooted in direct perception.

Helpfulness to the Fact-Finder (Rule 701(b))

The second requirement under Rule 701 is that the opinion must be helpful to the fact-finder—whether judge or jury—in understanding the witness's testimony or in determining a fact in issue. This prong ensures that lay opinions contribute meaningfully to the resolution of the case.

1. Clarifying Testimony

An opinion may be admitted under Rule 701(b) if it helps clarify the witness's testimony by providing context or explaining observations that might otherwise be ambiguous or difficult to understand.

For example, a witness might testify that a person seemed nervous because they were sweating and fidgeting during a conversation. This opinion helps the jury understand the witness's observations by linking specific behaviors to a general impression of nervousness, which is relevant to the case.

2. Determining a Fact in Issue

Lay opinions can also assist the fact-finder in determining a fact in issue by offering insights that are not apparent from the raw facts alone. The opinion must, however, relate directly to the issues at trial and not introduce irrelevant or confusing information.

For example, in a personal injury case, a witness might testify that, based on their observation, the plaintiff seemed to be in pain immediately after an accident. This opinion helps the jury assess the severity and immediate impact of the injury, which is a fact in issue in the case.

Exclusion of Specialized Knowledge (Rule 701(c))

The third prong of Rule 701 mandates that lay opinion testimony must not be based on scientific, technical, or other specialized knowledge within the scope of Rule 702. This requirement is intended to maintain a clear distinction between lay and expert testimony.

1. Distinguishing Lay and Expert Testimony

Rule 701(c) ensures that lay witnesses do not offer opinions that require the specialized knowledge, skills, or training typically associated with expert witnesses. Opinions that involve technical or scientific analysis, or that require an understanding of specialized fields, fall under the purview of expert testimony and are governed by Rule 702.

For instance, a lay witness cannot offer an opinion that someone was intoxicated based on a scientific understanding of blood alcohol levels or the effects of alcohol on the body. Such testimony would require an expert's analysis and fall outside the scope of Rule 701.

2. Ensuring Reliability and Relevance

By excluding specialized knowledge from lay opinions, Rule 701(c) helps ensure that lay testimony remains reliable and relevant to the witness's personal experience. This provision prevents lay witnesses from straying into areas where they lack the expertise to offer informed opinions, thereby protecting the integrity of the fact-finding process.

For example, if a witness without medical training offers an opinion about the cause of a medical condition, such testimony would be excluded under Rule 701(c) because it requires specialized medical knowledge.

Judicial Discretion in Applying Rule 701

Judges have significant discretion in determining whether lay opinion testimony meets the criteria outlined in Rule 701. This discretion allows judges to assess the relevance and reliability of such testimony on a case-by-case basis.

1. Evaluating the Basis for the Opinion

Judges must evaluate whether the lay opinion is truly based on the witness's personal perception, as required by Rule 701(a). This involves assessing the witness's familiarity with the facts and their ability to provide a rational opinion based on direct observation.

For instance, a judge might question whether a witness who was briefly at the scene of an incident can reliably offer an opinion about the overall demeanor of a person involved, considering the limited nature of their observation.

2. Assessing Helpfulness to the Fact-Finder

Judges must also consider whether the lay opinion will be helpful to the fact-finder, as required by Rule 701(b). This involves determining whether the opinion clarifies the witness's testimony or aids in resolving a fact in issue, without introducing unnecessary or confusing information.

For example, if a witness's opinion about someone's emotional state does not clearly relate to the issues being litigated, the judge might exclude the opinion on the grounds that it is not helpful to the fact-finder.

3. Ensuring Compliance with Rule 701(c)

Finally, judges must ensure that lay opinions do not stray into areas requiring specialized knowledge, as prohibited by Rule 701(c). This involves scrutinizing the content of the testimony to determine whether it is based on personal perception or whether it implicitly relies on technical or scientific understanding.

For instance, if a witness's opinion about the speed of a car at the time of an accident appears to be based on personal perception rather than on technical calculations, the judge would assess whether the opinion falls within the acceptable scope of lay testimony.

Strategic Considerations for Attorneys

Rule 701 presents both opportunities and challenges for attorneys. Understanding how to effectively introduce or challenge lay opinion testimony is crucial for building a persuasive case and for ensuring that the evidence presented is both admissible and compelling.

1. Crafting Lay Witness Testimony

Attorneys should carefully craft lay witness testimony to ensure that any opinions offered are clearly based on the witness's personal perceptions and that they contribute meaningfully to the fact-finder's understanding of the case. This involves preparing witnesses to articulate the basis for their opinions and to avoid straying into areas requiring specialized knowledge.

For example, when preparing a lay witness to testify about the behavior of a party during a contract negotiation, the attorney should focus on the witness's direct observations (e.g., tone of voice, facial expressions) and ensure that the witness does not offer opinions about the party's intentions or state of mind unless clearly grounded in what they personally observed.

2. Challenging Inadmissible Lay Opinions

When faced with potentially inadmissible lay opinion testimony, attorneys should be prepared to object based on the criteria outlined in Rule 701. This might involve arguing that the opinion lacks a rational basis, is unhelpful to the fact-finder, or encroaches on the domain of expert testimony.

For example, if opposing counsel attempts to introduce a lay witness's opinion about the cause of a mechanical failure, the attorney could object on the grounds that such an opinion requires specialized knowledge and is therefore inadmissible under Rule 701(c).

3. Using Lay Opinions Strategically

Attorneys can use lay opinion testimony strategically to reinforce key aspects of their case, particularly when such opinions provide valuable context or support the overall narrative. This might involve eliciting opinions from witnesses who observed critical events or interactions, provided that their testimony meets the requirements of Rule 701.

For instance, in a case involving alleged negligence, an attorney might use lay opinion testimony to establish that the defendant's behavior was unusual or reckless, based on the observations of a witness who was present at the time. By framing the opinion within the witness's personal experience, the attorney can provide the jury with a relatable and persuasive account of the events.

Rule 702 - Testimony by Expert Witnesses

Text of Rule 702

Rule 702. Testimony by Expert Witnesses
A witness who is qualified as an expert by knowledge, skill, experience, training, or education may testify in the form of an opinion or otherwise if:
(a) **the expert's scientific, technical, or other specialized knowledge will help the trier of fact to understand the evidence or to determine a fact in issue**;
(b) **the testimony is based on sufficient facts or data**;
(c) **the testimony is the product of reliable principles and methods**; and
(d) **the expert has reliably applied the principles and methods to the facts of the case**.

Introduction to Rule 702

Rule 702 of the Federal Rules of Evidence governs the admissibility of testimony by expert witnesses. Expert witnesses play a crucial role in legal proceedings by providing specialized knowledge, skills, or experience that can help the fact-finder understand complex issues that are beyond the common understanding of laypersons. Rule 702 establishes the criteria that must be met for expert testimony to be considered admissible, ensuring that such testimony is both relevant and reliable. This chapter provides a detailed analysis of Rule 702, exploring its text, interpretation, and broader implications for the administration of justice.

Analysis of Rule 702

Rule 702 outlines the foundational requirements for admitting expert testimony in court. The rule is designed to ensure that only qualified experts provide testimony, and that their opinions are based on sound reasoning and reliable methodologies.

Qualification of the Expert Witness

Before addressing the substance of the testimony, Rule 702 requires that the witness be qualified as an expert by virtue of their knowledge, skill, experience, training, or education. This qualification is the threshold requirement for admitting expert testimony.

1. **Criteria for Qualification**

The expert's qualifications must be directly related to the subject matter of the testimony. The qualification can arise from formal education, practical experience, specialized training, or a combination of these factors. The key is that the expert possesses a level of expertise that exceeds that of a layperson and is relevant to the issues in the case.

For example, in a medical malpractice case, a physician with years of experience in the relevant specialty would likely be qualified as an expert on the standard of care. Similarly, an engineer with specialized training in accident reconstruction could be qualified as an expert in a case involving a vehicular collision.

2. **Judicial Discretion in Determining Qualification**

The court has broad discretion in determining whether a witness is qualified to testify as an expert. This decision is based on the witness's credentials and the relevance of their expertise to the issues at trial. The court must ensure that the expert's qualifications are sufficient to support the opinions they intend to offer.

For instance, if a witness with a general engineering background is offered as an expert in a case involving highly specialized aerospace engineering issues, the court may require additional evidence of the witness's qualifications before allowing them to testify as an expert.

Helpfulness to the Trier of Fact (Rule 702(a))

Rule 702(a) requires that the expert's testimony be helpful to the trier of fact in understanding the evidence or determining a fact in issue. This provision emphasizes the necessity of expert testimony being relevant and aiding the court or jury in resolving the case.

1. **Relevance and Assistance**

The expert's testimony must provide insights that the trier of fact could not obtain without the expert's specialized knowledge. This means that the testimony must address issues that are beyond the common understanding of laypersons and that it directly relates to the matters at hand in the case.

For example, in a patent infringement case, expert testimony might be necessary to explain complex technical aspects of the patented technology and how the alleged infringing product operates. Such testimony would be considered helpful under Rule 702(a) because it assists the jury in understanding technical details that are crucial to determining infringement.

2. **Avoiding Needless Complication**

Expert testimony should not be admitted if it merely complicates the issues or confuses the trier of fact. The court must ensure that the testimony is not only relevant but also presented in a way that clarifies rather than obscures the issues.

For instance, if an expert's testimony involves overly technical jargon or concepts that are not directly related to the core issues, the court may exclude or limit the testimony to ensure that the jury remains focused on the pertinent facts.

Basis of the Testimony: Sufficient Facts or Data (Rule 702(b))

Rule 702(b) requires that the expert's testimony be based on sufficient facts or data. This requirement ensures that the expert's opinions are grounded in a reliable factual foundation and not merely speculative or conjectural.

1. Adequate Factual Foundation

The expert's opinion must be based on a thorough and reliable examination of the relevant facts or data. This could include the expert's own observations, the review of documents or physical evidence, or data provided by the parties. The court must be satisfied that the expert's opinion is supported by a sufficient factual basis.

For example, a forensic accountant offering testimony on financial fraud would need to base their opinions on a detailed analysis of financial records, bank statements, and other relevant data. The court would assess whether the expert had sufficient access to and understanding of these materials to form a reliable opinion.

2. Assessment by the Court

The court must evaluate whether the facts or data on which the expert relies are sufficient to support the opinions offered. This evaluation involves considering the quantity, quality, and relevance of the information used by the expert in forming their conclusions.

For instance, if an expert relies on outdated or incomplete data to form an opinion about market trends, the court might question the sufficiency of the data and consider excluding the testimony or limiting its scope.

Reliability of Principles and Methods (Rule 702(c))

Rule 702(c) requires that the expert's testimony be the product of reliable principles and methods. This provision ensures that the methodologies used by the expert are scientifically valid and generally accepted in the relevant field.

1. Scientific Validity

The principles and methods underlying the expert's testimony must be scientifically valid, meaning they are based on sound scientific principles that have been tested, peer-reviewed, and widely accepted in the relevant discipline. This requirement is particularly important in fields such as medicine, engineering, and the natural sciences.

For example, if an expert in environmental science testifies about the impact of a pollutant on public health, their testimony must be based on established scientific methods for measuring and analyzing pollutant exposure and its effects on human health.

2. General Acceptance

The methods used by the expert should be generally accepted by other professionals in the field. This criterion, often referred to as the "Daubert standard" (from the Supreme Court case *Daubert v. Merrell Dow*

Pharmaceuticals, Inc.), is used by courts to assess whether the expert's methods are reliable enough to be presented to the trier of fact.

For instance, if an expert uses a novel or unconventional method to analyze evidence, the court may require proof that the method is accepted within the relevant scientific community before allowing the testimony.

Application of Principles and Methods (Rule 702(d))

Rule 702(d) requires that the expert has reliably applied the principles and methods to the facts of the case. This provision ensures that the expert's methodology is not only reliable in theory but also applied correctly in the specific context of the case.

1. Consistency and Accuracy

The expert must apply their methods consistently and accurately to the facts at hand. This involves ensuring that the methods are used appropriately and that the expert's conclusions are logically derived from the application of these methods to the facts.

For example, if an expert in accident reconstruction testifies about the cause of a car crash, they must apply established principles of physics and engineering to the specific details of the accident (such as speed, angle of impact, and road conditions) to reach their conclusions.

2. Judicial Scrutiny

The court must scrutinize whether the expert has properly applied the principles and methods to the facts of the case. This includes evaluating whether the expert's conclusions follow logically from their analysis and whether any assumptions or extrapolations made by the expert are justified by the evidence.

For instance, if an expert makes assumptions about missing data or extrapolates findings from a limited dataset, the court may question whether these steps are scientifically valid and whether they undermine the reliability of the expert's conclusions.

Judicial Discretion and the Gatekeeping Role

Under Rule 702, judges serve as gatekeepers, ensuring that only reliable and relevant expert testimony is presented to the trier of fact. This gatekeeping function requires judges to evaluate the qualifications of the expert, the relevance of their testimony, the sufficiency of the underlying facts, and the reliability of the principles and methods used.

1. Gatekeeping Responsibilities

Judges must carefully assess whether the expert testimony meets all the criteria set forth in Rule 702. This involves conducting pre-trial hearings, known as *Daubert* hearings, to determine the admissibility of the expert testimony. During these hearings, the judge evaluates the expert's qualifications, the relevance of their testimony, and the reliability of the methodologies used.

For example, in a product liability case, the judge might hold a *Daubert* hearing to determine whether the plaintiff's expert, who intends to testify about the alleged defect in a product, is using scientifically valid methods to reach their conclusions.

2. Exclusion of Unreliable Testimony

If the judge determines that the expert's testimony does not meet the standards of Rule 702, they may exclude the testimony entirely or limit its scope. This exclusion is crucial for ensuring that the jury is not misled by unreliable or irrelevant expert opinions.

For instance, if an expert's testimony is based on speculative assumptions or untested methods, the judge may exclude the testimony to prevent the jury from giving undue weight to unreliable evidence.

Strategic Considerations for Attorneys

Rule 702 presents both opportunities and challenges for attorneys in managing expert testimony. Understanding how to effectively present or challenge expert testimony is essential for building a persuasive case.

1. Selecting the Right Expert

Attorneys must carefully select experts who are not only qualified but also capable of presenting their opinions in a clear and convincing manner. This involves considering the expert's credentials, experience, and ability to communicate complex ideas to a lay audience.

For example, in a medical malpractice case, an attorney might seek out a physician with extensive experience in the relevant specialty, as well as a strong track record of explaining medical concepts in understandable terms.

2. Preparing Expert Testimony

Attorneys should work closely with their experts to ensure that their testimony is based on sufficient facts or data, that they use reliable methods, and that they apply these methods appropriately to the facts of the case. This preparation is essential for meeting the requirements of Rule 702 and for withstanding challenges from the opposing party.

For instance, an attorney might conduct mock direct and cross-examinations with their expert to ensure that the expert's testimony is coherent, well-supported, and able to withstand scrutiny.

3. Challenging Opposing Experts

When faced with opposing expert testimony, attorneys must be prepared to challenge the qualifications of the expert, the relevance of their testimony, the sufficiency of the underlying data, or the reliability of the methods used. This often involves filing pre-trial motions to exclude or limit the testimony under Rule 702.

For example, if the opposing expert is using an unconventional method that lacks general acceptance in the relevant field, the attorney might file a motion to exclude the testimony on the grounds that it fails to meet the reliability standard set forth in Rule 702.

Rule 703 - Bases of an Expert's Opinion Testimony

Rule 703. Bases of an Expert's Opinion Testimony
An expert may base an opinion on facts or data in the case that the expert has been made aware of or personally observed. If experts in the particular field would reasonably rely on those kinds of facts or data in forming an opinion on the subject, they need not be admissible for the opinion to be admitted. But if the facts or data would otherwise be inadmissible, the proponent of the opinion may disclose them to the jury only if their probative value in helping the jury evaluate the opinion substantially outweighs their prejudicial effect.

Introduction to Rule 703

Rule 703 of the Federal Rules of Evidence addresses the foundational basis upon which expert witnesses may form their opinions. This rule allows experts to rely on various types of information when forming their opinions, even if that information would not be admissible in court on its own. Rule 703 is designed to ensure that expert testimony is grounded in reliable and relevant data, while also recognizing the unique nature of expert analysis, which often requires consideration of information that may not meet traditional evidentiary standards. This chapter provides a detailed analysis of Rule 703, exploring its text, interpretation, and broader implications for the administration of justice.

Analysis of Rule 703

Rule 703 provides the framework for determining the admissibility of the bases of an expert's opinion testimony. It allows experts to form opinions based on a wide range of information, recognizing the specialized nature of expert analysis while also setting boundaries to protect the fairness of the trial process.

Permissible Bases for Expert Opinions

Rule 703 allows experts to base their opinions on facts or data that they have been made aware of or have personally observed. This provision reflects the understanding that experts, due to their specialized knowledge, may need to rely on information from various sources to form a well-supported opinion.

1. Facts or Data Personally Observed

Experts may base their opinions on facts or data that they have personally observed. This includes information that the expert has directly witnessed or gathered through their own investigation or examination.

For example, a forensic pathologist might base their opinion on an autopsy they conducted, using the physical findings from the autopsy to determine the cause of death. This type of data, which the expert has directly observed, forms a reliable foundation for their opinion.

2. Facts or Data Made Aware Of

Experts may also base their opinions on facts or data that they have been made aware of, even if they did not personally observe this information. This can include information provided by other witnesses, documents, reports, or any other materials relevant to the case.

For instance, an economic expert might base their opinion on financial statements, market analyses, and statistical reports provided by the parties in a case. Although the expert did not create these documents, they are considered reliable sources of information in the expert's field, and thus, the expert can use them to form an opinion.

Reasonable Reliance Standard

Under Rule 703, the facts or data upon which an expert bases their opinion need not be admissible in court, provided that experts in the particular field would reasonably rely on those kinds of facts or data in forming an opinion on the subject. This "reasonable reliance" standard is a key aspect of Rule 703, as it acknowledges the unique methodologies and standards of practice in different expert fields.

1. Industry Standards for Reliance

The reasonable reliance standard means that the court must consider whether experts in the relevant field typically rely on similar types of information when forming their opinions. This involves evaluating whether the expert's reliance on certain facts or data is consistent with the practices and norms of their profession.

For example, medical experts often rely on patient histories, diagnostic tests, and medical literature to form their opinions. These sources of information may include hearsay or other types of evidence that would not be admissible in court, but they are considered reliable in the medical field.

2. Judicial Determination of Reasonableness

The court plays a crucial role in determining whether the expert's reliance on certain facts or data is reasonable. This determination is made on a case-by-case basis, considering the specific circumstances of the case and the standards of the expert's field.

For instance, if an expert in environmental science bases their opinion on data collected by third-party researchers, the court must assess whether it is standard practice in that field to rely on such data. If it is, the court will likely deem the expert's reliance reasonable and allow the opinion to be admitted.

Admissibility of Underlying Facts or Data

While Rule 703 allows experts to base their opinions on facts or data that are not admissible in court, it also provides guidelines for when and how this underlying information can be disclosed to the jury.

1. Disclosure to the Jury

If the underlying facts or data are themselves inadmissible, the proponent of the expert's opinion may disclose them to the jury only if their probative value in helping the jury evaluate the expert's opinion substantially outweighs their prejudicial effect. This provision ensures that the jury is not unduly influenced by information that would otherwise be excluded from the trial.

For example, if an expert's opinion is based in part on hearsay statements from witnesses who are not testifying in court, the court must carefully weigh whether disclosing these statements to the jury would help them understand the expert's opinion or whether it would create unfair prejudice.

2. Balancing Probative Value and Prejudice

The court must balance the probative value of the inadmissible facts or data against their potential prejudicial impact. This balancing test is crucial for maintaining the fairness of the trial while allowing the jury to fully understand the basis of the expert's opinion.

For instance, if an expert's opinion is based on a report that includes graphic or inflammatory details, the court may determine that the risk of prejudice outweighs the benefit of disclosing the report to the jury. In such cases, the expert may testify about their opinion without revealing the specific contents of the report.

Judicial Discretion in Applying Rule 703

Judges have significant discretion in applying Rule 703, particularly in determining whether the expert's reliance on certain facts or data is reasonable and whether the underlying information should be disclosed to the jury.

1. Evaluating Reasonableness

Judges must evaluate whether the expert's reliance on particular facts or data meets the reasonable reliance standard. This involves assessing the expert's field of expertise, the nature of the information relied upon, and the relevance of that information to the issues in the case.

For example, in a case involving complex financial transactions, the judge must determine whether the financial expert's reliance on certain market analyses or economic forecasts is consistent with standard practices in the financial industry.

2. Managing the Disclosure of Inadmissible Information

Judges are responsible for managing the disclosure of inadmissible facts or data to the jury. This requires careful consideration of the potential impact of such information on the jury's decision-making process and ensuring that any disclosure is necessary for the jury to understand the expert's opinion.

For instance, if an expert's opinion is based on a statistical study that includes sensitive or controversial data, the judge might decide to limit the disclosure of this information to the jury, providing only the portions that are directly relevant to the expert's conclusions.

Strategic Considerations for Attorneys

Rule 703 presents both opportunities and challenges for attorneys in managing expert testimony. Understanding how to effectively introduce or challenge the bases of an expert's opinion is crucial for building a persuasive case.

1. Selecting and Preparing Expert Testimony

Attorneys must carefully select experts who not only have the necessary qualifications but also rely on sound and generally accepted methods in their field. This involves ensuring that the expert's opinions are based on reliable and relevant data, even if some of that data would not be admissible in court.

For example, an attorney might work with an expert to identify the key sources of information that support the expert's opinion, ensuring that these sources are consistent with industry standards and that the expert can effectively explain their relevance to the case.

2. Challenging the Bases of Opposing Experts

When challenging opposing expert testimony, attorneys should focus on whether the expert's reliance on certain facts or data is reasonable and whether the information used is sufficiently reliable. This might involve questioning the expert's methodology, the quality of the data relied upon, or the general acceptance of the expert's approach within their field.

For instance, if an opposing expert bases their opinion on a study that has been widely criticized or is outdated, the attorney might challenge the admissibility of the expert's testimony by arguing that it fails to meet the reasonable reliance standard set forth in Rule 703.

3. Managing Disclosure Issues

Attorneys must also be strategic in managing the disclosure of inadmissible information underlying an expert's opinion. This involves weighing the benefits of disclosing such information to the jury against the risks of potential prejudice and being prepared to argue for or against disclosure based on the specific circumstances of the case.

For example, if an expert's opinion is based on confidential business records, the attorney might argue that disclosing the specific contents of these records to the jury would be prejudicial and unnecessary for understanding the expert's conclusions.

Rule 704 - Opinion on an Ultimate Issue

Text of Rule 704

Rule 704. Opinion on an Ultimate Issue
(a) **In General—Not Automatically Objectionable.** An opinion is not objectionable just because it embraces an ultimate issue.
(b) **Exception.** In a criminal case, an expert witness must not state an opinion about whether the defendant did or did not have a mental state or condition that constitutes an element of the crime charged or of a defense. Those matters are for the trier of fact alone.

Introduction to Rule 704

Rule 704 of the Federal Rules of Evidence addresses the admissibility of opinion testimony concerning an ultimate issue in a case. Traditionally, courts were cautious about allowing witnesses, particularly experts, to testify on issues that were considered to be the ultimate issues in a case— those that the trier of fact (judge or jury) is tasked with deciding. However, Rule 704 relaxes this restriction, allowing witnesses, including experts, to offer opinions on ultimate issues, provided that such opinions comply with other evidentiary rules and do not infringe on the trier of fact's role. This chapter provides a detailed analysis of Rule 704, exploring its text, interpretation, and broader implications for the administration of justice.

Analysis of Rule 704

Rule 704 allows for the admission of opinion testimony that addresses ultimate issues in a case, subject to specific limitations. This rule reflects a shift from earlier judicial practices that strictly limited such testimony, recognizing that opinions on ultimate issues can sometimes be helpful to the trier of fact.

Opinion on Ultimate Issues (Rule 704(a))

Rule 704(a) states that an opinion is not automatically objectionable merely because it embraces an ultimate issue in the case. This provision allows both lay and expert witnesses to offer opinions on matters that the trier of fact must ultimately decide.

1. Embracing the Ultimate Issue

The term "ultimate issue" refers to the key questions or conclusions that the trier of fact is responsible for resolving in a case. These might include determinations of liability, guilt, intent, or causation. Under Rule 704(a), a witness's opinion on such matters is admissible, provided it meets the other requirements for admissibility under the Federal Rules of Evidence.

For example, in a civil case involving a car accident, an expert witness in accident reconstruction may testify that, in their opinion, the defendant's vehicle was traveling at an excessive speed at the time of the accident, thus contributing to the collision. This opinion directly addresses an ultimate issue— whether the defendant's actions were negligent—but is not automatically objectionable under Rule 704(a).

2. Support for the Trier of Fact

The rationale behind Rule 704(a) is that opinions on ultimate issues can assist the trier of fact in understanding complex or technical matters, provided that the testimony does not usurp the trier of fact's role in making the final determination. The rule recognizes that expert testimony, in particular, can offer valuable insights into issues that require specialized knowledge or analysis.

For instance, in a medical malpractice case, an expert might testify that the defendant doctor's failure to diagnose a condition fell below the accepted standard of care and directly led to the patient's injury. This opinion on the ultimate issue of negligence aids the jury in making an informed decision based on the expert's specialized knowledge.

Limitation in Criminal Cases (Rule 704(b))

While Rule 704(a) permits opinion testimony on ultimate issues, Rule 704(b) imposes a significant limitation in criminal cases. Specifically, it prohibits expert witnesses from stating opinions about whether the defendant had a mental state or condition that constitutes an element of the crime charged or a defense. This limitation underscores the importance of preserving the trier of fact's role in making determinations about the defendant's state of mind.

1. Prohibited Testimony on Mental States

Rule 704(b) reflects the principle that certain determinations—specifically those related to a defendant's mental state—are the exclusive domain of the trier of fact. In criminal cases, questions of intent, knowledge, recklessness, or other mental states are often central to the case, and the rule prevents expert witnesses from directly opining on these matters.

For example, in a criminal trial where the defendant is charged with first-degree murder, an expert witness, such as a forensic psychologist, may testify about the defendant's mental health or cognitive abilities. However, the expert is prohibited from stating an opinion on whether the defendant actually intended to kill the victim, as this determination is reserved for the jury.

2. Protecting the Role of the Trier of Fact

The limitation in Rule 704(b) is designed to protect the integrity of the fact-finding process by ensuring that the trier of fact remains the sole arbiter of the defendant's mental state. This restriction prevents experts from unduly influencing the jury's decision by offering opinions on matters that require a subjective assessment of the defendant's intent or state of mind.

For instance, in a case where the defense is arguing that the defendant lacked the mental capacity to form the intent necessary for a conviction, an expert might explain the defendant's psychological condition and its potential effects on behavior. However, the expert cannot explicitly state that the defendant did not form the required intent, as this conclusion must be drawn by the jury based on all the evidence presented.

Judicial Discretion in Applying Rule 704

Judges have significant discretion in applying Rule 704, particularly in determining whether an opinion on an ultimate issue is admissible and whether it complies with the limitations set forth in the rule.

1. **Evaluating the Admissibility of Ultimate Issue Opinions**

Judges must assess whether an opinion on an ultimate issue meets the standards of relevance, reliability, and helpfulness as required by other rules of evidence, such as Rule 702 (testimony by expert witnesses) and Rule 403 (exclusion of evidence based on prejudice, confusion, or waste of time). This assessment ensures that the testimony is not only relevant but also appropriate for aiding the trier of fact.

For example, a judge might allow an expert in forensic accounting to testify that, in their opinion, the financial discrepancies in a case suggest fraudulent activity. However, the judge must ensure that the testimony is based on reliable methods and does not overstep into the jury's role by dictating a conclusion about the defendant's guilt.

2. **Ensuring Compliance with Rule 704(b)**

In criminal cases, judges must carefully monitor expert testimony to ensure that it does not violate Rule 704(b). This involves evaluating the expert's statements to determine whether they are offering an opinion on the defendant's mental state in a way that encroaches on the jury's responsibilities.

For instance, if an expert begins to testify in a manner that seems to suggest a conclusion about the defendant's intent, the judge might intervene, reminding the expert to refrain from making statements that would violate Rule 704(b) and to focus on describing the defendant's condition in general terms.

Strategic Considerations for Attorneys

Rule 704 offers both opportunities and challenges for attorneys in managing opinion testimony on ultimate issues. Understanding how to effectively introduce or challenge such testimony is crucial for shaping the narrative of a case.

1. **Introducing Opinion Testimony on Ultimate Issues**

Attorneys should strategically use opinion testimony on ultimate issues to reinforce key aspects of their case. This might involve carefully selecting expert witnesses who can provide clear, persuasive opinions that align with the case's theory while ensuring that these opinions comply with the rules of evidence.

For example, in a product liability case, an attorney might present an expert who testifies that the design defect in the product directly caused the plaintiff's injury. This opinion directly addresses the ultimate issue of causation and can be a powerful tool in persuading the jury.

2. **Challenging Improper Opinions**

When opposing opinion testimony on ultimate issues, attorneys should be prepared to challenge the admissibility of such testimony, particularly in criminal cases where Rule 704(b) applies. This might involve objecting to opinions that infringe on the trier of fact's role or that are not based on reliable methods.

For instance, if the prosecution in a criminal trial attempts to introduce expert testimony that implicitly suggests the defendant had the intent to commit the crime, the defense attorney should object on the grounds that this violates Rule 704(b) and oversteps the expert's role.

3. **Crafting Jury Instructions**

Attorneys should also consider how to address ultimate issue opinions in jury instructions. This might involve requesting specific instructions that clarify the jury's role in evaluating expert testimony and emphasize that the final determination of ultimate issues rests with the jury.

For example, in a case where expert testimony has addressed an ultimate issue, the attorney might request a jury instruction that reminds jurors they are not bound by the expert's opinion and must independently evaluate all the evidence presented.

Rule 705 - Disclosing the Facts or Data Underlying an Expert's Opinion

---

Rule 705. Disclosing the Facts or Data Underlying an Expert's Opinion

---

Unless the court orders otherwise, an expert may state an opinion—and give the reasons for it—without first testifying to the underlying facts or data. But the expert may be required to disclose those facts or data on cross-examination.

Introduction to Rule 705

Rule 705 of the Federal Rules of Evidence addresses the manner in which an expert witness may disclose the facts or data that underlie their opinion during testimony. This rule provides experts with flexibility in presenting their opinions without initially being required to disclose the underlying facts or data. However, it also protects the opposing party's right to probe the basis of the expert's opinion through cross-examination. Rule 705 balances the need for efficiency in expert testimony with the need for transparency and thoroughness in the fact-finding process. This chapter provides a detailed analysis of Rule 705, exploring its text, interpretation, and broader implications for the administration of justice.

Analysis of Rule 705

Rule 705 provides a framework for how expert witnesses may present their opinions in court, specifically addressing the disclosure of the facts or data that form the basis of those opinions. The rule allows for a streamlined presentation of expert testimony, while also ensuring that the underlying basis for the opinion can be fully explored during cross-examination.

Stating an Opinion Without Disclosing Underlying Facts or Data

The primary provision of Rule 705 allows an expert witness to state their opinion—and the reasons for that opinion—without first testifying to the underlying facts or data. This approach is designed to facilitate the efficient presentation of expert testimony, allowing the expert to focus initially on their conclusions rather than on the detailed factual foundation of those conclusions.

1. **Efficiency in Presentation**

By permitting experts to present their opinions without immediate reference to the underlying facts or data, Rule 705 aims to streamline the testimony process. This can be particularly useful in cases where the facts or data are complex or voluminous, and where a detailed exposition of those facts would unduly prolong the testimony or distract from the expert's main conclusions.

For example, in a complex financial fraud case, an expert accountant might testify that, in their opinion, the defendant engaged in fraudulent activities based on an analysis of financial records. Under Rule 705, the expert can initially present this conclusion without having to immediately explain each piece of financial data they reviewed.

2. **Judicial Discretion**

While Rule 705 generally allows experts to withhold the underlying facts or data initially, the court retains the discretion to require the expert to disclose these details before stating their opinion. This may occur in situations where the court determines that a full understanding of the expert's opinion requires a preliminary discussion of the underlying facts or data.

For instance, if an expert's opinion is highly dependent on specific, disputed data points, the court might order that the expert disclose these facts before offering their opinion to ensure that the jury or judge has a clear understanding of the basis for the testimony.

Cross-Examination and Disclosure of Underlying Facts or Data

While Rule 705 allows experts to present their opinions without initially disclosing the underlying facts or data, it also ensures that the opposing party has the opportunity to challenge the basis of the expert's testimony during cross-examination. This provision is crucial for maintaining the fairness and thoroughness of the trial process.

1. **Right to Cross-Examination**

The opposing party has the right to require the expert to disclose the facts or data underlying their opinion during cross-examination. This right is essential for testing the reliability and credibility of the expert's testimony, as it allows the opposing party to probe the foundation of the expert's conclusions and to identify any weaknesses, inconsistencies, or errors.

For example, if an expert witness testifies that a particular chemical caused an injury, the opposing counsel may cross-examine the expert by requiring them to disclose the studies, data, or other information that supports this conclusion. The cross-examination might reveal that the expert's opinion is based on a limited or flawed dataset, thereby weakening the testimony's impact.

2. **Impact on the Trier of Fact**

The ability to cross-examine an expert on the facts or data underlying their opinion helps ensure that the trier of fact—whether judge or jury—has a complete understanding of the expert's testimony. This process allows the fact-finder to weigh the expert's conclusions in light of the disclosed facts or data, leading to a more informed and balanced decision.

For instance, after an expert has been cross-examined on the basis of their opinion, the jury might find that the disclosed data does not fully support the expert's conclusions, leading them to give less weight to the testimony.

Strategic Considerations for Attorneys

Rule 705 presents strategic opportunities and challenges for attorneys in managing expert testimony. Understanding how to effectively present or challenge the disclosure of underlying facts or data is crucial for shaping the narrative of a case.

1. Strategic Use of Rule 705 by the Proponent

Attorneys who present expert witnesses may strategically use Rule 705 to focus the initial testimony on the expert's conclusions and reasoning, without becoming bogged down in the details of the underlying facts or data. This approach can help to present a clear and compelling narrative to the jury, while leaving the detailed examination of the facts or data for cross-examination.

For example, in a medical malpractice case, the plaintiff's attorney might have an expert witness testify that the standard of care was breached, initially focusing on the expert's professional judgment and reasoning. The detailed medical records and other data that support this opinion can then be addressed if and when the defense challenges the testimony during cross-examination.

2. Challenging Expert Testimony on Cross-Examination

For the opposing party, Rule 705 provides an opportunity to challenge the expert's testimony by probing the underlying facts or data during cross-examination. This strategy can be particularly effective in exposing weaknesses in the expert's conclusions or demonstrating that the expert's opinion is based on incomplete or questionable data.

For instance, if an expert's opinion is based on a small sample size or outdated research, the opposing attorney might focus cross-examination on these points to undermine the expert's credibility and the weight of their testimony.

3. Pre-Trial Preparation and Discovery

Attorneys must also consider the role of discovery in preparing for the application of Rule 705. Pre-trial discovery allows attorneys to obtain the facts or data that the expert relied upon, enabling them to prepare for effective cross-examination. By thoroughly understanding the basis of the expert's opinion before trial, the attorney can craft a more precise and targeted cross-examination.

For example, an attorney might use discovery to obtain all of the studies, reports, and data that an expert reviewed in forming their opinion. Armed with this information, the attorney can identify potential weaknesses or inconsistencies in the expert's analysis and prepare to exploit these during cross-examination.

Judicial Discretion in Applying Rule 705

Judges have significant discretion in applying Rule 705, particularly in determining whether to require the disclosure of underlying facts or data before an expert states their opinion, and in managing the scope of cross-examination.

1. Requiring Pre-Disclosure of Facts or Data

Judges may exercise discretion in deciding whether to require an expert to disclose the facts or data underlying their opinion before stating that opinion. This decision is typically made on a case-by-case basis, depending on the complexity of the issues, the clarity of the expert's testimony, and the potential for confusion or misunderstanding by the trier of fact.

For example, in a case where the expert's opinion hinges on a highly technical analysis that is difficult for laypersons to understand, the judge might order the expert to first explain the key data and methods used, thereby providing context for the opinion.

2. Managing Cross-Examination

Judges also have a role in managing cross-examination under Rule 705. This includes ensuring that cross-examination remains focused on relevant issues and that the opposing party's inquiry into the underlying facts or data is conducted in a fair and orderly manner. Judges must balance the need for thorough cross-examination with the risk of confusing or overwhelming the jury with excessive detail.

For instance, if an attorney's cross-examination becomes overly detailed or strays into irrelevant areas, the judge may limit the questioning to ensure that the testimony remains focused and comprehensible to the jury.

Rule 706 - Court-Appointed Expert Witnesses

Text of Rule 706

Rule 706. Court-Appointed Expert Witnesses
(a) **Appointment Process.** On a party's motion or on its own, the court may order the parties to show cause why expert witnesses should not be appointed and may ask the parties to submit nominations. The court may appoint any expert that the parties agree on and any of its own choosing. But the court may only appoint someone who consents to act.
(b) **Expert's Role.** The court must inform the expert of the expert's duties. The court may do so in writing and have a copy filed with the clerk or may do so orally at a conference in which the parties have an opportunity to participate. The expert:
• (1) must advise the parties of any findings the expert makes;
• (2) may be deposed by any party;
• (3) may be called to testify by the court or any party; and
• (4) may be cross-examined by any party, including the party that called the expert.
(c) **Compensation.** The expert is entitled to a reasonable compensation, as set by the court. The compensation is payable as follows:
• (1) in a civil case, by the parties in the proportion and at the time that the court directs—and the compensation is then charged like other costs; and
• (2) in a criminal case, or in any civil case in which law provides for compensation, the compensation is payable from any funds that are provided by law.
(d) **Disclosing the Appointment to the Jury.** The court may authorize disclosure to the jury that the court appointed the expert.
(e) **Parties' Choice of Their Own Experts.** This rule does not limit a party in calling its own experts.

Introduction to Rule 706

Rule 706 of the Federal Rules of Evidence provides the legal framework for the appointment of expert witnesses by the court. Unlike expert witnesses who are selected and retained by the parties to a case, court-appointed experts are chosen by the judge to provide an impartial and unbiased opinion on matters that require specialized knowledge. The use of court-appointed experts is relatively rare and typically reserved for cases where the issues are particularly complex or contentious, and where the court determines that an independent expert opinion would assist in the fair resolution of the case. This chapter provides a detailed analysis of Rule 706, exploring its text, interpretation, and broader implications for the administration of justice.

Analysis of Rule 706

Rule 706 establishes the procedures and guidelines for the appointment, role, and compensation of court-appointed expert witnesses. It ensures that such experts operate independently from the parties and that their input aids the court in resolving complex or technical issues fairly and impartially.

Appointment Process (Rule 706(a))

Rule 706(a) outlines the process by which a court may appoint an expert witness. This process can be initiated either on the court's own motion or at the request of a party. The rule provides the court with broad discretion in selecting experts, while also allowing the parties to participate in the nomination and selection process.

1. Initiating the Appointment

The court may decide to appoint an expert witness when it determines that an impartial expert opinion is necessary to resolve complex or technical issues that are beyond the common understanding of the court or jury. This decision can be made on the court's initiative or in response to a motion from one of the parties.

For example, in a case involving highly technical patent claims, the court might find that an independent expert in the relevant field of technology is needed to assist in understanding the intricacies of the patents at issue.

2. Party Participation

While the court has the authority to select an expert, Rule 706(a) encourages party involvement in the process. The court may ask the parties to submit nominations for potential experts and may appoint an expert that the parties agree upon. However, the court retains the ultimate discretion to appoint an expert of its own choosing, provided that the expert consents to serve in this capacity.

For instance, in a medical malpractice case, both parties might agree on a particular physician to serve as a court-appointed expert. If the court concurs and the physician consents, the court can formally appoint the physician as the expert witness.

Role and Duties of the Court-Appointed Expert (Rule 706(b))

Rule 706(b) defines the role and duties of a court-appointed expert. The court is responsible for informing the expert of their duties, which can be communicated either in writing or orally, and the expert's findings must be shared with all parties.

1. Communication of Duties

The court must clearly outline the expert's duties, ensuring that the expert understands the scope of their role, the nature of the issues they are to address, and the expectations for their conduct. This communication can occur in writing, with a copy filed with the clerk, or orally during a conference in which the parties have the opportunity to participate.

For example, the court may instruct a court-appointed economist to assess the economic impact of a proposed antitrust settlement, detailing the specific economic models and data the expert should consider.

2. Reporting and Testifying

The court-appointed expert is required to advise the parties of any findings they make. This transparency ensures that the parties have access to the expert's conclusions and can prepare for further examination. The expert may also be deposed by any party, called to testify by the court or any party, and cross-examined by any party, including the one that called the expert.

For instance, if a court-appointed forensic accountant finds evidence of financial irregularities in a case, they must inform both parties of their findings. The expert can then be called to testify and will be subject to cross-examination by both parties, allowing the adversarial process to test the expert's conclusions.

Compensation of the Court-Appointed Expert (Rule 706(c))

Rule 706(c) addresses the compensation of court-appointed experts, ensuring that they receive reasonable payment for their services, and it specifies how this compensation is to be allocated between the parties or paid from public funds.

1. Reasonable Compensation

The court is responsible for setting the amount of compensation for the expert, which must be reasonable given the nature and scope of the expert's work. This ensures that experts are fairly compensated for their time and expertise, reflecting the professional standards in their field.

For example, in a case requiring extensive scientific analysis, the court might set a higher rate of compensation for a court-appointed scientist than for an expert providing a straightforward financial assessment.

2. Allocation of Costs

In civil cases, the court may order the parties to share the costs of the expert's compensation in a manner it deems fair. The court's decision on cost allocation may consider factors such as the parties' financial resources and the extent to which each party benefits from the expert's testimony. The compensation is then charged like other court costs.

For instance, in a complex environmental litigation case, the court might direct that the costs of the court-appointed environmental expert be split equally between the plaintiff and the defendant.

In criminal cases, or civil cases where the law provides for compensation, the expert's payment is typically made from public funds. This provision ensures that the expert's services are accessible even in cases where the parties might not have the financial means to cover the costs.

Disclosure of the Appointment to the Jury (Rule 706(d))

Rule 706(d) permits the court to inform the jury that the expert witness has been appointed by the court. This disclosure can enhance the perceived impartiality and credibility of the expert's testimony, as the jury may view the court-appointed expert as a neutral figure without ties to either party.

1. Discretionary Disclosure

The decision to disclose the court-appointed status of the expert to the jury is at the discretion of the court. The court must weigh whether such disclosure will assist the jury in evaluating the expert's testimony or whether it might introduce potential biases or undue influence.

For example, in a highly contested medical malpractice trial, the court might inform the jury that the expert testifying about the standard of care was appointed by the court to ensure impartiality, thereby potentially lending greater weight to the expert's opinion.

2. Impact on Jury Perception

Informing the jury that an expert is court-appointed may lead the jury to view the expert's testimony as more objective or trustworthy. However, the court must also be cautious not to overemphasize this fact in a way that might unduly sway the jury or diminish the role of the experts retained by the parties.

For instance, the court might choose to simply mention the appointment during jury instructions or when the expert is first introduced, avoiding any suggestion that the court-appointed expert's testimony should be given more weight than that of the parties' experts.

Parties' Use of Their Own Experts (Rule 706(e))

Rule 706(e) clarifies that the appointment of a court-appointed expert does not preclude the parties from calling their own experts. This provision preserves the adversarial nature of the proceedings by allowing each party to present expert testimony that supports their respective positions.

1. Retaining and Presenting Party-Selected Experts

Even when the court appoints an expert, the parties retain the right to select and present their own experts to provide additional perspectives or to challenge the findings of the court-appointed expert. This ensures that the parties can fully advocate for their positions and that the trier of fact has access to a range of expert opinions.

For example, in a case involving disputed medical testimony, both the plaintiff and the defendant might present their own medical experts in addition to the court-appointed expert. The jury would then hear from all experts before making a determination.

2. Balancing Court-Appointed and Party-Selected Expert Testimony

The court must carefully balance the testimony of court-appointed experts with that of party-selected experts to ensure that the trial remains fair and that the jury is not unduly influenced by the status of the court-appointed expert. The goal is to allow all relevant expert testimony to be considered on its merits, without giving undue preference to any one expert.

For instance, during closing arguments, the court might instruct the jury to consider the qualifications and reasoning of all experts equally, regardless of whether they were appointed by the court or retained by the parties.

Judicial Discretion and Practical Considerations

Judges have broad discretion in applying Rule 706, particularly in deciding whether to appoint an expert, selecting the expert, and managing the expert's involvement in the case.

1. Deciding When to Appoint an Expert

Judges must carefully consider whether the appointment of an expert is necessary for resolving the issues in the case. Factors to consider include the complexity of the technical issues, the potential for bias in party-selected experts, and the need for an impartial assessment to aid the trier of fact.

For example, in a case involving highly technical environmental science, where the parties present conflicting expert testimony, the judge might decide that appointing an independent environmental expert is necessary to provide a neutral perspective.

2. Selecting and Managing the Expert

The selection of a court-appointed expert requires careful consideration of the expert's qualifications, impartiality, and willingness to serve. Once appointed, the judge must ensure that the expert's role is clearly defined and that their findings are communicated effectively to the parties and the court.

For instance, the judge might hold periodic status conferences with the court-appointed expert to ensure that the expert's work is progressing as planned and that any issues or concerns are addressed promptly.

ARTICLE VIII. HEARSAY

Rule 801 - Definitions That Apply to This Article; Exclusions from Hearsay

---

Text of Rule 801

Rule 801. Definitions That Apply to This Article; Exclusions from Hearsay
(a) **Statement.** "Statement" means a person's oral assertion, written assertion, or nonverbal conduct, if the person intended it as an assertion.
(b) **Declarant.** "Declarant" means the person who made the statement.
(c) **Hearsay.** "Hearsay" means a statement that:
• (1) the declarant does not make while testifying at the current trial or hearing; and
• (2) a party offers in evidence to prove the truth of the matter asserted in the statement.
(d) **Statements That Are Not Hearsay.** A statement that meets the following conditions is not hearsay:
• (1) **A Declarant-Witness's Prior Statement.** The declarant testifies and is subject to cross-examination about a prior statement, and the statement:
o (A) is inconsistent with the declarant's testimony and was given under penalty of perjury at a trial, hearing, or other proceeding or in a deposition;
o (B) is consistent with the declarant's testimony and is offered to rebut an express or implied charge that the declarant recently fabricated it or acted from a recent improper influence or motive in so testifying; or
o (C) identifies a person as someone the declarant perceived earlier.
• (2) **An Opposing Party's Statement.** The statement is offered against an opposing party and:
o (A) was made by the party in an individual or representative capacity;
o (B) is one the party manifested that it adopted or believed to be true;
o (C) was made by a person whom the party authorized to make a statement on the subject;
o (D) was made by the party's agent or employee on a matter within the scope of that relationship and while it existed; or
o (E) was made by the party's coconspirator during and in furtherance of the conspiracy.

Introduction to Rule 801

Rule 801 of the Federal Rules of Evidence provides foundational definitions and establishes critical distinctions regarding hearsay within the context of legal proceedings. Hearsay, generally defined as an out-of-court statement offered to prove the truth of the matter asserted, is typically inadmissible unless it falls within certain exceptions or exclusions. Rule 801 not only clarifies what constitutes hearsay but also delineates specific exclusions from hearsay, thereby setting the stage for the more detailed rules that follow. This chapter provides a detailed analysis of Rule 801, exploring its text, interpretation, and broader implications for the administration of justice.

Analysis of Rule 801

Rule 801 provides essential definitions that form the basis for understanding hearsay and its exclusions under the Federal Rules of Evidence. The rule outlines what constitutes a "statement," who is considered a "declarant," and what is considered "hearsay." Additionally, it details specific instances where certain statements, although seemingly hearsay, are explicitly excluded from the hearsay rule.

Definition of "Statement" (Rule 801(a))

The term "statement" is a crucial element in the hearsay analysis. Under Rule 801(a), a "statement" includes any oral or written assertion, as well as nonverbal conduct, provided that the nonverbal conduct was intended as an assertion.

1. Oral and Written Assertions

A "statement" typically involves a spoken or written communication that conveys information. These assertions are straightforward examples, such as a witness testifying that a person said, "I saw the defendant at the scene," or submitting a written document in which the declarant asserted a fact.

For instance, in a breach of contract case, if one party introduces an email from the other party stating, "I will deliver the goods by Monday," that email is a "statement" under Rule 801(a) because it is a written assertion made by a person.

2. Nonverbal Conduct Intended as an Assertion

Nonverbal conduct can also constitute a "statement" if the person performing the conduct intended it as an assertion. For example, nodding in agreement when asked a question, pointing to someone to identify them, or shaking one's head to indicate "no" can all be considered "statements" if the intent was to assert a fact.

For example, in a criminal trial, if a witness testifies that they saw the victim point to the defendant when asked who attacked them, that nonverbal action is a "statement" under Rule 801(a), assuming the victim intended it as an assertion of the attacker's identity.

Definition of "Declarant" (Rule 801(b))

The "declarant" is defined as the person who made the statement. This definition is straightforward and emphasizes that hearsay involves statements made by someone other than the witness currently testifying.

1. Identifying the Declarant

In applying Rule 801(b), the declarant is the individual whose out-of-court statement is being offered into evidence. Understanding who the declarant is helps determine whether the statement qualifies as hearsay and whether it fits within any of the exceptions or exclusions.

For example, if a witness testifies about what their friend said regarding the events of a case, the friend is the declarant under Rule 801(b). The relevance and admissibility of that friend's statement will be analyzed under the hearsay rule.

Definition of "Hearsay" (Rule 801(c))

Hearsay, as defined by Rule 801(c), is a statement that the declarant does not make while testifying at the current trial or hearing and that a party offers in evidence to prove the truth of the matter asserted in the statement. This definition is central to understanding what evidence is considered hearsay and, therefore, generally inadmissible unless an exception applies.

1. Out-of-Court Statement

The first part of the hearsay definition emphasizes that the statement must have been made outside of the current trial or hearing. This includes statements made in prior legal proceedings, written documents, or casual conversations.

For example, if a party offers into evidence a transcript of a statement made by a witness during a prior trial, and that statement is being used to prove the truth of what it asserts, it is considered hearsay under Rule 801(c).

2. Offered to Prove the Truth of the Matter Asserted

The second part of the hearsay definition requires that the statement be offered to prove the truth of the matter asserted within the statement. If the statement is being used to establish the truth of its content, it is considered hearsay. However, if it is offered for another purpose, such as to show the statement's effect on the listener or to prove that the statement was made (regardless of its truth), it may not be hearsay.

For instance, if a party introduces a witness's prior statement to show that the witness was aware of certain information (but not to prove that the information was true), the statement might not be considered hearsay because it is not being offered for its truth.

Exclusions from Hearsay (Rule 801(d))

Rule 801(d) identifies specific types of statements that, although they might appear to be hearsay, are explicitly excluded from the hearsay rule. These exclusions recognize certain circumstances where the reliability of the statement is sufficiently ensured or where its importance to the judicial process justifies its admission.

1. Declarant-Witness's Prior Statements (Rule 801(d)(1))

Rule 801(d)(1) excludes certain prior statements of a witness who is currently testifying and subject to cross-examination about the statement. These prior statements fall into three categories:

- **Inconsistent Statements Made Under Oath**: If a witness made a prior statement under penalty of perjury at a trial, hearing, deposition, or other proceeding, and that statement is inconsistent with their current testimony, it is not considered hearsay. This exclusion recognizes that prior statements made under oath in formal settings have a degree of reliability and can be used to challenge the witness's credibility.

For example, if a witness previously testified in a deposition that they saw the defendant at a crime scene, but now testifies differently at trial, the prior statement can be introduced to show inconsistency, and it is not considered hearsay under Rule 801(d)(1)(A).

- **Consistent Statements Offered to Rebut Charges of Fabrication**: If a prior statement is consistent with the witness's current testimony and is offered to rebut an implied or express charge of recent fabrication or improper motive, it is not considered hearsay. This provision allows parties to rehabilitate a witness's credibility when it is under attack.

For instance, if the defense suggests that a witness recently fabricated their testimony due to a new motive, the prosecution might introduce a prior consistent statement made before the alleged motive arose to show that the witness's story has been consistent over time, which is not considered hearsay under Rule 801(d)(1)(B).

- Statements of Identification: A prior statement identifying a person, made after perceiving that person, is not considered hearsay. This exclusion is particularly relevant in cases where a witness identified a suspect in a lineup or photo array and is now testifying about that identification.

For example, if a witness identified the defendant in a police lineup shortly after a crime occurred and now testifies about that identification, the prior statement is not hearsay under Rule 801(d)(1)(C).

2. Opposing Party's Statements (Rule 801(d)(2))

Rule 801(d)(2) excludes from hearsay statements made by an opposing party or those attributable to the opposing party. This exclusion recognizes that a party's own statements, or statements made on their behalf, carry an inherent reliability and relevance in legal proceedings.

- Individual or Representative Capacity: A statement made by a party in their individual or representative capacity is not hearsay when offered against that party. This includes admissions made by the party in connection with the case.

For example, in a contract dispute, if the defendant previously wrote in an email that they knew they had breached the contract, that statement can be introduced by the plaintiff as evidence and is not considered hearsay under Rule 801(d)(2)(A).

- Adopted Statements: If a party has manifested that they adopted or believed a statement to be true, that statement is not hearsay when offered against them. This can include explicit agreements or implicit endorsements of another's statement.

For instance, if the defendant nodded in agreement when another person accused them of a crime, that gesture could be considered an adoption of the statement, making it admissible under Rule 801(d)(2)(B).

- Statements by Authorized Persons: Statements made by a person authorized by the party to speak on a particular subject are not hearsay when offered against the party. This often applies in situations involving legal representatives, agents, or spokespersons.

For example, if a corporate executive authorized to speak on behalf of the company makes a statement about the company's policies, that statement can be introduced in litigation against the company and is not considered hearsay under Rule 801(d)(2)(C).

- Statements by Agents or Employees: Statements made by a party's agent or employee on a matter within the scope of their employment and during the existence of that relationship are not hearsay when offered against the party. This applies to statements made in the course of performing job duties.

For example, if an employee, while performing their job, admits to a mistake that caused harm, that statement can be introduced against the employer in a lawsuit and is not considered hearsay under Rule 801(d)(2)(D).

- Statements by Coconspirators: Statements made by a party's coconspirator during and in furtherance of a conspiracy are not hearsay when offered against the party. This exclusion applies in cases involving conspiracy charges, where coconspirator statements are often critical evidence.

For instance, if one member of a criminal conspiracy makes a statement during a meeting with others to plan a crime, that statement can be introduced against all members of the conspiracy and is not considered hearsay under Rule 801(d)(2)(E).

Strategic Considerations for Attorneys

Understanding Rule 801 is critical for attorneys in both the presentation and objection to evidence. The rule's definitions and exclusions from hearsay provide essential tools for constructing or challenging a case.

1. Leveraging Exclusions in Evidence Presentation

Attorneys can strategically use the exclusions in Rule 801(d) to introduce statements that might otherwise be excluded as hearsay. This includes carefully preparing witnesses to testify about prior statements that meet the conditions of Rule 801(d)(1) or introducing statements made by the opposing party or their representatives under Rule 801(d)(2).

For example, in a criminal case, the prosecution might introduce a coconspirator's statement under Rule 801(d)(2)(E) to establish the defendant's involvement in a conspiracy, framing the statement as direct evidence of the conspiracy's existence and the defendant's participation.

2. Challenging the Admissibility of Statements

Attorneys should also be vigilant in challenging the admissibility of statements that do not meet the exclusions outlined in Rule 801. This includes objecting to the introduction of hearsay evidence that does not fall within one of the exclusions or exceptions to the hearsay rule.

For instance, if the opposing party attempts to introduce a statement made by a non-party that does not fit within Rule 801(d)'s exclusions, the attorney should object on hearsay grounds, arguing that the statement is inadmissible because it is offered for the truth of the matter asserted and does not meet any of the specified exclusions.

3. Understanding the Role of Statements in Jury Perception

The strategic use of statements that qualify under Rule 801(d) can significantly impact how the jury perceives the evidence. Attorneys must carefully consider how introducing such statements will influence the jury's understanding of the case and whether it bolsters the credibility of the testimony.

Rule 802 - The Rule Against Hearsay

Text of Rule 802

Rule 802. The Rule Against Hearsay
Hearsay is not admissible unless any of the following provides otherwise:
•   a federal statute;
•   these rules;
•   other rules prescribed by the Supreme Court.

Introduction to Rule 802

Rule 802 of the Federal Rules of Evidence enshrines the fundamental principle that hearsay is generally inadmissible in court. Hearsay is defined as an out-of-court statement offered to prove the truth of the matter asserted, and the rule against hearsay is designed to protect the integrity and reliability of the judicial process. The rationale behind this rule is that hearsay statements are not subject to cross-examination, which is a key mechanism for testing the accuracy and credibility of testimony. However, the rule against hearsay is not absolute; it is subject to numerous exceptions and exclusions that recognize certain circumstances where hearsay may be sufficiently reliable to be admitted as evidence. This chapter provides a detailed analysis of Rule 802, exploring its text, interpretation, and broader implications for the administration of justice.

Analysis of Rule 802

Rule 802 establishes the general prohibition against hearsay, marking a critical boundary in the rules of evidence. The rule underscores the importance of firsthand testimony in legal proceedings while acknowledging that exceptions to this prohibition exist under certain circumstances.

The General Prohibition Against Hearsay

The core of Rule 802 is its straightforward declaration that hearsay is not admissible. This prohibition reflects the longstanding legal principle that statements made outside of the courtroom are generally unreliable because they are not subjected to the rigorous process of cross-examination, and the declarant's demeanor cannot be observed by the trier of fact.

1. Rationale for the Prohibition

The prohibition against hearsay is grounded in concerns about reliability and fairness. Hearsay evidence is typically viewed with suspicion because the declarant is not present in court to be cross-examined, and there is no opportunity for the opposing party to challenge the accuracy or credibility of the statement. Moreover, the trier of fact cannot observe the declarant's demeanor, which is often a critical factor in assessing the truthfulness of testimony.

For example, if a witness testifies that they heard someone else claim that the defendant committed a crime, this statement is hearsay because the declarant is not in court to confirm the statement or to be questioned about its accuracy. Rule 802 generally excludes such statements to prevent the introduction of unreliable evidence.

2. Preserving the Integrity of the Trial Process

By prohibiting hearsay, Rule 802 helps to preserve the integrity of the trial process. It ensures that the evidence presented in court is subject to cross-examination and that the trier of fact can fully assess the reliability of the testimony. This approach helps to prevent miscarriages of justice that could result from reliance on untested, out-of-court statements.

For instance, in a civil trial, if a party attempts to introduce a letter from a third party that makes factual assertions about the case, Rule 802 would typically bar the admission of the letter as hearsay, unless an exception applies. This ensures that the facts of the case are established through direct, in-court testimony that can be scrutinized by both parties.

Exceptions and Exclusions to the Hearsay Rule

While Rule 802 establishes the general rule against hearsay, it also explicitly acknowledges that hearsay may be admissible if permitted by a federal statute, the Federal Rules of Evidence, or other rules prescribed by the Supreme Court. These exceptions and exclusions are crucial because they recognize situations where hearsay may be reliable enough to be admitted into evidence.

1. Federal Statutes

Certain federal statutes provide specific exceptions to the hearsay rule. These statutory exceptions are often tailored to particular types of cases or evidence where hearsay is considered inherently reliable or where public policy favors its admission. Examples include exceptions for certain types of business records, public records, or statements made by witnesses who are unavailable due to death or incapacity.

For example, under the Federal Rules of Civil Procedure, business records may be admissible as an exception to the hearsay rule if they are created and kept in the ordinary course of business, and the record's reliability is supported by the circumstances of its creation.

2. Federal Rules of Evidence

The Federal Rules of Evidence themselves contain numerous exceptions to the hearsay rule, detailed in Rules 803, 804, and 807. These exceptions apply in both civil and criminal cases and cover a wide range of circumstances, from excited utterances and present sense impressions to statements against interest and dying declarations.

For instance, Rule 803(2) allows for the admission of excited utterances—statements made in response to a startling event while the declarant is still under the stress of excitement caused by the event—because such statements are considered to be spontaneous and less likely to be fabricated.

3. Other Rules Prescribed by the Supreme Court

In addition to federal statutes and the Federal Rules of Evidence, the Supreme Court may prescribe rules that provide for the admissibility of hearsay in specific contexts. These rules may arise from Supreme Court decisions or from procedural rules that govern particular types of legal proceedings.

For example, the Supreme Court has developed the "residual hearsay exception" under Rule 807, which allows for the admission of hearsay that does not fall within any specific exception but has equivalent guarantees of trustworthiness, is offered as evidence of a material fact, and serves the interests of justice.

Judicial Discretion in Applying Rule 802

Judges play a critical role in applying Rule 802, particularly in determining whether hearsay evidence should be admitted under an exception or exclusion. Judicial discretion is essential in balancing the need for reliable evidence with the practical realities of certain cases, where hearsay might be the best or only evidence available.

1. Assessing the Reliability of Hearsay

When considering whether to admit hearsay under an exception, judges must assess the reliability of the statement. This involves evaluating the circumstances under which the statement was made, the declarant's motivation and credibility, and the relevance of the statement to the issues in the case.

For example, in a case involving a dying declaration, the judge must determine whether the declarant genuinely believed they were near death when making the statement, as this belief is critical to the statement's reliability.

2. Balancing Probative Value and Prejudice

Even when hearsay evidence is potentially admissible under an exception, judges must also consider whether its probative value is substantially outweighed by the risk of unfair prejudice, confusion of the issues, or misleading the jury. This balancing act ensures that hearsay is only admitted when it contributes meaningfully to the case without compromising the fairness of the trial.

For instance, if a hearsay statement has significant probative value but also risks inflaming the jury's emotions against one of the parties, the judge may choose to exclude it under Rule 403, even if it technically qualifies under a hearsay exception.

Strategic Considerations for Attorneys

Rule 802 requires attorneys to be vigilant in both challenging and defending the admissibility of hearsay evidence. Understanding when and how to invoke or counter the hearsay rule is crucial for effective advocacy.

1. Objecting to Hearsay

Attorneys must be prepared to object to the introduction of hearsay evidence that does not fall within an exception or exclusion. This involves being able to quickly identify hearsay statements during testimony and articulating why the statement should be excluded under Rule 802.

For example, during a trial, if opposing counsel attempts to introduce a witness's out-of-court statement that does not fit within any recognized exception, the attorney should immediately object on hearsay grounds, requesting that the statement be stricken from the record.

2. Utilizing Hearsay Exceptions

Conversely, attorneys must also be adept at using hearsay exceptions to their advantage. This involves identifying potential hearsay evidence that supports their case and determining whether it can be admitted under one of the recognized exceptions. Preparing to argue for the admission of such evidence involves gathering supporting information that establishes the statement's reliability and relevance.

For instance, in a personal injury case, an attorney might seek to introduce medical records under the business records exception, demonstrating that the records were made in the regular course of business and are trustworthy reflections of the declarant's medical condition at the time.

3. Preparing for Hearsay Challenges

Attorneys should also anticipate potential hearsay objections to their evidence and prepare to counter them effectively. This preparation includes understanding the nuances of the hearsay exceptions and being ready to argue that the statement in question falls within one of those exceptions or serves a purpose other than proving the truth of the matter asserted.

For example, if a witness's prior statement is crucial to the case, the attorney should be prepared to argue that it is admissible as a prior consistent statement under Rule 801(d)(1)(B) or as an excited utterance under Rule 803(2), depending on the circumstances.

Rule 803 - Exceptions to the Rule Against Hearsay—Regardless of Whether the Declarant Is Available as a Witness

Text of Rule 803

Rule 803. Exceptions to the Rule Against Hearsay—Regardless of Whether the Declarant Is Available as a Witness

The following are not excluded by the rule against hearsay, regardless of whether the declarant is available as a witness:

1. **Present Sense Impression.** A statement describing or explaining an event or condition, made while or immediately after the declarant perceived it.

2. **Excited Utterance.** A statement relating to a startling event or condition, made while the declarant was under the stress of excitement that it caused.

3. **Then-Existing Mental, Emotional, or Physical Condition.** A statement of the declarant's then-existing state of mind (such as motive, intent, or plan) or emotional, sensory, or physical condition (such as mental feeling, pain, or bodily health), but not including a statement of memory or belief to prove the fact remembered or believed unless it relates to the validity or terms of the declarant's will.

4. **Statement Made for Medical Diagnosis or Treatment.** A statement that:

   o   (A) is made for—and is reasonably pertinent to—medical diagnosis or treatment; and

   o   (B) describes medical history; past or present symptoms or sensations; their inception; or their general cause.

5. **Recorded Recollection.** A record that:

   o   (A) is on a matter the witness once knew about but now cannot recall well enough to testify fully and accurately;

   o   (B) was made or adopted by the witness when the matter was fresh in the witness's memory; and

   o   (C) accurately reflects the witness's knowledge.

   o   If admitted, the record may be read into evidence but may be received as an exhibit only if offered by an adverse party.

6. **Records of a Regularly Conducted Activity.** A record of an act, event, condition, opinion, or diagnosis if:

   o   (A) the record was made at or near the time by—or from information transmitted by—someone with knowledge;

   o   (B) the record was kept in the course of a regularly conducted activity of a business, organization, occupation, or calling, whether or not for profit;

   o   (C) making the record was a regular practice of that activity;

   o   (D) all these conditions are shown by the testimony of the custodian or another qualified witness, or by a certification that complies with Rule 902(11) or (12) or with a statute permitting certification; and

   o   (E) the opponent does not show that the source of the information or the method or circumstances of preparation indicate a lack of trustworthiness.

7. **Absence of a Record of a Regularly Conducted Activity.** Evidence that a matter is not included in a record described in paragraph (6) if:

   o   (A) the evidence is admitted to prove that the matter did not occur or exist;

   o   (B) a record was regularly kept for a matter of that kind; and

   o   (C) the opponent does not show that the possible source of the information or other circumstances indicate a lack of trustworthiness.

8. **Public Records.** A record or statement of a public office if:

- o (A) it sets out:

  - ▪ (i) the office's activities;

  - ▪ (ii) a matter observed while under a legal duty to report, but not including, in a criminal case, a matter observed by law-enforcement personnel; or

  - ▪ (iii) in a civil case or against the government in a criminal case, factual findings from a legally authorized investigation; and

- o (B) the opponent does not show that the source of information or other circumstances indicate a lack of trustworthiness.

9. **Public Records of Vital Statistics.** A record of a birth, death, or marriage, if reported to a public office in accordance with a legal duty.

10. **Absence of a Public Record.** Testimony—or a certification under Rule 902—that a diligent search failed to disclose a public record or statement if:

  - o (A) the testimony or certification is admitted to prove that

    - ▪ (i) the record or statement does not exist; or

    - ▪ (ii) a matter did not occur or exist, if a public office regularly kept a record or statement for a matter of that kind; and

  - o (B) in a criminal case, a prosecutor who intends to offer a certification provides written notice of that intent at least 14 days before trial, and the defendant does not object in writing within 7 days of receiving the notice—unless the court sets a different time for the notice or the objection.

11. **Records of Religious Organizations Concerning Personal or Family History.** A statement of birth, legitimacy, ancestry, marriage, divorce, death, relationship by blood or marriage, or similar facts of personal or family history, contained in a regularly kept record of a religious organization.

12. **Certificates of Marriage, Baptism, and Similar Ceremonies.** A statement of fact contained in a certificate:

  - o (A) made by a person who is authorized by a religious organization or by law to perform the act certified;

  - o (B) attesting that the person performed a marriage or similar ceremony or administered a sacrament; and

  - o (C) purporting to have been issued at the time of the act or within a reasonable time after it.

13. **Family Records.** A statement of fact about personal or family history contained in a family record, such as a Bible, genealogy, chart, engraving on a ring, inscription on a portrait, or engraving on an urn or burial marker.

14. **Records of Documents That Affect an Interest in Property.** The record of a document that purports to establish or affect an interest in property if:

  - o (A) the record is admitted to prove the content of the original recorded document, along with its signing and its delivery by each person who purports to have signed it;

  - o (B) the record is kept in a public office; and

  - o (C) a statute authorizes recording documents of that kind in that office.

15. **Statements in Documents That Affect an Interest in Property.** A statement contained in a document that purports to establish or affect an interest in property if the matter stated was relevant to the document's purpose—unless later dealings with the property are inconsistent with the truth of the statement or the purport of the document.

16. **Statements in Ancient Documents.** A statement in a document that was prepared before January 1, 1998, and whose authenticity is established.

17. **Market Reports and Similar Commercial Publications.** Market quotations, lists, directories, or other compilations that are generally relied on by the public or by persons in particular occupations.

18. **Statements in Learned Treatises, Periodicals, or Pamphlets.** A statement contained in a treatise, periodical, or pamphlet if:

> o   (A) the statement is called to the attention of an expert witness on cross-examination or relied on by the expert on direct examination; and

> o   (B) the publication is established as a reliable authority by the expert's admission or testimony, by another expert's testimony, or by judicial notice.

> o   If admitted, the statement may be read into evidence but not received as an exhibit.

19. **Reputation Concerning Personal or Family History.** A reputation among a person's family by blood, adoption, or marriage—or among a person's associates or in the community—concerning the person's birth, adoption, legitimacy, ancestry, marriage, divorce, death, relationship by blood, adoption, or marriage, or similar facts of personal or family history.

20. **Reputation Concerning Boundaries or General History.** A reputation in a community—arising before the controversy—concerning boundaries of land in the community or customs that affect the land, or concerning general historical events important to that community, state, or nation.

21. **Reputation Concerning Character.** A reputation among a person's associates or in the community concerning the person's character.

22. **Judgment of a Previous Conviction.** Evidence of a final judgment of conviction if:

> o   (A) the judgment was entered after a trial or guilty plea, but not a nolo contendere plea;

> o   (B) the conviction was for a crime punishable by death or by imprisonment for more than a year;

> o   (C) the evidence is admitted to prove any fact essential to the judgment; and

> o   (D) when offered by the prosecutor in a criminal case for a purpose other than impeachment, the judgment was against the defendant.

> o   The pendency of an appeal may be shown but does not affect admissibility.

23. **Judgments Involving Personal, Family, or General History, or a Boundary.** A judgment that is admitted to prove a matter of personal, family, or general history, or boundaries, if the matter:

> o   (A) was essential to the judgment; and

> o   (B) could be proved by evidence of reputation.

24. **[Other exceptions covered elsewhere.]** (This category is reserved for exceptions not listed in Rule 803 but recognized in other parts of the Federal Rules or by statutes).

Introduction to Rule 803

Rule 803 of the Federal Rules of Evidence delineates numerous exceptions to the general prohibition against hearsay. Unlike other exceptions that require the declarant to be unavailable (as outlined in Rule 804), the exceptions under Rule 803 apply regardless of the declarant's availability. These exceptions recognize that certain types of statements possess inherent guarantees of trustworthiness, making them sufficiently reliable to be admitted as evidence even though they are hearsay. This chapter provides a detailed analysis of Rule 803, exploring its various exceptions, their rationale, and their broader implications for the administration of justice.

Analysis of Rule 803

Rule 803 provides a comprehensive list of exceptions to the rule against hearsay. These exceptions are grounded in the principle that certain statements are inherently reliable due to the circumstances under which they are made. This section provides an in-depth examination of each exception listed under Rule 803, highlighting the rationale behind their admissibility and the conditions under which they apply.

Present Sense Impression (Rule 803(1))

A present sense impression is a statement that describes or explains an event or condition made while the declarant is perceiving the event or immediately thereafter. The reliability of this type of statement stems from its contemporaneous nature, which reduces the likelihood of fabrication or faulty memory.

1.   **Conditions for Admissibility**

For a statement to qualify as a present sense impression, it must be made contemporaneously with the event or immediately after the event. The timing is crucial because the closer the statement is to the event, the less likely it is that the declarant had time to reflect or fabricate.

For example, if a witness immediately after a car accident exclaims, "The blue car ran the red light!" this statement may be admissible under Rule 803(1) because it describes the event as it was happening.

2. Rationale

The underlying rationale is that statements made in real-time are inherently trustworthy. The absence of time to deliberate or fabricate ensures a higher degree of reliability, making such statements valuable evidence even in the absence of the declarant's direct testimony.

Excited Utterance (Rule 803(2))

An excited utterance is a statement relating to a startling event or condition made while the declarant is under the stress of excitement caused by the event. The excitement of the moment is believed to prevent the declarant from engaging in reflective thought, thereby increasing the statement's reliability.

1. Conditions for Admissibility

The statement must be made in response to a startling event or condition, and the declarant must still be under the influence of the excitement or stress caused by that event. The timing of the statement, while flexible, must be sufficiently close to the event to ensure that the declarant was still affected by the stress or excitement.

For instance, a person who, after witnessing a robbery, exclaims, "He had a gun!" might be offering an excited utterance, admissible under Rule 803(2).

2. Rationale

The rationale for this exception lies in the belief that statements made under the influence of excitement or stress are less likely to be fabricated, as the declarant's reflective processes are overborne by the immediacy of the event.

Then-Existing Mental, Emotional, or Physical Condition (Rule 803(3))

This exception covers statements that reflect the declarant's then-existing state of mind, emotions, sensations, or physical condition. These statements are admissible because they are contemporaneous reflections of the declarant's internal state, making them less likely to be influenced by external factors or memory decay.

1. Conditions for Admissibility

The statement must pertain to the declarant's current mental, emotional, or physical condition at the time the statement was made. It cannot be used to prove a past event or condition, except in cases involving the declarant's will.

For example, if a person says, "I'm feeling dizzy," this statement could be admissible under Rule 803(3) as evidence of their physical condition at that moment.

2. Rationale

The reliability of these statements stems from their direct reflection of the declarant's state of mind or condition, which is less prone to distortion since the declarant is reporting on their immediate experience.

Statements Made for Medical Diagnosis or Treatment (Rule 803(4))

Statements made for the purpose of medical diagnosis or treatment are considered reliable because the declarant has a strong motive to be truthful in seeking accurate medical care.

1. Conditions for Admissibility

The statement must be made for—and reasonably pertinent to—medical diagnosis or treatment. It can include information about medical history, symptoms, pain, or the general cause of the condition, but it must be relevant to the treatment or diagnosis.

For instance, a patient's statement to a doctor, "I was hit on the head with a bat," may be admissible under Rule 803(4) because it is pertinent to diagnosing and treating the injury.

2. Rationale

The rationale behind this exception is that individuals seeking medical treatment are unlikely to fabricate symptoms or causes of injury because accurate information is crucial to receiving appropriate care. This inherent motivation for truthfulness supports the reliability of the statement.

Recorded Recollection (Rule 803(5))

A recorded recollection is a written or recorded statement that reflects a matter the witness once knew about but cannot recall well enough to testify fully and accurately. The record must have been made or adopted by the witness when the matter was fresh in their memory.

1. Conditions for Admissibility

The statement must have been made when the witness's memory was fresh, and it must accurately reflect the witness's knowledge at that time. If admitted, the record can be read into evidence, but it can only be entered as an exhibit if offered by the adverse party.

For example, if a witness wrote a note shortly after witnessing an event and now cannot recall the details, that note may be admissible under Rule 803(5) as a recorded recollection.

2. Rationale

The rationale is that a statement made when the memory was fresh is more likely to be accurate than a later recollection, particularly when the witness's current memory has faded. The document serves as a reliable substitute for in-court testimony.

Records of a Regularly Conducted Activity (Rule 803(6))

Commonly known as the "business records exception," this rule allows for the admission of records made in the regular course of business, provided certain conditions are met.

1. Conditions for Admissibility

The record must be made at or near the time of the event by someone with knowledge, and it must be kept as part of a regularly conducted business activity. The custodian or another qualified witness must testify to these conditions unless the record is self-authenticating under Rule 902.

For instance, a company's financial ledger maintained as part of its regular business operations could be admissible under Rule 803(6) to demonstrate financial transactions.

2. Rationale

The reliability of business records stems from the regularity and routine with which they are created and maintained. Because businesses rely on these records for their operations, there is a strong incentive to ensure their accuracy.

Absence of a Record of a Regularly Conducted Activity (Rule 803(7))

This exception allows for the introduction of evidence showing that a particular record, which would normally be kept in the regular course of business, is absent, thereby suggesting that the event or transaction did not occur.

1. Conditions for Admissibility

The absence of the record must be offered to prove that the matter did not occur, and the record must be one that is regularly maintained by the business or organization. The opponent has the opportunity to challenge the reliability of the absence.

For example, if a business regularly logs all customer complaints and a search reveals no record of a complaint on a specific date, that absence could be used as evidence that no complaint was made.

2. Rationale

The rationale is that if a business or organization routinely keeps records of certain activities, the absence of such a record is a strong indication that the activity did not occur.

Public Records (Rule 803(8))

Public records or statements of a public office are admissible under this exception, provided they set out the office's activities, matters observed under a duty to report, or factual findings from an investigation.

1. Conditions for Admissibility

The record must pertain to the activities of the office, observations made under a duty to report (excluding law enforcement observations in criminal cases), or factual findings from legally authorized investigations. The opponent may challenge the record's trustworthiness.

For example, a government report detailing the results of an environmental inspection could be admissible under Rule 803(8) in a civil case involving pollution.

2. Rationale

The reliability of public records comes from the assumption that public officials perform their duties responsibly and with accuracy, particularly when those duties involve recording information for official purposes.

Public Records of Vital Statistics (Rule 803(9))

This exception allows the admission of records of births, deaths, and marriages reported to public offices in accordance with legal requirements.

1. Conditions for Admissibility

The record must be created pursuant to a legal duty to report, typically involving vital statistics such as birth, death, or marriage certificates.

For example, a birth certificate recorded with the state could be admitted under Rule 803(9) to prove the birth of an individual.

2. Rationale

The rationale for this exception is the official and mandatory nature of the records, which are created as part of the government's duty to maintain vital statistics.

Absence of a Public Record (Rule 803(10))

Similar to Rule 803(7), this exception allows evidence that a diligent search failed to disclose a public record or statement, suggesting that the event or condition did not occur.

1. Conditions for Admissibility

The absence must be from a public office that regularly maintains such records, and the testimony or certification must demonstrate that a diligent search was conducted. In criminal cases, specific notice requirements apply.

For example, if a search of court records reveals no record of a defendant's prior conviction, this absence may be used to show that the conviction does not exist.

2. Rationale

The absence of a record in a context where one would normally be expected to exist suggests that the event or condition did not occur, providing reliable evidence of non-existence.

Records of Religious Organizations Concerning Personal or Family History (Rule 803(11))

This exception covers statements in records kept by religious organizations regarding personal or family history, such as birth, marriage, or death.

1. Conditions for Admissibility

The record must be regularly kept by the religious organization, and the statement must concern personal or family history.

For example, a church's baptismal records could be admissible under Rule 803(11) to prove the date and place of a person's baptism.

2. Rationale

Religious organizations often maintain detailed records of significant life events, and these records are generally considered reliable due to the importance of such events within the religious community.

Certificates of Marriage, Baptism, and Similar Ceremonies (Rule 803(12))

This exception allows for the admission of certificates issued by persons authorized to perform religious or legal ceremonies, attesting to the performance of such ceremonies.

1. Conditions for Admissibility

The certificate must be issued by someone authorized to perform the ceremony and must attest to the fact that the ceremony was performed. It must also have been issued at the time of the ceremony or shortly thereafter.

For instance, a marriage certificate issued by a clergy member could be admitted under Rule 803(12) to prove that a marriage took place.

2. Rationale

The rationale is that certificates of significant ceremonies are typically issued by trusted authorities at the time of the event, ensuring their accuracy and reliability.

Family Records (Rule 803(13))

This exception pertains to statements of fact regarding personal or family history contained in family records, such as Bibles, genealogies, or engravings.

1. Conditions for Admissibility

The statement must concern personal or family history and must be contained in a family record. Examples include inscriptions on a family tombstone or notes in a family Bible.

For example, an inscription in a family Bible noting a relative's birth date could be admitted under Rule 803(13) to prove the birthdate.

2. Rationale

Family records are often created and maintained over generations and are generally trusted as accurate reflections of family history, making them reliable sources of information.

Records of Documents That Affect an Interest in Property (Rule 803(14))

This exception allows for the admission of records of documents that establish or affect an interest in property, provided they meet certain conditions.

1. Conditions for Admissibility

The record must document a transaction that affects an interest in property, must be kept in a public office, and must be one that the law authorizes to be recorded.

For example, a deed recorded in the county clerk's office could be admitted under Rule 803(14) to prove the transfer of property.

2. Rationale

The public recording of property interests is a formal process with legal significance, ensuring that such records are reliable and accurately reflect the transactions they document.

Statements in Documents That Affect an Interest in Property (Rule 803(15))

Statements contained in documents affecting an interest in property are admissible if they were relevant to the document's purpose, unless later dealings with the property contradict the statement.

1. Conditions for Admissibility

The statement must be relevant to the document's purpose of establishing or affecting an interest in property, and there must be no subsequent actions that contradict the truth of the statement.

For example, a statement in a will that describes the distribution of property could be admissible under Rule 803(15) to prove the testator's intent regarding property distribution.

2. Rationale

Statements in documents that affect property interests are considered reliable because they are usually created with legal significance and are intended to have lasting effects, making them trustworthy.

Statements in Ancient Documents (Rule 803(16))

This exception applies to statements in documents prepared before January 1, 1998, whose authenticity is established.

1. Conditions for Admissibility

The document must be sufficiently old—prepared before January 1, 1998—and its authenticity must be established through evidence or stipulation.

For example, a land grant from the 19th century could be admitted under Rule 803(16) to prove historical land ownership.

2. Rationale

Ancient documents are often viewed as reliable due to their age and the presumption that if they were fraudulent, the fraud would have been exposed long before.

Market Reports and Similar Commercial Publications (Rule 803(17))

Market reports and similar publications relied upon by the public or professionals are admissible under this exception.

1. Conditions for Admissibility

The publication must be generally relied upon by the public or by those in a particular occupation for accurate information.

For instance, a stock market report published in a financial newspaper could be admitted under Rule 803(17) to show stock prices on a specific date.

2. Rationale

The reliability of these publications is based on their widespread use and the expectation that they provide accurate, up-to-date information for decision-making in commerce and other activities.

Statements in Learned Treatises, Periodicals, or Pamphlets (Rule 803(18))

Statements in learned treatises, periodicals, or pamphlets are admissible when relied upon by an expert witness or brought to their attention during cross-examination.

1. Conditions for Admissibility

The publication must be established as a reliable authority by expert testimony, admission by the expert witness, or judicial notice. The statement may be read into evidence but not received as an exhibit.

For example, a medical expert may rely on a statement from a respected medical journal during testimony, and that statement could be read into evidence under Rule 803(18).

2. Rationale

The rationale is that learned treatises and similar publications are considered reliable sources of information within their fields and are used by professionals to inform their practice.

Reputation Concerning Personal or Family History (Rule 803(19))

This exception allows for the admission of a person's reputation concerning their family history, such as birth, marriage, or death, among family members or the community.

1. Conditions for Admissibility

The reputation must concern personal or family history and be held among the person's family, associates, or community.

For instance, a person's reputation in their community as the legitimate child of a specific individual could be admissible under Rule 803(19).

2. Rationale

Reputation regarding family history is often passed down through generations and is typically based on collective knowledge, making it a reliable reflection of historical facts.

Reputation Concerning Boundaries or General History (Rule 803(20))

This exception applies to reputation in a community regarding land boundaries, customs affecting the land, or significant historical events.

1. Conditions for Admissibility

The reputation must concern boundaries, customs affecting land, or general historical events and must have arisen before the controversy at issue.

For example, the community's long-standing understanding of the boundary line between two properties could be admissible under Rule 803(20).

2. Rationale

Such reputations are formed over time and are based on the collective knowledge of the community, which is generally reliable, particularly in cases involving land and history.

Reputation Concerning Character (Rule 803(21))

This exception allows for the admission of a person's reputation concerning their character among their associates or within the community.

1. Conditions for Admissibility

The reputation must concern the person's character and be generally held among those who know the person well, such as associates or community members.

For example, a person's reputation for honesty within their community could be admissible under Rule 803(21) to support or challenge their credibility.

2. Rationale

A person's reputation for character is typically based on the collective observations and experiences of those who interact with them, providing a reliable gauge of their character.

Judgment of a Previous Conviction (Rule 803(22))

This exception permits the introduction of a final judgment of conviction to prove any fact essential to the judgment, particularly in criminal cases where the conviction relates to a crime punishable by death or imprisonment for more than a year.

1. Conditions for Admissibility

The judgment must have been entered after a trial or guilty plea (but not a nolo contendere plea), and the conviction must be for a crime punishable by death or imprisonment for more than a year. The pendency of an appeal may be shown but does not affect admissibility.

For instance, evidence of a defendant's prior conviction for fraud could be introduced under Rule 803(22) in a subsequent case to demonstrate a pattern of fraudulent behavior.

2. Rationale

A final judgment of conviction is considered reliable because it reflects a formal legal determination of guilt, made after the defendant had the opportunity to defend against the charges.

Judgments Involving Personal, Family, or General History, or a Boundary (Rule 803(23))

This exception allows the admission of judgments that pertain to personal, family, or general history, or boundaries, provided the matter was essential to the judgment and could be proven by evidence of reputation.

1. Conditions for Admissibility

The judgment must concern matters of personal, family, or general history, or boundaries, and these matters must have been essential to the judgment. Additionally, the matter must be one that could be proven by reputation evidence.

For example, a judgment that established the boundary between two properties in a previous legal dispute could be admitted under Rule 803(23) in a related case.

2. Rationale

Judgments involving historical facts or boundaries often require extensive evidence and are based on thorough judicial determinations, making them reliable sources of information.

Rule 804 - Exceptions to the Rule Against Hearsay—When the Declarant Is Unavailable as a Witness

Rule 804. Exceptions to the Rule Against Hearsay—When the Declarant Is Unavailable as a Witness

(a) **Criteria for Being Unavailable.** A declarant is considered to be unavailable as a witness if the declarant:

- (1) is exempted from testifying about the subject matter of the declarant's statement because the court rules that a privilege applies;

- (2) refuses to testify about the subject matter despite a court order to do so;

- (3) testifies to not remembering the subject matter;

- (4) cannot be present or testify at the trial or hearing because of death or a then-existing infirmity, physical illness, or mental illness; or

- (5) is absent from the trial or hearing and the statement's proponent has not been able, by process or other reasonable means, to procure:

  - (A) the declarant's attendance, in the case of a hearsay exception under Rule 804(b)(1) or (6); or

  - (B) the declarant's attendance or testimony, in the case of a hearsay exception under Rule 804(b)(2), (3), or (4).

But this subdivision (a) does not apply if the statement's proponent procured or wrongfully caused the declarant's unavailability as a witness in order to prevent the declarant from attending or testifying.

(b) **The Exceptions.** The following are not excluded by the rule against hearsay if the declarant is unavailable as a witness:

1. **Former Testimony.** Testimony that:

   - (A) was given as a witness at a trial, hearing, or lawful deposition, whether given during the current proceeding or a different one; and

   - (B) is now offered against a party who had—or, in a civil case, whose predecessor in interest had—an opportunity and similar motive to develop it by direct, cross-, or redirect examination.

2. **Statement Under the Belief of Imminent Death.** In a prosecution for homicide or in a civil case, a statement that the declarant, while believing the declarant's death to be imminent, made about its cause or circumstances.

3. **Statement Against Interest.** A statement that:

   - (A) a reasonable person in the declarant's position would have made only if the person believed it to be true because, when made, it was so contrary to the declarant's proprietary or pecuniary interest or had so great a tendency to invalidate the declarant's claim against someone else or to expose the declarant to civil or criminal liability; and

   - (B) is supported by corroborating circumstances that clearly indicate its trustworthiness, if it is offered in a criminal case as one that tends to expose the declarant to criminal liability.

4. **Statement of Personal or Family History.**

   - (A) A statement about the declarant's own birth, adoption, legitimacy, ancestry, marriage, divorce, relationship by blood, adoption, or marriage, or similar facts of personal or family history, even though the declarant had no way of acquiring personal knowledge about that fact; or

   - (B) A statement about another person concerning any of these facts, as well as death, if the declarant was related to the person by blood, adoption, or marriage or was so intimately associated with the person's family that the declarant's information is likely to be accurate.

5.	**[Other exceptions under Rule 804(b)(5)]** (This subdivision was transferred to Rule 807.)
6.	**Statement Offered Against a Party That Wrongfully Caused the Declarant's Unavailability.** A statement offered against a party that wrongfully caused—or acquiesced in wrongfully causing—the declarant's unavailability as a witness, and did so intending that result.

Introduction to Rule 804

Rule 804 of the Federal Rules of Evidence outlines specific exceptions to the general prohibition against hearsay in instances where the declarant is unavailable to testify as a witness. These exceptions recognize that certain statements may retain their reliability even in the absence of the declarant, often due to the circumstances under which the statements were made. Rule 804 is pivotal in ensuring that critical evidence is not excluded merely because the original speaker cannot be brought to court. This chapter provides a detailed analysis of Rule 804, exploring its text, interpretation, and broader implications for the administration of justice.

Analysis of Rule 804

Rule 804 provides specific exceptions to the hearsay rule, applicable only when the declarant is unavailable to testify. This section will provide an in-depth examination of the criteria for unavailability and each of the exceptions outlined in Rule 804(b), explaining their rationale and conditions for admissibility.

Criteria for Being Unavailable (Rule 804(a))

Before a hearsay statement can be admitted under Rule 804, it must be established that the declarant is unavailable as a witness. Rule 804(a) defines what constitutes "unavailability" by setting out five specific conditions under which a declarant is considered unavailable.

1. **Exemption Due to Privilege (Rule 804(a)(1))**

A declarant is unavailable if they are exempted from testifying about the subject matter of their statement because a privilege applies. This includes privileges such as attorney-client privilege, spousal privilege, or the Fifth Amendment right against self-incrimination.

For example, if a witness refuses to testify about a conversation with their attorney because of attorney-client privilege, and that testimony is crucial to the case, the witness may be considered unavailable under Rule 804(a)(1).

2. **Refusal to Testify Despite a Court Order (Rule 804(a)(2))**

A declarant is also considered unavailable if they refuse to testify about the subject matter, even after being ordered by the court to do so. This could occur in cases where the witness, despite being compelled by a subpoena and court order, still refuses to provide testimony.

For instance, a witness who refuses to testify in a criminal trial, despite being ordered by the judge to do so, can be deemed unavailable under Rule 804(a)(2).

3. **Lack of Memory (Rule 804(a)(3))**

If a declarant testifies that they cannot remember the subject matter, they are considered unavailable. This provision recognizes that genuine memory loss can impede a witness's ability to provide testimony, thereby justifying the use of prior statements.

For example, if a witness claims not to recall key details about an event that they previously described in a deposition, they may be considered unavailable under Rule 804(a)(3).

4. **Inability to Be Present Due to Death, Illness, or Infirmity (Rule 804(a)(4))**

A declarant is unavailable if they cannot testify because of death, a then-existing physical illness, mental illness, or infirmity. This criterion is straightforward, covering situations where the witness is deceased or too ill to attend court.

For example, if a key witness in a civil lawsuit passes away before trial, their prior testimony may be considered under Rule 804(b), given their unavailability due to death under Rule 804(a)(4).

5. **Absence from the Trial or Hearing (Rule 804(a)(5))**

A declarant is considered unavailable if they are absent from the trial or hearing, and the proponent of the statement has been unable to procure their attendance or testimony by reasonable means. This includes efforts to subpoena the witness or locate them.

For example, if a witness cannot be found despite diligent efforts, and their testimony is crucial to the case, the witness may be deemed unavailable under Rule 804(a)(5).

6. **Exceptions to Unavailability Due to Wrongful Conduct**

Rule 804(a) explicitly states that a declarant is not considered unavailable if their unavailability is the result of wrongful actions by the party seeking to introduce the hearsay statement. This provision is designed to prevent parties from benefiting from their own wrongdoing.

For instance, if a defendant in a criminal case intimidated a witness to prevent them from testifying, that witness would not be considered unavailable under Rule 804(a), and the defendant could not introduce the witness's prior statements under Rule 804(b).

Exceptions to the Hearsay Rule When the Declarant Is Unavailable (Rule 804(b))

Once a declarant is deemed unavailable, certain exceptions to the hearsay rule come into play under Rule 804(b). These exceptions allow for the admission of specific types of hearsay evidence that are considered reliable even in the absence of the declarant.

1. **Former Testimony (Rule 804(b)(1))**

Former testimony refers to testimony given as a witness at a prior trial, hearing, or lawful deposition, now offered against a party who had, or whose predecessor in interest had, an opportunity and similar motive to develop the testimony through direct, cross-, or redirect examination.

- **Conditions for Admissibility**

The prior testimony must have been given under oath at a legal proceeding, and the party against whom the testimony is offered must have had a prior opportunity to cross-examine the witness. This ensures that the testimony was subject to the adversarial process, which enhances its reliability.

For example, if a witness testified in a deposition during a civil case and later becomes unavailable due to illness, that testimony might be admissible under Rule 804(b)(1) in a related case where the opposing party had a similar motive to develop the testimony.

- ○ **Rationale**

The rationale behind this exception is that testimony subjected to cross-examination in a prior proceeding is reliable, even if the witness is now unavailable. The prior opportunity to challenge the testimony compensates for the witness's absence in the current proceeding.

2. **Statement Under the Belief of Imminent Death (Rule 804(b)(2))**

Commonly known as a "dying declaration," this exception applies to statements made by a declarant while believing their death was imminent, concerning the cause or circumstances of what they believed to be their impending death.

- ○ **Conditions for Admissibility**

The statement must be made under the belief of imminent death, and it must pertain to the cause or circumstances of the declarant's death. This exception is limited to prosecutions for homicide or civil cases, reflecting its historical roots in the common law.

For example, if a person, believing they are about to die from gunshot wounds, identifies their attacker, that statement could be admissible under Rule 804(b)(2) in a subsequent homicide trial.

- ○ **Rationale**

The rationale for admitting dying declarations is the belief that a person facing imminent death is unlikely to lie. The gravity of the situation is presumed to compel truthfulness, making such statements inherently reliable.

3. **Statement Against Interest (Rule 804(b)(3))**

This exception applies to statements that are so contrary to the declarant's interest—whether pecuniary, proprietary, or penal—that a reasonable person would not have made them unless they believed them to be true.

- ○ **Conditions for Admissibility**

The statement must be against the declarant's own interest, such that it would subject them to civil or criminal liability, or invalidate their legal claims. In criminal cases, the statement must be corroborated by additional evidence that indicates its trustworthiness.

For instance, a statement by an unavailable declarant admitting to committing a crime, which could subject them to criminal liability, might be admissible under Rule 804(b)(3) as a statement against interest, provided there is corroborating evidence of its trustworthiness.

- ○ **Rationale**

The rationale is that people generally do not make statements that are self-incriminating or otherwise detrimental to their own interests unless those statements are true. The self-inculpatory nature of the statement adds to its reliability.

4. **Statement of Personal or Family History (Rule 804(b)(4))**

This exception covers statements about the declarant's own personal or family history, such as birth, adoption, marriage, or other similar facts, even if the declarant had no direct personal knowledge of the fact.

- ○ **Conditions for Admissibility**

The statement can be about the declarant's own family history or the family history of someone closely related to the declarant, such as a blood relative or someone with whom the declarant had a close familial relationship.

For example, a statement made by a deceased family member about the birthdate of a relative might be admissible under Rule 804(b)(4) to establish the relative's age in a legal dispute.

- ○ **Rationale**

The rationale is that statements about personal or family history are often based on long-held family knowledge, passed down through generations. These statements are typically made without any motive to falsify and are therefore considered reliable.

5. **Statement Offered Against a Party That Wrongfully Caused the Declarant's Unavailability (Rule 804(b)(6))**

This exception allows for the admission of a statement against a party who wrongfully caused, or acquiesced in causing, the declarant's unavailability as a witness, with the intent to prevent the declarant from testifying.

- ○ **Conditions for Admissibility**

The proponent must show that the party against whom the statement is offered wrongfully caused the declarant's unavailability, and did so with the intent to prevent the declarant from testifying. This can include acts of violence, intimidation, or other wrongful conduct.

For instance, if a defendant in a criminal case threatened a witness to prevent them from testifying, any prior statements made by that witness could be admitted under Rule 804(b)(6) against the defendant.

- ○ **Rationale**

The rationale is to prevent parties from benefiting from their own wrongful conduct. This exception serves as a deterrent against tampering with witnesses and ensures that justice is not obstructed by the intimidation or silencing of key witnesses.

Strategic Considerations for Attorneys

Rule 804 requires attorneys to be vigilant in both establishing and challenging the unavailability of a declarant, as well as in arguing for or against the admissibility of hearsay statements under these exceptions.

1. **Establishing Unavailability**

Attorneys seeking to introduce hearsay evidence under Rule 804 must first convincingly establish the declarant's unavailability. This involves gathering and presenting evidence that meets the criteria outlined in Rule 804(a), such as proof of death, illness, or efforts to locate the witness.

For example, in preparing to introduce former testimony under Rule 804(b)(1), an attorney must document the declarant's death or the efforts made to procure their attendance at the trial, demonstrating due diligence.

2. **Challenging Unavailability**

Opposing counsel should scrutinize claims of unavailability to ensure that the proponent of the hearsay statement has genuinely met the burden of proof. This may involve questioning the sufficiency of efforts to locate or compel the witness or challenging the legitimacy of a claimed privilege or memory loss.

For instance, if the opposing party claims a witness is unavailable due to illness, the attorney might seek medical records or expert testimony to challenge the severity or legitimacy of the claimed illness.

3. **Leveraging Rule 804 Exceptions**

Attorneys must strategically use the exceptions under Rule 804(b) to introduce critical evidence that would otherwise be excluded under the hearsay rule. This involves carefully analyzing whether a statement meets the specific requirements of an exception and preparing to argue for its admissibility.

For example, in a criminal case, an attorney might seek to introduce a dying declaration under Rule 804(b)(2) by demonstrating the declarant's belief in imminent death and the relevance of the statement to the cause of death.

4. **Countering Rule 804 Exceptions**

When opposing the introduction of hearsay under Rule 804, attorneys should focus on undermining the reliability of the statement or the circumstances of its creation. This could involve challenging the trustworthiness of a statement against interest or questioning the corroboration required for such a statement in a criminal case.

For instance, if the opposing party seeks to introduce a statement against interest, the attorney might argue that the statement lacks sufficient corroborating circumstances, or that it was made under duress, thereby reducing its reliability.

Rule 805 - Hearsay Within Hearsay

Text of Rule 805

Rule 805. Hearsay Within Hearsay
Hearsay within hearsay is not excluded by the rule against hearsay if each part of the combined statements conforms with an exception to the rule.

Introduction to Rule 805

Rule 805 of the Federal Rules of Evidence addresses a specific and complex evidentiary issue known as "hearsay within hearsay," or double hearsay. This occurs when a statement contains another statement, and both are being offered as evidence. Rule 805 clarifies that such layered hearsay is admissible only if each part of the combined statements conforms with an exception to the hearsay rule. The rule is designed to maintain the integrity of evidence by ensuring that every level of hearsay meets the reliability standards required for admissibility. This chapter provides a detailed analysis of Rule 805, exploring its text, interpretation, and broader implications for the administration of justice.

Analysis of Rule 805

Rule 805 sets forth the principle that layered hearsay—where one hearsay statement includes another hearsay statement—can only be admitted if each level of hearsay is independently admissible under the hearsay rules. This section will examine the requirements for each layer of hearsay, the rationale behind the rule, and how it applies in practice.

Understanding Hearsay Within Hearsay

Hearsay within hearsay occurs when a statement made by one person (the first level of hearsay) includes another statement made by a different person (the second level of hearsay), and both statements are offered in court to prove the truth of the matters asserted. To admit such evidence, it is necessary to analyze each statement separately and determine whether it qualifies for an exception or exclusion under the hearsay rules.

1. Example of Hearsay Within Hearsay

Consider a scenario where a police report (a written statement by Officer A) includes a statement made by a witness (Witness B) who described an event. If the report is offered in court to prove the truth of what Witness B said, there are two levels of hearsay: (1) Officer A's report of Witness B's statement, and (2) Witness B's statement itself.

For this double hearsay to be admissible, each part of the statement must independently satisfy a hearsay exception. For instance, Officer A's report might be admissible as a business record under Rule 803(6), while Witness B's statement might qualify as an excited utterance under Rule 803(2).

Requirements for Admissibility Under Rule 805

To admit evidence containing hearsay within hearsay, the proponent of the evidence must demonstrate that each layer of hearsay falls within an exception or exclusion to the hearsay rule.

1. Independent Admissibility of Each Statement

Each hearsay statement within the layered statement must be analyzed individually. The court will determine whether the first statement and the embedded statement each independently qualify under a hearsay exception. If either part does not meet an exception, the entire statement is inadmissible.

For example, if a business record contains an entry that quotes a customer's complaint, the record itself may be admissible under the business records exception (Rule 803(6)), but the customer's complaint must also meet an exception, such as a present sense impression (Rule 803(1)), for the combined statement to be admissible.

2. Challenges in Application

The challenge in applying Rule 805 often lies in identifying the appropriate hearsay exceptions for each statement. The proponent must be prepared to argue the applicability of the exceptions for each layer, and the opposing party may challenge the sufficiency of those exceptions.

For instance, if a medical record includes a nurse's note that quotes a patient's statement about their symptoms, the court must evaluate both the record under the business records exception and the patient's statement under an exception like statements made for medical diagnosis or treatment (Rule 803(4)).

Rationale Behind Rule 805

The rationale for Rule 805 is to ensure that each component of a layered hearsay statement is reliable enough to be admitted as evidence. The rule maintains the integrity of the evidentiary process by preventing the introduction of statements that, while potentially reliable in one part, may include unreliable or unverified information at another level.

1. Ensuring Reliability

The primary concern with hearsay is the lack of opportunity to cross-examine the declarant. Rule 805 addresses this concern by requiring that each statement within the hearsay chain meets an exception that provides sufficient guarantees of trustworthiness.

For example, if a diary entry (potentially admissible under the recorded recollection exception) quotes a third party's casual remark, the rule ensures that the quoted remark must also meet an appropriate hearsay exception to be admissible.

2. Protecting the Integrity of the Evidence

By requiring that each hearsay statement conforms to an exception, Rule 805 prevents the admission of statements that could otherwise introduce untrustworthy or misleading information into the trial. This preserves the integrity of the trial process and ensures that the evidence considered by the trier of fact is as reliable as possible.

For instance, if a letter (hearsay) includes a quotation from a conversation (hearsay within hearsay), Rule 805 ensures that the reliability of both the letter and the quoted conversation is independently established before the evidence is admitted.

Strategic Considerations for Attorneys

Attorneys must be vigilant in both presenting and challenging evidence that involves hearsay within hearsay. Understanding how to navigate Rule 805 is crucial for effective advocacy.

1. Presenting Hearsay Within Hearsay

When presenting evidence that contains hearsay within hearsay, the proponent must be prepared to argue for the admissibility of each level of hearsay. This involves identifying applicable exceptions for each part of the statement and ensuring that the evidence is presented in a manner that clearly distinguishes the different layers.

For example, if an attorney seeks to introduce a police report that quotes a witness's statement, they must be prepared to argue that the report itself is admissible under the public records exception (Rule 803(8)) and that the witness's statement qualifies under a separate exception, such as a present sense impression (Rule 803(1)).

2. Challenging Hearsay Within Hearsay

Opposing counsel should be prepared to challenge the admissibility of any part of a layered hearsay statement that does not meet a recognized exception. This might involve attacking the reliability of the underlying statement or arguing that the proponent has failed to establish a valid hearsay exception.

For instance, if the opposing party introduces a business record that includes a customer's statement, the attorney might argue that while the record itself is admissible, the customer's statement does not meet any hearsay exception and should therefore be excluded.

3. Pre-Trial Preparation

Effective use of Rule 805 requires thorough pre-trial preparation. Attorneys should review all potential hearsay within hearsay in the evidence and be ready to address each layer's admissibility. This preparation involves understanding the nuances of hearsay exceptions and being ready to articulate why each level of hearsay meets the necessary criteria.

For example, during discovery, an attorney should identify any documents or statements that contain hearsay within hearsay and plan how to either support or challenge their admissibility based on the specific exceptions that apply.

Rule 806 - Attacking and Supporting the Declarant's Credibility

Text of Rule 806

Rule 806. Attacking and Supporting the Declarant's Credibility
When a hearsay statement—or a statement described in Rule 801(d)(2)(C), (D), or (E)—has been admitted in evidence, the declarant's credibility may be attacked, and then supported, by any evidence that would be admissible for those purposes if the declarant had testified as a witness. The court may admit evidence of the declarant's inconsistent statement or conduct, regardless of when it occurred or whether the declarant had an opportunity to explain or deny it. If the party against whom the statement was admitted calls the declarant as a witness, the party may examine the declarant on the statement as if on cross-examination.

Introduction to Rule 806

Rule 806 of the Federal Rules of Evidence provides the guidelines for attacking and supporting the credibility of a declarant whose hearsay statement has been admitted into evidence. In legal proceedings, hearsay statements are typically admitted under specific exceptions or exclusions to the hearsay rule. However, once a hearsay statement is admitted, the credibility of the declarant—the person who made the out-of-court statement—becomes a crucial factor in determining the weight that the trier of fact should give to the statement. Rule 806 allows parties to challenge or support the declarant's credibility in much the same way they would if the declarant were testifying live in court. This chapter provides a detailed analysis of Rule 806, exploring its text, interpretation, and broader implications for the administration of justice.

Analysis of Rule 806

Rule 806 provides a mechanism for addressing the credibility of a declarant whose out-of-court statement has been admitted into evidence. The rule ensures that the trier of fact can fully assess the reliability of the hearsay statement by allowing parties to introduce evidence that either undermines or bolsters the declarant's credibility. This section will examine the key components of Rule 806, including the types of evidence that can be used to attack or support credibility, the use of inconsistent statements, and the procedures for examining the declarant.

Scope and Application of Rule 806

Rule 806 applies whenever a hearsay statement or certain non-hearsay statements under Rule 801(d)(2)(C), (D), or (E) have been admitted into evidence. The rule recognizes that, because the declarant is not present in court to testify, the parties must be given an opportunity to challenge or support the declarant's credibility using the same methods that would be available if the declarant were on the witness stand.

1. Applicability to Hearsay Statements

The rule is primarily concerned with hearsay statements that have been admitted under one of the exceptions to the hearsay rule. For example, if a court admits a witness's out-of-court statement under the excited utterance exception (Rule 803(2)), Rule 806 allows the opposing party to attack the credibility of the declarant by introducing evidence that would be admissible if the declarant were testifying live.

For instance, if a declarant's statement identifying the defendant as the perpetrator is admitted as a present sense impression, the defense may seek to introduce evidence that

the declarant had a motive to lie, thus questioning the reliability of the identification.

2. Applicability to Statements under Rule 801(d)(2)(C), (D), or (E)

Rule 806 also applies to statements that are not considered hearsay under Rule 801(d)(2)(C), (D), or (E). These include statements made by a party's agent or employee, statements authorized by a party, and statements made by a coconspirator during and in furtherance of the conspiracy. When such statements are admitted, the rule allows for the same challenges to the declarant's credibility as would be permitted with hearsay statements.

For example, if a coconspirator's statement is admitted against a defendant, the defendant may introduce evidence of the coconspirator's prior convictions for dishonesty to challenge their credibility.

Methods of Attacking the Declarant's Credibility

Under Rule 806, a party may attack the credibility of the declarant using any evidence that would be admissible if the declarant were testifying as a witness. This includes, but is not limited to, evidence of the declarant's prior inconsistent statements, bias, lack of capacity, criminal convictions, or character for truthfulness.

1. Prior Inconsistent Statements

A key method for attacking a declarant's credibility under Rule 806 is through the introduction of prior inconsistent statements. These are statements made by the declarant at a different time that contradict the hearsay statement admitted into evidence. Such inconsistencies can cast doubt on the reliability of the hearsay statement and may significantly weaken its impact.

For instance, if a declarant previously stated that they did not see who committed a crime, but later made a hearsay statement identifying the defendant as the perpetrator, the prior inconsistent statement could be introduced to challenge the credibility of the identification.

2. Bias and Motive

Evidence of the declarant's bias or motive to fabricate is also admissible under Rule 806. This type of evidence is used to show that the declarant had a reason to lie or exaggerate, thereby undermining the credibility of the hearsay statement.

For example, if a declarant made a statement implicating the defendant in a crime but had a longstanding grudge against the defendant, evidence of this animosity could be introduced to suggest that the declarant's statement was motivated by bias.

3. Lack of Capacity

A party may also attack the declarant's credibility by introducing evidence that the declarant lacked the capacity to perceive, recall, or recount the events accurately. This includes evidence of mental illness, intoxication, or physical impairments that could affect the declarant's ability to provide reliable testimony.

For instance, if a declarant was intoxicated at the time they made a hearsay statement, the opposing party could introduce evidence of the declarant's intoxication to challenge the reliability of the statement.

4. Criminal Convictions

Evidence of the declarant's prior criminal convictions, particularly for crimes involving dishonesty or false statements, may be introduced under Rule 806 to attack credibility. Such evidence suggests that the declarant may have a propensity for untruthfulness, thereby casting doubt on the veracity of their hearsay statement.

For example, if a declarant has a prior conviction for perjury, the opposing party could introduce this conviction to argue that the declarant's hearsay statement should not be trusted.

5. Character for Truthfulness

Under Rule 806, evidence of the declarant's character for truthfulness or untruthfulness may be introduced to attack or support their credibility. This might include testimony from other witnesses who know the declarant and can speak to their reputation or specific instances of conduct that demonstrate truthfulness or deceit.

For example, if a declarant is known in their community for being untrustworthy, the opposing party could introduce testimony from someone familiar with the declarant's reputation to undermine the credibility of the hearsay statement.

Supporting the Declarant's Credibility

Once the declarant's credibility has been attacked, Rule 806 permits the party who introduced the hearsay statement to support the declarant's credibility with appropriate evidence. This might include presenting evidence that counters the attack, such as demonstrating the declarant's consistent behavior, character for truthfulness, or the absence of bias.

1. Rehabilitation After an Attack

After an opposing party attacks a declarant's credibility, the proponent of the hearsay statement may introduce evidence to rehabilitate the declarant. This could involve showing that the declarant had a consistent track record of truthfulness or that the alleged bias or motive to fabricate was nonexistent or overstated.

For example, if the defense attacks the credibility of a declarant by suggesting they had a motive to lie, the prosecution might introduce evidence showing that the declarant had no such motive and had consistently provided accurate information in the past.

2. Use of Consistent Statements

In some cases, the proponent may introduce prior consistent statements made by the declarant to support their credibility. These statements must meet the criteria for admissibility under Rule 801(d)(1)(B), such as being made before the alleged motive to fabricate arose, to be used for rehabilitating the declarant's credibility.

For instance, if a declarant made a statement consistent with their hearsay statement before any alleged bias or motive to fabricate emerged, that prior consistent statement might be introduced to support the credibility of the hearsay statement.

Use of Inconsistent Statements and Conduct

Rule 806 explicitly permits the admission of the declarant's inconsistent statements or conduct, regardless of when they occurred or whether the declarant had an opportunity to explain or deny them. This provision allows for a broad examination of the declarant's credibility, even if the inconsistent statements were made long before the current litigation.

1. Timing of Inconsistent Statements

The rule does not limit the use of inconsistent statements based on when they were made. This means that even if the declarant's inconsistent statement was made years before the current case, it may still be admissible to challenge the credibility of the declarant.

For example, if a declarant made an inconsistent statement in a prior, unrelated case, that statement could be introduced under Rule 806 to attack the credibility of the hearsay statement admitted in the current case.

2. Lack of Opportunity to Explain or Deny

Unlike the treatment of impeachment of live witnesses, Rule 806 does not require that the declarant be given an opportunity to explain or deny their inconsistent statements or conduct. This recognizes that the declarant is unavailable for cross-examination and that the opposing party should not be deprived of the ability to challenge credibility on that basis.

For instance, if a declarant is deceased and cannot be cross-examined, Rule 806 still permits the introduction of their inconsistent statements to challenge the credibility of their hearsay statement, even though the declarant cannot respond.

Rule 807 - Residual Exception

Rule 807. Residual Exception
(a) **In General.** Under the following conditions, a hearsay statement is not excluded by the rule against hearsay even if the statement is not admissible under a hearsay exception in Rule 803 or 804:
• (1) the statement has equivalent circumstantial guarantees of trustworthiness;
• (2) it is offered as evidence of a material fact;
• (3) it is more probative on the point for which it is offered than any other evidence that the proponent can obtain through reasonable efforts; and
• (4) admitting it will best serve the purposes of these rules and the interests of justice.
(b) **Notice.** The statement is admissible only if, before the trial or hearing, the proponent gives an adverse party reasonable notice of the intent to offer the statement and its particulars, including the declarant's name and address, so that the party has a fair opportunity to meet it.

Introduction to Rule 807

Rule 807 of the Federal Rules of Evidence, known as the "residual exception," provides a mechanism for admitting hearsay statements that do not fall within the specific exceptions enumerated in Rules 803 or 804 but nevertheless possess sufficient guarantees of trustworthiness. The residual exception is designed as a safety valve to ensure that highly reliable and probative evidence is not excluded merely because it does not fit neatly within a predefined category. This rule is intended to be used sparingly and only in exceptional circumstances where the interests of justice require the admission of the evidence. This chapter provides a detailed analysis of Rule 807, exploring its text, interpretation, and broader implications for the administration of justice.

Analysis of Rule 807

Rule 807 allows for the admission of hearsay statements that do not fall within the traditional exceptions but meet stringent criteria for reliability and necessity. This section will examine the conditions under which the residual exception may be invoked, the procedural requirements for its use, and the broader implications for the administration of justice.

Conditions for Admissibility Under Rule 807

For a hearsay statement to be admitted under the residual exception, it must satisfy several key conditions that together ensure the statement's reliability, relevance, and necessity.

1. **Equivalent Circumstantial Guarantees of Trustworthiness (Rule 807(a)(1))**

The first requirement is that the hearsay statement must have "equivalent circumstantial guarantees of trustworthiness" comparable to those found in the specific exceptions outlined in Rules 803 and 804. This means that the statement must be made under circumstances that suggest it is reliable, even though it does not fit within the traditional exceptions.

   o **Examples of Trustworthiness**

Trustworthiness may be found in statements made under oath, in the presence of others who could verify the accuracy, or in situations where the declarant had no motive to lie. For instance, a spontaneous statement made during a crisis, recorded on video with corroborating physical evidence, might be considered to have the necessary circumstantial guarantees of trustworthiness.

   o **Judicial Discretion**

The determination of whether a statement possesses equivalent guarantees of trustworthiness is largely within the discretion of the trial judge. Courts will carefully scrutinize the circumstances surrounding the statement to assess its reliability.

2. **Evidence of a Material Fact (Rule 807(a)(2))**

The hearsay statement must be offered as evidence of a material fact. A material fact is one that is significant or essential to the case's outcome. The rule ensures that the residual exception is used only for statements that are truly important to resolving the issues in the case.

   o **Relevance to the Case**

The statement must have a direct bearing on a key issue in the case. For example, a statement identifying a suspect in a criminal case would be considered material if it helps establish the identity of the perpetrator.

   o **Impact on the Decision**

The materiality of the statement also relates to its potential impact on the decision-making process of the trier of fact. If the statement could influence the outcome, it is more likely to meet this criterion.

3. **More Probative Than Other Evidence (Rule 807(a)(3))**

The statement must be "more probative on the point for which it is offered than any other evidence that the proponent can obtain through reasonable efforts." This requirement ensures that the residual exception is used only when the hearsay statement is the best available evidence on a particular issue.

○ Comparative Evaluation

The court will compare the probative value of the hearsay statement with that of other available evidence. If other evidence is equally or more probative, the hearsay statement may be excluded.

○ Reasonable Efforts

The proponent of the statement must demonstrate that they have made reasonable efforts to obtain other evidence but were unable to find anything as probative as the hearsay statement. For instance, if a key eyewitness is deceased and their statement is the most probative evidence available, it might be admitted under this rule.

4. Serves the Interests of Justice (Rule 807(a)(4))

Finally, admitting the hearsay statement must "best serve the purposes of these rules and the interests of justice." This broad criterion allows the court to consider the overall fairness and integrity of the trial process when deciding whether to admit the statement.

○ Balancing Test

The court will balance the need for the evidence against the potential for unfair prejudice, confusion, or delay. If admitting the statement promotes a fair and just resolution of the case, it may be deemed admissible under this rule.

○ Judicial Considerations

Judges will consider factors such as the seriousness of the case, the potential consequences of excluding the evidence, and the overall reliability of the judicial process in deciding whether to admit the statement under Rule 807.

Notice Requirement (Rule 807(b))

To ensure that the opposing party has a fair opportunity to contest the admissibility of the hearsay statement, Rule 807(b) imposes a notice requirement. The proponent of the statement must give the adverse party reasonable notice of their intent to offer the statement, along with details about the statement and the declarant.

1. Timing of Notice

Notice must be given "before the trial or hearing." The timing is crucial because it allows the opposing party adequate time to prepare arguments against the admission of the hearsay statement and to investigate its reliability.

○ Reasonable Notice

The rule requires "reasonable notice," which is typically interpreted to mean sufficient time to allow the opposing party to prepare. What constitutes reasonable notice may vary depending on the complexity of the case and the nature of the statement.

2. Particulars of the Statement

The notice must include the particulars of the statement, such as the content of the statement, the circumstances under which it was made, and the declarant's identity. This ensures that the opposing party can fully assess the statement's trustworthiness and relevance.

○ Declarant's Information

The proponent must provide the declarant's name and address, if known. This allows the opposing party to investigate the declarant's credibility, bias, or other factors that might affect the reliability of the statement.

○ Adequacy of Notice

If the proponent fails to provide sufficient details or gives notice too late, the court may exclude the statement on the grounds that the opposing party was unfairly disadvantaged in preparing their case.

Strategic Considerations for Attorneys

Rule 807 requires attorneys to carefully consider the strategic use of the residual exception. Because the rule is intended to be used sparingly, its application must be carefully justified, and attorneys must be prepared to meet the stringent requirements set forth in the rule.

1. When to Invoke the Residual Exception

Attorneys should consider invoking Rule 807 only when a critical piece of evidence does not fit within the established hearsay exceptions but is essential to their case. This often arises in situations where traditional evidence is unavailable, and the hearsay statement is the most reliable and probative evidence available.

○ Critical Evidence

The residual exception might be invoked in cases involving unique or extraordinary circumstances, such as a key witness's death or unavailability, where their statement is the best evidence available on a material fact.

2. Preparing to Satisfy the Rule's Requirements

Proponents of a hearsay statement under Rule 807 must be prepared to argue persuasively that the statement meets all four conditions: trustworthiness, materiality, probative value, and the interests of justice. This often requires extensive preparation, including gathering evidence to support the reliability of the statement and demonstrating that no better evidence is available.

○ Supporting Trustworthiness

Attorneys may need to gather corroborating evidence, such as documents or testimony from other witnesses, to bolster the trustworthiness of the hearsay statement. Additionally, they may need to provide context, such as the circumstances under which the statement was made, to persuade the court of its reliability.

ARTICLE IX. AUTHENTICATION AND IDENTIFICATION

Rule 901 - Authenticating or Identifying Evidence

Text of Rule 901

Rule 901. Authenticating or Identifying Evidence
(a) **In General.** To satisfy the requirement of authenticating or identifying an item of evidence, the proponent must produce evidence sufficient to support a finding that the item is what the proponent claims it is.
(b) **Examples.** The following are examples only—not a complete list—of evidence that satisfies the requirement:

- (1) **Testimony of a Witness with Knowledge.** Testimony that an item is what it is claimed to be.

- (2) **Nonexpert Opinion About Handwriting.** A nonexpert's opinion that handwriting is genuine, based on a familiarity with it that was not acquired for the current litigation.

- (3) **Comparison by an Expert Witness or the Trier of Fact.** A comparison with an authenticated specimen by an expert witness or the trier of fact.

- (4) **Distinctive Characteristics and the Like.** The appearance, contents, substance, internal patterns, or other distinctive characteristics of the item, taken together with all the circumstances.

- (5) **Opinion About a Voice.** An opinion identifying a person's voice—whether heard firsthand or through mechanical or electronic transmission or recording—based on hearing the voice at any time under circumstances that connect it with the alleged speaker.

- (6) **Evidence About a Telephone Conversation.** For a telephone conversation, evidence that a call was made to the number assigned at the time to:

  - (A) a particular person, if circumstances, including self-identification, show that the person answering was the one called; or

  - (B) a particular business, if the call was made to a business and the call related to business reasonably transacted over the telephone.

- (7) **Evidence About Public Records.** Evidence that:

  - (A) a document was recorded or filed in a public office as authorized by law; or

  - (B) a purported public record or statement is from the office where items of this kind are kept.

- (8) **Evidence About Ancient Documents or Data Compilations.** For a document or data compilation, evidence that it:

  - (A) is in a condition that creates no suspicion about its authenticity;

  - (B) was in a place where, if authentic, it would likely be; and

  - (C) is at least 20 years old when offered.

- (9) **Evidence About a Process or System.** Evidence describing a process or system and showing that it produces an accurate result.

- (10) **Methods Provided by a Statute or Rule.** Any method of authentication or identification allowed by a federal statute or a rule prescribed by the Supreme Court.

Introduction to Rule 901

Rule 901 of the Federal Rules of Evidence sets forth the foundational requirements for the authentication or identification of evidence. Authentication is a critical step in the evidentiary process, as it establishes that the evidence presented is what it purports to be. Without proper authentication, evidence cannot be admitted in court, regardless of its relevance or potential probative value. Rule

901 outlines the general principles for authentication and provides illustrative examples of how different types of evidence may be authenticated or identified. This chapter provides a detailed analysis of Rule 901, exploring its text, interpretation, and broader implications for the administration of justice.

Analysis of Rule 901

Rule 901 provides the framework for authenticating or identifying evidence in legal proceedings. This process is essential for establishing the legitimacy of evidence before it is considered by the trier of fact. This section will explore the general principles of Rule 901, the examples provided in the rule, and the implications of these requirements for the admission of various types of evidence.

General Requirement of Authentication (Rule 901(a))

The general requirement under Rule 901(a) is that the proponent of an item of evidence must produce sufficient evidence to support a finding that the item is what the proponent claims it is. This requirement applies to all types of evidence, including documents, physical objects, recordings, and digital data.

1. **Sufficiency of Evidence**

The standard for authentication is not absolute proof but rather the presentation of enough evidence to allow a reasonable jury to conclude that the item is genuine. This means that the proponent must provide a prima facie case of authenticity, after which the opposing party may challenge the evidence.

o **Prima Facie Case**

To establish a prima facie case of authenticity, the proponent might offer direct evidence, such as the testimony of a witness with firsthand knowledge, or circumstantial evidence, such as the distinctive characteristics of the item.

For example, if a party seeks to introduce a signed contract, the testimony of a witness who saw the contract being signed could provide sufficient evidence to support its authenticity.

2. **Role of the Trier of Fact**

The trier of fact—whether a judge in a bench trial or a jury—ultimately decides the authenticity of the evidence. The court's role under Rule 901 is to determine whether the proponent has provided enough evidence for the trier of fact to reasonably find that the item is what it purports to be.

o **Judicial Gatekeeping**

The judge acts as a gatekeeper, ensuring that only evidence with a sufficient foundation of authenticity is presented to the jury. If the judge finds that the proponent has not met the burden of establishing a prima facie case, the evidence may be excluded.

For instance, if a party attempts to introduce a letter without any evidence regarding its origin or the identity of the author, the judge may exclude the letter for lack of proper authentication.

Examples of Methods of Authentication (Rule 901(b))

Rule 901(b) provides a non-exhaustive list of examples of how various types of evidence can be authenticated. These examples illustrate common methods but do not limit the ways in which evidence can be authenticated.

1. **Testimony of a Witness with Knowledge (Rule 901(b)(1))**

The most straightforward method of authentication is through the testimony of a witness with firsthand knowledge of the item. This witness can confirm that the item is what it is claimed to be.

o **Application**

A witness who saw a photograph being taken can authenticate the photograph by testifying that it accurately depicts the scene as they observed it.

o **Relevance**

This method is relevant in situations where a witness is directly connected to the evidence, such as a person who witnessed a contract signing or someone who recorded a conversation.

2. **Nonexpert Opinion About Handwriting (Rule 901(b)(2))**

A nonexpert who is familiar with a person's handwriting, based on interactions that occurred before the litigation, can provide an opinion about the genuineness of the handwriting.

o **Familiarity Requirement**

The nonexpert must have acquired their familiarity with the handwriting independently of the current litigation. For example, a coworker who regularly received handwritten notes from the defendant could authenticate the handwriting in a disputed document.

o **Limitations**

The use of nonexpert opinion is limited to cases where the witness's familiarity with the handwriting is established, and the court may require additional evidence if the authenticity of the handwriting is particularly contested.

3. **Comparison by an Expert Witness or the Trier of Fact (Rule 901(b)(3))**

A document or other item can be authenticated by comparing it with an authenticated specimen. This comparison can be conducted by an expert witness or the trier of fact.

o **Expert Analysis**

An expert in handwriting, for example, might compare a disputed signature with a known sample to determine its authenticity.

o **Jury Comparison**

In cases where the differences or similarities are apparent to a layperson, the trier of fact might directly compare the evidence without expert assistance.

4. **Distinctive Characteristics and the Like (Rule 901(b)(4))**

The appearance, contents, substance, internal patterns, or other distinctive characteristics of an item, taken together with the surrounding circumstances, can serve as a basis for authentication.

- ○ **Internal Consistency**

For instance, a letter's content might refer to specific, known events or details that only the purported author would likely know, supporting its authenticity.

- ○ **Circumstantial Evidence**

The combination of physical features and contextual evidence can be persuasive, especially when no direct evidence is available.

5. **Opinion About a Voice (Rule 901(b)(5))**

A voice, whether heard firsthand or through a recording, can be authenticated by someone who is familiar with the voice, provided the familiarity was gained in circumstances that connect the voice to the alleged speaker.

- ○ **Voice Identification**

For example, a witness who has regularly spoken with the declarant over the phone may identify their voice in a recorded conversation.

- ○ **Application**

This method is often used in cases involving audio recordings where the identity of the speaker is a key issue.

6. **Evidence About a Telephone Conversation (Rule 901(b)(6))**

Authentication of a telephone conversation can be established by showing that a call was made to the number assigned to a particular person or business and that the conversation related to matters typically associated with that person or business.

- ○ **Self-Identification**

If a call was made to a specific number and the person answering identified themselves as the intended recipient, this could suffice for authentication.

- ○ **Business Calls**

Calls made to a business number where the conversation relates to business transactions can be authenticated by the nature of the conversation and the number dialed.

7. **Evidence About Public Records (Rule 901(b)(7))**

Public records can be authenticated by evidence that a document was recorded or filed in a public office as authorized by law, or that a purported public record is from the office where such records are kept.

- ○ **Official Records**

For example, a birth certificate can be authenticated by showing that it was issued by a government agency responsible for maintaining such records.

- ○ **Certification**

In many cases, a certified copy of a public record, issued by the custodian of the records, will be sufficient for authentication.

8. **Evidence About Ancient Documents or Data Compilations (Rule 901(b)(8))**

An ancient document or data compilation (at least 20 years old) can be authenticated if it is in a condition that creates no suspicion about its authenticity, was found in a place where such documents are typically kept, and meets the age requirement.

- ○ **Condition and Location**

The condition of the document and its storage location are crucial factors in determining its authenticity. A will found in a law firm's archives, in good condition and over 20 years old, might be authenticated under this rule.

- ○ **No Suspicion**

The document must not show signs of tampering or forgery, and there should be no other circumstances that cast doubt on its authenticity.

9. **Evidence About a Process or System (Rule 901(b)(9))**

A process or system used to produce an accurate result can be authenticated by describing the process or system and demonstrating that it produces reliable outcomes.

- ○ **Technological Systems**

This method is commonly used to authenticate digital records, such as emails or electronic data, where the proponent must show that the system used to generate or store the data is reliable.

- ○ **Chain of Custody**

In cases involving complex processes, such as DNA analysis, the proponent must often establish a clear chain of custody and demonstrate that the process was correctly followed.

10. **Methods Provided by a Statute or Rule (Rule 901(b)(10))**

Any method of authentication or identification authorized by a federal statute or Supreme Court rule is acceptable under Rule 901. This provision allows for flexibility in the authentication process, accommodating various types of evidence that may not be specifically addressed in Rule 901(b)(1)-(9).

- ○ **Statutory Methods**

Certain types of evidence may be authenticated under specific federal statutes, such as those governing electronic records or certified copies of official documents.

- ○ **Supreme Court Rules**

Additional methods of authentication may be prescribed by Supreme Court rules, providing a legal basis for the admission of evidence that requires specialized authentication procedures.

Implications for Legal Practice

The requirements of Rule 901 have significant implications for legal practice, as they impose a burden on the proponent of evidence to establish its authenticity before it can be admitted. Attorneys must be diligent in gathering the necessary evidence to satisfy Rule 901 and must be prepared to challenge the authenticity of evidence presented by the opposing party.

1. **Preparation for Authentication**

Attorneys must anticipate the need for authentication and prepare their cases accordingly. This may involve securing witnesses who can testify to the authenticity of documents, objects, or recordings, or obtaining certified copies of public records.

o **Documentary Evidence**

When dealing with documentary evidence, attorneys should ensure that they have the necessary supporting testimony or certifications to establish authenticity.

For example, an attorney introducing emails as evidence should be prepared to authenticate them by showing that they were sent from the defendant's known email address and that the content is consistent with other communications.

2. **Challenging Authentication**

Opposing parties may challenge the authenticity of evidence by questioning the reliability of the methods used to authenticate it or by presenting evidence that contradicts the proponent's claims of authenticity.

o **Cross-Examination**

During cross-examination, an attorney might challenge the credibility of a witness testifying to the authenticity of a document, particularly if there are inconsistencies in the witness's testimony or if the document's condition raises suspicions.

o **Expert Testimony**

In some cases, attorneys may call upon expert witnesses to challenge the authenticity of evidence, such as handwriting experts or forensic analysts who can dispute the claims made by the proponent.

3. **Strategic Considerations**

The process of authentication can be a strategic element of trial preparation, as the success or failure of authenticating key evidence can significantly impact the outcome of a case.

o **Early Identification**

Identifying potential authentication issues early in the case allows attorneys to address them proactively, whether by gathering additional evidence or by preparing to argue for alternative methods of authentication under Rule 901(b)(10).

o **Preserving Objections**

Attorneys should be vigilant in preserving objections to the authenticity of evidence, as failure to do so may result in the admission of evidence that could otherwise have been excluded.

Rule 902 - Evidence That Is Self-Authenticating

Text of Rule 902

Rule 902. Evidence That Is Self-Authenticating

The following items of evidence are self-authenticating; they require no extrinsic evidence of authenticity in order to be admitted:

1. **Domestic Public Documents That Are Sealed and Signed.** A document that bears:

   - o (A) a seal purporting to be that of the United States; any state, district, commonwealth, territory, or insular possession of the United States; the former Panama Canal Zone; the Trust Territory of the Pacific Islands; a political subdivision of any of these entities; or a department, agency, or officer of any entity named above; and
   - o (B) a signature purporting to be an execution or attestation.

2. **Domestic Public Documents That Are Not Sealed but Are Signed and Certified.** A document that bears no seal if:

   - o (A) it bears the signature of an officer or employee of an entity named in Rule 902(1)(A); and
   - o (B) another public officer who has a seal and official duties within that same entity certifies under seal—or its equivalent—that the signer has the official capacity and that the signature is genuine.

3. **Foreign Public Documents.** A document that purports to be signed or attested by a person who is authorized by a foreign country's law to do so. The document must be accompanied by a final certification as to the genuineness of the signature and official position:

   - o (A) of the signer or attester; or
   - o (B) of any foreign official whose certificate of genuineness relates to the signature or attestation or is in a chain of certificates of genuineness relating to the signature or attestation.

   The certification may be made by a secretary of a United States embassy or legation; by a consul general, vice consul, or consular agent of the United States; or by a diplomatic or consular official of the foreign country assigned or accredited to the United States. If all parties have been given a reasonable opportunity to investigate the document's authenticity and accuracy, the court may, for good cause, either:

   - o (A) order that it be treated as presumptively authentic without final certification; or
   - o (B) allow it to be evidenced by an attested summary with or without final certification.

4. **Certified Copies of Public Records.** A copy of an official record—or a copy of a document that was recorded or filed in a public office as authorized by law—if the copy is certified as correct by:

   - o (A) the custodian or another person authorized to make the certification; or
   - o (B) a certificate that complies with Rule 902(1), (2), or (3), a federal statute, or a rule prescribed by the Supreme Court.

5. **Official Publications.** A book, pamphlet, or other publication purporting to be issued by a public authority.

6. **Newspapers and Periodicals.** Printed material purporting to be a newspaper or periodical.

7. **Trade Inscriptions and the Like.** An inscription, sign, tag, or label purporting to have been affixed in the course of business and indicating origin, ownership, or control.

8. **Acknowledged Documents.** A document accompanied by a certificate of acknowledgment that is lawfully executed by a notary public or another officer who is authorized to take acknowledgments.

9. **Commercial Paper and Related Documents.** Commercial paper, a signature on it, and related documents, to the extent allowed by general commercial law.

10.	**Presumptions Under a Federal Statute.** A signature, document, or anything else that a federal statute declares to be presumptively or prima facie genuine or authentic.
11.	**Certified Domestic Records of a Regularly Conducted Activity.** The original or a copy of a domestic record that meets the requirements of Rule 803(6)(A)–(C), as shown by a certification of the custodian or another qualified person that complies with a federal statute or a rule prescribed by the Supreme Court. Before the trial or hearing, the proponent must give an adverse party reasonable written notice of the intent to offer the record—and must make the record and certification available for inspection—so that the party has a fair opportunity to challenge them.
12.	**Certified Foreign Records of a Regularly Conducted Activity.** In a civil case, the original or a copy of a foreign record that meets the requirements of Rule 902(11), modified as follows: the certification must be signed in a manner that, if falsely made, would subject the maker to a criminal penalty in the country where the certification is signed. The proponent must also meet the notice requirements of Rule 902(11).
13.	**Certified Records Generated by an Electronic Process or System.** A record generated by an electronic process or system that produces an accurate result, as shown by a certification of a qualified person that complies with the certification requirements of Rule 902(11) or (12). The proponent must also meet the notice requirements of Rule 902(11).
14.	**Certified Data Copied from an Electronic Device, Storage Medium, or File.** Data copied from an electronic device, storage medium, or file, if authenticated by a process of digital identification, as shown by a certification of a qualified person that complies with the certification requirements of Rule 902(11) or (12). The proponent must also meet the notice requirements of Rule 902(11).

Introduction to Rule 902

Rule 902 of the Federal Rules of Evidence provides a list of categories of evidence that are considered self-authenticating, meaning they require no extrinsic evidence of authenticity in order to be admitted into evidence. This rule simplifies the process of admitting certain types of documents and records by presuming their authenticity, thus eliminating the need for additional witness testimony or other evidence to establish their genuineness. Rule 902 is essential in streamlining the evidentiary process, especially in cases involving routine or commonly accepted documents. This chapter provides a detailed analysis of Rule 902, exploring its text, interpretation, and broader implications for the administration of justice.

Analysis of Rule 902

Rule 902 streamlines the evidentiary process by providing a clear list of documents and items that are considered self-authenticating, thus eliminating the need for additional proof of authenticity. This section examines each category of self-authenticating evidence, explaining its application, rationale, and implications for legal practice.

Domestic Public Documents That Are Sealed and Signed (Rule 902(1))

Public documents bearing an official seal and a signature of an authorized officer are self-authenticating. This category includes documents issued by federal, state, or local governments, such as birth certificates, court records, or official correspondence.

1. **Seals and Signatures**

The presence of an official seal and signature provides inherent credibility to the document, presuming it to be genuine and eliminating the need for further authentication.

   o **Application**

A certified copy of a marriage license issued by a state government, bearing the state seal and the signature of the issuing officer, would be self-authenticating under Rule 902(1).

   o **Rationale**

The use of official seals and signatures is a widely accepted method of ensuring the authenticity of public documents, making additional proof unnecessary.

Domestic Public Documents That Are Not Sealed but Are Signed and Certified (Rule 902(2))

Documents that lack an official seal but are signed by an officer or employee of a public entity can be self-authenticating if accompanied by a certification from another public officer with official duties within the same entity.

1. **Certification Process**

The certification confirms that the signer holds the official capacity claimed and that the signature is genuine. This additional layer of certification ensures the document's reliability.

   o **Application**

A document issued by a municipal clerk, signed by the clerk but without a seal, can be self-authenticating if another public officer certifies the authenticity of the signature and the official capacity of the clerk.

   o **Rationale**

The certification process provides sufficient assurance of the document's authenticity, obviating the need for further proof.

Foreign Public Documents (Rule 902(3))

Foreign public documents are self-authenticating if they are signed or attested by an authorized person and accompanied by a final certification regarding the genuineness of the signature and the official position of the signer or attester.

1. **Final Certification**

The final certification can be made by a U.S. diplomatic or consular officer, or by an official of the foreign country assigned to the United States. This certification ensures that the foreign document meets the standards of authenticity recognized by U.S. courts.

o **Application**

A birth certificate issued by a foreign government, accompanied by a certification from a U.S. consulate verifying the authenticity of the signature and the official capacity of the issuer, would be self-authenticating under Rule 902(3).

o **Rationale**

The requirement of a final certification by a recognized authority provides a high degree of assurance regarding the authenticity of foreign public documents, facilitating their use in U.S. courts.

58.3.4 Certified Copies of Public Records (Rule 902(4))

Copies of official records, or documents recorded or filed in a public office, are self-authenticating if certified as correct by the custodian or another authorized person.

1. **Certification by Custodian**

The certification process confirms that the copy is a true and accurate representation of the original record or document held in a public office.

o **Application**

A certified copy of a property deed from a county recorder's office would be self-authenticating under Rule 902(4), provided it includes the necessary certification from the custodian of records.

o **Rationale**

Certified copies of public records are widely accepted as authentic, given the official nature of the certification and the responsibility of the custodian to maintain accurate records.

Official Publications (Rule 902(5))

Official publications issued by public authorities are self-authenticating. This includes books, pamphlets, and other publications that purport to be issued by a government entity.

1. **Presumption of Authenticity**

The presumption of authenticity arises from the fact that these publications are produced and distributed by public authorities, making additional proof unnecessary.

o **Application**

A government-issued report on public health, printed and distributed by a state health department, would be self-authenticating under Rule 902(5).

o **Rationale**

Official publications are considered reliable sources of information due to their governmental origin, and their authenticity is generally unquestioned.

Newspapers and Periodicals (Rule 902(6))

Printed material purporting to be a newspaper or periodical is self-authenticating. This category includes widely circulated publications that are generally accepted as reliable sources of news and information.

1. **Purported Authenticity**

The authenticity of newspapers and periodicals is presumed based on their widespread distribution and public accessibility, which provides a measure of credibility.

o **Application**

A copy of a newspaper article from a major national newspaper would be self-authenticating under Rule 902(6), without the need for further evidence to prove its authenticity.

o **Rationale**

The public nature of newspapers and periodicals, coupled with their regular publication and broad readership, supports their presumption of authenticity.

Trade Inscriptions and the Like (Rule 902(7))

Inscriptions, signs, tags, or labels purporting to have been affixed in the course of business and indicating origin, ownership, or control are self-authenticating. This category includes trademarks, brand labels, and other commercial markings.

1. **Commercial Authenticity**

The authenticity of trade inscriptions is presumed based on their use in commerce, where accurate representation of origin and ownership is crucial for business operations.

o **Application**

A label on a product indicating the manufacturer's name and trademark would be self-authenticating under Rule 902(7).

o **Rationale**

Trade inscriptions are integral to commercial transactions, and their authenticity is generally accepted in business contexts, reducing the need for additional proof.

Acknowledged Documents (Rule 902(8))

Documents accompanied by a certificate of acknowledgment that is lawfully executed by a notary public or another officer authorized to take acknowledgments are self-authenticating.

1. **Notarial Acknowledgment**

The acknowledgment by a notary or other authorized officer provides a formal attestation of the document's authenticity, ensuring that it was executed by the person whose signature appears on it.

o **Application**

A contract signed and notarized, with an acknowledgment certificate from the notary, would be self-authenticating under Rule 902(8).

o **Rationale**

The process of notarization, which involves verifying the signer's identity and willingness to execute the document, provides a high level of assurance regarding the document's authenticity.

Commercial Paper and Related Documents (Rule 902(9))

Commercial paper, signatures on it, and related documents are self-authenticating to the extent allowed by general commercial law. This category includes negotiable instruments such as checks, promissory notes, and bills of exchange.

1. Commercial Law Standards

The authenticity of commercial paper is governed by established commercial law principles, which presume the validity of signatures and related documents in the course of business.

○ **Application**

A check signed by a bank customer and presented for payment would be self-authenticating under Rule 902(9), based on the presumption that the signature and the document are genuine.

○ **Rationale**

Commercial paper operates under a legal framework that assumes the authenticity of documents used in financial transactions, facilitating their use in commerce without the need for additional proof.

Presumptions Under a Federal Statute (Rule 902(10))

Any signature, document, or other item that a federal statute declares to be presumptively or prima facie genuine or authentic is self-authenticating.

1. Statutory Authentication

Federal statutes may provide specific methods of authentication for certain types of evidence, creating a presumption of authenticity that is recognized by Rule 902.

○ **Application**

A certified mail receipt that is deemed presumptively authentic under a federal statute would be self-authenticating under Rule 902(10).

○ **Rationale**

Statutory presumptions of authenticity are designed to streamline the admission of evidence in federal courts, reflecting legislative determinations of reliability and authenticity.

Certified Domestic Records of a Regularly Conducted Activity (Rule 902(11))

Domestic records that meet the requirements of Rule 803(6)(A)–(C), supported by a certification of the custodian or another qualified person, are self-authenticating. The proponent must give reasonable written notice to the adverse party before trial.

1. Certification Process

The certification must comply with federal statutes or rules prescribed by the Supreme Court and must demonstrate that the record meets the criteria for admissibility under Rule 803(6).

○ **Application**

A business record, such as a ledger or invoice, certified by the company's record custodian, would be self-authenticating under Rule 902(11), provided the opposing party receives timely notice.

○ **Rationale**

The certification process, coupled with the notice requirement, ensures that the record is reliable and that the opposing party has an opportunity to challenge its authenticity before trial.

Certified Foreign Records of a Regularly Conducted Activity (Rule 902(12))

Similar to Rule 902(11), this provision applies to foreign records, with the additional requirement that the certification must be signed in a manner that subjects the signer to criminal penalties for falsification in their country.

1. International Standards

The certification process ensures that foreign records meet the same standards of authenticity as domestic records, while accounting for the legal framework of the country where the record was created.

○ **Application**

A certified foreign bank statement, accompanied by a certification that meets the requirements of Rule 902(12), would be self-authenticating in a U.S. court.

○ **Rationale**

By requiring certification that subjects the signer to criminal penalties, this rule ensures that foreign records are as trustworthy as domestic records, facilitating their admission in U.S. courts.

Certified Records Generated by an Electronic Process or System (Rule 902(13))

Records generated by an electronic process or system that produces an accurate result are self-authenticating if certified by a qualified person. The proponent must provide notice to the adverse party before trial.

1. Digital Authentication

This rule addresses the increasing use of electronic records and systems in modern litigation, providing a method for their authentication without the need for extrinsic evidence.

○ **Application**

A digitally signed and certified email, generated by a reliable electronic system, would be self-authenticating under Rule 902(13), provided the opposing party is given proper notice.

○ **Rationale**

The certification by a qualified person, combined with the notice requirement, ensures that electronic records are reliable and that the opposing party has the opportunity to contest their authenticity.

Certified Data Copied from an Electronic Device, Storage Medium, or File (Rule 902(14))

Data copied from an electronic device, storage medium, or file is self-authenticating if authenticated by a process of digital identification and certified by a qualified person. The proponent must provide notice to the adverse party before trial.

1. **Digital Identification**

This rule facilitates the admission of data from electronic devices, ensuring that such data is authenticated through a reliable process of digital identification.

  o **Application**

A forensic copy of a hard drive, authenticated through digital identification and certified by a qualified forensic expert, would be self-authenticating under Rule 902(14), with proper notice to the opposing party.

  o **Rationale**

The rule recognizes the importance of digital evidence in modern litigation and provides a streamlined method for its authentication, while ensuring reliability and fairness through the certification and notice requirements.

Strategic Considerations for Attorneys

Rule 902 has significant implications for the practice of law, particularly in the preparation and presentation of evidence. Attorneys must be familiar with the categories of self-authenticating evidence and the procedures for introducing such evidence at trial.

1. **Leveraging Self-Authenticating Evidence**

Attorneys can streamline the evidentiary process by leveraging self-authenticating evidence under Rule 902, reducing the need for witness testimony and other forms of authentication.

  o **Efficiency in Trial Preparation**

By identifying self-authenticating evidence early in the case, attorneys can focus their efforts on other aspects of trial preparation, knowing that these items will likely be admitted without challenge.

  o **Tactical Use**

The use of self-authenticating evidence can be a tactical advantage, allowing attorneys to present a clear and uncontested case without the risk of authenticity disputes.

2. **Challenging Self-Authenticating Evidence**

While Rule 902 presumes the authenticity of certain evidence, opposing counsel may still challenge the admissibility of self-authenticating evidence on other grounds, such as relevance, hearsay, or unfair prejudice.

  o **Cross-Examination and Objections**

Attorneys should be prepared to cross-examine the basis for the certification or to object to the evidence on grounds other than authenticity, particularly if the evidence is prejudicial or lacks probative value.

  o **Notice and Preparation**

Attorneys should closely monitor the notice requirements under Rule 902, ensuring they are adequately prepared to address any self-authenticating evidence presented by the opposing party.

Rule 903 - Subscribing Witness's Testimony

Text of Rule 903

Rule 903. Subscribing Witness's Testimony
A subscribing witness's testimony is necessary to authenticate a writing only if required by the law of the jurisdiction that governs its validity.

Introduction to Rule 903

Rule 903 of the Federal Rules of Evidence addresses the circumstances under which the testimony of a subscribing witness is required to authenticate a writing. A subscribing witness is an individual who has signed a document, usually to attest that the primary signer executed the document voluntarily and with the required formalities. Historically, such witnesses were often required to testify to authenticate the document before it could be admitted into evidence. However, Rule 903 simplifies this process by establishing that the testimony of a subscribing witness is generally not necessary unless required by the law of the jurisdiction governing the document's validity. This chapter provides a detailed analysis of Rule 903, exploring its text, interpretation, and broader implications for the administration of justice.

Analysis of Rule 903

Rule 903 clarifies the conditions under which the testimony of a subscribing witness is required for the authentication of a writing. By default, the rule eliminates the need for such testimony unless it is specifically mandated by the relevant jurisdictional law. This section will explore the historical context of subscribing witness testimony, the impact of Rule 903, and its practical implications for legal practice.

Historical Context of Subscribing Witness Testimony

Traditionally, many legal systems required the testimony of a subscribing witness to authenticate certain documents, particularly those involving significant transactions such as wills, contracts, and deeds. The subscribing witness would testify to the circumstances under which the document was executed, providing assurance that the document was signed by the party it purports to bind and that the signing complied with any formal legal requirements.

1. **Role of the Subscribing Witness**

The subscribing witness typically played a key role in the execution of legal documents, ensuring that the signer was competent, that the signature was genuine, and that the document was executed in accordance with legal formalities.

   o **Execution of Wills**

For example, in the case of a will, the subscribing witnesses would attest that the testator signed the document willingly and was of sound mind at the time of signing. Their testimony was often required to probate the will.

   o **Authentication of Deeds**

Similarly, deeds often required subscribing witnesses to ensure that the transfer of property was legally binding. The witnesses would later testify, if necessary, to the authenticity of the deed.

2. **Evolving Legal Practices**

Over time, the legal requirement for subscribing witnesses has diminished, especially with the advent of notarization and other methods of document authentication. The need for a subscribing witness's testimony has become increasingly rare, except in specific circumstances dictated by jurisdictional law.

   o **Notarization**

The use of notaries public, who verify the identity of signers and the voluntary nature of their signatures, has largely supplanted the role of subscribing witnesses in many contexts.

   o **Self-Authenticating Documents**

Modern rules, such as those in Rule 902, have introduced categories of self-authenticating documents, further reducing the need for subscribing witness testimony.

Rule 903's Approach to Subscribing Witness Testimony

Rule 903 streamlines the evidentiary process by establishing that the testimony of a subscribing witness is generally not required to authenticate a writing. This reflects the modern trend toward simplifying document authentication, except in cases where the governing law explicitly requires such testimony.

1. **General Elimination of the Requirement**

Under Rule 903, subscribing witness testimony is not necessary to authenticate a document unless the law of the jurisdiction that governs the document's validity specifically mandates it. This significantly reduces the burden on parties seeking to introduce documents into evidence.

   o **Default Position**

The rule assumes that documents can be authenticated through other means, such as through the testimony of a custodian, comparison with authenticated specimens, or certification under Rule 902.

   o **Jurisdictional Exceptions**

However, if the law governing the document imposes a requirement for subscribing witness testimony, Rule 903 defers to that requirement, acknowledging the supremacy of local or state law in such matters.

2. **Implications for Legal Practice**

The primary impact of Rule 903 is to streamline the evidentiary process by eliminating unnecessary testimonial requirements, thereby facilitating the admission of documents. However, attorneys must remain vigilant about the specific requirements of the jurisdiction governing the document, as some jurisdictions may still require subscribing witness testimony for certain documents.

- ○ **Jurisdictional Awareness**

Attorneys must be aware of the laws of the jurisdiction where the document was executed or is being enforced. For example, certain states may still require subscribing witness testimony for the authentication of wills or deeds.

- ○ **Practical Considerations**

In cases where subscribing witness testimony is required, attorneys must ensure that such witnesses are available and prepared to testify, or that alternative means of authentication are considered.

Examples of When Subscribing Witness Testimony May Be Required

While Rule 903 generally eliminates the need for subscribing witness testimony, there are specific scenarios where such testimony may still be necessary due to jurisdictional requirements.

1. **Wills and Testamentary Documents**

In some jurisdictions, the testimony of subscribing witnesses is still required to probate a will. This ensures that the will was properly executed and that the testator was competent and free from undue influence at the time of signing.

- ○ **State Law Requirements**

For instance, some states may require that at least one of the subscribing witnesses testify in court to authenticate the will before it can be admitted to probate.

- ○ **Alternative Procedures**

Where subscribing witnesses are unavailable, jurisdictions may allow for alternative methods of authentication, such as affidavits or deposition testimony.

2. **Real Estate Deeds**

Certain states may require subscribing witness testimony to authenticate real estate deeds, particularly in cases involving older deeds or specific types of property transfers.

- ○ **Title Examination**

In the context of real estate transactions, title examiners may require proof that the deed was properly executed, which could necessitate subscribing witness testimony.

- ○ **Historical Documents**

For historical deeds or documents executed before modern notarization practices, subscribing witness testimony might still be relevant or required by law.

3. **Contracts Requiring Formal Execution**

In rare cases, contracts that require formal execution, such as certain corporate agreements or international contracts, might necessitate subscribing witness testimony if required by the jurisdiction's law.

- ○ **Corporate Formalities**

Some corporate charters or bylaws may stipulate that certain contracts must be executed with subscribing witnesses, especially for significant transactions like mergers or acquisitions.

- ○ **International Agreements**

International contracts governed by foreign law may require subscribing witness testimony, depending on the formal execution requirements of the foreign jurisdiction.

Strategic Considerations for Attorneys

Attorneys must consider the implications of Rule 903 when preparing to authenticate documents in court. Understanding when subscribing witness testimony is required and when it is not can significantly impact the strategy for admitting evidence.

1. **Determining the Governing Law**

The first step for attorneys is to identify the law governing the validity of the document in question. This will determine whether subscribing witness testimony is required under Rule 903.

- ○ **Jurisdictional Research**

Attorneys should conduct thorough research on the jurisdictional requirements for document authentication, particularly in cases involving wills, deeds, or contracts with formal execution requirements.

- ○ **Advising Clients**

When drafting or executing documents, attorneys should advise clients on the potential need for subscribing witness testimony, depending on the governing law, to ensure future enforceability.

2. **Preparation of Witnesses**

In cases where subscribing witness testimony is required, attorneys must ensure that witnesses are available, competent, and prepared to testify regarding the execution of the document.

- ○ **Witness Availability**

Attorneys should confirm the availability of subscribing witnesses early in the litigation process to avoid delays or challenges in authenticating the document.

- ○ **Witness Preparation**

Witnesses should be thoroughly prepared to testify about the circumstances of the document's execution, including the identification of signatories and the observance of legal formalities.

.

ARTICLE X. CONTENTS OF WRITINGS, RECORDINGS, AND PHOTOGRAPHS

Rule 1001 - Definitions That Apply to This Article

Text of Rule 1001

Rule 1001. Definitions That Apply to This Article
In this article:
(a) **Writing.** A "writing" consists of letters, words, numbers, or their equivalent set down in any form.
(b) **Recording.** A "recording" consists of letters, words, numbers, or their equivalent recorded in any manner.
(c) **Photograph.** A "photograph" means a photographic image or its equivalent stored in any form.
(d) **Original.** An "original" of a writing or recording means the writing or recording itself or any counterpart intended to have the same effect by the person who executed or issued it. For electronically stored information, "original" means any printout—or other output readable by sight—if it accurately reflects the information. An "original" of a photograph includes the negative or a print from it.
(e) **Duplicate.** A "duplicate" means a counterpart produced by a mechanical, photographic, chemical, electronic, or other equivalent process or technique that accurately reproduces the original.

Introduction to Rule 1001

Rule 1001 of the Federal Rules of Evidence provides key definitions that apply specifically to Article X, which governs the admissibility of evidence regarding the contents of writings, recordings, and photographs. The definitions outlined in Rule 1001 are fundamental to understanding and applying the rules related to the best evidence principle, which requires the production of original documents, recordings, or photographs, or an acceptable duplicate, when the contents are in dispute. This chapter provides a detailed analysis of Rule 1001, exploring each definition, its interpretation, and its broader implications for the administration of justice.

Analysis of Rule 1001

Rule 1001 provides the foundational definitions for terms used throughout Article X of the Federal Rules of Evidence, which deals with the admissibility of evidence pertaining to writings, recordings, and photographs. These definitions are crucial for applying the rules related to the best evidence doctrine, which prioritizes the use of original documents and other forms of media in legal proceedings. This section will examine each definition in detail, explaining its meaning, interpretation, and application in the context of the broader evidentiary rules.

Definition of "Writing" (Rule 1001(a))

The term "writing" is defined in Rule 1001(a) as consisting of "letters, words, numbers, or their equivalent set down in any form." This definition is broad and encompasses various forms of written communication, whether on paper, electronically stored, or otherwise recorded.

1. **Scope of "Writing"**

The broad definition of "writing" ensures that all forms of written expression, regardless of the medium, are covered by the rules governing the admissibility of evidence. This includes traditional handwritten or typed documents, as well as digital text files, emails, and even coded messages.

o **Traditional Documents**

Traditional forms of writing, such as letters, contracts, and legal documents, clearly fall within this definition. For example, a written contract between two parties is considered a "writing" under Rule 1001(a).

o **Electronic Writings**

The definition also extends to electronic forms of writing, such as emails, text messages, and word processing files. These are considered "writings" even though they may not exist in a physical form until printed.

o **Equivalents**

The rule's reference to "equivalents" acknowledges that writing can take various forms, including non-alphabetic symbols or characters, as long as they convey information similarly to letters, words, or numbers.

2. **Implications for Legal Practice**

Attorneys must recognize the expansive scope of what constitutes a "writing" when dealing with evidence. This broad definition requires careful consideration of all potential sources of written communication when preparing for litigation.

o **E-Discovery**

In the context of electronic discovery (e-discovery), this definition ensures that electronic documents and communications are treated as "writings" and thus subject to the same rules of evidence as physical documents.

- o **Document Authentication**

The definition also affects the authentication process, as all forms of writings, whether digital or physical, must be properly authenticated before being admitted as evidence.

Definition of "Recording" (Rule 1001(b))

A "recording" under Rule 1001(b) consists of "letters, words, numbers, or their equivalent recorded in any manner." This definition is similarly broad and includes any method by which information is captured and stored for later retrieval.

1. **Forms of Recordings**

The definition encompasses all forms of recorded information, whether audio, visual, or data-based. This includes traditional audio recordings, such as tapes or digital audio files, as well as video recordings and other media that capture information.

- o **Audio Recordings**

Traditional audio recordings, such as those on cassette tapes or digital audio files (e.g., MP3s), are covered by this definition. For example, a recorded phone conversation would be considered a "recording" under Rule 1001(b).

- o **Video Recordings**

Video recordings, whether on film, tape, or digital formats (e.g., MP4), are also included. A security camera recording of an event would fall within this definition.

- o **Data Recordings**

The definition extends to data that is recorded and stored in electronic formats, such as digital logs, system recordings, and other forms of electronically stored information (ESI).

2. **Implications for Legal Practice**

The broad definition of "recording" ensures that all types of recorded information can be subject to the best evidence rule. Attorneys must be diligent in identifying and preserving recordings that may be relevant to their case.

- o **Preservation of Evidence**

Given the broad scope of what constitutes a recording, parties must ensure that all relevant recordings are preserved during litigation, particularly in the context of e-discovery and digital evidence.

- o **Admissibility Considerations**

When introducing recordings into evidence, attorneys must ensure that the recordings meet the requirements for authenticity and accuracy, as they fall under the rules governing writings, recordings, and photographs.

Definition of "Photograph" (Rule 1001(c))

The term "photograph" in Rule 1001(c) refers to "a photographic image or its equivalent stored in any form." This definition includes both traditional photographic prints and digital images, as well as any other form of visual media that captures an image.

1. **Forms of Photographs**

The definition of "photograph" covers a wide range of visual media, including traditional photographs, digital images, and other visual representations that capture a likeness or scene.

- o **Traditional Photographs**

Traditional photographic prints, such as those produced from film negatives, clearly fall within this definition. For example, a printed photograph of an accident scene would be considered a "photograph" under Rule 1001(c).

- o **Digital Images**

Digital images, including those captured by digital cameras, smartphones, or other electronic devices, are also covered. A JPEG file of a photograph taken with a smartphone would be considered a "photograph" under this rule.

- o **Equivalent Visual Media**

The rule's reference to "equivalent" visual media includes other forms of images, such as those stored in electronic formats or even screen captures. This ensures that all visual representations, regardless of how they are stored, are treated as photographs.

2. **Implications for Legal Practice**

The definition of "photograph" has significant implications for how visual evidence is treated in court. Attorneys must be prepared to authenticate and introduce a wide range of visual media under this broad definition.

- o **Digital Photography**

The increasing use of digital photography and videography in legal proceedings requires attorneys to be proficient in handling digital images and ensuring they are properly authenticated and admitted into evidence.

- o **Chain of Custody**

For photographs, especially those in digital form, maintaining a clear chain of custody is crucial to ensure that the image has not been altered or tampered with before being presented as evidence.

Definition of "Original" (Rule 1001(d))

The term "original" is defined in Rule 1001(d) to mean the writing or recording itself or any counterpart intended to have the same effect by the person who executed or issued it. For electronically stored information (ESI), "original" includes any printout or other output readable by sight if it accurately reflects the information. In the case of photographs, an "original" includes the negative or a print from it.

1. **Understanding "Original"**

The definition of "original" is critical for applying the best evidence rule, which generally requires the production of the original document or recording when the contents are in dispute.

- o **Writings and Recordings**

For writings and recordings, an "original" includes not only the primary document or recording but also any duplicate that was intended to have the same legal effect as the original.

For example, carbon copies or duplicates made by the original signer could be considered originals under this definition.

o Electronically Stored Information

For ESI, an "original" includes printouts or other outputs that accurately reflect the stored information. This means that a printed email or a digital file that is presented in a readable format can be considered an original.

o Photographs

For photographs, the original includes the negative from which prints are made, as well as any print made directly from the negative. This ensures that the first-generation image is treated as the original.

2. Implications for Legal Practice

The definition of "original" is foundational for determining what evidence must be produced under the best evidence rule. Attorneys must ensure that they are presenting the correct version of a document, recording, or photograph as the original.

o Production of Originals

In cases where the contents of a document or recording are disputed, attorneys must be prepared to produce the original or justify why a duplicate or secondary evidence should be admitted instead.

o Handling ESI

With the prevalence of electronic records, understanding what constitutes an original for ESI is essential. Attorneys must be able to demonstrate that digital printouts or outputs accurately reflect the original electronic information.

Definition of "Duplicate" (Rule 1001(e))

Rule 1001(e) defines "duplicate" as a counterpart produced by a mechanical, photographic, chemical, electronic, or other equivalent process or technique that accurately reproduces the original.

1. Understanding "Duplicate"

The definition of "duplicate" allows for the use of copies of documents, recordings, and photographs when the accuracy of the reproduction is not in question. This definition is crucial for applying the rules that permit the admission of duplicates under certain circumstances.

o Mechanical and Electronic Copies

Duplicates can be created through a variety of methods, including photocopying, scanning, digital duplication, or other techniques that produce an accurate reproduction of the original. For example, a scanned copy of a contract that accurately reproduces the original document would be considered a "duplicate" under Rule 1001(e).

o Accuracy Requirement

The key requirement is that the duplicate must accurately reproduce the original. If the accuracy of the duplication process is in question, the court may require the original to be produced instead.

2. Implications for Legal Practice

Understanding when and how duplicates can be used is essential for efficiently managing evidence in legal proceedings. Attorneys must ensure that the duplicates they present are accurate and meet the criteria set forth in Rule 1001(e).

o Use of Duplicates in Court

In many cases, duplicates are admissible without the need to produce the original, particularly when the original is lost, destroyed, or otherwise unavailable. Attorneys should be prepared to justify the use of duplicates when necessary.

o Challenging Duplicates

If an opposing party challenges the accuracy of a duplicate, attorneys must be ready to either defend the accuracy of the duplication process or produce the original document or recording.

Rule 1002 - Requirement of the Original

Rule 1002. Requirement of the Original
An original writing, recording, or photograph is required in order to prove its content unless these rules or a federal statute provides otherwise.

Introduction to Rule 1002

Rule 1002 of the Federal Rules of Evidence, often referred to as the "best evidence rule," establishes the foundational principle that, to prove the content of a writing, recording, or photograph, the original document or item must be produced, unless an exception applies. This rule is designed to ensure the accuracy and reliability of evidence by prioritizing the use of the original over copies or other secondary forms of evidence. The rule is rooted in the idea that the original document is the most reliable source of its content and that copies, even if accurate, may be more susceptible to error or tampering. This chapter provides a detailed analysis of Rule 1002, exploring its text, interpretation, and broader implications for the administration of justice.

Analysis of Rule 1002

Rule 1002 articulates the general principle that, when the content of a writing, recording, or photograph is at issue, the original must be produced to prove that content. This requirement is central to maintaining the integrity of the evidence presented in court, as it minimizes the risk of inaccuracies that might arise from the use of copies or summaries. This section examines the key elements of Rule 1002, including its application, exceptions, and the strategic considerations it entails for legal practice.

The General Requirement of the Original

The primary mandate of Rule 1002 is that, to prove the content of a writing, recording, or photograph, the original item must be produced. This requirement applies broadly to all forms of written, recorded, or photographic evidence when the content of the document or item is directly in dispute.

1. **Application to Writings, Recordings, and Photographs**

The rule applies to any situation where the content of a writing, recording, or photograph is being introduced as evidence to prove a particular fact. The term "content" refers to the specific information contained within the document, recording, or photograph, such as the text of a contract, the words spoken in an audio recording, or the image depicted in a photograph.

- ○ **Examples of Application**

  - ▪ **Written Documents:** If a party seeks to prove the terms of a contract, the actual signed contract must be produced.

  - ▪ **Audio Recordings:** If a conversation recorded on an audio tape is central to the case, the original tape must be presented.

  - ▪ **Photographs:** If the visual details in a photograph are contested, the original photograph or its negative should be used.

- ○ **Purpose of the Rule**

The requirement to produce the original ensures that the evidence is as accurate and reliable as possible. The rule is particularly important in cases where the content of the document, recording, or photograph is disputed, as the original is presumed to be the best representation of that content.

2. **Rationale Behind the Rule**

The rationale for requiring the original is based on the assumption that the original document or item is less likely to have been altered or corrupted than a copy. Copies, even if well-made, can introduce errors, omissions, or distortions that might affect the evidence's reliability. The original, therefore, is considered the most trustworthy source for proving the content.

- ○ **Potential for Error in Copies**

Copies may suffer from various issues, such as degradation in quality, transcription errors, or even intentional alterations. By requiring the original, Rule 1002 aims to prevent these problems from compromising the integrity of the evidence.

- ○ **Legal Precedent**

The best evidence rule has deep roots in common law, where courts historically emphasized the importance of original documents to avoid disputes over the accuracy of evidence.

Exceptions to the Requirement of the Original

While Rule 1002 establishes a general preference for the original, there are several exceptions where secondary evidence may be admissible in place of the original. These exceptions are outlined in other rules within Article X and include situations where the original is unavailable, duplicates are accepted, or public records are involved.

1. **Admissibility of Duplicates (Rule 1003)**

Rule 1003 allows for the use of duplicates in place of the original unless there is a genuine question raised about the authenticity of the original or it would be unfair to admit the duplicate in lieu of the original.

- ○ **Definition of Duplicate**

A duplicate is defined as a counterpart produced by a process that accurately reproduces the original, such as photocopying, digital scanning, or other mechanical or electronic reproduction methods.

○ **When Duplicates Are Acceptable**

Duplicates are generally admissible if they accurately reflect the content of the original, and no party disputes their accuracy. For example, a photocopy of a signed lease agreement might be admissible if there is no reason to doubt its fidelity to the original.

2. **Exceptions for Lost or Destroyed Originals (Rule 1004)**

Rule 1004 permits the use of other evidence to prove the content of a writing, recording, or photograph when the original has been lost or destroyed, provided the loss or destruction was not the result of bad faith by the proponent of the evidence.

○ **Conditions for Admissibility**

- **Lost or Destroyed:** If the original is lost or destroyed without bad faith, secondary evidence, such as a copy or oral testimony, may be used.

- **Unavailable Original:** If the original is outside the jurisdiction of the court and cannot be obtained by any available judicial process, other evidence may be admitted.

○ **Good Faith Requirement**

The rule requires that the loss or destruction of the original be unintentional. If the party seeking to introduce secondary evidence is responsible for the loss or destruction of the original in bad faith, the court may exclude the secondary evidence.

3. **Public Records (Rule 1005)**

Rule 1005 allows for the use of certified copies of public records in place of the original, recognizing that public records are often voluminous and difficult to produce in their original form.

○ **Certified Copies**

Certified copies of public records, such as birth certificates, property deeds, or court judgments, are admissible under this rule. The certification process ensures that the copy accurately reflects the original.

○ **Rationale for the Exception**

Public records are typically kept under strict conditions and are presumed to be accurate and reliable. The use of certified copies is practical and avoids the logistical challenges of handling original public records in court.

4. **Summaries (Rule 1006)**

Rule 1006 permits the use of summaries to prove the content of voluminous writings, recordings, or photographs that cannot be conveniently examined in court.

○ **Use of Summaries**

When dealing with large amounts of data or extensive records, a summary may be presented to provide an overview of the content, provided that the original or a duplicate is made available for examination or copying by the opposing party.

○ **Conditions for Use**

Summaries are admissible when the underlying documents are too voluminous to be practically reviewed in court. However, the party presenting the summary must make the original or duplicates available to the other party.

Strategic Considerations for Attorneys

Understanding Rule 1002 and its exceptions is critical for attorneys as they prepare to introduce or challenge evidence. The requirement of the original can have significant implications for case strategy, particularly when the content of a document, recording, or photograph is central to the dispute.

1. **Preparation and Discovery**

Attorneys must be diligent in obtaining and preserving original documents and other forms of evidence during the discovery process. Ensuring access to the original can prevent challenges to the admissibility of evidence based on the best evidence rule.

○ **Obtaining Originals**

During discovery, attorneys should prioritize obtaining originals or certified copies of key documents, particularly when their content is likely to be contested. If an original cannot be obtained, the attorney should be prepared to explain its absence and justify the use of secondary evidence.

○ **Preservation of Evidence**

Preserving the integrity of original documents and recordings is essential. Attorneys must ensure that originals are protected from loss, destruction, or tampering, as any such issues could undermine the admissibility of the evidence.

2. **Challenging the Admission of Secondary Evidence**

When the opposing party seeks to introduce a duplicate or other secondary evidence, attorneys should scrutinize the circumstances under which the original is unavailable and challenge the admissibility of the secondary evidence if there are doubts about its accuracy or fairness.

○ **Questioning the Authenticity**

If a duplicate is presented, the opposing party may challenge its admission by questioning its authenticity or the accuracy of the duplication process. If successful, this could compel the production of the original or lead to the exclusion of the evidence.

○ **Bad Faith Destruction**

If there is evidence that the original was lost or destroyed in bad faith, the attorney should argue against the admission of any secondary evidence on the grounds that it would be unjust to allow such evidence in place of the original.

Rule 1003 - Admissibility of Duplicates

Rule 1003. Admissibility of Duplicates

A duplicate is admissible to the same extent as the original unless a genuine question is raised about the original's authenticity or the circumstances make it unfair to admit the duplicate.

Introduction to Rule 1003

Rule 1003 of the Federal Rules of Evidence governs the admissibility of duplicates in legal proceedings. While Rule 1002 establishes the general requirement that the original document, recording, or photograph must be produced to prove its content, Rule 1003 provides an exception that allows for the admission of duplicates in place of the original. This rule reflects the practical recognition that duplicates, when accurately produced, can serve as reliable substitutes for originals, especially in a legal system where the efficient administration of justice is paramount. However, Rule 1003 also includes safeguards to ensure that the use of duplicates does not compromise the integrity of the evidence. This chapter provides a detailed analysis of Rule 1003, exploring its text, interpretation, and broader implications for the administration of justice.

Analysis of Rule 1003

Rule 1003 allows duplicates to be admitted as evidence in lieu of the original, provided certain conditions are met. This provision is crucial in modern legal practice, where the use of photocopies, digital reproductions, and other forms of duplicates is common. The rule is designed to balance the need for efficiency with the need to ensure that evidence is reliable and trustworthy. This section examines the key components of Rule 1003, including the conditions under which duplicates are admissible, the exceptions to their admissibility, and the strategic considerations for legal practice.

General Admissibility of Duplicates

Under Rule 1003, a duplicate is generally admissible to the same extent as the original document, recording, or photograph. The rule assumes that duplicates produced by reliable processes are sufficiently accurate to stand in for originals in most legal contexts.

1. **Definition of Duplicate**

A "duplicate" is defined in Rule 1001(e) as a counterpart produced by a mechanical, photographic, chemical, electronic, or other equivalent process or technique that accurately reproduces the original. This includes photocopies, digital scans, and other forms of reproduction that ensure a faithful representation of the original.

  o **Types of Duplicates**

  ▪ **Photocopies:** Commonly used in legal practice, photocopies are considered duplicates under this rule.

  ▪ **Digital Scans:** Scanned images of documents, often used in electronic discovery, are admissible as duplicates.

  ▪ **Mechanical Reproductions:** Processes such as carbon copies or facsimile transmissions also fall under the category of duplicates.

  o **Accuracy Requirement**

The key requirement for a duplicate to be admissible is that it must accurately reproduce the content of the original. This accuracy is presumed when the duplication process is reliable and the resultant duplicate is a faithful representation of the original.

2. **Rationale for Admitting Duplicates**

The rationale behind Rule 1003 is the recognition that modern duplication technologies are generally reliable, making it unnecessary to require the original in every case. This approach facilitates the efficient handling of evidence, especially when originals may be difficult to obtain or when the original and duplicate are indistinguishable in quality.

  o **Efficiency in Legal Proceedings**

By allowing duplicates to be admissible, Rule 1003 reduces the burden on courts and litigants, who might otherwise need to manage and produce large volumes of original documents.

  o **Practicality and Accessibility**

In many cases, the original document may be stored far from the court or may be part of a large collection of documents, making the use of a duplicate more practical and cost-effective.

Exceptions to the Admissibility of Duplicates

While Rule 1003 generally allows for the admission of duplicates, it also includes two critical exceptions: when a genuine question is raised about the original's authenticity, or when the circumstances make it unfair to admit the duplicate.

1. **Genuine Question About the Original's Authenticity**

A duplicate may not be admissible if there is a genuine question raised about the authenticity of the original document, recording, or photograph. This exception addresses situations where the accuracy or integrity of the original is in dispute, potentially undermining the reliability of any duplicates made from it.

  o **Challenging the Authenticity**

If a party challenges the authenticity of the original, they may argue that the duplicate should not be admitted until the authenticity of the original is established. For example, if there is evidence that the original document may have been tampered with, the court may require the production of the original rather than relying on a duplicate.

- ○ **Burden of Proof**

The burden of raising a genuine question about the original's authenticity rests on the party challenging the duplicate. This typically requires some evidence or indication that the original is not what it purports to be.

2. **Unfairness in Admitting the Duplicate**

Even if the original's authenticity is not in question, a duplicate may still be excluded if the circumstances make it unfair to admit the duplicate in place of the original. This exception addresses concerns about fairness and justice in the use of evidence.

- ○ **Examples of Unfairness**

    - **Quality Discrepancies:** If the duplicate is of significantly lower quality than the original, such that it may misrepresent the content or omit important details, the court may find it unfair to admit the duplicate.

    - **Incomplete Reproduction:** If the duplication process failed to capture the entirety of the original document or recording, leading to a misleading or incomplete representation, it may be unfair to admit the duplicate.

    - **Contextual Concerns:** In some cases, the context in which the duplicate was created might raise concerns about its reliability or the fairness of its use. For instance, if the duplicate was made under circumstances that suggest potential bias or manipulation, the court may choose to exclude it.

- ○ **Judicial Discretion**

The determination of unfairness is within the court's discretion, allowing judges to consider the specific circumstances of each case and decide whether admitting the duplicate would compromise the fairness of the proceedings.

Strategic Considerations for Attorneys

Understanding Rule 1003 and its exceptions is crucial for attorneys as they prepare to introduce or challenge duplicates in court. The strategic use of duplicates can streamline the presentation of evidence, but attorneys must also be prepared to address any challenges to their admissibility.

1. **Proving the Reliability of Duplicates**

When introducing a duplicate into evidence, attorneys should be prepared to demonstrate the reliability of the duplication process and the accuracy of the duplicate. This may involve presenting evidence about the methods used to create the duplicate and ensuring that the duplicate accurately reflects the content of the original.

- ○ **Documentation of the Duplication Process**

Attorneys should maintain thorough records of how the duplicate was created, including details about the equipment and methods used. This documentation can be crucial in establishing the reliability of the duplicate.

- ○ **Expert Testimony**

In cases where the duplication process is complex or where the accuracy of the duplicate is critical, attorneys may consider using expert testimony to explain and verify the duplication process.

2. **Challenging the Use of Duplicates**

If the opposing party seeks to introduce a duplicate, attorneys should scrutinize the circumstances under which the original is unavailable and assess whether the duplicate meets the standards set by Rule 1003. If there are doubts about the authenticity of the original or concerns about the fairness of admitting the duplicate, attorneys should be prepared to challenge its admissibility.

- ○ **Raising Questions About Authenticity**

If there is reason to believe the original may have been altered, forged, or otherwise compromised, attorneys should challenge the admissibility of the duplicate by questioning the original's authenticity.

- ○ **Arguing Unfairness**

Attorneys should evaluate whether the admission of the duplicate would be unfair to their client. This might involve demonstrating that the duplicate is of poor quality, incomplete, or created under questionable circumstances.

3. **Preparing for Objections**

When relying on duplicates, attorneys must anticipate potential objections from the opposing party. Being prepared to address challenges regarding the authenticity of the original or the fairness of the duplication process can help ensure that the evidence is admitted.

- ○ **Preemptive Measures**

Attorneys can take preemptive measures to minimize the likelihood of objections, such as providing the opposing party with copies of the duplicates well in advance of the trial and offering to make the original available for inspection if possible.

- ○ **Responding to Objections**

If an objection is raised, attorneys should be ready to respond with evidence supporting the reliability and fairness of the duplicate, including testimony, documentation, and, if necessary, a request for the court to view the original.

Rule 1004 - Admissibility of Other Evidence of Content

Text of Rule 1004

Rule 1004. Admissibility of Other Evidence of Content
An original is not required, and other evidence of the content of a writing, recording, or photograph is admissible if:
(a) **All the originals are lost or destroyed, and not by the proponent acting in bad faith;**
(b) **An original cannot be obtained by any available judicial process;**
(c) **The party against whom the original would be offered had control of the original; was at that time put on notice, by pleadings or otherwise, that the original would be a subject of proof at the trial or hearing; and fails to produce it; or**
(d) **The writing, recording, or photograph is not closely related to a controlling issue.**

Introduction to Rule 1004

Rule 1004 of the Federal Rules of Evidence addresses the circumstances under which secondary evidence—other than the original document, recording, or photograph—may be admitted to prove the content of that item. While Rule 1002, the "best evidence rule," generally requires the production of the original to prove the content of a writing, recording, or photograph, Rule 1004 recognizes that there are situations in which the original is unavailable or cannot be produced. In such cases, Rule 1004 allows for the admission of other evidence of the content, such as duplicates or even oral testimony, provided certain conditions are met. This chapter provides a detailed analysis of Rule 1004, exploring its text, interpretation, and broader implications for the administration of justice.

Analysis of Rule 1004

Rule 1004 sets forth specific conditions under which secondary evidence may be used to prove the content of a writing, recording, or photograph, despite the general preference for originals established in Rule 1002. This section examines each condition under which secondary evidence may be admitted, exploring the legal principles and practical implications of the rule.

Loss or Destruction of the Original (Rule 1004(a))

Under Rule 1004(a), secondary evidence of the content of a writing, recording, or photograph is admissible if all originals have been lost or destroyed, provided that the loss or destruction was not the result of bad faith by the proponent of the evidence.

1. **Conditions for Admissibility**

   o **Loss or Destruction:** The rule allows for the use of secondary evidence when the original is lost or destroyed, making it impossible to produce the original in court. This applies regardless of how many originals were created, as long as all are unavailable.

   o **No Bad Faith:** The key limitation is that the loss or destruction must not be due to bad faith by the party seeking to introduce the secondary evidence. If the proponent of the evidence intentionally destroyed or

negligently lost the original, they may be precluded from using secondary evidence.

2. **Implications for Legal Practice**

   o **Proof of Loss or Destruction:** The party seeking to introduce secondary evidence must provide evidence or testimony that the original was lost or destroyed without bad faith. This might involve affidavits, witness testimony, or documentation showing the circumstances of the loss.

   o **Challenge by Opposing Party:** The opposing party may challenge the admissibility of secondary evidence by arguing that the original was not actually lost or that the loss was due to bad faith. In such cases, the court will assess the credibility of the evidence presented.

Inability to Obtain the Original (Rule 1004(b))

Rule 1004(b) permits the admission of secondary evidence when the original cannot be obtained by any available judicial process, such as through a subpoena or other court order.

1. **Conditions for Admissibility**

   o **Unobtainable Original:** This provision applies when the original is in the possession of a third party who is outside the jurisdiction of the court, or when the original is otherwise unavailable despite reasonable efforts to obtain it.

   o **Judicial Process:** The rule presupposes that the party seeking the original has made reasonable attempts to obtain it through judicial means, such as issuing a subpoena or requesting a court order. If these efforts fail, secondary evidence may be admissible.

2. **Implications for Legal Practice**

   o **Demonstrating Unavailability:** Attorneys must be prepared to demonstrate that they have exhausted all reasonable judicial processes to obtain the original. This might include evidence of attempts to subpoena the document or a showing that the original is held by a party outside the court's jurisdiction.

- o **Strategic Use of Secondary Evidence:** When an original cannot be obtained, attorneys should ensure that the secondary evidence they present is as accurate and reliable as possible, minimizing the potential for objections from the opposing party.

Failure to Produce the Original by the Opposing Party (Rule 1004(c))

Rule 1004(c) allows for the admission of secondary evidence when the party against whom the original would be offered had control of the original, was notified that it would be a subject of proof, and fails to produce it.

1. **Conditions for Admissibility**

   - o **Control of the Original:** The rule applies when the opposing party has control over the original document, recording, or photograph, meaning that they have possession or the legal ability to produce it.

   - o **Notice and Failure to Produce:** The opposing party must have been put on notice—through pleadings or other formal communications—that the original would be relevant at trial. If, despite this notice, the party fails to produce the original, secondary evidence may be used.

2. **Implications for Legal Practice**

   - o **Notifying the Opposing Party:** Attorneys must ensure that they properly notify the opposing party of the need to produce the original. This notification should be documented in pleadings, discovery requests, or other formal communications.

   - o **Holding the Opposing Party Accountable:** If the opposing party fails to produce the original after being put on notice, attorneys can leverage Rule 1004(c) to introduce secondary evidence, potentially shifting the burden onto the opposing party to explain the absence of the original.

The Writing, Recording, or Photograph Is Not Closely Related to a Controlling Issue (Rule 1004(d))

Rule 1004(d) provides that secondary evidence is admissible when the writing, recording, or photograph is not closely related to a controlling issue in the case. This provision reflects the principle that, in cases where the content of the document is not crucial to the outcome, the rigorous standards of the best evidence rule may be relaxed.

1. **Conditions for Admissibility**

   - o **Relevance to Controlling Issue:** The rule applies when the document, recording, or photograph in question is not central to the

key issues of the case. In such instances, the court may allow secondary evidence to be admitted without requiring the original.

- o **Discretion of the Court:** The court has discretion to determine whether the content of the document is closely related to a controlling issue. If the court finds that the document is not central to the case, secondary evidence may be admitted.

2. **Implications for Legal Practice**

   - o **Arguing Non-Centrality:** Attorneys may argue that the document in question is not closely related to a controlling issue, thereby justifying the use of secondary evidence. This argument might be particularly relevant in cases involving minor or ancillary issues.

   - o **Judicial Discretion:** Attorneys should be prepared to address the court's discretion in determining whether a document is closely related to a controlling issue. Understanding how courts have interpreted this provision in similar cases can inform the strategy for introducing or challenging secondary evidence.

Strategic Considerations for Attorneys

Understanding Rule 1004 and its exceptions to the best evidence rule is crucial for attorneys as they prepare to introduce or challenge secondary evidence in court. The strategic use of Rule 1004 can allow attorneys to admit necessary evidence when originals are unavailable, while also providing a basis for challenging the admissibility of secondary evidence presented by the opposing party.

1. **Preparing to Use Secondary Evidence**

When relying on secondary evidence under Rule 1004, attorneys must be prepared to demonstrate that one of the rule's conditions is met. This requires thorough preparation, including gathering evidence of the original's loss, destruction, unavailability, or the opposing party's failure to produce it.

- o **Documentation of Efforts:** Attorneys should meticulously document all efforts to locate and produce the original, including correspondence, discovery requests, and attempts to obtain the document through judicial process.

- o **Selection of Secondary Evidence:** The chosen secondary evidence should be as accurate and reliable as possible. Attorneys may consider using certified copies, corroborating witness testimony, or expert analysis to support the authenticity and accuracy of the secondary evidence.

2. **Challenging the Admissibility of Secondary Evidence**

When the opposing party seeks to introduce secondary evidence, attorneys should scrutinize whether the conditions of Rule 1004 are truly met. Challenges may focus on the availability of the original, the completeness and accuracy of the secondary evidence, or the relevance of the document to a controlling issue.

- o **Questioning Bad Faith:** If there is any indication that the original was lost or destroyed in bad faith, attorneys should argue that secondary evidence should not be admitted, as the proponent of the evidence bears responsibility for the unavailability of the original.

- o **Demanding the Original:** If the original could reasonably be obtained, attorneys should challenge the use of secondary evidence and insist on the production of the original. This is particularly relevant when the original is central to the case and its content is in dispute.

3. **Responding to Objections**

If an objection to the use of secondary evidence is raised, attorneys should be prepared to respond with evidence and arguments that demonstrate compliance with Rule 1004. This might include testimony about the loss or destruction of the original, evidence of unsuccessful attempts to obtain the original, or arguments that the document is not central to the case.

- o **Building a Strong Foundation:** Ensuring that the foundation for admitting secondary evidence is strong and well-documented can help attorneys overcome objections and secure the admission of crucial evidence.

- o **Mitigating Risks:** Attorneys should also consider the potential risks of relying on secondary evidence, such as challenges to its accuracy, and take steps to mitigate these risks through corroboration and thorough preparation.

Rule 1005 - Copies of Public Records to Prove Content

Rule 1005. Copies of Public Records to Prove Content
The proponent may use a copy to prove the content of an official record—or of a document that was recorded or filed in a public office as authorized by law—if these conditions are met: the record or document is otherwise admissible; and the copy is certified as correct in accordance with Rule 902(4) or is testified to be correct by a witness who has compared it with the original. If no such copy can be obtained by reasonable diligence, then the proponent may use other evidence to prove the content.

Introduction to Rule 1005

Rule 1005 of the Federal Rules of Evidence addresses the use of copies of public records to prove the content of those records in legal proceedings. Public records are essential sources of information in many cases, and their authenticity and reliability are generally assumed due to the official nature of their creation and maintenance. Rule 1005 provides a practical mechanism for introducing evidence from public records without the need to produce the original document, thus facilitating the efficient administration of justice. This chapter provides a detailed analysis of Rule 1005, exploring its text, interpretation, and broader implications for the use of public records in court.

Analysis of Rule 1005

Rule 1005 provides specific guidelines for using copies of public records to prove the content of those records in legal proceedings. This rule acknowledges the practical challenges of producing original public records in court and offers a structured approach for using certified copies or, when necessary, other forms of secondary evidence.

Use of Copies to Prove Content

Rule 1005 permits the use of a copy to prove the content of an official record or a document recorded or filed in a public office, provided certain conditions are met. This provision is crucial for allowing parties to introduce evidence efficiently, especially when dealing with public records that are often bulky, difficult to transport, or too valuable to remove from their location.

1. **Scope of Application**

   o **Official Records:** Rule 1005 applies to official records, which include documents generated and maintained by government entities, such as birth certificates, death certificates, marriage licenses, court judgments, and property deeds.

   o **Filed Documents:** The rule also covers documents that have been recorded or filed in a public office as authorized by law, such as contracts, liens, and other legal instruments that are required to be filed with a government agency.

2. **Conditions for Admissibility**

   o **Otherwise Admissible:** The record or document itself must be admissible under the rules of evidence. This means it must meet the general criteria for relevance,

authenticity, and any other applicable evidentiary standards.

   o **Certified or Testified as Correct:** The copy must be certified as correct in accordance with Rule 902(4), which deals with self-authenticating documents, or it must be testified to as correct by a witness who has compared it with the original. This ensures that the copy is an accurate reproduction of the original document.

   o **Certified Copies (Rule 902(4)):** A certified copy is a reproduction of a public record that has been authenticated by the custodian of the record or another authorized person. Certification typically involves an official seal and a statement that the copy is a true and accurate reproduction of the original.

   o **Testified to by a Witness:** Alternatively, a witness who has compared the copy with the original can testify to the copy's accuracy. This provides a secondary means of verifying the authenticity of the copy when a certified copy is not available.

Reasonable Diligence and Use of Other Evidence

If a certified copy or a copy testified to as correct cannot be obtained despite reasonable diligence, Rule 1005 allows the proponent to use other evidence to prove the content of the public record. This provision is important for situations where the original record is inaccessible, and no certified copy is available.

1. **Reasonable Diligence Requirement**

   o **Efforts to Obtain a Copy:** The rule requires the proponent to demonstrate that they have made reasonable efforts to obtain a certified copy or a copy that can be verified by comparison with the original. This might include requesting the document from the relevant public office, attempting to access it through legal channels, or showing that the original is in a location that cannot be accessed.

   o **Documentation of Efforts:** The proponent should be prepared to document their efforts to obtain the copy, as this may be necessary to satisfy the court that reasonable diligence was exercised.

2. **Other Evidence to Prove Content**

   ○ **Use of Secondary Evidence:** If a proper copy cannot be obtained, the rule permits the use of other evidence to prove the content of the public record. This might include oral testimony, uncertified copies, or other forms of secondary evidence that can establish the content of the record.

   ○ **Court Discretion:** The court has discretion to determine whether the proponent has exercised reasonable diligence and whether the secondary evidence is sufficiently reliable to be admitted.

Strategic Considerations for Attorneys

Rule 1005 offers attorneys a practical method for introducing public records into evidence, but it also requires careful attention to the procedures for obtaining and certifying copies. Understanding how to effectively use Rule 1005 can streamline the presentation of evidence and avoid unnecessary challenges to its admissibility.

1. **Obtaining Certified Copies**

   ○ **Requesting Certification:** Attorneys should routinely request certified copies of public records from the appropriate government offices when preparing for trial. This ensures that the evidence will meet the admissibility standards of Rule 1005 and reduces the likelihood of challenges based on authenticity.

   ○ **Verification by Witnesses:** In situations where a certified copy is not available, attorneys should identify and prepare witnesses who can testify to the accuracy of a copy by comparing it with the original.

This provides an alternative means of satisfying Rule 1005's requirements.

2. **Preparing for Challenges**

   ○ **Documenting Efforts:** When a certified copy or a witness-verified copy cannot be obtained, attorneys must be ready to document their efforts to obtain the record and to argue that they have exercised reasonable diligence. This documentation is critical for justifying the use of secondary evidence.

   ○ **Using Secondary Evidence:** Attorneys should carefully select and prepare secondary evidence that can reliably prove the content of a public record. This might involve gathering corroborative testimony, identifying related documents, or using expert analysis to support the secondary evidence.

3. **Challenging the Use of Copies**

   ○ **Scrutinizing Certification:** When opposing counsel seeks to introduce a copy of a public record, attorneys should scrutinize the certification or witness testimony to ensure that the copy is accurate and that it meets the requirements of Rule 1005. Any discrepancies or lapses in the certification process may be grounds for objection.

   ○ **Questioning Diligence:** If the proponent of secondary evidence claims that a proper copy could not be obtained, the opposing party may challenge the sufficiency of the efforts made. Attorneys should be prepared to argue that reasonable diligence was not exercised if the circumstances warrant such a challenge.

Chapter 65: Rule 1006 - Summaries to Prove Content

Rule 1006. Summaries to Prove Content
The proponent may use a summary, chart, or calculation to prove the content of voluminous writings, recordings, or photographs that cannot be conveniently examined in court. The proponent must make the originals or duplicates available for examination or copying, or both, by other parties at a reasonable time and place. And the court may order the proponent to produce them in court.

Introduction to Rule 1006

Rule 1006 of the Federal Rules of Evidence provides a mechanism for parties to present summaries of voluminous writings, recordings, or photographs when it is impractical to examine these items in court due to their sheer volume. This rule is designed to facilitate the efficient presentation of evidence without compromising the accuracy or integrity of the information conveyed. By allowing the use of summaries, Rule 1006 balances the need for thorough evidence presentation with the practical limitations of court proceedings, ensuring that the trier of fact can effectively comprehend and evaluate complex or extensive evidence. This chapter provides a detailed analysis of Rule 1006, exploring its text, interpretation, and broader implications for the administration of justice.

Analysis of Rule 1006

Rule 1006 provides clear guidelines for the use of summaries, charts, or calculations to prove the content of extensive evidence that would be impractical to present in its entirety during trial. This section will examine the conditions under which summaries are admissible, the requirements for making originals or duplicates available, and the strategic considerations involved in utilizing or challenging summaries in court.

Use of Summaries, Charts, or Calculations

Rule 1006 allows a party to use summaries, charts, or calculations to present the content of voluminous writings, recordings, or photographs. The key consideration under this rule is whether the materials are so extensive that presenting them in their entirety would be impractical for the court.

1. **Voluminous Evidence**

   o **Definition and Scope:** The rule applies to evidence that is voluminous, meaning that it consists of a large number of documents, recordings, or photographs, making it impractical to review each item in detail during court proceedings. Examples might include financial records, business logs, extensive correspondence, or large sets of photographs.

   o **Impracticality of Examination:** The proponent must demonstrate that the sheer volume of the evidence would make it difficult, if not impossible, to conveniently examine each piece in court. This impracticality is a fundamental criterion for the use of summaries.

2. **Types of Summaries**

   o **Summaries:** A summary condenses the essential content of the voluminous evidence into a more manageable form, focusing on the key points that are most relevant to the case. For example, a summary might condense hundreds of pages of financial transactions into a concise report showing overall trends.

   o **Charts:** Charts often represent data visually, such as through graphs or tables, making complex information easier to understand. A chart might be used to illustrate the flow of funds in a financial fraud case.

   o **Calculations:** Calculations involve mathematical computations derived from the voluminous evidence, such as computing totals, averages, or other statistical measures based on detailed financial records.

3. **Admissibility Criteria**

   o **Accuracy and Reliability:** The summary, chart, or calculation must accurately reflect the content of the underlying evidence. The proponent must ensure that the summarized information is not misleading and that it represents the data fairly and accurately.

   o **Relevance:** As with all evidence, the summary must be relevant to the issues in the case. It should aid the trier of fact in understanding complex or extensive information that would be difficult to digest in its original form.

Requirement to Make Originals or Duplicates Available

A crucial requirement of Rule 1006 is that the proponent must make the originals or duplicates of the summarized evidence available for examination or copying by other parties. This provision ensures that the opposing party has the opportunity to verify the accuracy of the summary and challenge its contents if necessary.

1. **Availability for Examination**

   o **Reasonable Time and Place:** The proponent must provide the opposing party with reasonable access to the originals or duplicates at a time and place that is convenient. This allows the opposing party to inspect the evidence and ensure that the summary accurately reflects the content of the original materials.

- ○ **Access for Verification:** Providing access to the originals or duplicates is essential for maintaining transparency and fairness in the use of summaries. It allows the opposing party to verify the summary and prepare any challenges or objections based on their examination of the original evidence.

2. Court's Discretion

- ○ **Order to Produce Originals in Court:** The court may order the proponent to produce the originals or duplicates in court, especially if there are disputes about the accuracy or completeness of the summary. This ensures that the trier of fact can review the original materials if necessary.

- ○ **Judicial Oversight:** The court's discretion in ordering the production of originals or duplicates serves as a check on the use of summaries, ensuring that the integrity of the evidence is preserved and that the opposing party's rights are protected.

Strategic Considerations for Attorneys

The use of summaries under Rule 1006 can be a powerful tool in presenting complex evidence, but it also requires careful preparation and attention to detail. Attorneys must ensure that summaries are accurate, relevant, and compliant with the rule's requirements, while also being prepared to address potential challenges from the opposing party.

1. Preparation and Presentation of Summaries

- ○ **Accuracy and Completeness:** Attorneys must ensure that the summaries, charts, or calculations they prepare are accurate and complete, reflecting the underlying evidence without distortion or omission. This requires a thorough review of the original materials and careful attention to how the information is presented.

- ○ **Documentation of Methodology:** Attorneys should document the methodology used to create the summary, including the selection of data, any calculations performed, and how the summary was constructed. This

documentation can be crucial in defending the summary against challenges.

2. Anticipating and Addressing Challenges

- ○ **Verification by Opposing Party:** Attorneys should anticipate that the opposing party will seek to verify the accuracy of the summary by examining the originals or duplicates. Providing timely and adequate access to these materials can help mitigate challenges and demonstrate transparency.

- ○ **Responding to Objections:** If the opposing party challenges the accuracy or fairness of the summary, attorneys should be prepared to defend the summary by explaining how it accurately reflects the original evidence and why it is a reliable representation of the content.

3. Challenging the Use of Summaries

- ○ **Scrutinizing the Summary:** When the opposing party introduces a summary under Rule 1006, attorneys should carefully scrutinize the summary for accuracy, completeness, and potential bias. If discrepancies or omissions are found, they can form the basis for an objection or cross-examination.

- ○ **Demanding Production of Originals:** If there are doubts about the accuracy or fairness of the summary, attorneys may request that the court order the production of the originals or duplicates in court. This can be particularly important if the summary plays a critical role in the case.

4. Use of Expert Testimony

- ○ **Supporting or Challenging Summaries:** In complex cases, attorneys may use expert testimony to support the accuracy of a summary or to challenge the methodology used by the opposing party. Experts can provide valuable insights into whether the summary accurately reflects the underlying evidence and whether the calculations or charts are based on sound principles.

Rule 1007 - Testimony or Statement of a Party to Prove Content

Rule 1007. Testimony or Statement of a Party to Prove Content
The proponent may prove the content of a writing, recording, or photograph by the testimony, deposition, or written statement of the party against whom the evidence is offered. The proponent need not account for the original.

Introduction to Rule 1007

Rule 1007 of the Federal Rules of Evidence provides an exception to the best evidence rule by allowing the content of a writing, recording, or photograph to be proved through the testimony or deposition of the party against whom the evidence is offered, or through that party's written statement. This rule simplifies the process of proving content in situations where the opposing party has already acknowledged the content in a manner that the court deems reliable. By permitting such testimony or statements to serve as proof of content, Rule 1007 facilitates the admission of evidence and enhances judicial efficiency without compromising the fairness of the proceedings. This chapter provides a detailed analysis of Rule 1007, exploring its text, interpretation, and broader implications for the administration of justice.

Analysis of Rule 1007

Rule 1007 establishes that a party's own testimony, deposition, or written statement can be used to prove the content of a writing, recording, or photograph, and that there is no requirement to produce the original document or item when such evidence is offered. This rule is an exception to the general requirement of Rule 1002, which mandates the production of the original to prove content. Rule 1007 recognizes the reliability of admissions made by a party against their own interest and therefore relaxes the stringent requirements typically associated with the best evidence rule.

Scope of Rule 1007

Rule 1007 applies specifically to situations where the content of a writing, recording, or photograph is at issue and where that content has been acknowledged by the party against whom the evidence is offered. The rule permits the use of the party's own statements, whether oral, written, or recorded, to establish the content without needing to produce the original document or item.

1. **Types of Statements Covered**

   o **Testimony:** Oral statements made by a party during trial or in a deposition can be used to prove the content of the writing, recording, or photograph. This includes statements made under oath that directly address the content in question.

   o **Depositions:** Statements made during a deposition, which are typically transcribed, can also be used to prove content under Rule 1007. Depositions are often conducted prior to trial and provide a recorded account of the party's knowledge and admissions.

   o **Written Statements:** Any written statement made by the party, whether in the form of letters, emails, affidavits, or other documents, can be used to establish the content. The written statement must be attributable to the party and must directly acknowledge or describe the content of the item in question.

2. **No Requirement to Produce the Original**

   o **Exception to the Best Evidence Rule:** Rule 1007 provides an exception to the general requirement under Rule 1002 that the original writing, recording, or photograph must be produced to prove its content. When the content has been acknowledged by the party against whom it is offered, the rule dispenses with the need to account for the original.

   o **Reliability of Admissions:** The rationale behind this exception is that a party's own admissions, whether in testimony, deposition, or writing, are considered sufficiently reliable to prove the content of the evidence, thereby obviating the need for the original.

Strategic Considerations for Attorneys

Rule 1007 provides attorneys with a powerful tool for proving the content of documents, recordings, or photographs through the admissions of the opposing party. However, attorneys must carefully consider how to effectively use or challenge such evidence under this rule.

1. **Using Rule 1007 to Prove Content**

   o **Identifying Relevant Statements:** Attorneys should review all testimony, depositions, and written statements made by the opposing party to identify admissions that can be used to prove the content of the evidence. These admissions should be clearly documented and presented to the court.

   o **Avoiding the Need for Originals:** By relying on Rule 1007, attorneys can avoid the potential difficulties associated with locating and producing original documents, particularly when the originals are unavailable, difficult to obtain, or not crucial to the case's outcome.

   o **Presenting Clear and Convincing Evidence:** When using a party's statement to prove content, it is important to ensure that the statement is clear, unambiguous, and directly addresses the content in question. This minimizes the risk of objections or challenges based on the reliability of the statement.

2. **Challenging the Use of Rule 1007**

   o **Questioning the Clarity of the Admission:** If the opposing party seeks to use a statement under Rule 1007, attorneys should scrutinize the statement for any ambiguities or inconsistencies. If the statement is not clear or does not directly address the content of the evidence, it may be possible to challenge its admissibility under Rule 1007.

   o **Disputing the Context or Accuracy:** Attorneys may also challenge the context in which the statement was made or argue that the statement does not accurately reflect the content of the original evidence. For example, if a statement was made under duress or without full knowledge of the content, it may be less reliable.

   o **Requesting the Original:** In some cases, attorneys may argue that the original document, recording, or photograph should still be produced, particularly if there is any doubt about the accuracy or completeness of the statement being used to prove content.

Legal Implications and Case Law

Rule 1007 has been the subject of various judicial interpretations, with courts generally upholding the principle that a party's own admissions can serve as a reliable basis for proving content. However, the application of Rule 1007 may vary depending on the specifics of the case and the jurisdiction.

1. **Judicial Interpretation**

   o **Reliability of Admissions:** Courts have consistently held that statements made by a party against their own interest are inherently reliable and can be used to prove content under Rule 1007. This is because such statements are generally not made lightly and are often viewed as more trustworthy than other forms of evidence.

   o **Limits on Rule 1007:** While Rule 1007 provides a significant exception to the best evidence rule, courts may still require the original if there is evidence that the statement is unreliable, ambiguous, or taken out of context. The rule does not override the need for a fair and accurate presentation of evidence.

2. **Practical Application**

   o **Effective Use in Litigation:** Rule 1007 is most effectively used in situations where the opposing party has made clear and unequivocal statements about the content of the evidence. Such admissions can streamline the litigation process by eliminating the need for additional proof.

   o **Challenges in Application:** Attorneys must be cautious when relying on Rule 1007, as the opposing party may attempt to discredit the statement or argue for the necessity of the original evidence. Careful preparation and a thorough understanding of the statement's context are essential.

Rule 1008 - Functions of the Court and Jury

Rule 1008. Functions of the Court and Jury
Ordinarily, the court determines whether the proponent has fulfilled the factual conditions for admitting other evidence of the content of a writing, recording, or photograph under Rule 1004 or 1007. But in a jury trial, the jury determines—in accordance with Rule 104(b)—any issue about whether:
(a) an asserted writing, recording, or photograph ever existed;
(b) another one produced at the trial or hearing is the original; or
(c) other evidence of content accurately reflects the content.

Introduction to Rule 1008

Rule 1008 of the Federal Rules of Evidence delineates the respective roles of the court and the jury in determining issues related to the admissibility of evidence, particularly concerning writings, recordings, and photographs. While the judge typically decides preliminary questions of admissibility, such as whether a document is authentic or whether an original is required, Rule 1008 provides that certain factual determinations are reserved for the jury. This rule ensures that the jury, as the trier of fact, plays its crucial role in resolving disputes over the evidence presented during the trial. This chapter provides a detailed analysis of Rule 1008, exploring its text, interpretation, and broader implications for the administration of justice.

Analysis of Rule 1008

Rule 1008 provides guidance on the division of responsibilities between the court and the jury when issues arise concerning the admissibility of evidence related to writings, recordings, or photographs. This rule ensures that while the judge oversees the application of the law, the jury maintains its essential role in deciding factual disputes that are central to the case.

Court's Role in Determining Admissibility

Under Rule 1008, the court generally determines whether the proponent of the evidence has satisfied the factual conditions necessary for admitting other evidence of content under Rule 1004 (which concerns the admissibility of secondary evidence when the original is unavailable) or Rule 1007 (which concerns the use of a party's testimony or statements to prove content).

1. **Judicial Determination of Admissibility**

   o **Preliminary Questions:** The court decides preliminary questions about the admissibility of evidence, such as whether the conditions for admitting secondary evidence under Rule 1004 or using a party's testimony under Rule 1007 have been met. This involves assessing whether the proponent has provided sufficient evidence to justify the use of such evidence instead of the original.

   o **Legal Standards:** The court applies legal standards to determine whether the evidence meets the requirements set forth

in the Federal Rules of Evidence. This may involve considering the authenticity of the evidence, the reliability of the secondary evidence, or the credibility of the party's statement.

2. **Function Under Rule 104(a):**

   o **Rule 104(a) Considerations:** The court's role under Rule 104(a) involves making determinations based on a preponderance of the evidence, considering all relevant factors, including the credibility of witnesses and the reliability of the evidence. The judge's decision in this context is final and determines whether the evidence will be presented to the jury.

Jury's Role in Determining Factual Issues

Rule 1008 reserves certain factual determinations for the jury, reflecting the jury's essential role as the trier of fact in a trial. These determinations include whether an asserted writing, recording, or photograph ever existed; whether the item produced in court is the original; and whether other evidence of content accurately reflects the content of the original.

1. **Existence of the Evidence (Rule 1008(a))**

   o **Determining Existence:** The jury is tasked with deciding whether the asserted writing, recording, or photograph actually exists. This issue might arise when there is a dispute about whether a document or recording ever existed in the first place, which is a factual matter that the jury must resolve.

   o **Examples:** For instance, in a case where a party claims that a contract was created but the other party denies its existence, the jury must decide whether the contract in question ever existed based on the evidence presented.

2. **Originality of the Evidence (Rule 1008(b))**

   o **Identifying the Original:** The jury also determines whether the item produced at trial is the original. This determination is crucial in cases where there are multiple copies or versions of a document, and the authenticity of the original is in question.

- o **Examples:** If a party presents a document as the original contract, but the opposing party argues that it is a copy or a forgery, the jury must decide which version, if any, is the true original.

3. **Accuracy of Other Evidence (Rule 1008(c))**

- o **Assessing Accuracy:** The jury is responsible for deciding whether the other evidence of content—such as a summary, chart, or testimony—accurately reflects the content of the original. This issue might arise when secondary evidence is introduced in place of the original, and there is a dispute about its accuracy.

- o **Examples:** If a summary of financial records is introduced as evidence, and the opposing party disputes whether the summary accurately reflects the content of the original records, the jury must resolve this factual dispute.

Strategic Considerations for Attorneys

Understanding the division of responsibilities between the court and the jury under Rule 1008 is crucial for attorneys as they prepare and present their cases. Attorneys must be prepared to address both the legal and factual aspects of evidence admissibility, recognizing when to argue before the judge and when to present issues to the jury.

1. **Arguing Before the Court**

- o **Preliminary Admissibility:** Attorneys should be prepared to argue before the court on preliminary questions of admissibility under Rule 1004 or 1007. This involves presenting evidence and legal arguments to convince the judge that the conditions for admitting secondary evidence or using a party's statement have been met.

- o **Framing Legal Issues:** Attorneys must carefully frame the legal issues for the court, focusing on the application of the rules of evidence and the standards for admissibility. Success at this stage can determine whether crucial evidence will be considered by the jury.

2. **Presenting Factual Issues to the Jury**

- o **Factual Disputes:** When factual disputes are reserved for the jury under Rule 1008, attorneys must effectively present their case to persuade the jury. This involves providing clear, compelling evidence on issues such as the existence of the document, the authenticity of the original, or the accuracy of the secondary evidence.

- o **Cross-Examination and Witness Testimony:** Attorneys should use cross-examination and witness testimony to challenge the opposing party's evidence and to support their own arguments about the factual issues before the jury.

3. **Challenging the Opposing Party's Evidence**

- o **Objections and Motions:** Attorneys should be vigilant in challenging the opposing party's evidence on both legal and factual grounds. This might involve filing motions to exclude evidence, objecting to the introduction of secondary evidence, or arguing that the opposing party has not met the conditions for admissibility under Rule 1004 or 1007.

- o **Jury Instructions:** When factual issues are presented to the jury, attorneys should request appropriate jury instructions that clearly explain the jury's role in deciding these issues. Proper jury instructions can help ensure that the jury understands its responsibilities and the legal standards it must apply.

Legal Implications and Case Law

Rule 1008 has been interpreted and applied in various cases, with courts emphasizing the distinct roles of the judge and the jury in determining issues related to evidence admissibility. Understanding how courts have applied Rule 1008 can provide valuable insights for attorneys in developing their case strategy.

1. **Judicial Precedent**

- o **Separation of Functions:** Courts have consistently upheld the principle that the judge decides preliminary questions of law, while the jury resolves factual disputes. This separation of functions is fundamental to ensuring that both legal and factual issues are properly addressed in a trial.

- o **Balancing Roles:** In applying Rule 1008, courts have emphasized the need to balance the judge's role in ensuring that evidence meets legal standards with the jury's role in determining the credibility and weight of the evidence.

2. **Practical Application in Trials**

- o **Effective Use of Rule 1008:** Attorneys who effectively navigate the division of responsibilities under Rule 1008 can better manage the presentation of evidence and address potential challenges. By understanding when to argue before the court and when to appeal to the jury, attorneys can enhance their ability to present a strong case.

ARTICLE XI. MISCELLANEOUS RULES

Rule 1101 - Applicability of the Rules

Text of Rule 1101

Rule 1101. Applicability of the Rules
(a) **To Courts and Judges.** These rules apply to proceedings before:
•   United States district courts;
•   United States bankruptcy and magistrate judges;
•   United States courts of appeals;
•   the United States Court of Federal Claims; and
•   the district courts of Guam, the Virgin Islands, and the Northern Mariana Islands.
(b) **To Cases and Proceedings.** These rules apply in:
•   civil cases and proceedings, including bankruptcy, admiralty, and maritime cases;
•   criminal cases and proceedings; and
•   contempt proceedings, except those in which the court may act summarily.
(c) **Rules on Privilege.** The rules on privilege apply to all stages of a case or proceeding.
(d) **Exceptions.** These rules—except for those on privilege—do not apply to the following:
•   (1) the court's determination, under Rule 104(a), on a preliminary question of fact governing admissibility;
•   (2) grand-jury proceedings; and
•   (3) miscellaneous proceedings such as:

o	extradition or rendition;
o	issuing an arrest warrant, criminal summons, or search warrant;
o	a preliminary examination in a criminal case;
o	sentencing;
o	granting or revoking probation or supervised release; and
o	considering whether to release on bail or otherwise.

Introduction to Rule 1101

Rule 1101 of the Federal Rules of Evidence outlines the scope and applicability of the Federal Rules of Evidence, clarifying the contexts in which these rules govern the admissibility of evidence and the proceedings to which they apply. This rule is essential in establishing the boundaries within which the Federal Rules of Evidence operate, providing guidance on when and how the rules are to be applied in various legal proceedings, including civil and criminal cases, as well as certain specialized and administrative contexts. By delineating the scope of the rules, Rule 1101 ensures consistency and clarity in the application of evidentiary standards across different types of legal proceedings. This chapter provides a detailed analysis of Rule 1101, exploring its text, interpretation, and broader implications for the administration of justice.

Analysis of Rule 1101

Rule 1101 provides a comprehensive overview of the applicability of the Federal Rules of Evidence, specifying the courts and proceedings in which these rules govern, the cases to which they apply, and the exceptions where the rules, apart from those on privilege, do not apply. This section will examine each component of Rule 1101 in detail, discussing its implications and practical significance.

Applicability to Courts and Judges (Rule 1101(a))

Rule 1101(a) establishes the scope of the Federal Rules of Evidence in terms of the courts and judges to which they apply. The rule specifies that the Federal Rules of Evidence govern proceedings before various federal courts and judges.

1. **Courts Covered by the Rule**

   o **United States District Courts:** The rules apply to all proceedings in United States district courts, which are the general trial courts of the federal judicial system.

   o **United States Bankruptcy and Magistrate Judges:** The rules also apply to proceedings before United States bankruptcy judges, who oversee bankruptcy cases, and United States magistrate judges, who handle various pretrial matters and certain types of cases.

   o **United States Courts of Appeals:** The rules extend to proceedings before the United States courts of appeals, which review decisions made by district courts and other lower courts.

   o **United States Court of Federal Claims:** The rules govern proceedings in the United States Court of Federal Claims, a court that handles monetary claims against the federal government.

   o **Territorial Courts:** The rules apply to the district courts of Guam, the Virgin Islands, and the Northern Mariana Islands, which are federal courts with jurisdiction over their respective territories.

2. **Implications for Legal Practice**

   o **Uniform Application:** Rule 1101(a) ensures that the Federal Rules of Evidence are uniformly applied across a broad range of federal courts, promoting consistency in the handling of evidentiary issues.

   o **Judicial Compliance:** Judges in the specified courts are required to adhere to the Federal Rules of Evidence when presiding over relevant proceedings, ensuring that evidentiary standards are consistently enforced.

Applicability to Cases and Proceedings (Rule 1101(b))

Rule 1101(b) outlines the types of cases and proceedings in which the Federal Rules of Evidence apply, including civil and criminal cases, as well as certain contempt proceedings.

1. **Civil Cases and Proceedings**

   o **Scope:** The rules apply to all civil cases and proceedings, including bankruptcy,

admiralty, and maritime cases. This broad application ensures that evidentiary standards are consistently applied in all types of civil litigation.

   o **Specific Contexts:** Bankruptcy cases involve the handling of insolvent debtors and their assets, while admiralty and maritime cases pertain to issues arising on navigable waters. The inclusion of these specialized areas underscores the wide applicability of the rules in civil matters.

2. **Criminal Cases and Proceedings**

   o **Application:** The rules also govern criminal cases and proceedings, ensuring that evidence presented in criminal trials meets the same rigorous standards as in civil cases. This includes all phases of a criminal case, from pretrial motions to the trial itself.

   o **Fair Trial:** The application of the Federal Rules of Evidence in criminal cases is crucial for ensuring a fair trial, as it governs the admissibility of evidence that may affect the outcome of the case.

3. **Contempt Proceedings**

   o **Summary Contempt Excluded:** The rules apply to contempt proceedings except those in which the court may act summarily. Summary contempt proceedings typically involve immediate punishment for contemptuous behavior occurring in the presence of the court, where the need for formal evidentiary rules is less pronounced.

Rules on Privilege (Rule 1101(c))

Rule 1101(c) states that the rules on privilege apply to all stages of a case or proceeding, ensuring that privileged communications and information are protected throughout the judicial process.

1. **Comprehensive Application**

   o **Privilege at All Stages:** The rules on privilege, which protect certain communications from disclosure, apply at every stage of a case or proceeding. This includes pretrial, trial, and post-trial phases, ensuring consistent protection of privileged information.

   o **Types of Privilege:** Privileges covered by this rule include attorney-client privilege, doctor-patient privilege, and other recognized privileges that safeguard confidential communications.

2. **Implications for Legal Practice**

   o **Protection of Privileged Information:** Attorneys must be vigilant in asserting and protecting privileges throughout all stages of a case. This rule reinforces the importance of maintaining the confidentiality of privileged communications.

- o **Judicial Enforcement:** Courts are required to enforce privilege rules consistently, ensuring that privileged information is not improperly disclosed or used against a party.

Exceptions to the Applicability of the Rules (Rule 1101(d))

Rule 1101(d) lists specific exceptions where the Federal Rules of Evidence, except for those on privilege, do not apply. These exceptions reflect situations where the formal evidentiary rules are deemed unnecessary or impractical.

1. **Preliminary Questions of Fact (Rule 104(a))**

   - o **Court's Determination:** The rules do not apply to the court's determination of preliminary questions of fact governing admissibility under Rule 104(a). In such situations, the court may consider any relevant information, even if it would not be admissible under the Federal Rules of Evidence.

   - o **Flexibility:** This exception allows the court to exercise flexibility in making preliminary determinations about the admissibility of evidence without being bound by the strict rules of evidence.

2. **Grand-Jury Proceedings**

   - o **Grand Jury Function:** The rules do not apply to grand-jury proceedings, which are investigative and conducted in secret. Grand juries determine whether there is sufficient evidence to indict a suspect, and the formal rules of evidence are not required in this context.

   - o **Broad Evidence Consideration:** Grand juries may consider a wider range of evidence, including hearsay, that would not be admissible in a trial.

3. **Miscellaneous Proceedings**

   - o **Specific Proceedings Listed:** The rules do not apply to various miscellaneous proceedings, including extradition or rendition, issuing arrest warrants, criminal summonses, or search warrants, preliminary examinations in criminal cases, sentencing, granting or revoking probation or supervised release, and considering bail or other release conditions.

   - o **Practical Considerations:** These proceedings often involve urgent or administrative matters where the full application of the Federal Rules of Evidence would be impractical. The focus in these contexts is on expediency and practicality rather than formal evidentiary standards.

Strategic Considerations for Attorneys

Understanding the applicability of the Federal Rules of Evidence under Rule 1101 is crucial for attorneys as they navigate different types of proceedings. Attorneys must be aware of when and where the rules apply and when exceptions might allow for more flexible approaches to evidence.

1. **Application in Federal Courts**

   - o **Consistency in Practice:** Attorneys practicing in federal courts must consistently apply the Federal Rules of Evidence in the contexts specified by Rule 1101(a) and (b). This requires a thorough understanding of the rules and how they influence the admissibility of evidence in civil and criminal cases.

   - o **Preparation for Contempt and Other Proceedings:** In cases involving contempt or other specialized proceedings, attorneys must be prepared to apply or challenge the rules as appropriate, particularly when dealing with summary contempt or other exceptions.

2. **Privilege Considerations**

   - o **Vigilant Protection of Privileges:** Given that the rules on privilege apply at all stages of a case, attorneys must be diligent in asserting privileges and protecting confidential communications from disclosure. This includes understanding the scope of applicable privileges and anticipating challenges from opposing counsel.

   - o **Strategic Use of Privileges:** Attorneys should strategically use privilege to protect their clients' interests, ensuring that privileged information remains confidential and is not subject to discovery or use in court.

3. **Navigating Exceptions**

   - o **Understanding Exceptions:** Attorneys must be familiar with the exceptions outlined in Rule 1101(d) and know when the formal rules of evidence do not apply. This knowledge is essential for effectively navigating preliminary hearings, grand-jury proceedings, and other miscellaneous proceedings where flexibility is allowed.

   - o **Arguing for or Against Applicability:** In situations where the rules may or may not apply, attorneys should be prepared to argue for the appropriate standard of evidence, whether that involves invoking the formal rules or relying on more flexible evidentiary principles.

Rule 1102 - Amendments

Text of Rule 1102

Rule 1102. Amendments
These rules may be amended as provided in 28 U.S.C. §§ 2072 and 2075.

Introduction to Rule 1102

Rule 1102 of the Federal Rules of Evidence establishes the process by which these rules may be amended. The Federal Rules of Evidence, like other sets of procedural rules governing the judiciary, must be adaptable to changes in legal practice, societal values, and technological advancements. Rule 1102 provides the framework for the amendment process, ensuring that any modifications to the rules are carried out in a structured and deliberate manner, subject to the oversight of both the judiciary and the legislative branches of the federal government. This chapter provides a detailed analysis of Rule 1102, exploring its text, interpretation, and the broader implications for the evolution of evidentiary standards in the federal legal system.

Analysis of Rule 1102

Rule 1102 is a succinct rule that refers directly to the statutory framework governing the amendment of the Federal Rules of Evidence, as well as other procedural rules within the federal judiciary. The rule itself does not provide specific procedures for amendment but instead incorporates by reference the relevant provisions of the United States Code, specifically 28 U.S.C. §§ 2072 and 2075. This section will examine these statutes in detail, explaining how they structure the amendment process for the Federal Rules of Evidence.

Amendment Process Under 28 U.S.C. § 2072

28 U.S.C. § 2072, commonly referred to as the Rules Enabling Act, grants the Supreme Court of the United States the authority to prescribe general rules of practice and procedure for cases in the federal courts, including the Federal Rules of Evidence. This statute outlines the procedural framework for the amendment of these rules.

1. **Authority of the Supreme Court**

    o **Prescribing Rules:** The Supreme Court is authorized to prescribe rules for the federal courts, including rules related to evidence, as long as these rules do not modify substantive rights. The Court's authority extends to creating, amending, and abrogating rules as necessary to ensure the fair and efficient administration of justice.

    o **Limitations:** The rules prescribed by the Supreme Court must be procedural rather than substantive. This distinction is crucial, as substantive rights are typically within the purview of Congress rather than the judiciary. Rules that affect substantive rights are beyond the scope of the Court's rule-making authority under 28 U.S.C. § 2072.

2. **Procedural Requirements for Amendments**

    o **Consultative Process:** The process for amending the Federal Rules of Evidence involves extensive consultation, including input from advisory committees, public comments, and the Judicial Conference of the United States. These committees are composed of judges, practitioners, and scholars who provide expertise and recommendations on proposed changes.

    o **Publication and Comment Period:** Proposed amendments are published for public comment, allowing stakeholders, including members of the legal profession and the public, to provide feedback. This process ensures transparency and broad participation in the rule-making process.

3. **Transmission to Congress**

    o **Congressional Review:** After the Supreme Court approves an amendment, it is transmitted to Congress. Congress has the authority to modify or reject the proposed amendment. If Congress does not act within a specified period (usually seven months), the amendment automatically takes effect.

    o **Legislative Oversight:** This requirement ensures that the legislative branch retains ultimate control over the rules governing federal courts, maintaining the balance of power between the judiciary and Congress.

Amendment Process Under 28 U.S.C. § 2075

28 U.S.C. § 2075 specifically addresses the amendment of rules related to bankruptcy procedure, which includes evidentiary rules applicable in bankruptcy cases. This statute operates in conjunction with § 2072, ensuring that the process for amending the Federal Rules of Evidence, as they apply to bankruptcy cases, follows a similar framework.

1. **Bankruptcy Rules and Evidence**

    o **Bankruptcy Context:** The Federal Rules of Evidence apply in bankruptcy proceedings, subject to the specific provisions of the Bankruptcy Rules.

Section 2075 provides the mechanism for amending both procedural and evidentiary rules within the context of bankruptcy law.

- **Amendment Procedure:** The amendment procedure under § 2075 mirrors that of § 2072, involving the Supreme Court's rule-making authority, advisory committees, public comment, and Congressional review.

2. **Integration with Broader Amendments**

- **Consistency Across Contexts:** Amendments to the Federal Rules of Evidence that affect bankruptcy proceedings are integrated into the broader framework of federal procedural rules, ensuring consistency across different types of cases and courts. This integration is crucial for maintaining uniform standards of evidence across the federal judiciary.

Strategic Considerations for Legal Practitioners

Understanding the amendment process outlined in Rule 1102 and the referenced statutes is important for legal practitioners, particularly those involved in federal litigation or who have a role in commenting on or advocating for changes to the Federal Rules of Evidence.

1. **Staying Informed on Proposed Amendments**

- **Monitoring Changes:** Attorneys should stay informed about proposed amendments to the Federal Rules of Evidence, as these changes can significantly impact litigation strategy and the handling of evidence in federal courts. This involves regularly reviewing publications from the Judicial Conference and other relevant bodies.

- **Participating in the Comment Process:** Legal practitioners have the opportunity to participate in the amendment process by submitting comments on proposed changes. Engaging in this process allows attorneys to influence the development of the rules and advocate for changes that reflect practical realities in legal practice.

2. **Adapting to Amendments**

- **Implementation of New Rules:** Once amendments are adopted, attorneys must quickly adapt to the new rules, understanding how they alter the evidentiary landscape in federal courts. This may require updating legal strategies, revising training materials, and educating clients about the implications of the changes.

- **Continuing Legal Education:** Participating in continuing legal education (CLE) programs focused on recent amendments to the Federal Rules of Evidence can help attorneys stay current with the latest developments and ensure that they are fully prepared to apply the new rules in practice.

3. **Strategic Use of Amendments in Litigation**

- **Leveraging Rule Changes:** Attorneys can strategically use amendments to the Federal Rules of Evidence to their advantage in litigation. This might involve exploiting new evidentiary standards or challenging opposing counsel's use of outdated practices.

- **Anticipating Future Changes:** By understanding the trends in rule amendments and the issues currently under consideration, attorneys can anticipate future changes and begin adapting their practices in advance, positioning themselves to better serve their clients.

Broader Implications for the Federal Judicial System

The amendment process governed by Rule 1102 and the referenced statutes has broader implications for the federal judicial system, ensuring that the Federal Rules of Evidence evolve in response to new legal challenges, technological advancements, and shifts in societal values.

1. **Dynamic Nature of Evidentiary Standards**

- **Adapting to Change:** The ability to amend the Federal Rules of Evidence allows the judiciary to respond to changes in legal practice and societal expectations. This adaptability is crucial for maintaining the relevance and effectiveness of the rules in a rapidly changing world.

- **Examples of Recent Amendments:** Recent amendments to the rules, such as those addressing electronic evidence or changes in privilege law, demonstrate the judiciary's responsiveness to emerging issues that affect the fair and efficient administration of justice.

2. **Maintaining Judicial Integrity**

- **Balancing Tradition and Innovation:** The amendment process strikes a balance between maintaining the integrity of long-standing evidentiary principles and embracing necessary innovations. This balance ensures that the Federal Rules of Evidence continue to serve the dual purposes of justice and efficiency.

Rule 1103 - Title

Rule 1103. Title
These rules may be cited as the Federal Rules of Evidence.

Introduction to Rule 1103

Rule 1103 of the Federal Rules of Evidence provides a succinct yet important declaration: it formally designates the collective set of these rules as the "Federal Rules of Evidence." While brief, Rule 1103 carries significance in terms of the official nomenclature and recognition of the rules within the broader legal framework. The title not only serves as an identifier but also encapsulates the comprehensive nature of the evidentiary standards that govern proceedings in federal courts across the United States. This chapter provides a detailed analysis of Rule 1103, exploring its text, implications, and the broader context within which the title operates.

Analysis of Rule 1103

Rule 1103, though brief, serves an essential function by formally establishing the title of the rules as the "Federal Rules of Evidence." This designation ensures consistency in how the rules are referenced in legal documents, court opinions, academic writings, and everyday legal practice. The title also signifies the rules' authoritative status as the governing standards for the admissibility of evidence in federal courts.

Purpose and Function of the Title

The title "Federal Rules of Evidence" serves multiple purposes, both practical and symbolic, in the context of the U.S. legal system.

1. **Uniformity and Consistency**

   o **Standardized Citation:** By formally designating the title, Rule 1103 ensures that all references to the rules are uniform across various legal contexts. This standardization simplifies communication among legal professionals, ensuring that there is no ambiguity about the set of rules being referenced.

   o **Citation Practices:** In legal practice, proper citation is crucial for clarity and precision. The title "Federal Rules of Evidence" provides a clear, concise reference that can be consistently used in legal briefs, court orders, and scholarly articles, thereby enhancing the precision of legal discourse.

2. **Recognition and Authority**

   o **Authoritative Source:** The title emphasizes the authoritative nature of the rules as the official guidelines for evidentiary matters in federal courts. It signals that these rules are the definitive source for determining the admissibility of evidence in legal proceedings, carrying the weight of federal law.

   o **Institutional Identity:** The title also contributes to the institutional identity of the rules, distinguishing them from other sets of rules, such as the Federal Rules of Civil Procedure or the Federal Rules of Criminal Procedure. This distinction is important for practitioners and scholars who may be navigating multiple bodies of procedural law.

3. **Symbolic Importance**

   o **Embodiment of Legal Standards:** The title "Federal Rules of Evidence" embodies the entire body of legal standards that govern evidence in federal courts. It reflects the culmination of decades of legal development, judicial interpretation, and legislative refinement that have shaped these rules into a coherent and comprehensive framework.

   o **Continuity and Tradition:** The formal title also reflects the continuity and tradition of the federal judicial system. It signals that the rules are part of an ongoing legal tradition that dates back to the adoption of the Federal Rules of Evidence in 1975 and continues to evolve through amendments and judicial interpretation.

Practical Implications for Legal Practice

While Rule 1103 is primarily concerned with the title of the rules, its implications extend into various aspects of legal practice, particularly in terms of citation, reference, and legal research.

1. **Citing the Federal Rules of Evidence**

   o **Legal Documents:** In legal documents, such as briefs, motions, and opinions, proper citation of the Federal Rules of Evidence is essential for clarity and authority. Rule 1103's formal designation of the title ensures that legal professionals have a clear and consistent way to reference these rules, which in turn supports the effective communication of legal arguments.

   o **Court Opinions:** When courts reference the rules in their opinions, the use of the official title reinforces the rules' authority and helps standardize judicial language. This uniformity aids in legal research and ensures that practitioners can easily locate and understand references to the rules in case law.

2. **Legal Education and Scholarship**

- o **Teaching and Learning:** In legal education, the title "Federal Rules of Evidence" is commonly used to refer to the set of rules studied by law students, discussed in legal seminars, and analyzed in scholarly articles. The formal recognition of this title supports the consistent teaching and understanding of evidentiary law across educational institutions.

- o **Academic Research:** Scholars who write about evidentiary issues rely on the formal title when citing the rules in their research. The standardization provided by Rule 1103 ensures that academic discussions are clear and that references to the rules are easily recognizable and accessible to readers.

3. **Legal Research and Databases**

- o **Research Tools:** Legal research databases and tools, such as Westlaw, LexisNexis, and online federal legal repositories, organize and categorize the Federal Rules of Evidence under this official title. Rule 1103's designation facilitates efficient research by ensuring that users can quickly find and reference the rules within these platforms.

- o **Cross-Referencing:** The consistent use of the title also aids in cross-referencing the Federal Rules of Evidence with other legal materials, such as case law, treatises, and annotations. This interconnectedness enhances the utility of legal research tools and supports comprehensive legal analysis.

Broader Context and Historical Significance

Rule 1103, by providing the formal title "Federal Rules of Evidence," connects these rules to a broader historical and legal context. Understanding this context is important for appreciating the significance of the rules and their role in the federal judicial system.

1. **Historical Development**

- o **Adoption in 1975:** The Federal Rules of Evidence were officially adopted in 1975, following years of development by the Advisory Committee on Rules of Evidence and approval by the Supreme Court and Congress. The title "Federal Rules of Evidence" has since become synonymous with the codified principles that govern evidence in federal courts.

- o **Evolution Through Amendments:** Since their adoption, the rules have undergone numerous amendments to address changes in legal practice, technological advancements, and evolving societal values. The continuity of the title reflects the ongoing relevance and adaptability of the rules in the face of these changes.

2. **Influence on State Evidence Rules**

- o **Model for State Rules:** The Federal Rules of Evidence have served as a model for the evidence rules adopted by many states. The formal title distinguishes the federal rules while highlighting their influence on state-level legal standards.

- o **Uniformity Across Jurisdictions:** While states may adapt the federal rules to their specific needs, the use of a similar title (e.g., "State Rules of Evidence") in many jurisdictions reflects the uniformity and coherence of evidentiary principles across the United States.

Evidentiary Objections and Responses

Introduction to Evidentiary Objections and Responses

Evidentiary objections and responses are critical components of trial practice, as they directly impact the admissibility of evidence and the overall presentation of a case. The ability to effectively raise objections, as well as to respond to those raised by opposing counsel, requires a deep understanding of the rules of evidence, strategic thinking, and an awareness of courtroom dynamics. This chapter provides a comprehensive analysis of evidentiary objections and responses, exploring their types, purposes, and the strategic considerations involved in making and addressing them. The goal is to equip legal practitioners with the knowledge and tools necessary to navigate these crucial aspects of trial practice with confidence and precision.

Purpose and Function of Evidentiary Objections

Evidentiary objections serve multiple purposes within the trial process, ensuring that only legally permissible evidence is presented to the trier of fact. These objections help to maintain the integrity of the judicial process by enforcing the rules of evidence, preventing the introduction of prejudicial, irrelevant, or otherwise improper material.

Ensuring Compliance with the Rules of Evidence

The primary purpose of an evidentiary objection is to enforce the Federal Rules of Evidence (or their state equivalents). These rules establish the standards for the admissibility of evidence, governing aspects such as relevance, hearsay, character evidence, and privilege. By objecting to evidence that fails to meet these standards, attorneys help to ensure that the trial is conducted fairly and that the evidence presented is reliable and appropriate for consideration by the jury or judge.

Protecting the Rights of the Parties

Objections are also crucial for protecting the rights of the parties involved in the trial. An objection can prevent the introduction of evidence that might unfairly prejudice the jury against a party, or that might otherwise compromise the fairness of the proceedings. For example, objections to character evidence, hearsay, or evidence obtained in violation of a party's rights are common mechanisms for safeguarding the interests of the parties.

Shaping the Presentation of Evidence

Strategically, objections can be used to shape the narrative presented to the jury. By excluding certain pieces of evidence, an attorney can influence how the jury perceives the facts of the case. Additionally, the act of objecting can signal to the jury that certain evidence is contested or controversial, potentially affecting how the jury weighs that evidence.

Preserving Issues for Appeal

Raising timely objections is essential for preserving issues for appeal. If an attorney fails to object to the admission of improper evidence during the trial, they may forfeit the right to challenge that evidence on appeal. Properly raising and responding to objections on the record ensures that potential errors can be reviewed by an appellate court.

Types of Evidentiary Objections

There are numerous types of evidentiary objections, each corresponding to specific rules or principles of evidence. This section will detail the most common objections, explaining their legal basis, proper usage, and potential exceptions.

Relevance Objections

Relevance is a foundational principle of evidence law, requiring that all evidence presented must be pertinent to the issues being decided in the case.

1. **Legal Basis (Rule 401 and Rule 402)**

   o **Rule 401** defines relevant evidence as any evidence that has any tendency to make a fact more or less probable than it would be without the evidence, and that is of consequence in determining the action.

   o **Rule 402** provides that relevant evidence is generally admissible unless the United States Constitution, a federal statute, the Federal Rules of Evidence, or other rules prescribed by the Supreme Court provide otherwise.

2. **Grounds for Objection**

   o An objection based on relevance asserts that the evidence in question does not relate to any fact that is material to the issues in the case. If the evidence does not meet the criteria of relevance under Rule 401, it should be excluded under Rule 402.

3. **Exceptions**

   o Even relevant evidence may be excluded if its probative value is substantially outweighed by the risk of prejudice, confusion, or waste of time, as outlined in Rule 403.

Hearsay Objections

Hearsay objections address the admissibility of out-of-court statements offered to prove the truth of the matter asserted.

1. **Legal Basis (Rule 801, Rule 802)**

   o **Rule 801** defines hearsay as a statement that the declarant does not make while testifying at the current trial or hearing, and that a party offers in evidence to prove the truth of the matter asserted in the statement.

   o **Rule 802** states that hearsay is generally not admissible unless an exception applies.

2. **Grounds for Objection**

- o An objection based on hearsay asserts that the evidence in question is an out-of-court statement being offered to prove the truth of the matter asserted and does not fall within any recognized exception.

3. **Exceptions**

- o Numerous exceptions to the hearsay rule exist, including those found in **Rule 803** (which applies regardless of whether the declarant is available), **Rule 804** (which applies when the declarant is unavailable), and **Rule 807** (the residual exception).

Objections to Character Evidence

Character evidence is generally inadmissible to prove that a person acted in conformity with a character trait on a particular occasion.

1. **Legal Basis (Rule 404)**

- o **Rule 404(a)** generally prohibits the use of character evidence to prove that on a particular occasion, the person acted in accordance with the character or trait.

- o **Rule 404(b)** limits the use of evidence of other crimes, wrongs, or acts to prove character, although it may be admissible for other purposes such as proving motive, opportunity, intent, or knowledge.

2. **Grounds for Objection**

- o An objection based on character evidence asserts that the evidence is being improperly used to suggest that a person acted in conformity with a particular character trait, which is prohibited under Rule 404(a).

3. **Exceptions**

- o Exceptions to the general prohibition on character evidence include cases involving the character of the accused in criminal trials (where the accused may offer evidence of a pertinent trait), the character of the victim in self-defense cases, and evidence of character for truthfulness or untruthfulness in credibility determinations (under **Rule 608**).

Objections to Leading Questions

Leading questions are questions that suggest the desired answer, typically prohibited during direct examination.

1. **Legal Basis (Rule 611(c))**

- o **Rule 611(c)** generally prohibits the use of leading questions during the direct examination of a witness, except as necessary to develop the witness's testimony. Leading questions are typically allowed on cross-examination and when examining a hostile witness.

2. **Grounds for Objection**

- o An objection based on leading questions asserts that the question posed by counsel is improperly suggesting the desired answer to the witness, thereby undermining the fairness of the examination.

3. **Exceptions**

- o Exceptions to the prohibition against leading questions include situations where the witness is hostile, uncooperative, or a child, or when the witness's memory needs to be refreshed.

Objections Based on Privilege

Privilege objections protect certain communications from being disclosed in court.

1. **Legal Basis (Rule 501)**

- o **Rule 501** governs the recognition of privileges in federal courts, often deferring to common law unless superseded by the Constitution, federal statutes, or court rules.

2. **Grounds for Objection**

- o An objection based on privilege asserts that the evidence in question involves a communication that is protected by a recognized privilege, such as attorney-client privilege, doctor-patient privilege, or spousal privilege.

3. **Exceptions**

- o Exceptions to privileges may apply, such as the crime-fraud exception to the attorney-client privilege, where the communication was made in furtherance of a crime or fraud.

Responses to Evidentiary Objections

When an opposing counsel raises an objection, the attorney who offered the evidence must be prepared to respond effectively. Responses to objections can involve arguing the admissibility of the evidence, pointing to an applicable exception, or addressing the relevance or probative value of the evidence.

Arguing Admissibility

The primary response to an objection is to argue that the evidence is admissible under the relevant rules of evidence. This may involve:

1. **Citing the Rule:** Referring to the specific rule that permits the admission of the evidence.

2. **Establishing Relevance:** Demonstrating that the evidence is relevant and that its probative value outweighs any potential prejudicial effect.

3. **Clarifying the Purpose:** Explaining the purpose for which the evidence is being offered, particularly in

cases where the evidence might be misconstrued as inadmissible for one purpose but admissible for another (e.g., using character evidence to prove intent rather than conformity).

Pointing to Exceptions

If the objection is based on hearsay, character evidence, or privilege, the attorney may respond by identifying a specific exception that applies to the case:

1. **Hearsay Exceptions:** Arguing that the evidence falls within one of the exceptions to the hearsay rule (e.g., excited utterance, present sense impression, or business records).

2. **Character Evidence Exceptions:** Pointing out that the evidence is being offered under one of the exceptions to the character evidence rule, such as proving motive or intent.

3. **Privilege Exceptions:** Demonstrating that an exception to the privilege applies, such as the crime-fraud exception or waiver of the privilege.

Relevance and Probative Value

In response to objections based on relevance or potential prejudice, the attorney may argue that:

1. **Relevance:** The evidence is relevant because it makes a fact of consequence more or less probable, and thus should be admitted.

2. **Probative Value:** The probative value of the evidence outweighs any potential prejudicial effect, confusion, or waste of time, thereby justifying its admission under Rule 403.

Preserving the Record

If the objection is sustained and the evidence is excluded, the attorney should take steps to preserve the issue for appeal:

1. **Offer of Proof:** An offer of proof allows the attorney to make a record of what the evidence would have shown had it been admitted, ensuring that the appellate court has the necessary information to review the trial court's ruling.

2. **Making a Record:** The attorney should ensure that the objection, the ruling, and the grounds for the objection and response are clearly recorded in the trial transcript.

Strategic Considerations in Raising and Responding to Objections

Effective use of objections and responses requires careful strategy, considering both the short-term impact on the trial and the long-term implications for appeal.

Timing and Frequency of Objections

1. **Selective Objection:** Overuse of objections can alienate the judge or jury, leading to perceptions of obstruction or desperation. Attorneys should be selective, raising objections that are most likely to succeed or that address critical evidence.

2. **Timing:** Objections should be raised promptly, ideally before the answer is given or the evidence is introduced. Failure to object in a timely manner may result in the waiver of the objection.

The Impact on the Jury

1. **Jury Perception:** Attorneys should be mindful of how objections might be perceived by the jury. Persistent objections may cause the jury to question the strength of the case, while well-placed objections can enhance the attorney's credibility.

2. **Minimizing Prejudice:** In cases where potentially prejudicial evidence is admitted despite an objection, the attorney may request a limiting instruction to minimize its impact on the jury.

Building a Record for Appeal

1. **Preserving Issues:** Ensuring that all objections and responses are properly recorded is crucial for preserving issues for appeal. This includes making offers of proof when necessary.

2. **Strategic Objections:** Attorneys may choose to raise certain objections specifically to preserve them for appeal, even if they do not expect the trial court to sustain the objection.

Special Considerations in Digital Evidence

Introduction to Digital Evidence

The rise of technology has profoundly impacted the legal landscape, particularly in the realm of evidence. Digital evidence, which encompasses data stored or transmitted in digital form, has become increasingly prevalent in both civil and criminal litigation. This category of evidence includes emails, text messages, social media posts, electronic documents, digital photographs, databases, and other forms of electronically stored information (ESI). Given the unique characteristics of digital evidence, its use in legal proceedings presents a range of special considerations that differ from traditional forms of evidence. This chapter provides a comprehensive examination of the challenges and legal issues associated with digital evidence, focusing on its admissibility, authentication, preservation, and the implications for privacy and security.

Understanding Digital Evidence

Digital evidence differs from traditional forms of evidence in several key ways, necessitating special attention to its handling, storage, and presentation in court.

Definition and Types of Digital Evidence

Digital evidence refers to any information that is stored or transmitted in binary form and can be used in court. The following are common types of digital evidence:

1. **Electronic Documents:** Files such as Word documents, PDFs, and spreadsheets that are created and stored electronically.

2. **Emails and Text Messages:** Communications transmitted via electronic means, often used to establish timelines, intent, or communication between parties.

3. **Social Media Content:** Posts, messages, images, and videos shared on platforms like Facebook, Twitter, and Instagram, which can be used to demonstrate behavior, statements, or relationships.

4. **Digital Photographs and Videos:** Visual evidence captured and stored electronically, often subject to questions of authenticity and tampering.

5. **Databases and Logs:** Large collections of data, such as transaction logs, server logs, and customer databases, which may be used to track activities or establish patterns.

6. **Metadata:** Information about data, such as timestamps, file origins, and access logs, which can provide context and help authenticate digital evidence.

Characteristics of Digital Evidence

Digital evidence possesses several unique characteristics that distinguish it from traditional physical evidence:

1. **Intangibility:** Digital evidence exists in a virtual form, making it intangible and requiring specialized tools and methods to access and present in court.

2. **Volume and Complexity:** The sheer volume of digital evidence can be overwhelming, with large datasets and extensive communications requiring careful analysis and management.

3. **Malleability:** Digital evidence can be easily altered, duplicated, or deleted, raising concerns about its authenticity and integrity.

4. **Permanence and Transience:** While digital evidence can be permanently stored, it can also be easily deleted or corrupted, making timely preservation and collection critical.

Admissibility of Digital Evidence

The admissibility of digital evidence in court is governed by the same general principles that apply to other forms of evidence, but the unique nature of digital evidence requires careful attention to specific issues such as relevance, authenticity, and hearsay.

Relevance (Rule 401 and Rule 402)

As with any evidence, digital evidence must be relevant to be admissible. Under **Rule 401**, evidence is relevant if it has any tendency to make a fact more or less probable than it would be without the evidence, and if the fact is of consequence in determining the action. **Rule 402** states that all relevant evidence is admissible unless otherwise provided by law.

1. **Establishing Relevance:** The proponent of digital evidence must demonstrate that the evidence is directly related to the issues in the case. For example, emails between parties may be relevant to establish intent, while metadata might be relevant to establish the timing of certain actions.

2. **Challenges to Relevance:** Opposing counsel may challenge the relevance of digital evidence by arguing that it is too tangential or speculative to be of probative value, or that it confuses the issues rather than clarifying them.

Authentication (Rule 901 and Rule 902)

Authentication is a critical hurdle for digital evidence. Under **Rule 901**, the proponent must produce evidence sufficient to support a finding that the item is what the proponent claims it is. **Rule 902** provides for certain self-authenticating evidence that requires no extrinsic evidence of authenticity.

1. **Methods of Authentication (Rule 901(a))**

   o **Testimony of a Witness with Knowledge:** A witness familiar with the digital evidence, such as the author of an email or the custodian of a digital document, can testify to its authenticity.

   o **Distinctive Characteristics:** Features such as email addresses, IP addresses, and metadata can help authenticate digital evidence by linking it to a specific individual or event.

- o **Hash Values:** A hash value, which is a unique digital fingerprint of a file, can be used to demonstrate that the digital evidence has not been altered since it was created or last accessed.

2. **Self-Authenticating Evidence (Rule 902(13) and (14))**

   - o **Certified Records Generated by an Electronic Process:** Under **Rule 902(13)**, records generated by an electronic process that produces an accurate result, such as data from a well-maintained computer system, may be self-authenticating.

   - o **Certified Data Copied from an Electronic Device: Rule 902(14)** allows data copied from an electronic device to be self-authenticating if it is accompanied by a certificate of authenticity.

3. **Challenges to Authentication:** Opposing counsel may challenge the authenticity of digital evidence by arguing that it has been tampered with, altered, or that it cannot be definitively linked to the relevant parties or events.

Hearsay Considerations (Rule 801 and Rule 802)

Digital evidence often involves statements made out of court, raising potential hearsay issues under **Rule 801** and **Rule 802**.

1. **Definition of Hearsay (Rule 801)**

   - o **Hearsay:** Digital communications such as emails, text messages, and social media posts may be considered hearsay if they are offered to prove the truth of the matter asserted. These are generally inadmissible unless an exception applies.

2. **Hearsay Exceptions (Rule 803 and Rule 804)**

   - o **Business Records Exception:** Emails or other records made in the regular course of business may be admissible under the business records exception to the hearsay rule (Rule 803(6)).

   - o **Party Admissions:** Statements made by a party-opponent in digital form, such as in emails or text messages, may be admissible as non-hearsay under Rule 801(d)(2).

   - o **Other Exceptions:** Digital evidence may also fall under other hearsay exceptions, such as present sense impressions, excited utterances, or statements against interest.

3. **Challenges to Hearsay:** Opposing counsel may challenge the admissibility of digital evidence on hearsay grounds by arguing that the evidence is an out-of-court statement and does not meet any recognized exception.

The Best Evidence Rule (Rule 1002)

The best evidence rule, as articulated in **Rule 1002**, requires that to prove the content of a writing, recording, or photograph, the original or a duplicate is generally required. This rule applies to digital evidence in specific contexts.

1. **Original Digital Evidence:** The "original" of digital evidence is often the data itself, such as an electronic file or email stored on a server or device.

2. **Duplicates and Copies:** Under **Rule 1003**, a duplicate is generally admissible to the same extent as an original unless a genuine question is raised about the original's authenticity or if it would be unfair to admit the duplicate in place of the original.

3. **Challenges to the Best Evidence:** Opposing counsel may argue that the proponent has not produced the original digital evidence or that the duplicate lacks reliability or accuracy.

Preservation and Collection of Digital Evidence

The preservation and collection of digital evidence are critical steps in ensuring that such evidence is admissible and reliable in court. Mishandling digital evidence can result in its exclusion or can lead to spoliation claims.

Legal Requirements for Preservation

1. **Duty to Preserve:** Once litigation is anticipated, parties have a duty to preserve relevant digital evidence. This duty requires parties to take steps to prevent the destruction or alteration of potentially relevant data.

2. **Litigation Holds:** Implementing a litigation hold involves notifying relevant personnel and departments within an organization to preserve all potentially relevant digital evidence, including emails, documents, and other electronically stored information.

3. **Spoliation and Sanctions:** Failure to preserve digital evidence can result in sanctions, including adverse inference instructions, fines, or even dismissal of claims or defenses. Courts may impose sanctions under **Rule 37(e)** of the Federal Rules of Civil Procedure when parties fail to preserve electronically stored information.

Collection Methods

1. **Forensic Imaging:** Forensic imaging involves creating an exact, bit-by-bit copy of a storage device, capturing all data, including deleted files and slack space. This method preserves the integrity of the evidence and ensures that it can be analyzed without altering the original data.

2. **Chain of Custody:** Maintaining a clear and documented chain of custody is essential to ensure that digital evidence is admissible. The chain of custody tracks the evidence from the time it is collected until it is presented in court, documenting every transfer and handling of the evidence.

3. **Search and Seizure:** In criminal cases, the collection of digital evidence must comply with the Fourth Amendment, which protects against unreasonable searches and seizures. Warrants must be specific in describing the place to be searched and the items to be seized, including digital evidence.

Technical Challenges

1. **Encryption and Access Control:** Encryption and other security measures can complicate the collection of digital evidence. Legal and technical solutions, such as obtaining decryption keys or using specialized forensic tools, may be necessary to access encrypted data.

2. **Data Volume and Filtering:** The sheer volume of digital evidence can be challenging to manage. Filtering tools and techniques, such as keyword searches or date-range filtering, can help narrow down the data to relevant material.

Privacy, Security, and Ethical Considerations

Handling digital evidence raises significant privacy, security, and ethical issues that must be addressed to ensure compliance with legal standards and professional responsibilities.

Privacy Concerns

1. **Personal Data Protection:** Digital evidence often contains personal data, which may be protected by privacy laws such as the General Data Protection Regulation (GDPR) in Europe or the California Consumer Privacy Act (CCPA) in the United States. Legal practitioners must ensure that the collection, processing, and presentation of digital evidence comply with applicable privacy regulations.

2. **Minimization:** Minimization involves limiting the scope of data collection to what is strictly necessary for the case, thereby reducing the impact on individuals' privacy. This approach is especially important when dealing with sensitive or personal information.

Security Considerations

1. **Data Security:** Digital evidence must be securely stored and transmitted to prevent unauthorized access, tampering, or loss. This includes using secure storage solutions, encryption, and secure communication channels.

2. **Preventing Data Breaches:** Legal practitioners must take steps to prevent data breaches that could compromise the integrity of digital evidence or expose sensitive information. This includes following best practices for cybersecurity and responding promptly to any suspected breaches.

Ethical Obligations

1. **Competence in Technology:** Attorneys handling digital evidence must be competent in the relevant technology. The American Bar Association's Model Rule 1.1 on competence has been interpreted to require that attorneys understand the technology used in their cases, including the preservation, collection, and presentation of digital evidence.

2. **Duty of Candor:** Attorneys have an ethical duty of candor to the court, which includes ensuring that digital evidence is not altered or manipulated. Any potential issues with the authenticity or integrity of digital evidence must be disclosed to the court and opposing counsel.

3. **Confidentiality:** Attorneys must also ensure that digital evidence containing confidential information is protected in accordance with ethical rules, including maintaining the confidentiality of client information and complying with court orders regarding the handling of sensitive evidence.

Presentation of Digital Evidence in Court

The presentation of digital evidence in court requires careful planning and the use of appropriate technology to ensure that the evidence is clear, understandable, and persuasive to the trier of fact.

Visual Aids and Demonstratives

1. **Using Screenshots and Visualizations:** Screenshots, charts, and visualizations can help make complex digital evidence more accessible to the jury. These tools can be used to highlight key information, demonstrate patterns, or simplify large datasets.

2. **Interactive Presentations:** Interactive presentations, such as digital timelines or databases that can be navigated in real-time, can be effective in demonstrating the relevance and context of digital evidence.

Expert Testimony

1. **Role of Digital Forensic Experts:** Digital forensic experts may be called to testify about the methods used to collect and analyze digital evidence, authenticate the evidence, and explain technical aspects to the jury. Experts can provide credibility to the evidence and help the jury understand its significance.

2. **Challenging Expert Testimony:** Opposing counsel may challenge the qualifications of the expert or the methods used to analyze the digital evidence, particularly if the expert's conclusions are central to the case.

Jury Considerations

1. **Simplifying Complex Evidence:** Given the potential complexity of digital evidence, attorneys must find ways to present the evidence in a manner that is easily understood by the jury. This may involve breaking down technical concepts, using analogies, or focusing on the most salient points.

2. **Jury Instructions:** Jury instructions regarding the evaluation of digital evidence can be critical. Instructions may need to address issues such as the reliability of digital records, the significance of metadata, and the importance of considering the evidence within the broader context of the case.

Recent Amendments and Their Impact

Introduction to Recent Amendments

The Federal Rules of Evidence, like other procedural rules governing the U.S. legal system, are subject to periodic amendments designed to reflect evolving legal standards, address emerging challenges, and incorporate advancements in technology and legal practice. These amendments ensure that the rules remain relevant and effective in promoting fairness and efficiency in the administration of justice. Understanding recent amendments is crucial for legal practitioners, as these changes can have significant implications for litigation strategies, evidentiary procedures, and the overall conduct of trials. This chapter provides a comprehensive analysis of the most recent amendments to the Federal Rules of Evidence, examining their content, rationale, and impact on legal practice.

Overview of Recent Amendments

Recent amendments to the Federal Rules of Evidence have focused on various aspects of evidence law, including the admissibility of expert testimony, the use of digital evidence, and the handling of prior consistent statements, among others. Each amendment is typically driven by the need to address specific legal issues or to clarify existing rules in response to judicial interpretations or emerging trends.

Amendment to Rule 106: Remainder of or Related Writings or Recorded Statements

Effective Date: December 1, 2023

Key Changes:

- The amendment to Rule 106 clarifies the application of the rule regarding the admissibility of the remainder of or related writings or recorded statements when only part of a statement is introduced into evidence. The amendment emphasizes that when a party introduces a part of a writing or recorded statement, the opposing party has the right to introduce any other part or any other writing or recorded statement that in fairness ought to be considered at the same time.

Rationale:

- The amendment addresses concerns that selective introduction of statements could mislead the jury or judge by presenting a skewed or incomplete version of events. The revised rule ensures that evidence is presented in a manner that allows the factfinder to consider the full context of the statement.

Impact:

- The amendment strengthens the ability of parties to present evidence in its entirety, reducing the risk of misinterpretation. Legal practitioners must now be more vigilant in preparing to introduce related statements or writings when only a portion of a statement is initially presented by the opposing party.

Amendment to Rule 615: Excluding Witnesses from the Courtroom

Effective Date: December 1, 2023

Key Changes:

- The amendment to Rule 615 clarifies the procedures for excluding witnesses from the courtroom to prevent them from hearing the testimony of other witnesses. The rule now explicitly states that a party who is not a natural person (such as a corporation or government entity) may designate an officer or employee to remain in the courtroom even when other witnesses are excluded.

Rationale:

- The amendment aims to resolve ambiguity regarding the application of Rule 615 to parties that are not natural persons. By allowing these entities to designate a representative to remain in the courtroom, the rule recognizes the practical needs of such parties in managing and understanding the proceedings.

Impact:

- This change affects how legal teams representing corporations or government entities approach trial strategy, particularly in selecting which representative will remain in the courtroom. It also clarifies the procedural rights of non-natural persons in litigation.

Amendment to Rule 702: Testimony by Expert Witnesses

Effective Date: December 1, 2023

Key Changes:

- The amendment to Rule 702 focuses on the admissibility of expert testimony, specifically reinforcing the gatekeeping role of the court in ensuring that such testimony is both reliable and relevant. The amendment clarifies that the court must determine that the expert's testimony reflects a reliable application of the principles and methods to the facts of the case.

Rationale:

- The amendment responds to ongoing concerns about the admission of expert testimony that may be speculative or not adequately grounded in reliable methodology. By emphasizing the court's role in scrutinizing the application of the expert's methods, the amendment seeks to enhance the reliability of expert evidence presented in court.

Impact:

- Legal practitioners must be more rigorous in preparing expert testimony, ensuring that the methodology and its application are clearly articulated and defensible under scrutiny. This amendment may also lead to increased challenges to expert testimony during pretrial motions.

Analysis of the Impact of Recent Amendments

The recent amendments to the Federal Rules of Evidence have a wide-ranging impact on trial practice, affecting both procedural and substantive aspects of evidence law. This section provides an in-depth analysis of how these changes influence legal strategy, court proceedings, and the overall administration of justice.

Enhancing Fairness and Context in Evidence Presentation

The amendments to Rule 106 aim to ensure that evidence is presented in a context that allows the factfinder to understand the full scope of a statement or series of statements. This change promotes fairness by preventing the selective introduction of evidence that could otherwise mislead the jury or judge.

1. **Strategic Considerations:**

   o Attorneys must anticipate the need to introduce related statements or writings whenever opposing counsel introduces only part of a statement. This requires careful preparation and a thorough understanding of the context in which statements were made.

   o The amendment also encourages the use of pretrial motions or stipulations to resolve potential disputes over the admissibility of related statements, reducing the risk of mid-trial objections and delays.

2. **Judicial Considerations:**

   o Judges must be vigilant in applying the amended Rule 106, ensuring that the rule is used to provide a complete and fair context for the evidence without allowing unnecessary or extraneous material to be introduced.

Clarifying Procedures for Witness Exclusion

The amendment to Rule 615 provides clarity on the treatment of non-natural persons in the context of witness exclusion. By allowing such parties to designate a representative to remain in the courtroom, the rule acknowledges the unique challenges faced by corporate and government litigants.

1. **Strategic Considerations:**

   o Legal teams must carefully select the most appropriate representative to remain in the courtroom, considering factors such as the individual's knowledge of the case, ability to assist counsel, and potential impact on the jury.

   o This amendment may also influence decisions regarding trial strategy, particularly in cases involving complex organizational structures or where the presence of a high-ranking official could sway the jury.

2. **Judicial Considerations:**

   o Judges must ensure that the designation of a representative under Rule 615 does not undermine the purpose of witness exclusion, which is to prevent witnesses from tailoring their testimony based on what they hear in court.

Strengthening the Reliability of Expert Testimony

The amendment to Rule 702 reinforces the court's role as a gatekeeper in evaluating expert testimony. By focusing on the reliability of the expert's methods and their application to the facts of the case, the rule aims to prevent the admission of speculative or unsubstantiated expert opinions.

1. **Strategic Considerations:**

   o Attorneys must work closely with their experts to ensure that their testimony is grounded in reliable methodology and that this methodology is clearly and convincingly applied to the facts of the case. This may involve more extensive pretrial preparation and the use of mock trials or hearings to test the strength of the expert's testimony.

   o Opposing counsel should be prepared to challenge expert testimony through Daubert motions, questioning both the methodology and its application to the case at hand.

2. **Judicial Considerations:**

   o Judges must be diligent in applying the amended Rule 702, thoroughly evaluating the reliability and relevance of expert testimony before admitting it into evidence. This may involve holding more frequent pretrial hearings to assess the admissibility of expert evidence.

Broader Implications for Legal Practice

The recent amendments reflect a broader trend towards enhancing the rigor and fairness of evidence law in federal courts. Legal practitioners must adapt to these changes by refining their approaches to evidence preparation, presentation, and challenge.

1. **Continuing Legal Education:**

   o Attorneys should seek out continuing legal education (CLE) opportunities focused on the recent amendments to the Federal Rules of Evidence. Staying informed about these changes is essential for effective advocacy and compliance with evolving legal standards.

2. **Impact on Case Management:**

   o The amendments may lead to changes in how cases are managed, particularly with regard to pretrial motions, evidentiary hearings, and trial strategy. Attorneys must be proactive in addressing these changes to ensure that their cases proceed smoothly and effectively.

Landmark Cases Involving the Federal Rules of Evidence

Introduction to Landmark Cases

The Federal Rules of Evidence (FRE) have been central to the development of American jurisprudence since their adoption in 1975. Through landmark cases, the courts, particularly the United States Supreme Court, have interpreted and applied these rules, shaping the contours of evidence law in profound ways. These cases not only clarify the application of specific rules but also establish precedents that guide lower courts and legal practitioners. This chapter explores key landmark cases that have significantly influenced the interpretation and application of the Federal Rules of Evidence, examining the facts, legal issues, and enduring impact of each case.

Daubert v. Merrell Dow Pharmaceuticals, Inc. (1993)

Citation: 509 U.S. 579 (1993)

Rule(s) Involved: Rule 702 - Testimony by Expert Witnesses

Case Overview

Facts: The plaintiffs, Jason Daubert and Eric Schuller, were minors born with serious birth defects allegedly caused by their mothers' ingestion of Bendectin, a prescription drug manufactured by Merrell Dow Pharmaceuticals. The plaintiffs sought to introduce expert testimony that Bendectin could cause birth defects based on reanalyzed epidemiological studies and animal studies.

Legal Issue: The primary legal issue was whether the expert testimony proffered by the plaintiffs met the admissibility standard under Rule 702 of the Federal Rules of Evidence, which governs the admissibility of expert testimony.

Court's Holding and Reasoning

The Supreme Court held that the "general acceptance" test from Frye v. United States (1923) was superseded by the adoption of the Federal Rules of Evidence, specifically Rule 702. The Court introduced a new standard, now known as the "Daubert standard," which requires that scientific testimony must be both relevant and reliable to be admissible. The Court outlined several factors for judges to consider when determining the reliability of expert testimony, including:

1. **Testability:** Whether the theory or technique can be and has been tested.

2. **Peer Review and Publication:** Whether the theory or technique has been subjected to peer review and publication.

3. **Error Rate:** The known or potential error rate of the theory or technique.

4. **General Acceptance:** While not the sole criterion, the degree of acceptance within the relevant scientific community remains a factor.

Impact on Legal Practice

The Daubert decision significantly changed the landscape of expert testimony in federal courts by placing a stronger gatekeeping role on judges to assess the relevance and reliability of scientific evidence. This case has led to the exclusion of "junk science" and has required that expert testimony be grounded in scientifically valid reasoning and methodology. The Daubert standard has been widely adopted in many state courts and remains a cornerstone of evidence law in evaluating expert testimony.

Crawford v. Washington (2004)

Citation: 541 U.S. 36 (2004)

Rule(s) Involved: Rule 801 - Definitions That Apply to This Article; Exclusions from Hearsay, Rule 802 - The Rule Against Hearsay

Case Overview

Facts: Michael Crawford was charged with assault and attempted murder. His wife, Sylvia, who was unavailable to testify due to spousal privilege, had given a recorded statement to the police that implicated her husband. The prosecution sought to admit this statement under a hearsay exception, arguing that it bore adequate "indicia of reliability."

Legal Issue: The issue was whether the admission of Sylvia Crawford's recorded statement violated the Confrontation Clause of the Sixth Amendment, despite its admissibility under the hearsay rules.

Court's Holding and Reasoning

The Supreme Court held that the Confrontation Clause of the Sixth Amendment requires that testimonial statements of witnesses who do not appear at trial are admissible only where the defendant has had a prior opportunity to cross-examine the witness, and the witness is unavailable to testify at trial. The Court rejected the "indicia of reliability" test from Ohio v. Roberts (1980) and emphasized that the Constitution guarantees a defendant's right to confront their accusers, which includes cross-examination.

Impact on Legal Practice

Crawford v. Washington dramatically altered the admissibility of hearsay evidence, particularly in criminal cases, by establishing a stricter standard for the admission of testimonial statements. The decision has led to greater scrutiny of hearsay exceptions in criminal cases and has underscored the importance of cross-examination in ensuring the reliability of evidence. This case has prompted courts to more carefully analyze whether a statement is testimonial in nature and whether the requirements of the Confrontation Clause have been satisfied.

Kumho Tire Co. v. Carmichael (1999)

Citation: 526 U.S. 137 (1999)

Rule(s) Involved: Rule 702 - Testimony by Expert Witnesses

Case Overview

Facts: Patrick Carmichael's minivan overturned, resulting in a fatal accident. The plaintiffs sued Kumho Tire Company, alleging that the tire's defect caused the accident. The plaintiffs sought to introduce the testimony of a tire failure analyst, who would testify that the tire was defective based on visual and tactile inspections.

Legal Issue: The key issue was whether the Daubert standard applied only to scientific testimony or whether it extended to all expert testimony, including that based on technical and specialized knowledge.

Court's Holding and Reasoning

The Supreme Court held that the Daubert standard applies to all expert testimony, not just to scientific testimony. The Court clarified that the judge's gatekeeping obligation under Rule 702 extends to the admissibility of all expert testimony, whether it is scientific, technical, or based on other specialized knowledge. The Court also emphasized the flexibility of the Daubert factors, indicating that they should be applied in a manner consistent with the particular circumstances of the case.

Impact on Legal Practice

Kumho Tire expanded the application of the Daubert standard, ensuring that all forms of expert testimony are subject to rigorous scrutiny for relevance and reliability. This case reinforced the role of the trial judge as the gatekeeper for expert evidence and highlighted the importance of applying the Daubert criteria flexibly, depending on the context and type of expertise involved. As a result, legal practitioners must ensure that all expert testimony, regardless of the field, is prepared to meet the stringent requirements of admissibility under Rule 702.

Michigan v. Bryant (2011)
Citation: 562 U.S. 344 (2011)

Rule(s) Involved: Rule 801 - Definitions That Apply to This Article; Exclusions from Hearsay, Rule 803 - Exceptions to the Rule Against Hearsay

Case Overview

Facts: Responding to a report of a shooting, police officers found Anthony Covington mortally wounded. Covington identified Richard Bryant as his shooter in a conversation with the police. Covington's statement was admitted at trial under the hearsay exception for dying declarations.

Legal Issue: The primary issue was whether Covington's statement was testimonial in nature and therefore inadmissible under the Confrontation Clause, or whether it was admissible under the dying declaration exception to the hearsay rule.

Court's Holding and Reasoning

The Supreme Court held that Covington's statement was not testimonial because it was made during an ongoing emergency, where the primary purpose was to enable police assistance in responding to the situation rather than to establish or prove past events potentially relevant to later criminal prosecution. The Court emphasized that the "primary purpose" test must be used to determine whether a statement is testimonial and thus subject to the Confrontation Clause.

Impact on Legal Practice

Michigan v. Bryant clarified the application of the Confrontation Clause in cases involving statements made during emergencies. The decision emphasized the context in which statements are made and provided guidance on distinguishing between testimonial and non-testimonial statements. This case has significant implications for criminal prosecutions, particularly in determining the admissibility of statements made to law enforcement officers during the course of their investigations.

Jaffee v. Redmond (1996)
Citation: 518 U.S. 1 (1996)

Rule(s) Involved: Rule 501 - Privilege in General

Case Overview

Facts: Mary Lu Redmond, a police officer, shot and killed a suspect while on duty. In the aftermath, Redmond received counseling from a licensed clinical social worker. The plaintiff sought to obtain the therapist's notes, arguing that they were necessary for cross-examination and impeachment.

Legal Issue: The central issue was whether communications between Redmond and her therapist were protected by a federal evidentiary privilege, thus making them inadmissible in court.

Court's Holding and Reasoning

The Supreme Court recognized a federal psychotherapist-patient privilege under Rule 501, holding that confidential communications between a licensed psychotherapist and their patients in the course of diagnosis or treatment are protected from compelled disclosure. The Court emphasized the importance of privacy in therapeutic relationships and the necessity of such privilege for effective treatment.

Impact on Legal Practice

Jaffee v. Redmond established a new federal evidentiary privilege, significantly impacting cases involving mental health treatment. The decision underscores the importance of confidentiality in therapeutic settings and provides clear protection for communications between patients and licensed psychotherapists. Legal practitioners must now consider the implications of this privilege when seeking to obtain or introduce evidence related to mental health treatment.

Hypothetical Scenarios and Practical Exercises

Introduction to Hypothetical Scenarios and Practical Exercises

Theoretical knowledge of the Federal Rules of Evidence is foundational to the practice of law, but the ability to apply this knowledge in real-world situations is essential for effective advocacy. Hypothetical scenarios and practical exercises provide an invaluable opportunity for legal practitioners, students, and scholars to engage with complex evidentiary issues in a simulated environment. By working through these scenarios, individuals can refine their understanding of the rules, develop strategic thinking, and enhance their ability to analyze and respond to evidentiary challenges in a courtroom setting.

This chapter presents a series of hypothetical scenarios followed by practical exercises designed to test and deepen the reader's comprehension of the Federal Rules of Evidence. Each scenario is accompanied by questions and exercises that encourage critical thinking and application of the rules.

Hypothetical Scenario 1: The Case of the Disputed Contract

Scenario: In a civil case, ABC Corporation is suing XYZ, Inc. for breach of contract. The dispute centers on a sales agreement in which XYZ, Inc. allegedly agreed to purchase 1,000 units of a specialized component from ABC Corporation. XYZ, Inc. contends that no binding agreement was ever reached, arguing that their discussions were preliminary and never formalized into a contract.

ABC Corporation seeks to introduce an email exchange between the parties as evidence of the contract's existence. The emails contain discussions about the terms of the deal, including price, quantity, and delivery dates. XYZ, Inc. objects to the admission of the emails on several grounds, including hearsay, lack of authenticity, and relevance.

Practical Exercises:

1. **Authenticity Challenge:**

   o **Question:** Under Rule 901, what steps must ABC Corporation take to authenticate the email exchange? What evidence might XYZ, Inc. present to challenge the authenticity of the emails?

   o **Exercise:** Draft a motion in limine seeking to admit the emails into evidence, addressing the authenticity requirements and preemptively countering potential objections from XYZ, Inc.

2. **Hearsay Objection:**

   o **Question:** Consider whether the email exchange constitutes hearsay under Rule 801. If it does, are there any applicable exceptions under Rule 803 or Rule 804 that ABC Corporation could invoke to admit the emails?

   o **Exercise:** Prepare an argument for a hearing on the hearsay objection, identifying specific exceptions that apply and explaining why the emails should be admissible.

3. **Relevance and Rule 403:**

   o **Question:** Analyze whether the emails are relevant under Rule 401 and Rule 402. Could XYZ, Inc. argue that the probative value of the emails is substantially outweighed by the risk of prejudice, confusion, or waste of time under Rule 403?

   o **Exercise:** Write a memorandum assessing the relevance of the emails and responding to any potential Rule 403 objections.

Hypothetical Scenario 2: The Case of the Missing Witness

Scenario: In a criminal case, the defendant, Jane Doe, is charged with armed robbery. The prosecution's case hinges on the testimony of an eyewitness, John Smith, who claims to have seen Doe fleeing the scene of the crime. However, Smith has recently relocated to another country and is unwilling to return to testify in person. The prosecution seeks to introduce a videotaped deposition of Smith's testimony, taken before his departure, in lieu of his live testimony at trial.

The defense objects to the use of the deposition, arguing that it violates Doe's Sixth Amendment right to confront the witnesses against her and that it should be excluded as hearsay.

Practical Exercises:

1. **Confrontation Clause Analysis:**

   o **Question:** How does the Confrontation Clause, as interpreted in cases such as Crawford v. Washington, apply to the use of the videotaped deposition in this case? What arguments can the defense make to exclude the deposition on constitutional grounds?

   o **Exercise:** Draft a motion to exclude the videotaped deposition, focusing on the Confrontation Clause and relevant case law.

2. **Hearsay Considerations:**

   o **Question:** Is the videotaped deposition considered hearsay under Rule 801? If so, what hearsay exceptions might the prosecution argue under Rule 804 to justify its admissibility?

   o **Exercise:** Prepare a response to the defense's motion to exclude, arguing why the deposition should be admitted under the hearsay exceptions.

3. **Preliminary Questions Under Rule 104:**

   o **Question:** What preliminary questions might the judge need to resolve under Rule 104 before deciding whether to admit the videotaped deposition?

   o **Exercise:** Role-play a pretrial hearing in which the judge must rule on the admissibility of the deposition, considering the preliminary questions of fact and law involved.

Hypothetical Scenario 3: The Case of the Expert Witness

Scenario: In a products liability case, the plaintiff, Sarah Lee, claims that a defective automobile part manufactured by the defendant, AutoCo, caused her vehicle to crash, resulting in serious injuries. The plaintiff's case relies heavily on the testimony of Dr. Alan Green, an engineering expert who will testify that the design of the part was inherently flawed and that this defect was the direct cause of the accident.

The defense challenges the admissibility of Dr. Green's testimony, arguing that his methodology is not scientifically valid and that his conclusions are speculative. They file a Daubert motion under Rule 702, seeking to exclude his testimony on the grounds that it fails to meet the standards of reliability and relevance.

Practical Exercises:

1. **Daubert Motion Preparation:**

   o **Question:** What factors will the court consider in ruling on the Daubert motion? How can the plaintiff support the admissibility of Dr. Green's testimony by addressing these factors?

   o **Exercise:** Draft a memorandum in opposition to the Daubert motion, outlining the reliability of Dr. Green's methodology and the relevance of his testimony to the issues in the case.

2. **Expert Qualification Under Rule 702:**

   o **Question:** Evaluate Dr. Green's qualifications as an expert under Rule 702. How can the defense argue that Dr. Green is not qualified to offer the opinions he intends to present?

   o **Exercise:** Prepare an argument for the defense challenging Dr. Green's qualifications and the basis for his expert opinions.

3. **Evidentiary Hearing Role-Play:**

   o **Question:** Consider the procedures and evidentiary issues that might arise during a Daubert hearing. How should the parties present their arguments and evidence to persuade the judge?

   o **Exercise:** Conduct a mock Daubert hearing, with one participant acting as the judge, another as the plaintiff's attorney defending the expert's testimony, and a third as the defense attorney challenging it.

Hypothetical Scenario 4: The Case of the Digital Evidence

Scenario: In a complex commercial litigation case, TechCorp is suing its former employee, James Brown, for allegedly stealing proprietary software code and selling it to a competitor. TechCorp has obtained digital evidence from Brown's company-issued laptop, including email correspondence, code fragments, and access logs that purportedly show unauthorized downloads.

Brown's defense team objects to the admission of this digital evidence, arguing that it was obtained in violation of his privacy rights and that the evidence is not properly authenticated. They also contend that the data may have been altered and is therefore unreliable.

Practical Exercises:

1. **Authentication of Digital Evidence:**

   o **Question:** How can TechCorp authenticate the digital evidence under Rule 901? What types of evidence or testimony will be necessary to establish the chain of custody and the integrity of the data?

   o **Exercise:** Draft a brief in support of the admission of the digital evidence, detailing the methods used to authenticate the data and addressing potential objections related to its reliability.

2. **Privacy and Fourth Amendment Issues:**

   o **Question:** Analyze the privacy and Fourth Amendment implications of the digital evidence collection. How can the defense argue that the evidence was obtained unlawfully, and what exceptions might TechCorp invoke to justify its admissibility?

   o **Exercise:** Write a motion to suppress the digital evidence, citing relevant case law on privacy rights and the lawful collection of digital evidence.

3. **Chain of Custody and Spoliation Concerns:**

   o **Question:** What challenges might arise regarding the chain of custody and potential spoliation of digital evidence? How should TechCorp respond to these concerns to ensure the evidence is admitted?

   o **Exercise:** Create a detailed chain of custody report for the digital evidence, and prepare a response to any allegations of spoliation, demonstrating that the data was preserved and handled correctly.

Hypothetical Scenario 5: The Case of the Impeached Witness

Scenario: In a high-profile defamation case, the plaintiff, a well-known public figure, is suing a media company for publishing a story that allegedly contained false and damaging statements about his personal life. The defense plans to call a witness, Mary Johnson, who will testify that she has first-hand knowledge of the events described in the article and that the statements are true.

The plaintiff's attorney, however, has discovered that Johnson made contradictory statements in a previous deposition in an unrelated case. The plaintiff intends to use these prior statements to impeach Johnson's credibility when she testifies.

Practical Exercises:

1. **Impeachment by Prior Inconsistent Statement:**

   o **Question:** Under Rule 613, how can the plaintiff's attorney use Johnson's prior inconsistent statements to impeach her testimony? What steps must be taken to properly introduce the prior statements into evidence?

   o **Exercise:** Prepare an outline for cross-examining Johnson, including the specific questions that will highlight her inconsistent statements and undermine her credibility.

2. **Rehabilitation of the Witness:**

   o **Question:** If Johnson's credibility is successfully impeached, how can the defense attempt to rehabilitate her under Rule 608 or Rule 801(d)(1)(B)? What evidence or testimony might be introduced to support her credibility?

   o **Exercise:** Draft a plan for rehabilitating Johnson's credibility, identifying potential witnesses or evidence that could be used to counter the impeachment.

3. **Jury Instructions on Impeachment:**

   o **Question:** What jury instructions might be necessary to guide the jury's consideration of Johnson's impeachment? How can these instructions ensure that the jury properly weighs the credibility of her testimony?

   o **Exercise:** Draft proposed jury instructions regarding the impeachment of a witness and the use of prior inconsistent statements, ensuring that the instructions are clear and balanced.

Made in the USA
Coppell, TX
29 October 2024

39329471R00109